TROUT FISHERMEN'S DIGEST

Edited by David Richey

DBI BOOKS, INC., NORTHFIELD, ILLINOIS

(Formerly Digest Books, Inc.)

TROUT FISHERMEN'S DIGEST STAFF

David Richey
Editor

Wanda Sahagian
Production Manager

Ed Park
Cover Photographer

Sheldon L. Factor
Associate Publisher

DEDICATION

To Carol—my wife:

She has watched my trout fishing comings and goings for many years. Last year she learned what trout fishing excitement can lead to when she battled and finally landed a 10-pound brown. Now she's a confirmed trout addict . . . just like me.   *D.R.*

CONTENTS

INTRODUCTION

Trout fishing means many things to many people. To one fisherman it could be a nymph drifted slowly through a deep run to a heavily feeding brown while another angler chooses to brave the rushing water and torrential downpours of the Pacific Northwest while winter steelheading.

Baitfishing for trout captures the imagination of many young trout fishermen while the more advanced angler often drifts into flyfishing as a matter of course. Each fisherman feels his method of taking trout to be the best.

Actually, trout fishing has endured for many centuries simply because there are so many facets to the sport that no one can become a master of all. Consequently, this book was written by a select group of trout fishermen. Each discusses his favorite type of trout fishing experience. Each chapter is packed with useful "how to" information for beginning and advanced trout fishermen alike.

The editor and contributing authors wish to express a common goal for all trout fishermen: Become interested and actively involved in helping clean up our trout lakes and streams. Pollution of our waterways has been set back in many areas but there is still much that needs to be done. Many trout areas are rapidly being destroyed by industrial pollution. We need to clean up our act now.

Join an organization such as Trout Unlimited, determine what needs to be done in your area, and work toward a cleaner environment for trout. The sport of trout fishing has provided us with many enjoyable days and years. It's about time we did something to assure our children and grandchildren that trout fishing, as we know it, will still be available for future generations.

David Richey

How to Read a Trout Stream

by TOM WENDELBURG

IT WAS MY companion's first crack at fishing a trout stream so I started him at a trout lair which was easily fished with a short cast. He made his cast, kept a tight line and the offering drifted downstream naturally in the current. A 14-inch brown trout took and provided a thrilling battle before being netted.

Very few first casts on a strange stream will produce a chunky brown unless you first know how to read a stream. Learning where trout are found in a stream is the first step to catching fish you can't see actively feeding. Every stream has certain areas where trout hold and/or feed and the savvy trout fisherman learns these spots and knows when each should be productive.

Trout lurk in waters where they have safety from predators, where currents are comfortable, and ideally, where food is plentiful. Though they spend most of their time in shady lairs, they may move to waters which have more food when conditions are favorable for feeding. Visible "keys" will help identify the various surface currents, underwater cover and streambank habitats, which create feeding and holding areas for trout.

Pools are areas of deeper water. They may be only a few

Author nets a nice brownie which was hiding under a shallow, grassy-edged bank. Currents erode some surprisingly deep undercut banks, and good-sized trout as this 18-incher will seek their gentle currents, concealment for safety, and have food such as grasshoppers tumble off the banks and other food drift to them. Shallow undercuts are especially productive in summer, when food is most plentiful there.

A trout stream, large or small, is a collection of myriad current paths and eddies, holes, pools, obstructions such as rocks and overhanging foliage which create small buffers of quiet water called pockets, and other physical features. The angler who "reads" the signs along a stream learns where trout hold, where they move to feed at certain times and with this knowledge he can avoid the barren water. The angler who spends his fishing time where the trout are catches fish when they aren't visibly feeding at the surface.

yards long on small brooks or blocks long on a large river. A pool usually begins where shallow, often rippling or choppy water, drops off forming the head (upstream end) of the deep water. The lower end of a pool usually shallows up again before spilling over into the next riffle. Depth alone may provide cover and trout will lie on bottom where currents are slower and less forceful.

Some pools have swift running surfaces, with choppy water, which diffuses light. This adds up to additional cover for trout. Direct shade from debris such as logs, surface logjams, overhanging foliage or evergreen boughs may attract trout. Any change in the bottom structure such as rocks or boulders, or a ledge or dropoff, may hold trout.

Along the shallower portion of a river, such instream and shoreline cover creates mini-pools called pockets. During the spring through summer months, pocket water along a stream may provide better fishing than larger pools.

I refer to pocket water, and cover in pools, simply as "edges" along flowing water. *Edges* generally attract the most trout in any stream.

An edge *may* hold just one trout but with this approach to "reading" a stream, I frequently catch numerous trout from one edge. Generally all trout from an edge will run to similar sizes and this includes larger fish—all but the oversize trophies in a stream.

The grouping of trout I'm speaking of is dependent on the habitat. Locate an ideal edge and careful fishing will produce a number of trout from the area.

I've found this to be true in winter's waters which are often only a few degrees above the freezing mark. Trout will congregate in deep, lower ends of pools. Toward spring, with warming temperatures, the fish may feed more actively at times but they'll still be found near deeper, gentler flows.

With the arrival of high, often muddy snowmelt runoff waters, trout will spread around a stream and be numerous in the same comfortable waters but also in deep pockets which flow quietly along the stream edge. As waters lower and clear, many trout move to the shallower pockets. These pockets offer plenty of cover through summer months. The reason is simple: Pocket water provides cover, highly oxygenated water and an abundance of food such as small fish and insects. Deep pockets produce well during autumn months. This general seasonal pattern gives a trout fisherman places to seek productive edges along almost any stream.

As early as 6 weeks before trout spawn they may begin moving upstream. You'll see them two or more at a time, and a rule of thumb I use is that when I catch one fish, my next cast goes to the same place. These movements of trout occur in inland streams which do not receive new supplies of spawning-run trout from a larger river, lake or reservoir. Unlike some other spawning species of fish, trout do feed and in fact they often become bolder in striking. Keep in mind I'm referring to native trout populations with which I've had the most experience.

The movements of these fish correspond with the warming trend in early spring (rainbows) and the cooling time of late summer and early autumn. Thus the fishing for browns and brookies will pick up markedly as early as late August and become increasingly better through October. I mention this seasonal spawning trend because it means good fishing whenever you locate the edges harboring these colorful trout—regardless of season.

Food is another reason trout congregate. For example, where insects are abundant and trout have adequate water and shelter, there'll likely be good fishing. There needn't be a hatch and feeding trout present because trout can be effectively caught in their lairs. A particular hatch of caddis flies occurs for several weeks at about the same time each spring along a stream I fish. The trout are in the area in great numbers for this food and can be caught merely by adapting methods to conditions. When the waters run murky after rains and trout "hole up" under the banks I catch them with a deep-drifted attractor wet fly. Later on, after the hatch wanes, this section of stream doesn't produce steady trout fishing.

A quiet approach and keeping hidden from the fish is important to catching one trout and increasingly important when it comes to taking several fish from one small area.

I recall a boulder lying in 3 feet of water which showed

several edges to fish. My first cast to the bulging pocket behind the boulder produced a 15-inch trout. I took several steps to one side for a better angle to drop my next cast alongside the big rock. The offering drifted a yard downstream and a 16-inch trout slashed the water to grab the fly. The largest trout often hold in front of cover when looking for food so I moved upstream a bit and fished to the cushion of water in front of the boulder. My reward was a spunky 2½-pounder.

I wouldn't be without my polarized sunglasses when locating edges and underwater cover. They cut glare and provide a window to habitat below the surface. Sometimes they enable me to see trout. When trout are located in a group or line, hooking one usually spooks the others so I normally fish for the largest trout I can see.

Eddies are circles or partial circles of water which form around any current-breaker. Insects drift through eddies and pile up in the slow water where trout are resting or looking for food. Patches of foam often mark these spots. Eddies may be any size and I've taken large trout from an eddy just 2 feet wide. The better trout available in a river are likely to be found in a shallow eddy which is located near its deepwater lair.

There are numerous other surface signs of edges which hold trout. Here are a few:

● Trout hold beneath the sometimes nearly undefinable line where choppy water edges flat water. This food line may roughly parallel the streamflow. Often this indicates an underwater ledge which follows the contour of the stream which is a favorite deep edge for trout.

● Similarly, where the choppy-topped water simmers down and flattens across the width of a pool, is a hotspot for trout. Think of this line of fanning-out water as running in generally an across-stream direction.

● An underwater rock or other current-breaker may create a ripple on the water's surface. The currents scour a dish-like pocket downstream from the obstruction. Such pockets also are formed whenever the current flows over a hard rubble bottom and then surges across a softer bottom. Such pockets may be small but often a trout will hold in them. Sometimes the smallest surface sign leads to a larger deeper area. A large sunken log in a sandy stretch of water may shift currents enough to form a large pool downstream.

● Trout seek the highly oxygenated broken waters during the summer months when stream waters run warmer. This is

A spin angler fishes the trout cover along a small stream; trout might lie under snag (see arrow), under grassy bank, or in deep hole fed by riffle. Sometimes they'll be up in riffle, for oxygen on a hot summer day, or other times to grub for aquatic nymphs in the gravel and rubble.

Knowing how to read a trout stream will enable an angler to duplicate this brook trout catch.

Where fast water edges slower water, trout lie on bottom. The lunkers (such as the brown trout below) will likely be under the heavy, rolling current behind underwater rocks which form pockets. And some will be under the deeply undercut bank on the side nearest the photographer, which is shaded by overhanging foliage.

because broken water mixes with the air and brings fresh oxygen into the stream. Sometimes trout will hold in the shallow riffles behind rocks under choppy water for the extra oxygen found there.

Larger trout are usually a bit deeper, at the dropoff of the fast water entering the head of the pool, in the eddies curling off to the sides or along a deep edge.

Rainbows are thought of as fast-water trout but some hefty browns will join them during summer months to capitalize on the extra oxygen. Many browns are caught in quieter water edging the heavy flowing current, where bubbles are bursting and the foam fizzles out. This is the type of water which produces some of the largest hot-weather trout every summer.

Surface signs get you started but underwater edges can guide you to larger trout. Locating an underwater edge during low, clear water, is one way to scout a stream for times when the stream may be murky and visibility limited. Any cover such as a rock or boulder which is a foot higher than the stream bottom may have a trout resting or feeding in the quiet water directly behind it. In turbulent deep running water there will be large trout behind almost any cover which forms a pocket of gentler flow. Hooking one may require patient fishing.

I'll say I've heard more stories of trout estimated at 5 to 10 pounds being hooked in such deepwater pockets than in any other lair, during daylight, along fast water. I've hooked a few such trophy trout myself which have simply stayed deep and refused to budge or have run out all my line in one frightened downstream run.

I earlier spoke of the underwater ledge which parallels the stream contour. This ledge is usually a little ways away from a bank. The ledges can often be identified only in low water when the surface runs smooth. The deep side of the ledge is home for lunkers and I've hooked a half-dozen good-sized trout without moving from these areas.

Mossy vegetation which grows in large beds forms deep edges and trout hold around the cover to feed on the abundant insect larvae present. Such habitat is common in the mineral rich waters of limestone streams meandering through open meadows. Trout hold behind or even inside the vegetation. Fish the edges and the narrow slots of open water between the moss beds.

While trout may occupy lairs across the width of a stream, the edges along the banks will produce many fish. In high water, trout hold in the brushy undercuts away from the

Rainbow trout nose up into the oxygenated riffle, a hotspot on hot summer days.

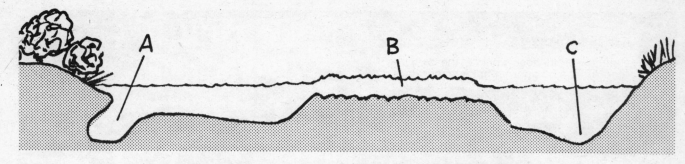

Cross section of river showing (A) undercut bank, a good hiding place for large trout, (B) riffle caused by shallow water and rough bottom, (C) deep pocket at stream edge.

Angler fishing under shady overhanging tree catches trout holding near undercut bank.

Casting to pocket water behind and to the sides of rocks produced this jumping trout.

heavy flow of water. In murky water, they'll sometimes be at lower ends of pools in even flowing water along open banks. During summer and autumn low water periods, a shady undercut bank or deep bend is cool and comfortable and there is a substantial insect food present which drops from overhanging grasses.

Usually it's necessary to fish right up tight against the bank to catch trout. There are times when it becomes necessary to float the offering beneath overhanging grasses. Many banks are deeply undercut and trout won't always come out to the edge to take an offering. So if my bait, lure or fly doesn't catch a trout by fishing the edge of the bank, I find a way to fish it beneath the bank. A low, snappy, across-stream cast may accomplish this. Other times I'll cast upstream or downstream as needed so the current will drift my lure through the undercut area.

The stream flow generally erodes undercut banks along straight sections and deep outside bends of rivers. The average fisherman passes up one good spot at every bend in the river—the inside elbow or bend of the stream. This lair is often a feeding station and good sized trout often will be found using this spot.

Another place sure to hold at least one trout is immediately below a cool feeder stream entering the river. Such areas offer trout more than just comfortable water—often there is food present. The smallest incoming springs may harbor trout. Patches of bankside moss may mark a trickling spring entering the stream.

Springs also upwell from sandy stream bottoms. Trout are usually found nearby and often in very shallow water. Springs can be found by wading fishermen simply by the change in coolness on wader-clad legs.

Holes or pools with fresh spring water may host numbers of trout. Transparent spring holes offer some of the most difficult places to fish and this type of angling requires a long,

light line and a great deal of patience.

Bridges over a stream often create a shady deep hole which may hold large trout. Fishing under the bridge will catch trout. Many times the fish will drop back to the nearby shallows to feed. It pays to fish from under a bridge because the dark area offers concealment to the fisherman while casting. Fish the water both above and below the bridge.

When a trout wants to feed, it will often move out of its lair and take up a feeding station nearby. This may be at the edge of the lair, or the trout may forage in a riffle on insect larvae or small fish. Sometime during the morning warming period and again as light dims toward evening, trout will be looking for food—whether there's a supply of insects on the water or not.

Hatching periods change through the season due to such factors as stream temperature, barometric pressure, fishing pressure or weather conditions. A substantial hatch of aquatic insects may bring on rises of trout at anytime. When the day warms enough and hatches occur I've enjoyed excellent dry-fly fishing to rising trout during winter months.

Night feeding trout become bolder but remember these lunkers feed to a great extent by using their acute sense of hearing and feeling to detect food such as swimming baitfish. Any unnatural sound such as splashy wading or tremors from footsteps on the bank may spook fish.

Lunker trout may cruise the shallows at night and they also forage heavily in pools. I locate likely hangouts of big trout during daylight hours and then come after darkness falls to fish. Knowing how to read a stream can lead to good catches of trout day or night.

Streams are composites of varied habitat and any one area may provide better fishing than another at any given time. Though bait, lures and various flies each have times and places where a particular one will do a better job than another, the versatile angler who can read a trout stream will be able to find fishing success.

High Peaks and Golden Trout

by CHARLES J. FARMER

DANGLE the word "golden trout" in front of me and I squirm and jump like a kid in front of an ice cream shop. I can almost taste the alpine sweetness of the high country. And I see clearly those touted rascals flicking their slender copper bodies at me as I study them from above. Prima donnas, that's what those golden fish are. Maybe they have more brains than I do. Sometimes it seems that way. They make a fisherman work hard just to touch the divine waters in which they swim. And to top it all off, the golden boys, as I like to call them, have an irritating habit of snubbing my best casts and choicest imitations. Why do I put up with them, you ask. That's a good question.

The place was Grizzly Lake, west of Laramie, Wyoming in the Medicine Bow National Forest. To reach Grizzly, a 3-mile hike is necessary . . . a picnic of a walk compared to golden trout standards. There is no established trail to the lake but it is easy to find on a good topographic map. My wife, Kathy, and I found Grizzly resting quietly in a setting of steep talus cliffs mixed with sparse clusters of Alpine Fir. At 10,000-plus feet, we nudged timberline with a simple, but comfortable, backpack camp. Soon I was casting "North Platte" streamers into the deep, inky waters and the platter-size swirls that pocked the lake.

Three days and an awesome barrage of casts went by before Kathy and I decided to give up the rods. During that time I managed to seduce one 4-inch golden on a 2-inch Mepps spinner—I was pooped and downright discouraged too. With fly rod and ultra light spin gear, we penetrated

Above and below—Backpacking is often most enjoyable and economical way to get to goldens.

the best looking golden water imaginable. The fish were there though. Good ones. Several I estimated to weigh-in at 2 pounds cruised within inches of a silver bladed spinner. They always turned away slowly when the lure neared the shoreline. That's golden fishing . . . sometimes.

Wall Lake, in the Bridger Wilderness of northwestern Wyoming, was a different story. But success did not come easy. After a 2-day, 14-mile backpack trip into Wall, my-self and four fishing partners, were eager to sample a deep, glassy pool directly below our camp.

To our amazement, large goldens were thick in the pool. They cruised about casually in search of nymphs while the five of us laid out every imaginable fly and lure. When dark-ness and cold, damp weather finally did us in for the night, we did not have a single fish to show for our efforts. We crawled into down sleeping bags at 9 PM, stomachs filled with dehydrated macaroni and cheese instead of coral-pink trout fillets . . . exhausted. My weary dreams were filled with the sulking, dark forms whose broad tails slapped away my lures and flies. A net, that's what we need. Did anyone bring a net?

Dwayne Smith was up early. From the cozy warmth of my sleeping bag, I could hear him moaning as he slipped into trousers chilled by the damp, cold of night air. "Go get 'em, Smitty," I whispered. I snuggled deeper in the bag. Tough fish would require an extra 40 winks.

Secretly we had hoped that Dwayne would return with golden fillets for breakfast. Despite giving him a half-hour or so alone at the pool, no such luck. "Nothing works," he muttered in between sips of coffee. "Those fish are weird."

Goldens are funny fish. Their trophy status may very well be based on their rarity and inaccessibility. But even when found, on many occasions, they remain wary and finicky. Temperamental. Take a golden lake that is seldom fished and an angler would expect a fish race to the bait. Not true with goldens. They're weird!

We had been offering our Wall Lake teasers the best casts and the finest flies and lures we had. But the gourmet treat-ment, because there was nothing left to try, came to a halt. I tied on a big (No. 8) gaudy, Platte River Special streamer and about a foot above it, clamped on a pea-size shot. That changed our luck.

For the next three days we caught as many goldens as we wished. They inhaled big, gaudy streamers and wet flies as if they were foraging for their last meals. The secret? The biggest, ugliest flies caught the most fish. Unusual? No.

Since those initial treks for golden trout, I have been continually amazed at the fish's propensity for large (No. 12s and bigger) gaudy wets and streamers. When I say big and gaudy I really do not mean to reflect upon the skill of the tier as much as the ironical twist associated with the seemingly finicky golden and its lack of concern for delicately tied, properly hackled, midge-sized imitations. Big and bold that's the way the goldens I know like them. Fish the patterns deep and slow and don't worry too much about presentation. Goldens don't seem bashful.

Another case in point. I have, during the course of 10, full fledged, backpack bouts with goldens, given somewhat equal time to lures and flies. And I have not been so pure, that worms and grasshoppers were not tested thoroughly. My findings are this. If forced to choose among flies, lures and live bait for goldens, I would select a boxful of gaudy flies every time. These I would stick with even under fishless conditions (and those conditions are inevitable) because they work better, most of the time, than lures and bait.

Here are some "good gaudies" to have on hand for your golden trip. Streamers in sizes 6 to 12. The North Platte Special has worked well for me. But any streamer "dace" or "minnow" imitation, in brown and gold should get the job done. White, black, and red and white maribou combina-tions are effective also.

Muddler Minnows, weighted imitation grasshoppers and Maribou Muddlers are dynamite. Use enough weight to fish them slow and close to the bottom.

If you do not use a fly rod, try spinning gear with a clear, plastic bubble to present the fly. Or you can use ultra-

Below—Anglers study map on route to high altitude golden trout.

Opposite page—Backpack camp set up on shore of a Wyoming golden lake. ▶

Opposite page—Golden Lakes are still rare gems, often nestled in craggy pine mountains. Right—Ordinarily there is not easy route to golden water. Angler fords swollen stream.

light spin gear which will enable you to adequately cast a fly and splitshot. These methods seem to work with equal effectiveness.

How to Find Golden Lakes

Remembering that goldens usually favor lakes above the 10,000-foot mark, prospects can be narrowed down to the western, mountain states. Originally native only to California, western game and fish departments transplanted and stocked California goldens in clear, high altitude lakes. Much of the stocking was successful. Although far from being plentiful or as widespread as rainbow trout, the golden can be found in every western state. However, due to the fish's rigid habitat demands and difficult accessibility for anglers, pinpointing the exact locations of golden lakes can be a challenge.

Keep in mind that game and fish departments, through transplanting and stocking, are continually adding new golden lakes to their lists of fishable waters. Airplane and helicopter stockings of fry and fingerlings have, in comparison to the old days when fish were carried in milk cans lashed to mules and pack horses, facilitated stocking. More and more golden prospects are being discovered.

To find good, current lists of *fishable* golden trout lakes, write to game and fish departments in the western states (see accompanying list). Department stocking records will indicate when fish were planted and fisheries biologists can advise anglers as to what size fish they can expect to catch. In the past, some golden lakes have had winter kills from enduring ice cover and depletion of oxygen. Contacting game and fish personnel can sometimes prevent wasted trips to winter killed lakes.

Some pure strain golden lakes have been "ruined" when brook trout or rainbows have been accidentally introduced. Brookies will take over a golden lake due to their ability to reproduce and grow faster than goldens. And when rainbows and goldens get together they interbreed with most fish taking on the snubbed head, rainbow stripe and square-tail appearance of the rainbow trout. I caught several such crosses at Wall Lake 4 years ago which is a bad sign for the future of that golden fishery. There is nothing wrong with the beauty, fighting or eating qualities of the rainbow-golden but the pure golden strain is gone.

Cook Lake, a few hundred yards below the outlet of Wall Lake still holds the world record for golden trout, 11 pounds, 4 ounces, 28 inches long, caught by C. S. Reed in 1948. The golden fishery is virtually nonexistent now as the lake is presently filled with stunted brook trout.

I have dwelled on the possibility of the disappearance and cross-breeding of goldens in lakes said to contain established populations because it is wise for fishermen to thoroughly check out this information first. Otherwise, long, rugged trips may be in vain.

Ask game and fish personnel to be as specific as possible when locating golden lakes. Request local contacts such as area wardens or forest rangers, who may be able to further help to pinpoint golden prospects. Finally, locate and mark the lakes on topographic maps you can purchase for the area. A listing of western Game and Fish Departments is included at the end of this article.

Topo maps show land contours, significant natural features, rivers, streams and lakes. For golden trout prospect-

Left—This photo was taken on July 4 with plenty of snow still in high country and ice partially covering lake. Opposite page—A dandy fish . . . but a threat to a golden lake. This is a rainbow-golden trout cross taken from Wall Lake in Wyoming.

ing, they are a must. The maps are easy to read with a little practice and can put fishermen right on the mark of golden treasure.

You can obtain topo maps by writing to Map Information Offices, United States Geological Survey, Washington, D.C. 20242 and requesting an *Index Circular* of the state you are interested in. After studying the circular, you can decide what maps you need. For specific maps *west* of the Mississippi River send your order to: Distribution Section, Geological Survey, Denver Federal Center, Denver, Colorado 80225. Most copies will cost 50 cents while maps scaled 1:250,000 are 75 cents. Some maps are available also at ranger stations and sporting goods stores in the area you will be fishing.

How to Get to Golden Trout

The majority of golden lakes are located in roadless national forests, wilderness or primitive areas. That means you are going to have a hike or a horseback ride to get to good fishing.

Backpacking is the most economical way to go and can be the most enjoyable provided you are in good physical shape. Altitudes and terrain at and above timberline are taxing. If you have a weight, heart, breathing or lung problem, don't risk the chance of hoofing it. Horseback may be your only alternative.

If you backpack, go as light as possible and have the best gear available. A good, brand-name down or Fiberfill-II sleeping bag with a comfort range down to zero or lower is a necessity. A lightweight pack tent is handy. A good pair of sturdy, Vibram-soled hiking boots is a must. A compact, lightweight stove will prove valuable in areas where wood is scarce. And dehydrated food, along with fresh golden trout fillets, will keep you nourished.

Because the terrain above 10,000 feet is rugged and because snow and cold weather are relatively common, even in the summer, you will need the best equipment you can afford. That way, you will enjoy the experience. If you skimp, the best fishing in the world won't make up for sleepless nights and exhausted minds and bodies.

Allow yourself enough time to challenge goldens and enjoy the great scenery that surrounds you. For a one-way hike, of 3 to 6 miles, allow at least 3 days of fishing. Allow 5 to 10 days for hikes over 10 miles. If you try to cram a golden fishing trip into a short weekend, you may end up too exhausted to enjoy it. Pace yourself coming and going. And choose fishing partners with similar physical capabilities as your own.

Horseback trips are another alternative to reaching high lakes. But, unless you personally know a horse concessionaire or outfitter, don't count on being able to rent the horses and ride into the sunset on your own. Most horse renters do not trust "dudes" alone. And most require that you be accompanied by an outfitter. And outfitters usually cost anywhere from $50 to $100 a day for high country fishing trips.

You might be able to save some money by having a guide pack you into an alpine camp and then return for you and your gear on a designated day. There are advantages and disadvantages to outfitted trips for goldens depending on your particular taste. Lists of fishing outfitters can usually be obtained from state game and fish departments and choosing the right one is up to you.

When to Fish for Golden

The season on goldens is ruled by mother nature. The number of fishermen who have set off in June and July, only to find a foot of ice on their golden lake, is overwhelming. Summer and ice out come late in altitudes above 10,000 feet. And a good safe rule to follow for the time to go is from mid-July through the end of August . . . unless you don't mind packing an ice auger.

WESTERN GAME AND FISH DEPARTMENTS
(For Golden Prospects)

Arizona—P.O. Box 9095, Phoenix, Ariz. 85020
California—1416 Ninth Street, Sacramento, Calif. 95814
Colorado—6060 N. Broadway, Denver, Colo. 80216
Idaho—660 South Walnut St., Boise, Id. 83707
Montana—Fish & Game Dept., Helena, Mont. 59601
Nevada—P.O. Box 10678, Reno, Nev. 89510
New Mexico—State Capitol, Santa Fe, N.M. 87501
Oregon—P.O. Box 3503, Portland, Ore. 97208
Utah—1596 West North Temple, Salt Lake City, Utah 84116
Washington—600 North Capitol Way, Olympia, Wash. 98504
Wyoming—P.O. Box 1589, Cheyenne, Wyo. 82002

Spinning Gear Basics For The Beginner

by MALCOLM HART

NO TYPE of rod-and-reel combination can match spinning tackle for its versatility and ease of use. Even a neophyte to fishing can quickly learn to cast effectively with a spinning outfit. Spinning gear has revolutionized fishing since its introduction to North America some three decades ago. It has become one of the most popular ways of casting a lure or bait.

The essential difference between the spinning reel and the older bait-casting reel is the spool which holds the line on a spinning reel is stationary during the cast. On a bait-casting reel, the spool revolves during the cast. On a flyfishing outfit, the reel plays no role in casting at all. It is solely a device for storing line.

When a cast is made with a spinning reel, the line slips or spins freely over the rim of the spool. The only time the spool on a spinning reel moves is when the lure is being reeled back or when a fish is taking out line. When a fish is running with line, the spool rotates on a spindle which offers resistance by means of a "drag."

The fixed spool concept has several important advantages over the revolving spool. The lack of restraint on the line allows long casts to be made with relatively light and small lures, making possible the design of very light tackle. The revolving spool on the bait casting reel in the hands of a tyro frequently causes a "backlash" of tangled line. There is no threat of backlash with a spinning reel. Spinning equipment also allows a more sensitive response and feel from fish.

There was, at one time, a belief that spinning tackle had been invented to replace the older bait-casting tackle. This is not true. Spinning tackle compliments bait-casting tackle; it cannot replace it. There are many fishing situations where bait-casting tackle is a better choice than spinning tackle.

With spinning tackle, an angler retrieves line by turning a crank with his less-skilled hand—the left hand in the case of a right-handed person. The rod is held in the right hand, and the fish is fought with the right hand. For a left-handed person the process is, of course, the reverse.

Spinning Reels

There are two basic types of spinning reels on the market —the "open-faced" reel and the "closed-faced" reel. In appearance, the two are quite different, despite the fact that on both types the line spins off a stationary spool. On an open-faced reel, the spool of line is visible; on a closed-faced reel, the spool is enclosed in a cone-shaped housing. On an open-faced reel, the line runs off in large spirals. But on a

No other type of rod and reel can match spinning tackle for versatility.

closed-faced reel, the line runs out of a hole in the cone, which eliminates large loose spirals of line.

The essential difference between these two reels lies in their method of retrieving line. On an open-faced reel, the line is wound back on the spool by a bail. On a closed-faced reel, the line is wound back by a lug or pin which picks up the line inside the housing.

In casting with an open-faced reel, the bail is pushed back over the end of the spool. The free line is then held with the index finger. When the lure hits the water, or if you want to shorten the cast while the lure is still flying through the air, the bail is flicked back to the retrieving position by a turn of the handle. The lure can be "feathered" down by allowing the index finger to lightly strike the coils of line as they come off the spool.

In casting with a closed-faced reel, a push-button on the reel is pressed and held down with the thumb. This retracts the pick-up pin and leaves the line free to slip off the spool. But the line is held until it is released on the forward movement of the cast. When the rod tip reaches the end of its arc during the motion of the cast, the thumb is lifted off the push-button and the line is free to shoot out from the momentum of the lure. When the lure hits the water, or while it is still in the air, the push-button is pressed down again to engage the line pick-up pin so that the line can be retrieved.

The closed-faced spinning reel is easier to operate than the open-faced reel. For this reason, it's a good choice for beginners. Also, because the cone of the closed-faced reel eliminates loose coils of line, there is less chance of tangles due to spilled spirals of line. For this reason, the closed-faced reel is frequently chosen for night fishing or for very windy days.

Many fishermen believe that the cone of the closed-faced reel restricts or inhibits the free flow of line from the spool and thus decreases casting distance. There is no evidence to indicate that this is true. Tests show no practical difference between the two types of reels as far as casting distance is concerned.

Spinning Rods

Most spinning rods today are made of tubular glass fiber with cork handles. But, graphite rods have already appeared on the market and one can expect that graphite will be a more popular material for fishing rod construction in the future. Now and then, a spinning rod of split bamboo is seen. Such rods are the handiwork of custom rod makers and are very expensive.

Spinning rods are made in a variety of lengths, from 5-foot ultralights to heavy, 10½-foot saltwater rods. The choice of length and action depends on the type of fishing and the weight of lures you use.

Rods with parametric action are generally chosen for big steelhead and lakers. Such rods cushion the runs of these fish and wear them down. The most popular action is the universal, sometimes called the omni-action. It is designed to handle lures of various weights. The single-action rods, on the other hand, are basically designed for lures of one weight range. Universal action rods have a progressive taper. The butt portion of the rod is swelled to give the rod body and backbone. From the butt, the rod tapers to a flexible tip.

One feature all spinning rods have in common is guides that are wider in diameter than those of bait-casting rods. When one looks down through the guides from the butt, one can see that they gradually decrease in diameter as they progress towards the tip. The purpose of the large guides is to gather the loops of line as they come off the spool and reduce them in size a little at a time, so the line is not hampered by too much friction.

The open-faced spinning reel comes in a variety of sizes, from ultralight for small waters to big reels for surf casting in the ocean.

Closed-faced spinning reels also come in various sizes.

Open-faced and closed-faced spinning reels each use a rod of different design. Rods for closed-faced reels are much like bait-casting rods. The butt may be slightly offset, and there is a finger hook on the other side of the reel seat. They have the same type of reel seat, and the reel is mounted in the same position as on a bait-casting reel. The major difference between rods for closed-faced spinning reels and bait-casting reels is that spinning rods are longer and have wider guides.

Rods for open-faced reels look somewhat like flyrods with larger guides. The reel seat may be nothing more than two sliding metal rings on the handle. These are slipped over the foot of the reel to keep it in place. The reel may be placed almost anywhere along the butt. However, a more common type of reel seat is one that is built into the rod handle. The foot of the reel is held by threaded double locking rings which rotate around the barrel of the reel seat.

Choosing a Rod and Reel

The combination of rod and reel should make a balanced outfit. The accompanying table will help in achieving a balanced system of rod, reel, line, and lures.

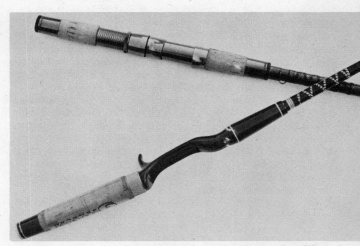

Rods for closed- and open-faced spinning reels differ. On those for the former, the butt is offset and the reel rest is similar to those found on bait casting rods. The rod is also shorter and has smaller guides.

ROD and REEL COMBINATIONS

TYPE OF FISHING	REEL	ROD	LINE (Pound Test)	LURES (Weight in Ounces)
—Brook trout, in small streams	ultralight	ultralight 5' to 6'6"	2 to 4	1/16 to 1/4
—Brook trout, cutthroat trout, rainbow trout, Dolly Varden, in streams	light	extra-light 6'6" to 7'	4 to 6	1/8 to 3/8
—Brown trout, rainbow trout, brook trout, in rivers and lakes	medium-light	light 6'6" to 7'	6 to 8	1/4 to 1/2
—Arctic char, steelhead	medium	medium 6'6" to 7'	8 to 10	3/8 to 3/4
—Lake trout, steelhead in big rivers	medium-heavy	saltwater 7' to 8'	10 to 15	1/2 to 1
—Salt water surf	heavy	saltwater 8'6" to 10'6"	12 to 20	1 to 4

There are a number of features that a prospective buyer of a spinning rod should look for. Action is very important. It should be crisp and snappy with a fair amount of backbone. Casting with a spinning outfit demands a quick, double snap of the wrist. A rod without backbone, a rod that is limp and slow, does not have the right action for proper casting. It will not respond to a snap of the wrist.

The next thing to look over is construction of the rod. Windings that hold the guides to the rod should be smooth and even. This indicates good workmanship. The varnish

The drag on an open-faced spinning reel is adjusted by means of a spool nut on top of the spool.

The drag on a closed-faced reel can be adjusted either by a micrometer ring just below the cone, or by a coin-slotted nut on the crank, as in the case of this reel.

The roller guide of a spinning reel should be checked often for signs of wear. Worn guides can cut monofilament line quickly.

around the bindings should be evenly spread and should form a shiny bond. The reel seat and ferrules must be made of rust-resistant material. The reel must fit firmly on the seat.

The handle should be comfortable in your hand. Most handles on rods for open-faced reels are made of cork rings. On good quality rods, the joints between the cork rings are almost invisible. The cork should be free of pits.

The length of the rod is not an overly-important consideration. Most freshwater fishing can be handled with rods of 6½ to 7 feet in length. However, a longer rod is capable of making longer casts. Likewise, a longer rod is better if you intend to use your rod for flyfishing with a plastic bubble. Longer rods are generally more limber and take the shock of casting and playing a fish much better than stiff rods.

There are a number of features a buyer should look for when purchasing a new reel. The reel should feel sturdy, even if it is a tiny ultralight. The finish on the reel should be corrosion-resistant, and if it's a closed-faced reel, the cone should be made of stainless steel or a similar non-corrosive material.

Turn the handle or crank to check for smooth, quiet operation. High quality reels use ball-bearing anchor gear trains—they are particularly smooth in operation. The anti-reverse control lever should be easily accessible—this will prevent the handle from flying backwards when you hook a big fish.

The bail on an open-faced reel should open and close smoothly. It should be of sound construction and made of stainless steel or similar metal because bails take a lot of punishment.

Be sure to check the drag control, not only to see that it operates smoothly and efficiently, but also to see how easy it is to reach and adjust. The spool should be easy to take out and interchange. The entire reel should be easy to oil and lubricate.

One final suggestion about buying spinning tackle, or any tackle for that matter. Get the best equipment you can afford. Junk never lasts. It always proves more expensive in the long run. Stick to well-known brands. No well-known manufacturer can afford to turn out shoddy equipment. He wouldn't be in business for very long.

Filling the Reel

Most spinning reels pick up and distribute line on the spool in a clockwise direction. To fill a reel with line from a regular spool, someone must hold the spool in such a position that the line spirals off the facing of the spool edge and is wound up onto the reel. This will insure that the line is wound onto the reel without a twist. Then, tie a slipknot around the spool on the reel and tighten the drag on the reel so there is no slippage. Apply a little tension on the line with your thumb and index finger to make certain that the line is wound on tightly.

A few manufacturers also put line in containers called "spin packs." The position of the line in a spin pack is ready for reels that pick up line in a clockwise direction. If you have a reel that picks up line in a counterclockwise direction, the line in the spin pack is reversed so that it feeds off the bottom end. The procedure then is the same as for line on a regular spool. A spin pack has the added convenience that no one is required to hold it while you wind the line on. The spin pack is simply placed on the floor and you can hold it down with your foot.

At least one manufacturer of line and spinning reels sells line on spools that can also serve as spare reel spools. All an angler has to do to change worn-out line (or change

The spinning reel was not invented to compete with the older flyrod or bait casting outfit, but rather to complement them.

from a light line to a heavier one) is to slip the line spool into the reel, and he's ready to cast.

A spinning reel should be filled within ⅛-inch of the spool flange. Overloading or underloading should be avoided. A reel that is underloaded will cause shorter casts because the line will not spin off the spool quite as easily. On the other hand, an overloaded reel often causes snarls of line and always makes the line more difficult to handle.

Once the reel has been filled, the line should not be allowed to uncoil when the reel is not being used. Some reel spools have clips or grooves that hold the end of the line so that it cannot uncoil or snarl. But a rubber band with a small loop in it can be used for the same purpose. The loop in the rubber band is used to remove the band when the reel is to be put to use.

Drag—Your Biggest Ally

Most fishermen, even after having their lines snapped by trophy fish, rarely try to determine why they lost the lunker. There are a number of reasons why a line may snap but the most common is an improperly set drag.

The principle of proper drag is less understood by anglers, even some experienced anglers, than any other element of fishing tackle. Proper drag is the amount of resistance which allows the fish to take line during sudden, swift rushes, but allows the angler to retrieve line when the fish is less vigorous in its attempts to get away.

Most fishermen don't realize that it frequently takes about twice as much force to start a drag slipping on some reels than is required once the spool starts to slip. A drag set at 2 pounds of pull may require 4 pounds to start it. A rule-of-thumb in setting a drag is to adjust for no more than one-quarter of the weight or test strength of the line.

An experienced angler will use the least amount of mechanical drag he can. He'll use his fingers and hands for additional pressure if required. This is particularly true when using ultralight spinning tackle. However, too light a drag will also cause you to lose fish. The drag must be adjusted tightly enough to offer resistance when a fish strikes and you whip the rod back to set the hooks.

The amount of line on the spool determines how much pull is required to make the spool slip. The drag works best on a spinning reel when the spool is filled to maximum capacity. The less line there is on a spool, the greater is the pull required to make the line slip. If a big steelhead suddenly goes on a long run, it's wise to lighten the drag a little as the fish is running and taking out line. Unfortunately, many fishermen don't think of this. When the fish takes off, their excitement rises and obliterates cool thinking.

The drag on an open-faced reel is adjusted by the spool nut on top of the spool. Closed-faced spinning reels have a micrometer ring just below the cone. There are several ways the drag can be adjusted. The easiest is to tie a lure on the line and hook in onto a tree or post. Then put the reel in the retrieve position and step backwards with the rod under stress, so that you can feel the amount of drag being exerted. If the line pulls taut and the clutch refuses to slip and release line, or if the line is released with a great deal of difficulty, lessen the drag until the line rolls off smoothly. Each time a spool of line is changed, the drag must be adjusted.

A good drag must be adjustable and maintain its adjustment while fighting a fish. It must have a low starting ratio and must release line smoothly. High quality reels can generally be relied upon to possess all of these features. Cheap reels rarely ever do.

There is a simple test that every angler can use to determine whether his reel has a smooth drag. Thread the line through the rod guides and set the drag so that it is about one-quarter the strength of the line. Hold the rod butt at about a 45-degree angle. Then ask someone to run out with the line for 50 to 60 yards. As the line starts out, your rod will bend forward because of the greater pressure required to start the drag. Once the line starts slipping out, the rod tip will rise to a running position. If the rod tip stays in one position and does not bounce around, the drag is smooth and even. If however, the rod tip bounces and weaves about like a willow branch in a high wind, the drag is poor and jerky.

A jerky drag may be caused by worn out washers or oil on the washers. Have them replaced. New reels sometimes have jerky drags because the drag has not been broken in. One of the main reasons for poor performance of drags on some reels is storing the reel with the drag on. Heed the manufacturer's recommendations on storage. Drags are made of alternating soft and hard washers. The life of the washers on some reels is considerably shortened if they are squeezed together for a long time. After a day of fishing, release the tension on the drag so that the washers can relax and return to their original shape.

If you maintain the drag on your reel properly, you'll be rewarded with bigger fish and more of them. A properly maintained drag is the best ally a fisherman has in fighting big fish.

Family Trout Fishing—It's Fun!

by DAVID RICHEY

KIMMY'S rod tip was playing footsie with the surface of the lake as the unseen brown trout dashed for bottom. She'd bring the rod tip up slightly and the hefty trout would yank it back down again.

"Dad, my arms are getting tired," she complained, as the brown surged off on another line-ripping run.

"I know babe but stick with it. This is a nice fish."

She hung in there like the 9-year old veteran she is and soon the monstrous brown was cutting figure eights far below the boat. "Is he big?" she asked as the fish was slowly pumped toward the surface.

"He's a dandy, Kim. Just keep steady pressure on him and don't yank hard on the line. We've got all day," I cautioned. She groaned at the thought of the battle continuing much longer. She'd had the fish on for 15 minutes and was rapidly getting tired.

She would slowly raise the rod tip to a vertical position and then quickly reel in the slack on the way down. Another lift, more reeling and I could see the exhausted brown easing toward the surface.

The brown broke the surface about 10 feet from the boat and I cautioned Kimmy again to take it slow and easy. This was certainly her largest trout to date and I didn't want her to lose it.

A minute later I slid the wide-mouthed net under the brown and laid it gently in the bottom of the boat. "We did it! We did it!" she hollered. I gave her a congratulatory hug and kiss and we hung the trout from a pair of small scales.

The scales quivered slightly and then settled on 12½ pounds—a fantastic brown trout for anyone to catch, especially a 9-year old girl. Kimmy went on to catch four other browns in the 6- to 10½-pound range that day. She considers it the best fishing trip she's ever had.

Many families feel trout fishing is too demanding for youngsters and that they lose their concentration and desire too quickly. I've found family trout fishing trips to be a great way for children and their parents to spend a healthy day on the water and still catch fish.

As in all types of participant sports, there are certain rules that must be followed—both by children and adults.

My wife and I have four children and Kimmy is the oldest. I've found the quickest way to have a discouraging day trout fishing is to take all four children at once. This usually results in either the children or me becoming upset. I've found it impossible for me to cope with four different sets of problems at once and still put the kids into trout.

The easiest solution to this problem is to either take them individually or, second best, to take two kids at one time.

25

Author David Richey feels that family trout fishing trips are a great way for children and their parents to spend a healthy day on the water and still catch fish. Pictured here is daughter

Kimmy catching a 12½-pound brown and her envious mother Carol. Note that Kimmy wears her life jacket when afloat—an important detail when fishing with children.

This cuts the problems in half and makes it much easier for everyone to have a good time.

Parents should take children together only if there is no real sense of competition. Over the years I've found it difficult to explain to one child why the other youngster caught the only trout of the day. It's okay to take a child that obtains as many thrills from watching a brother or sister catch a fish as he would if he were landing it himself.

My children offer two extremes; one boy and one girl are easy going, will tackle any fishing problem, and do not complain if another catches a fish. Another girl and boy are more withdrawn, highly competitive, and are harder to please. I've found it best to either take the more competitive children by themselves or with one of the easier going kids. The problems tend to iron themselves out easily when the competitive spirit is removed.

Children have a very short attention span during their younger years. Kimmy, for instance, will fish all day without complaining but Guy, our youngest, is bored stiff after 2 hours of uneventful fishing. He likes action and plenty of it —that's what keeps youngsters' enthusiasm stirred up.

Parents should realize that attention spans vary from child to child. It becomes necessary to plan trout fishing trips accordingly. Some youngsters will tolerate wading a trout stream just one time where they can't readily catch fish, but will sit for hours in a boat and troll without complaining.

Personally, I feel the best method of getting a family into trout fishing is to purchase or rent a boat and troll. Trolling means movement and children are geared to moving from one place to another and they settle more comfortably into trolling for trout than any other method.

Of primary importance to any trout fishing family is the need to expose children to a method of fishing that stands the best chance of putting a trout on the ends of their lines. I've found the best bet is to query the Department of Natural Resources' Fish Division with direct questions as to where the best trolling spots are located for trout. Determine the type of trout available, best times of year and the best method of trolling to take these trout.

Once the best locations have been found in your state, it is vitally important to determine the peak periods of activity. In Michigan where I live, brown trout are found in the shallows of Lake Michigan during June. I geared my trip with Kimmy and my wife Carol for the end of June because I felt this was the optimum time to produce a trophy brown for my daughter. As it turned out, I couldn't have hit the fishing at a better time.

Parents reading this article shouldn't get the impression I'm advocating trophy fishing for children. Trout are pretty difficult to creel consistently and I feel it's much more important to expose kids to catching trout than it is to try and push trophy trout fishing down their throats.

On the other hand, I'm also not advocating exposing children to the philosophy that an angler is entitled to a limit catch of fish just because he went trout fishing. Children should learn early in their fishing careers that some days the trout cooperate and some days they don't. They must learn to be philosophical about trout fishing and learn there is more to the sport than just catching fish.

Once the location of the trout fishing hotspot has been determined and the peak periods solved, there comes a period of getting ready for the trip. Children should be encouraged to help in the preliminary work to prepare for the trip. This will help set the mood of the sport and teach them that trout fishing involves more than just fishing.

I try to delegate jobs according to the sex of the child. Girls usually help Mom pack the lunch basket, fill the Thermoses with coffee and cold drinks, and prepare other

A sonar unit and proper tackle add up to a nice rainbow for this youngster.

When youngsters get older they can get into stream fishing. The author guided this young man to these nice steelhead.

facets for the outing. Boys generally help me work out snarls in the lines for the boat, sort out the tackle boxes, help grease wheel bearings on the boat trailer and do other outside jobs.

Family planning is a key part of the trip and I generally show the kids a map to orient them with the area to be fished. I've heard my youngsters telling their friends about fishing at such and such a place. The neighbor kids haven't a clue as to what my kids are talking about, but it makes my youngsters happy to be able to talk about where they fish.

There are important rules to be followed when parents take children fishing in a boat. I bought each of my kids a Stearns life jacket and they are expected to wear it. Even my 6-year old son can swim, but he's expected to wear the life jacket whenever he's in the boat. Tragedies can be avoided simply by planning ahead and taking necessary precautions before the need to act arises. My kids know that if they shed that life jacket while we're on the water they'll be on shore promptly. I find absolutely no pleasure in quarreling with a child over something as necessary as safety precautions.

Another rule I insist on is calm behavior. Horseplay has no place on a fishing boat. It can lead to lack of attention on the part of the boat operator and this can lead to an accident. Parents should keep unnecessary in-boat activities to a minimum.

Conversely, I will allow my children to stand up in my boat while landing a fish. They are directly involved in the battle and it aids them to be able to see what is going on. They are always cautioned against getting too close to the gunwales but my boat is large enough so a youngster can stand up inside it without danger of falling overboard.

We always try to have some snacks aboard for the kids while fishing—a can of pop or handful of potato chips will allay any restlessness for a period of time.

A radio or tape deck goes a long way toward relieving boredom induced by long hours on the water when trout aren't biting. Let the kids listen to the radio and sing the familiar songs. It will keep their minds occupied until the fish decide to cooperate.

Trolling is the best method of putting youngsters into trout. They don't have to learn current speeds, how to wade, how to cast and how to fight trout in current. Trolling puts the lures or bait in front of trout and the speed of the boat brings out the action. Wary trout are less likely to spook from the sound of a foot scraping the bottom of the boat than they are from the sounds of a foot banging clumsily against an underwater rock.

One of the best points in favor of trolling is that it allows the fisherman to cover much more water than any other method. Shallow and deep water can both be explored by merely turning the wheel. Once a pattern of trout activity has been determined, it becomes much easier to catch trout by trolling.

The trolling family should have some type of sonar unit with which to keep track of the depth of water. I have a recording graph on my boat and my kids get a big kick out of watching the graph mark fish. This, in itself, affords a break in the normal trolling routine. The youngsters holler and carry on whenever a fish mark shows on the paper. "Trout at 18 feet," they shout. They've learned to read the unit and this can be a big asset when the pilot is busy setting lines or steering the boat.

I'm a firm believer in allowing the children to set their own lines. I show them the proper way to release line to put the lures behind the boat, how to check and adjust the drag, how to operate the free-spool mechanism and how to take the rod out of the rodholder on the strike. I watch them intently until I'm sure they completely understand the procedures and then I leave 'em alone. If they make a mistake, I'll counsel them, but they learn it was their mistake that cost them a fish. I haven't seen them make the same mistake twice.

The parents must be familiar enough with trout and trout habits to know how and where to look for fish. Part of this knowledge can come from reading books on the subject while the bulk of the experience is best attained from previous trout fishing trips. Visits to local tackle shops can often pinpoint best locations for fishing.

I'm a firm believer in allowing children to fight their own fish. I can't see how a youngster can learn about trout fishing by their parents cranking in hooked trout for them. My kids take the rod from the time the fish is hooked until it's either lost or safely in the boat.

Fishing trips can be both fun and pandemonium. I remember one time my wife and I took three youngsters out on Lake Michigan for a day of fishing. I set two downriggers and we trolled two flat lines in hopes of latching onto a lake trout.

We trolled for nearly an hour without any action. The kids were lulled into a mood of not watching the lines. Suddenly the two downriggers snapped to attention. "Fish on!" I yelled, as the kids looked from one rod to the other. I vaulted over the seat, grabbed one bucking rod and handed it to my youngest son. "Crank hard," I advised, as Guy fought to control the large rod.

The second rod was given to Dave, Jr. and he found himself tangled up with a jumping steelhead. Guy's fish bored for bottom and later turned out to be a 9-pound lake trout.

Dave gets real determined when a fish is on and he tussled with his steelhead through four jumps. Finally the trout tired and he slid the fish into my net. Two minutes later I scooped up Guy's fish and the day quickly took on a new meaning for the boys.

Stacey, the comic in our family, spoke up with the quiet observation: "I've never seen you move so fast Dad." Trout fishing action comes hot and heavy and the parents should do their best to keep the kids into the action as long as possible.

One thing I caution parents against is landing trout themselves. We let the children land all the fish because I feel it's important to expose them to as much success as possible. Days when everything goes like clockwork are far outnumbered by days when Jr. and Sr. anglers spend a long stretch on the water with nothing to show for their efforts except a sunburn.

Children actively seek praise and we find the quiet congratulations of a job well done in landing a trout really perks up a child's spirits. Bestow praise for a good cast, a job well done when battling a trout or for just being good kids in a crowded boat. Kids enjoy this and you'll find them much more eager to please and do a good job when they are happy in their sport.

Family trout fishing trips involves little more than some advance planning, familiarization with tackle and equipment, a boat and the willingness to troll for long hours in areas known to harbor good concentrations of trout.

My family loves trolling because they've found it produces good catches of trout with a minimum amount of effort. As my children grow older I'll expose them to stream fishing and the special situations involved in that type of sport.

There is no reason why a trout fishing parent cannot expose his youngsters to his favorite sport. Try it and I'm sure the satisfaction you'll derive will more than make up for a day away from your trout fishing buddies.

Blueback trout, once thought to be extinct, do not grow to behemoth sizes. Largest pictured here is a 14½-incher, weighing a bit over 1 pound.

Blueback Comeback

by NICK KARAS

UNLESS YOU ARE a fairly dedicated trout fisherman you probably never heard of a blueback trout. And even if you are, there's a good chance that the blueback has slipped past your attention. Bluebacks don't grow to behemoth sizes, they are not extremely plentiful and their range and distribution is pretty sorry when compared to lake trout or brook trout. In fact, you couldn't even find one until a few years ago . . . they were thought to be extinct for nearly 50 years.

So, why go fishing for bluebacked trout? Most anglers don't need an excuse to fish, but when it comes to the blueback you might be looking for one. I've been fishing now for more years than I care to recall. In those years, I've tangled with almost every species of game fish that swims and a few that wouldn't. When I heard rumors, a few years ago, that the blueback trout had been sighted again, my curiosity was aroused. I guess I was a lot like the big-game trophy hunter who, after collecting all of the common heads or trophies, begins looking around for something new to shoot. Like the bird-watcher, I wanted to

add the blueback to my life list of fishes.

Delving into the rumor, I located where it had been stemming from and luckily found an established hunting and fishing camp deep in the land of the blueback from which I could work. The camp is on Maine's Island Pond and is operated by a retired Maine game warden, "Sleepy" Atkins. His Red River camps were first built near the turn of the century and Island Pond is only half a mile from Pushineer Pond, the body of water that was supposed to have produced the blueback trout.

But, before attempting to catch a blueback, I had to spend some time in the archives. The blueback trout has another name, oquassa trout. It was first discovered near the village of Oquossoc on the Rangeley Lakes and the name simplified to oquassa. It was thought to exist only in these Rangeley Lakes when it was first discovered in 1853.

The blueback trout, unlike its char cousins, was a sly and seldom-seen fish. It preferred to search for its food in the deep and cold parts of a lake or pond rather than make a commotion by jumping for flies on the water's surface. It did come to the top and along the shore only late in the afternoon and evening to feed, when most trout fishermen had left the water.

Because of its secretive life-style it was seldom caught by fishermen of old. But, come October and November of every year, bluebacks abandoned the deep water and headed for the

The state of Maine maintains several campsites on Pushineer Pond that can be reached by fording the shallow Red River.

"Sleepy" Atkins (left), operator of Red River Camps and a retired
Maine game warden, helps author, Nick Karas, ready a spin rod.

shallows at the mouths of streams and along the shore, ready-ing themselves for a spawning migration up the feeders. How-ever, in stepped man with little care for a resource that he believed inexhaustible. He moved with nets and spears. Bluebacks intent with the business at hand had lost their wary ways at spawning time and became easy prey for the netters. Each year they were taken in great quantities; by the bushel-ful and even by the wagon-load to be used as cheap fertilizer on nearby farm fields.

This practice continued until the turn of the century when unexpectedly the bluebacks suddenly became scarce. Farm-ers had to turn to other fertilizers. But as far as the fish was concerned, it was too late. By 1904, the blueback had disap-peared from the Rangeley Lakes of Maine.

So ends the story of how the blueback disappeared, a sad tale that has been repeated too often with many species of fish, birds and animals. Though the tale may end, the story does not. Biologists in Maine conducted a state-wide study during the 1940s of all its waters to determine what fish still existed where. At this time, the blueback trout was still con-sidered an extinct species. Soon after the survey got under way, however, reports from the northern counties, at the headwaters of the Penobscot and Red Rivers, were indicating that a fish resembling the old blueback, was still around—a lingering population of blueback trout had been found.

Today, the heart of the blueback trout country has shifted from the Rangeley Lakes in west-central Maine to the far north. Due north of Mount Katahdin and less than 20 miles south of the Maine-Canada border, a group of small, mountain ponds form the headwaters of the Red River that eventually flows into the St. John River. The land surrounding these numerous ponds and lakelets is still wild and isolated and has been held in trust for many years by lumber companies.

Until just a few years ago, the only way to reach these waters was over a wet and winding logging road. In part, this isolation helped preserve the blueback trout. Today these ponds: Gardiner, Deboulie, Pushineer and Fish Pond on one chain, and Little Black Ponds and Black Pond on another linking chain form the last stronghold of the blueback.

Bluebacks are not a large or fast-growing trout. While they were still present in the Rangeley Lakes, seldom were they reported larger than 10 inches in length, with an average nearer 8 inches. "It took four or five of these little fish to weigh a pound," according to the old records. Compared to their ancestors, the newly-discovered blueback are giants. Some of the fish taken by biologists during the sampling measured 15 inches.

Size in the blueback trout, really a char like the brook trout and lake trout, is controlled largely by the amount of food in the waters these fish now inhabit. Typically, the blueback is a dweller of the deep, oligotrophic lakes of Maine that are sparse in food. The fish are then forced to feed primarily on plankton and microscopic organisms. In lakes richer in food, the landlocked salmon thrive and bluebacks cannot compete successfully against this more aggressive fish.

Red River Camps are located about 25 miles southwest of Fort Kent on the Canadian Border. To get there, I drove due north from Bangor in the southern part of the state and near Houlton turned onto Route 11 that heads north. Just south of the village of Eagle Lake we spotted the sign to Red River Camps and turned west for an 18-mile drive through the original primeval forest.

I had no idea how to catch bluebacked trout nor did anyone else to whom I first talked. So, I took along my cousin, Joe Drahos of Binghamton, N.Y. Joe is a dyed-in-the-wool fisherman and I hoped that between us we could solve the riddle. When we arrived in camp, we were told that we could have turned off Route 11 at Portage on another marked road. It was 29 miles long, but a much better road.

The next morning dawned clear, bright and typically cool for northern Maine during the waning days of June. Our goal for the day was Pushineer Pond, several hundred yards from Red River Camps and just over the hill. I drove my camp-er van over the remnants of a road to where several canoes were cached on the lake shore. As Joe readied one canoe I hauled out a small outboard and attached it to a side mount on the canoe.

Pushineer Pond isn't large; half-a-mile at its greatest length

Author fights and lands
a blueback from trolling canoe.
All it took was the
simple trick of trolling
at faster pace.

Left—Closeup of a blueback trout's head. The fish, also known as the oquassa trout, was once harvested in great quantities by Maine farmers for use as fertilizer. Opposite page—An immature blueback as indicated by the parr markings along the side of its body.

across the base and roughly triangular in shape. Pushineer is at the bottom of a chain formed by Gardiner and Deboulie Ponds and then connected by small links or streams. The amount of run-off water is small and the connecting streams have nominal flows of water. Most of the water that keeps them filled comes from large springs on the lakes' bottoms. This accounts for their lack of the typically acid-tan or coffee-colored water that is a mark of most Maine lakes. In part, the lack of a flowing stream also limits the sedimentation and accounts for some of the greater depths. These ponds have stayed deep since they were glacially formed more than 5,000 years ago. Pushineer reaches almost 60 feet and Deboulie nearly 90 feet and thus form ideal waters for blueback trout that prefer to range the cold water depths.

As we launched the canoe, we spotted a boat on the southwest corner and worked our way to them to see what they had caught. They didn't mind the interruption because they had just filled out their trout limit and were heading in. One of the fishermen held up the stringer and among the square-tails hung one, silver, bluebacked trout. They asked if we knew what kind of fish it was. I wasn't sure at the time; I had never seen a bluebacked trout but the conclusion was almost automatic. It was a char but lacked the vermiculations across the back like a brook trout and the mottled pattern along the side like a lake trout. It had the typical char pipings along the ventral fins . . . it had to be what we were after.

"Joe," I said, "the bluebacks are here. All we need to do is figure out how to catch them."

From reading the research material, I knew that these char were a deep-water fish; seeking water below ten feet and they preferred their food small. It seemed an easy task, All we had to do was find the deepest part of the lake, use small lures or bait and we'd catch fish.

An old log slide planked a high bank on the south side of the lake and we'd been told that deep water existed here just a few feet from shore. The anglers we had talked with had been trolling this piece of water when we first spotted them, so Joe and I figured that this had to be a good spot for the bluebacks.

I rigged a small, double-bladed gold spinner to the end of a light spinning line and adorned the hook with a bit of fresh garden hackle. A few feet ahead of the spinner I added a three-way swivel and then a 2-foot dropper line to which I tied a light dipsey sinker. It would help pull the affair into the realm of the bluebacks.

Joe did the same and then we moved the canoe upwind of where we wanted to fish, cut the outboard and allowed the wind to drift us back. I had attached the transducer of a portable depth sounder to the side of the canoe and then turned on the fish locator to see where the bottom was located. A quick sounding showed the water was nearly 35 feet

deep just 50 feet from shore. This had to be blueback water.

We tried several wind drifts over the spot with our rigs somewhere near bottom but received little response from the fish. Maybe we were drifting too fast, so I tried the slowest trolling speed possible with the little outboard and into the wind so our lures bumped bottom. But still no trout. The entire morning sped by and we were fishless.

We ate our lunch on the eastern porch of an old abandoned trapper's cabin and tried to figure out what we had been doing wrong. "Maybe those fishermen never caught the blueback on Pushineer Pond," Joe suggested. "We just assumed that they had." "Or maybe that wasn't a blueback trout we saw." I said. "Or maybe we aren't fishing the deepest water in the lake. It's time to make our own map."

After lunch, we did just that. I sketched out the shape of the pond on a piece of paper and then began running ranges back and forth with the depth sounder working. In just a short time we saw the bottom of the lake taking shape. After the last range, I connected the similar depths in contour lines and they revealed that there was deep water just off the log slide, but farther into the southwest bay, right in the middle of it, the water reached 50 feet. We would have to troll down the middle of the bay to find our bluebacks.

We trolled all right, all afternoon, after dinner until 10 o'clock and darkness and even the next two days without getting a look at a bluebacked trout. The fish was quickly becoming a mystery to us. We tried everything from spinner, flies, spoons, plugs and even more garden hackle in big balls, but nothing worked. We fished at all times of the day, from early morning to late in the evening. We caught some good brook trout, the only other fish, excepting a few perch, that inhabit the lake. We must have been doing something wrong, but what? With one more day left for fishing, we were becoming desperate.

That evening in camp we met the game warden for the district we had been fishing. John Crabtree was from Eagle Lake and even agreed to spend his only day off fishing with us. The next day, as John suggested, we tried Deboulie Pond.

We had high hopes for Deboulie the next morning, and with John to guide us, we felt confident that we'd find our first blueback. Deboulie is a pretty lake. A large stone slide, off the face of Deboulie Mountain to the north, continues from near the top well into the depths of the lake. It is the only break in the dense green mantle of spruce and hemlock trees that cover the mountains that surround the lake. The water is clear and deeper than Pushineer and the lake is nearly 2 miles long. We found the depth of the water near the slide to be over 50 feet and easily filled the requirements for bluebacks. The three of us worked the hole for the entire morning, but again no trout.

We concentrated our trolling for most of the afternoon over a deep hole and even anchored and still-fished, but still no trout. Joe caught a square-tail from just under the boat as he was pulling up his line to check the bait and for a moment we had a scare, thinking that at last it might be a blueback.

We heard the the evening dinner bell toll over the hills. John, never late for a meal, started the motor before Joe's line was in, Joe hauled faster but on the first few cranks the line wrapped around the bail. The accident saved the trip. The fast troll caught us a fish. Joe hardly knew it was on at first, the drag was so slight. Finally, John stopped the motor and I netted the fish, though it hardly needed netting, it was only 6 inches long. At first glance, it didn't look like a trout but resembled a chub. Then John yelled, "It's a blueback."

We wolfed down dinner that evening, eager to get back onto the water. We had the trick of catching bluebacks all figured out. All we needed was a faster troll through about 30 feet of water and we'd catch bluebacks.

The sun was already hiding behind some higher peaks when we returned to the lake. The western shore was in shadows. We started dropping our lures into the water just as the canoe trolled past the now familiar log-slide landmark. At that point, the depth fell off from 30 to 50 feet over the bottom. This time, however, we kept the little 3-horse motor purring at a faster rate and as we passed the white birch stump where Joe had the first strike, he hauled in another blueback. This time it was a little larger than the 6-incher he had caught during the afternoon. I made a turn at the end of the lake and we made another trolling pass across the same water. My rod bobbed sharply as we passed the birch stump and a fish hung on. I cut the motor and settled down to land my first blueback.

Bluebacks must have been schooled in one spot because just as we passed the lone birch stump again, Joe's reel sang out. It was a big fish but too lightly colored for a brookie. Moments later it neared the surface. It was a deep-bellied blueback, every bit a fighting match for the same size brookie. As Joe swung it to the net I had extended, I saw that it wouldn't easily fit. It was 18 inches long and when Joe saw it he goofed. In his desire to land the trophy blueback he tightened-up too much on the line and lifted the trout's head out of the water. That's all the fish needed as it rolled over once and was gone.

We picked up more fish until it was too dark to see. When we returned to camp, we had eight bluebacks in the packbasket. I couldn't believe it. We had fished so hard for the three previous days and missed them continuously and a simple trick like a faster troll was all that was needed.

The largest fish was a beauty that measured 14¾ inches long and weighted 1¼ pounds. The hook in the lower jaw had started to form and we knew it was a male. "Blueback" is a poor name for the fish because it acquires the deeper bluish hues only in the fall when spawning is near. It is a late spawner, becoming active late in November and December. The rest of the season, the fish is more of an opalescent salmon color, with metallic hues shifting color in the light. They change from a gold along the sides to a tanner dark brown on the back in the fish we caught.

The larger male showed the characteristic markings of the fish. It contained the white stripes along the leading edge of the fins that are characteristic of all chars. The lake trout and brookie are a little more pronounced, but similarly marked. The fish is delicate in shape when compared to a brook trout and closely resembles a salmon. The head is often small in proportion to the rest of the body and the tail is often forked, even more so than in lake trout.

The blueback is perfectly compatible with the brook trout and co-exists in waters at the head of the Red River system. The blueback being a deep water fish usually claims the stratum from 30 to 50 feet. The brook fish is seldom found below 30 to 50 feet. Food-wise, the blueback feeds on small crustaceans and plankton found in the depths. Later, I found it will rise to the surface during the evening and will take flies, but this type of feeding accounts only for about 10 per cent of its diet. The lakes aren't extremely fertile at these depths and this is one reason a blueback of comparable age is usually shorter and lighter in weight than a brook trout.

The ponds and Red River Camps are easily reached today over a new logging road just completed by the Great Northern Paper Company. The state maintains several campsites on Pushineer that can be reached by fording the shallow Red River just at the outlet of the lake. Several other campsites are located on Deboulie, but you need a canoe or boat to reach them unless you come in on a back road that is passable only by jeep. Immediately intermingled with Gardiner, Black, Deboulie and Pushineer Ponds are Perch, Togue and Mud Ponds. These waters, however, don't connect with the Red River, but drain west, eventually flowing into the Allagash as it heads north. Bluebacks are unknown in these ponds but togue or lake trout are there and this is probably the reason bluebacks are not.

Blueback trout, according to several icthyologists, are a land-locked Arctic char that was isolated from the more northern Arctic chars after the last glacier moved north. Since that time, they have developed on their own and have given up the yen for salt-water their larger cousins desire. Though exterminated in the Rangeleys, the blueback in Aroostook County are holding their own. Wise bag limitations and strict enforcement are helping the bluebacks stay around. This time, we've been lucky and given a second chance to holding onto a rare fish.

Playing and Landing Trout

by MARK SOSIN

Right—When a trophy trout takes off downstream, work into shallower water and chase the fish. There's no safe way to get a big fish back against the current. Opposite page— In landing a stream caught trout, push rod behind you with one hand and reach for fly with the other if you intend to release your quarry. Otherwise, simply net fish head first and the trophy is yours.

WHETHER you wade the well-trampled bottom of a hatchery stocked stream or cast for trophy trout in waters only accessible by float plane, handling your quarry once it is hooked demands a special awareness. Even the pen-reared trout can present a problem if it is hooked on light tippet in a fast riffle.

The instant a fish feels the barb of a hook, it goes into a panic situation. Escape is paramount and, since this is a new experience for your quarry, it is going to follow the easiest route. Usually, that's downstream. If a fish maintained a lie in some type of cover such as a log or under a brush pile, it might try to reach this sanctuary, hoping to sever the tethering leader in the process.

Even before they make the cast, top anglers know instinctively what will happen if they hook a trout right now. They have learned through experience to stay alert and to think about what might take place if a heavyweight rises to the fly or engulfs a natural bait. The trick is to eliminate the elements of surprise where you suddenly discover that the husky denizen on the other end already is in control. Sometimes, you have to be fast to salvage the ballgame.

Trout fishing is often a slow-paced sport in which the angler perfects a delicate presentation and a gentle reaction when the fish strikes. This is often carried over into fighting a fish. Many enthusiasts are quite content to gingerly pressure a fish, hoping it will either fall asleep from boredom or turn on its side from old age. It is precisely this attitude that often gives the fish the advantage.

Fish are lost because of tackle failure or angler error. The longer you play a fish, the greater the chances for an item of gear to give out or for you to zig when you should have zagged. If you want the fish on the end of your line, you should apply maximum pressure and lead the fish to you as quickly as you can.

There's another reason. Trout fishermen have been in the forefront of conservation, urging other anglers to release

unwanted fish and turning a percentage of their own catches loose. During normal swimming, the bloodstream of a fish provides enough oxygen to the muscles and carries away wastes. When a fish swims at burst speed for a prolonged period or gives its all to do battle against an angler, lactic acid often builds up in the muscles. This can be poisonous to a fish and death may take place several hours after the trout is released.

The well-meaning angler who permits the trout to exhaust itself before freeing the fish may be defeating his own purpose. If you want to share the resources of trout fishing, the more sensible approach is to get the fish in and turn it loose in the shortest time possible.

In a stream, you not only have to fight the fish, but you must counter the force of the current as well. A trout that moves below you and then turns broadside to the flowing water can become a problem. If the fish isn't too big, you can often work it toward you by first easing the fish toward

the surface. Pumping is the key ingredient. Too many anglers with spinning or spin casting tackle insist on cranking a fish to them using the reel as a winch. This will work with small fish in relatively calm water, but it can cost you a trophy.

A better approach is to pull the fish toward you by lifting the rod. Then lower the rod as you turn the handle of the reel to regain line. By repeating the procedure, you can work the fish toward you and lead it out of the current. Beginners tend to panic and often apply too much pressure. Yet, it is surprising how much pressure you can put on a fish if you do it correctly and use the rod as a spring or cushion.

The fly fisherman prefers to use the strip method in playing a small fish. He clamps the first or second finger of his rod hand against the line and holds the line against the foregrip of the flyrod. Then, with the other hand, he pulls in line and the fish moves toward him. A number of anglers erroneously believe that the spring in the rod eventually

Above—Fly fishermen should play large trout directly from the reel. By palming the spool flange or holding a finger against the inside of the spool, you can add drag manually. Below—Drag settings on a reel should be measured with a scale on a straight pull directly off the spool. The correct setting should be 15-25 percent of the unknotted line strength.

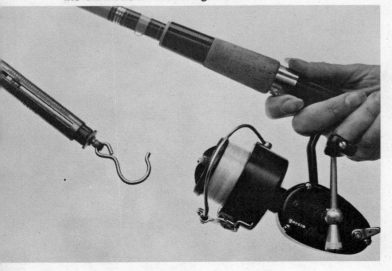

tires the fish. Perhaps over a long period of time that may be a factor, but the direct pressure you can put on a fish does the damage. The rod is really a shock absorber to help adjust the pressure and yield when necessary.

Stripping a fish toward you with a flyrod can be done much more easily if you use the rod to pump the fish. Instead of simply pulling the flyline, lift the rod and pull the fish toward you with the rod. Then, strip in the excess flyline as you lower the rod tip again. Repeat the procedure and you can move the fish without undue strain on the leader.

The toughest situation occurs with a trophy-sized fish in swiftly flowing water. Once the fish gets below you, there is little chance of working your quarry back up stream. This is where you must think in advance and react quickly. Your initial objective is to lead the fish out of the fast water. That's not always easy to do, but if you can handle a rod well and can get the jump on the trout, you can sometimes succeed.

Assuming that you can't work the fish into the shallows or out of the current, the second objective is to stay abreast of the fish and keep it from getting below you. You often have to move fast to do it, crashing and stumbling downstream while exerting all the pressure that you can on the fish.

The problem often becomes compounded by the route of the stream. Frequently, the water plunges into a gorge or follows a dogleg into rougher terrain, making it virtually impossible to follow very far. When that happens, you don't have much choice. Your only hope is to pressure the fish to the maximum and force it out of the current or break the leader in the attempt. If the fish gets beyond the beaching or netting point and continues downstream, there is no way you can get it back to you.

The textbook case occurred in an Arctic char river in Greenland that turned sharply to the right and plunged into a gorge. There was less than 100 feet from the spot where the fish were hooked to the turn and one had to ease the fish out of the current and keep them from making the bend in the river or all was lost.

Flyfishermen should always play big trout from the reel. Even if there is slack flyline on the water, hold the line against the grip of the rod and reel in the extra line. There is an exception, of course, since all rules have them. In this case, you might not have time to get the fish "on the reel" if the stream drops into a set of rapids or a gorge where you can't follow. If it's a choice between keeping the fish out of the current by manually handling the line or playing the fish from the reel, the first alternative is the way to go. I've saved a few trophy fish by simply clamping on the line, dropping the rod tip to let the fish ease off a few feet and then pulling the rod up and forcing the fish back. It's unorthodox, but it works—particularly when you are desperate.

If your flyreel has a built in drag system, it should be set relatively light. The rule of thumb is about 15 percent of the unknotted strength of the lightest tippet material. This should be measured on a straight pull from the reel with the rod tip pointing directly at the scale. You'll discover that as you raise the rod tip, the amount of drag increases. A flyline moving through the water also adds drag and, as the line on the reel spool decreases in diameter, drag increases.

It's well to keep all of these factors in mind because they can be important. Remember that the least amount of drag occurs when you point the rod tip directly at the fish. And, as the fish gets farther and farther away from you, the amount of drag is increasing. By dropping the rod tip, you can ease the amount of drag on the fish at any time.

Smaller fish are usually played by stripping them in. If you lift the rod and pull the fish toward you, you can actually pump your adversary. Then, recover line as you drop the rod tip.

Husky lake trout in shallow water can be a problem, but a reel with a smooth drag can even the score. The trick is to get on the fish quickly, move the boat to the trout, and stay on top until the fish is whipped.

Veteran anglers prefer a very light preset drag and then apply additional drag with the fingers of their left hand. Depending on the flyreel you are using, you can either use your hand against the flange of the spool or reach in front of the reel and put your fingers against the line itself. If the fish should surge suddenly, you need only pull your hand away and the drag is removed. At the same time, if the surge is significant, you can drop the rod tip and push the rod toward the fish to reduce the pressure. As soon as the fish settles down, raise the rod tip and you should have your quarry back under control.

The same basic principles of drag apply to any other type of tackle. Spinning enthusiasts often tighten the drag on the reel well beyond a safe setting. For general fishing, you can get by with 15-25 percent of the unknotted line strength. This means that 10-pound-test line should carry a drag setting of 1½ to 2 pounds on a straight pull. Additional drag can be applied with the hands by cupping the spool of the spinning reel. As you pump the fish toward you, you can hold the spool to keep it from slipping and ease the fish your way. If the fish resists or surges, drop the rod tip and release the hand pressure.

All of us have heard the warning of keeping a tight line at all times. That's not necessarily true all the time and one -

exception is when a fish jumps. There are some who would argue that it is best to pull the fish down or push the rod tip under water and try to keep the fish from becoming airborne in the first place. Saltwater specialists have learned long ago that it makes sense to drop the rod tip and push the rod toward the fish when it jumps. They call this "bowing to a fish" and it makes sense.

Under the surface, a fish has neutral buoyancy, but in the air, a fish weighs the same as it would on a scale. That means that an aerial acrobat puts more strain on the leader. At the same time, the fish is moving and the velocity adds to the problem. If the leader doesn't break from sudden impact, the fish could land on it and part it easily. If you give the fish controlled slack, however, the trout might land on a limp leader instead of a taut one and the leader might not break. Chances are that the lure will stay in the fish's mouth regardless of what you do.

If you've been successful in playing the fish, you'll have an opportunity to land your quarry. You can almost bet that the instant the fish sees your hand, the net, shallow water, or a gravel bar, it will make a final bid for freedom. This is a critical moment and you should be ready for it. When the fish moves off, just drop the rod tip and let it go for a very short distance until you can regain control.

Control is really the key to playing and landing a fish. By badgering your adversary and putting constant pressure on it, you can often force the fish to give up long before it normally would. Experienced fish fighters never stop slugging until the fish is netted or turned loose.

Small fish are seldom a problem, but with a trophy you should think about where you will land your prize. If you're in a boat, pick the side and the position. In a stream, you want fairly shallow water out of the main current. If the fish is small and you intend to release it, it is best not to use a net or touch the fish at all. Fly fishermen can merely hold the hook and shake it. That's usually enough for the fish to free itself and you don't have to worry about touching it.

When you put your hands on a fish or net a trout, some of the protective slime is removed from the fish's body. This usually leads to infection and the fish can die. If you have to handle the fish, latest theory dictates that you do so with dry hands. It was once felt that wet hands would help to eliminate removing the protective coating, but that led to other complications. Not only did the slime still come off, but the angler had to squeeze the fish harder and often damaged internal organs in the process. When you hold a trout, do so gently, but firmly and don't put your hands or fingers in the gills.

If you want to keep the trout you catch, the best procedure is to use a net. Make sure the opening in the net is large enough for the largest trout you might catch. Trophies are often lost by trying to cram them into nets that wouldn't hold fish half that size. Netting, of course, is always done head first. A fish can't swim backward. If you put the net in the water at a 45-degree angle and swim the fish into the net, you're following the correct procedure. Don't try to scoop the fish with the net and, if someone else offers to net your trophy for you, make certain he knows what he's doing before you allow him to try.

In open water, you can lead the trout over the net from any direction, but even with a slight current, you'll probably be easing the fish upstream into the net. Be sure to work your quarry into fairly shallow water. If the water is too deep, the fish can easily dive under the net and you can become a loser if the leader gets nicked.

You always have the alternative of beaching a fish and you can do this best on a gravel bar or any projection of land that eases into the water. The key is to keep the fish in the water and prevent it from lying on the shallow bottom and thrashing. Pick the place ahead of time and, once the fish is fairly tired, swim it right up into the shallows and lift it on the bar with your hand or by pushing it with your boot. Once the belly of the fish touches the gravel or bottom, you have to move quickly and get the fish on dry land.

When you net a fish, the procedure is to push the rod back behind one shoulder and reach out with the net using the other hand. If you are using a fairly long leader, you might discover that you can't reach the fish no matter how far back you push the rod. The answer is to reel part of the leader through the guides. This can be somewhat dangerous if the fish surges away from you. That's why old timers use long butt sections on their leaders and a minimum of knots. If the fish does move off, rotate your wrist and turn the flyrod so that the guides are pointing up instead of down. The leader will move through and the knots won't hang up.

Most trout anglers tend to ignore the fine points of playing and landing fish and that's one reason there are plenty of trophy trout still swimming around that once tasted the steel of a hook. If you remember only one thing, don't forget that you should plan your strategy before you made the first cast. That way, you won't be surprised regardless of the size fish that engulfs your offering.

Landing husky trout is always an exciting experience, but you have to get on the fish quickly and keep it from seeking the sanctuary of an obstruction or getting downstream on you.

CLASSIC TROUT STREAMS

The East Branch of the Ausable River in New York contains some excellent trout fishing.

OF THE NORTHEAST

by JIM STABILE

TROUT FISHING in the classic streams of the Northeast has a special attraction that is difficult, if not impossible, to match at other top-rated streams elsewhere in the United States.

The famous northeastern rivers cannot match in quantity or size of trout the rivers of Montana or Michigan, but they offer a long and rich tradition and history in an area where American trout fishing was born.

It was on these classic waters that fly fishing for trout began in the United States, where brown trout were first introduced and where the noted trout authors of the past century gained the knowledge and skill that led to countless volumes on the sport.

Today's trout angler can mend the drift of his line as his Quill Gordon floats through the same currents where Theodore Gordon first developed this fly.

There are but a few truly classic streams, most of them within a 3-hour drive of New York City, and a handful of other streams which hold special places in the history of trout fishing.

Well-read fishermen with a knowledge of trouting's beginnings in the U.S. fish the classic waters not only because they still provide quality fishing, but also in recognition of the fact that the classics are firmly enshrined in annals of fishing history. Many make annual pilgrimages to fish the classics with an almost-religious fervor.

They go to streams like the Neversink and Beaverkill Rivers of lower New York State, the first American homes of the brown trout, imported in the 1880s.

Theodore Gordon, considered by many to be the father of trout fishing in the U.S., spent years fishing the Neversink and writing about it. Some of his favorite stretches of the stream now lie deep below the Neversink Reservoir.

The East and West branches of the Neversink begin on Slide Mountain in the Catskills. Slide is a wild, rocky, wooded 4,204-foot-high mountain that is the largest of that region.

Native brook trout abound in the upper reaches of the Neversink but much of the land bordering the upper branches is privately owned.

Downstream, the public has more access to the waters and their brown trout in the mainstream, between the point where the stream enters the Delaware River and the reservoir upstream.

Some of the best public stream fishing in the East can still be found on the nearby Beaverkill, which is joined by the Willowemoc Creek at the famed Junction Pool in Roscoe, home of the legendary Two-Headed Trout—a fish that cannot decide which fine stream it should ascend.

Private clubs control most of the fishing above Junction

A jumping trout on the Willowemoc Creek proves this angler has done everything right.

Above—Fisherman cleans a trout on the famous Beaverkill in New York. This is where flyfishing in America had its origin. Below—The Yellow Breeches Creek in Cumberland County, Pennsylvania is home to some pretty big brown trout and is rapidly coming on strong as a classic northeastern stream.

Pool, but there is a popular 2½-mile stretch below where only artificial lures can be used and all trout caught must be returned to provide sport for others. Fifteen-trout-per-hour catches are possible.

Fishermen can keep trout caught below this special-regulation area, and more than a dozen miles of river are open to the public. Fishing is very good, despite the heavy pressure generated by its proximity to high-population areas.

Both the Beaverkill and the Willowemoc are heavily stocked, easily wadable, and located in picturesque, forested valleys. The Hendrickson is a fly that was born on the Beaverkill, a stream whose famous pools include Painter Bend, Cairns, Wagon Wheel, Hendrickson's and others. These streams contain mostly browns and rainbows, plus some brookies.

Farther north, the Esopus Creek is a classic that starts tumbling down the northwest slope of Slide Mountain, winds through steep hemlock and pine valleys, then rushes for miles before it flows into the Ashokan Reservoir.

This stream's history, and the esteem in which it is held today, has been dimmed somewhat by tremendous fishing pressure, especially during the spring, and its place as a conduit for water destined to wind up in New York City.

A spring run of rainbows out of Ashokan Reservoir still attracts anglers, and heavy stockings of brown trout, in addition to smaller rainbows, provide sport through the summer months.

During the high-water conditions often found during the spring rainbow run, fishermen who try the tributaries such as Stony Clove and the Chichester gain easier access to the spawners. New York's trout season always opens on April 1.

The mainstream can be treacherous to wade even later in the season, however, because of the transfer of water from the Schoharie Reservoir, via a tunnel through the mountains, to the Esopus.

When the tunnel's portal is gushing water north of Phoenicia, the Esopus runs bank full and discolored. Both the Schoharie and Ashokan Reservoirs are part of New York City's water supply system. Still, there is ample public access to the Esopus, and it was frequently fished and written about by top angling writers earlier in this century.

Below the Ashokan Reservoir, trout are relatively rare, although some are occasionally caught downstream in the Esopus, which empties into the Hudson River.

The Ausable River is one of northern New York State's most popular and most publicized rivers. Numerous magazine articles have extolled the Ausable's outstanding brown trout fishing.

The Ausable has its headwaters in the northern Adirondack Mountains, some of the wildest country in the state, and it winds its way through the valleys to drain into Lake Champlain.

For those who don't mind hiking, the upper reaches of the Ausable support good populations of brook trout. As the river flattens, browns and rainbows are more common.

The East and West branches of the river provide a variety of stream conditions, from difficult to easy, with plenty of pocket water in some areas, to long, smooth pools and runs in others. The Flume Pool in Essex County is a spectacular, if not always productive, place to fish.

The Ausable is one of the most heavily fished streams in the Adirondacks, and with good reason. State officials say it

A rushing waterfall on an Adirondack trout stream is one of the primary reasons why anglers flock to the classic regions of Vermont, New York and Pennsylvania.

This fisherman reaches way out to net a trout on the Neversink.

A skillful cast with the proper fly will provide a hookup on any northeastern stream. ▶

is one of the Adirondacks' top streams for both productivity and angler success.

A 2.2-mile section of the West Branch, downstream from Monument Falls, has been set aside as a trophy stretch, limited to fishing with artificial lures only, with a daily limit of one trout, 14 inches or larger.

Fishermen who prefer using worms or other live bait have ample areas, and find best success early in the season. Dry fly fishing is excellent in late spring and early summer, while terrestrial patterns are productive in late summer and during September.

Interstate I-87, the "Northway," makes the stream easy to reach, and public access is plentiful.

Vermont officials say the Battenkill is the best trout stream of its size in the southern part of the state, and one of the best in the U.S.

A portion of the Battenkill in New York State, from the Vermont line to the covered bridge downstream at Eagleville, has been given special regulations, with a daily limit of three trout 12 inches or larger and only artificial lures permitted.

Vermont fisheries biologists believe the Battenkill's high-quality fishing results from a large volume of cold ground water entering the stream through its bed, high natural reproduction and a relatively stable watershed that tempers flooding and scouring.

The stream contains mostly browns, with these fish providing most of the action in the lower section. The

brookies are upstream. Clear water and brown trout that feed very selectively make the Battenkill especially challenging during summer.

Some regulars say the "easy" fish are taken early on live bait. Later, as the browns zero-in on insects, long fine leaders and tiny dry flies catch trout for skillful anglers.

The abundance of trout the year-around was proved one August, after most of the fishing pressure had subsided. A pool 150 feet long and 60 feet wide was net sampled. It yielded 56 browns, half of them more than 12 inches long.

Northeastern Pennsylvania's Pocono Mountains contain many fine trout streams, but none so rich in history and tradition as Brodheads Creek.

Teddy Roosevelt, Calvin Coolidge, Gifford Pinchot, Buffalo Bill Cody and Annie Oakley were among those who enjoyed the bounty of the Brodheads.

Coolidge Hole is a pool named after the president; Annie Oakley's favorite was Pine Tree Pool, and just about every famed angling author of the past century has fished the Brodheads on occasion.

Brook trout population was high in the 1700s, when the area was first settled, and it remained the predominant species until the late 1800s, when browns were introduced. Brown trout fishing continues to be excellent, with insect life again abundant as the stream continues to recover from damaging flood waters in 1955.

Noted angler-writers who were regulars on the Brodheads include Edward Ringwood Hewitt, George LaBranche, Ray Bergman, John Alden Knight, Preston Jennings and dozens more.

Pennsylvania also holds streams that are the nearest in comparison to England's chalk streams—the limestone streams in the central and southern part of the state.

These streams feature an abundance of insect life, plentiful freshwater shrimp and trout that are among the largest in the East.

The Letort, Yellow Breeches and Big Spring Creeks are south of the Penns, Spring, and Spruce Creeks. They are generally smooth and gently flowing streams.

There's a special fly stretch on the Yellow Breeches where anglers are not allowed to kill a trout unless it is at least 20 inches long.

Fly fishermen face a real test in trying to fool big, sophisticated browns and rainbows. Long, light leaders and flies on Nos. 18, 20 and 22 hooks are often necessary. The big trout are there, but they're not easy to catch.

A 3.5-mile stretch of Penns Creek is open all year on a "fish for fun" basis, and it is growing in popularity. Parts of the creek, which rises in a large spring and flows through Penns Cave, are stocked heavily with browns and rainbows.

Much of what has been written about Pennsylvania's limestone streams is of relatively recent vintage, compared to other classic streams of the Northeast. But the history and traditions of the limestone streams are growing at a fantastic rate.

While these and other streams have growing traditions, if one had to chose the ones with the shrine-like qualities because their place is so secure in history, waters such as those of New York's Catskills and the Brodheads of Pennsylvania's Poconos, will live on as long as they can support trout life.

The classics will continue to draw anglers new and old who seek the enjoyment and fulfillment of trout fishing in waters where the greatest names in angling's past have cast, caught trout and learned about them, and whose words still ring true today.

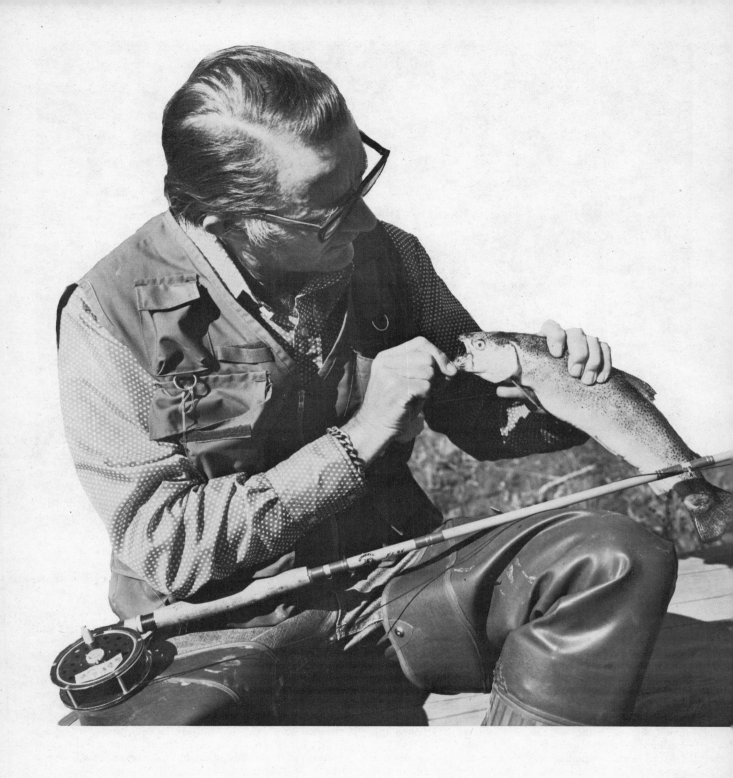

SEA RUNS ARE

I PARKED my car as close as I could to the bridge, grabbed my fly rod out of the back seat and headed down over the bank of the Naselle River.

It was late August and there was a bite to the chill of the morning. Fog and mist curled around the willows along the far side. I headed downstream, looking for the pool I knew was just ahead, hoping nobody had beat me to the spot.

Nobody there! My heart danced to a quickened rhythm of anticipation. I stopped this side of the pool, pushed the green line through the guides, then tied a brightly colored No. 6 bucktail to the end of my leader.

Ever so carefully I worked my way into position. The fly curved out over the surface of the river, flicked out of sight in the current and then was swimming its way along the far shore, flitting and working through the slowly moving water of the big pool.

Ready as I was for the strike, it came with smashing surprise. One second there was nothing. Then k-a-s-l-u-r-s-h! Fish on! My line slapped tight against the guides of my rod. Then the surface of the pool was shattered as almost 20 inches of glittering silver flashed out and fell back.

Five minutes later I paused to admire and examine the fine sea run cutthroat which I'd just taken. The beauty of these fish, trout that were spawned in the fresh waters of a Columbia River tributary but grew up in the Pacific Ocean, are a sight calculated to appeal to the most discriminating angler. And they don't only appeal from a standpoint of beauty. The sea run cutthroat is one of the top game fish to be found along the Pacific coast from the timbered slopes of southeastern Alaska on down to Northern California.

Exactly what is a sea run cutthroat? Just what the name implies. It's a strain of cutthroat trout with a life cycle much like that of the steelhead. The fish is spawned in fresh water and remains there until it reaches a length of 4 or 5 inches. Then it moves on down and out of the parent stream and heads for the vast salty pasturelands of the Pacific Ocean. In the Pacific the fish take on muscle and maturity. Then they head back for the parent stream to spawn.

It's when these bright beauties return from the Pacific that they provide terrific sport for western anglers who are fortunate enough to live near one of the rivers which support such a run. I'm outdoor editor of *The Daily News* in Longview, Washington. My home town sets right on the shore of the Columbia River. That's how come I'm so familiar with these fish. The Columbia and its tributaries, you see, just happen to provide some of the very best action to be found anywhere for these migratory gamesters.

The fish return from the sea beginning in July and the run peaks in late August and September. You'll hear the fish referred to as "harvest trout" along the Washington side of the Columbia River. In Oregon, anglers call them "bluebacks." Whatever name you pin on these hard fighting, good eating trout, there's just no doubt but that they deserve

Bucktail patterns like these are favorites for sea run cutthroats in western waters.

by STAN FAGERSTROM

method. This kind of fishing is especially productive during the early part of the run. That's also when the largest fish appear and those first harvest trout are a sight to behold. They shine like a new dime and their meat is a delightful firm pink.

Almost any kind of rod and reel that will handle up to

Left, below and opposite page—Author eases 13-inch cutthroat into the shallows—fish came from slow water near the end of old log in background (see photo, left). Sea reared cutthroat are fine fighters and make excellent eating; this one fell for bucktail.

a place with the better known steelhead and salmon as premier fish of far western waters.

In many ways I think of the sea run cutthroat as the ideal fish for the newcomer to trout angling. Why do I say that? Partly because the fish can be caught by such a wide variety of methods. The tackle can be just about as primitive or refined as one chooses to make it and still have a reasonable chance for success.

Let's take a look at the way many people who don't care to put much effort into their fishing go after sea run cutts. These fishermen head for wide beaches of a river like the Columbia, hang a couple of nightcrawlers on their hook, use a sinker heavy enough to hold the line against the pull of the big river's current and just plunk the worms out there to wait for a fish to come along.

In my country we call these cast-and-wait anglers "plunkers." The name fits. That's exactly what they do. They just plunk their bait out there and sit and wait. And they do more waiting than anything else. That's not to say, however, that they don't take fish. The first harvest trout I ever caught came from the Columbia via the plunking

a couple of ounces of weight will do for harvest time plunking along the lower Columbia for sea runs. I favor using two hooks and oftentimes I'll bait one with worms and the other with a small cluster of salmon eggs or perhaps a little piece of flesh cut from a chub sucker.

I was using such a two hooked outfit on the Columbia one day and had my back to my rod when the little warning bell I'd attached to the tip when I placed it in the sand spike started to ring.

"Hey, Stan! You got a bite!" my dad hollered.

And indeed I did. I quickly lifted the rod out of its holder, took up the slack and hit the fish. For a while I didn't know what I had hold of. The line leading down into the water seemed to be trying to go in two directions at once. Perhaps it was. You see, when I finally managed to get control of the situation I found I had a harvest trout on one hook and a nice summer steelhead on the other.

Most plunkers concentrating on harvest trout rig up with No. 6 worm hooks on about 3 feet of leader. Be sure the hooks have something similar to the bait holder barbs like those marketed by Eagle Claw. Be generous with the worms.

Sea run cutthroat favor a sizeable bait and it's a good idea to change worms often enough to make sure you're always presenting one that's fresh and lively.

I mentioned using little dabs of white meat cut from the flesh of a chub sucker. Don't worry about locating such bait. You'll probably find more chubs than you want. They are noted bait stealers, sometimes nibbling away at your worm the minute it hits the water. When you catch one, kill and skin it. Then fillet little strips from along the backbone to use for bait. Sometimes harvest trout hit best on a combination of worm and white meat. As is wise in any kind of fishing, don't use the same bait hour after hour. If worms

don't produce, try eggs. If eggs don't work, try white meat or mixing combinations of the two.

Actually, this plunking is a darn good way for anybody to introduce himself to sea run cutthroat angling. It's an easy way to learn what these fish look like and just listening to the old-timers who invariably will be scattered among the crowds that come to fish during the main part of the run will be of benefit. Once a fellow makes a couple of plunking trips he'll be better prepared for the more demanding methods of harvest trout angling.

One of those more sophisticated methods, and it's a productive one, is the use of spinning tackle. I say spinning tackle because the lures employed are usually on the light side and it was lightweight work that spinfishing was designed for in the beginning and it's still the one job that it does best of all.

Spin fishing is done on smaller streams, rivers like the many which are tributaries of the Columbia. Right in my own part of Washington state there are streams like the Toutle, Kalama, East Fork of the Lewis, the North Fork of the Lewis, the Elochoman and the Naselle to name

just a few. Oregon has almost as many and there are others, as I've indicated, scattered all along the Washington and Oregon coast as well as parts of California, British Columbia and Alaska.

Little wobblers and some of the smaller plugs can be excellent for the spin fisherman after harvest trout. So can bait. I was walking down the bank of the Toutle one wet September afternoon, feeling sorry for myself because the water wasn't in very good shape for me to use the fly rod which is my favorite method for ocean-going cutthroat. I rounded a bend near one of the favorite holes just as my friend the late Blaine Albert, of Longview, was trying to stuff an 18-incher through the hole in the top of his creel.

"He ain't gona fit, I guess," Blaine laughed. Then he opened the creel to show me six of the prettiest trout you could ever hope to find anyplace. The fish ranged from 13 to 18 inches and I suppose they ran from 2 to 3 pounds.

"I got 'em on this spinner and worm set up," Blaine said, and displayed a little double Indiana with worms trailing 6 inches behind the spinner. He had drifted this combination at the head end of the pools and in the roily water the spinner and bait was just what the fish wanted. I've made that same set-up work on other occasions and it's one well worth remembering when water clarity is less than perfect.

Small metal wobblers are another good bet for sea run cutthroat. Cast them across and slightly upstream, then let them work back down along the bottom, occasionally ticking the rocks and boulders jutting up from the stream floor.

Once I saw a fellow with spinning tackle take a beautiful catch on the smallest of the Lazy Ike plugs. The little lure he was using couldn't have been an inch long. He used about 2 feet of leader behind a sinker heavy enough to take the little plug to the bottom. Then he simply reeled in slowly across the pools, the tiny Ike wiggling and wobbling along

Author prefers to go after cutthroat with the fly rod, however a wide variety of tackle and techniques including spinning gear and plunking will land the sea run.

just off the bottom. The angler in question had a Washington state limit of 6½ pounds of trout.

As I indicated earlier, I don't really spend a lot of time either plunking or spin fishing for sea run cutthroat. I prefer to go after them with the fly rod. It's one of the most efficient methods of all to take these cutts and for my money by far the most pleasurable for the angler with a little experience.

As is the situation with spinning or plunking, fly fishing for cutthroat will be best when the fish are moving in from the Pacific to spawn. Along much of the Washington and Oregon coasts that will run from July on through October. A few cutthroat will hang around off the mouths of streams and move in and out all season long. These fish aren't prime specimens like those that are making the migration back from the Pacific and you can tell the difference in the appearance of the fish, the way they fight and the color and flavor of the flesh. Long time Pacific Northwest residents invariably rank the sea run cutthroat right at the top of their list of fish which are excellent for the table.

As in many other kinds of freshwater fishing, knowing where to find cutthroat is going to solve many of the problems. The fish like pools. Look for them around log jams or brush clumps, someplace where the water deepens, yet there is current both going in and out of the hole.

Never fail to note carefully where you take fish or where you have hits. You'll be able to return another day or another season with excellent odds of finding fish in the same spot. If you're a newcomer to a West Coast cutthroat stream, don't spend your first day beating the water into a froth. Take time to get your bearings. Hike up and down the river, note how the other fishermen are operating, the kind of flies they are using, how those flies are fished and anything else that could be of importance later on. You'll learn more spending a few hours in this fashion than you will in a half-dozen trips where you pay no attention to what experienced anglers are doing.

You'll see a variety of fly outfits being used for sea run cutthroat. I personally do most of my fishing with an 8½-foot rod and a weight-forward No. 8 line. I go with either a floater or a slow sinking line and from 7½ to 9 feet of leader. I'll use the floating line if conditions indicate I'll be able to fish fairly shallow. If I find I have to get down deeper, I'll switch to the sinking line. Either one will get me by a large share of the time.

In many ways the sleek sided sea run cutthroat reminds

Cutthroats love big quiet pools such as this one.

The fall of the year is a top time for sea run cutthroats in Washington or Oregon coastal streams.

me of an ugly old bigmouth bass with a belly ache. Their disposition is much the same at least a portion of the time. I say that partly because of the way a cutthroat flails into a fly, especially if it's up near the surface. If you've ever watched a 3- or 4-pound bass smash into a Lucky 13 you'll know what I mean. He just flat busts the hell out of things! That's the way it is with a cutthroat. He'll come sizzling up out of nowhere and the surface just erupts.

Even the fight of these fish is a little more basslike than trout. The cutthroat is a slugger, an in-fighter. He'll jump now and then, but more often the battle will be underwater with sizzling runs and strong surges into the current. I rarely go under 4-pound-test leader in Washington cutthroat waters. There are a couple of reasons. One is that the relatively large flies I use most of the time will wear a lighter leader too rapidly. The second is that in my country one never knows when a summer run steelhead or a coho salmon might whack into his offering and if that happens next to white water in a big river you want to have a fighting chance. Some of my buddies knot 6-pound leader to the end of their fly line and never change all season long. Yes, they get their share of fish.

How about actual flies? Be sure to include a selection of bucktails and streamers. The Royal Coachman bucktail has caught a wad of sea run cutthroat. Probably the most popular pattern of all in my own bailiwick is one called the Kalama Special. This fly is tied with a red tag, yellow body, white bucktail wing and badger hackle. I've had excellent success over the years with a brilliant pattern I tie myself. This one has a red and yellow tag, a yellow yarn body ribbed with either gold or silver tinsel, white bucktail and red and yellow hackle. The thing looks like a floating Christmas tree in the water but I've had cutthroat tear them up in some of the finest fly fishing it's ever been my good fortune to enjoy.

The Muddler Minnow is another excellent pattern. So is a grey hackle with a yellow body. On other occasions I've done very well using a bee pattern bucktail tied to my own specs with polar bear hair for a wing.

Don't despair if you raise a harvest trout and he doesn't take. It's characteristic of the fish. And when you see that flash of silver or the water boils behind your fly, reel in and change patterns. Don't fool around with a dozen more casts before you make such a change. Do it right now. Then cast again and get back over the same spot. The chances are better than average that the harvest trout you just got a glimpse of a moment before will come flashing back like he'd been waiting for you all summer long.

There's hardly any ocean fishery for sea run cutthroat. And the fish are too small to figure in the commercial catch in the coastal rivers or offshore. They can be artificially propogated and that's exactly what the Washington State Game Department is doing. Such a program makes sense. Raise a sea run cutthroat to migratory size and he'll head out for sea and won't come back until he's a hell raising adult, full of vinegar and as salty as the sea he's just left. He'll average around 13 inches, often will run 15 to 18 and might even be a whopping 6-pounder like the Washington state record.

If the sea run cutthroat existed in a land which didn't already have the steelhead and the Pacific salmon you'd find books being written about them. They are standouts, even in the face of such fabulous competition. Come to think of it, I might get around to that sea run cutthroat book someday anyhow. It might be as good an excuse as any for spending more time with these glistening migratory beauties which brighten the autumn harvest season for anglers of the Pacific Northwest.

Bait Fish Temperature– the Key to Big Trout

by RANDALL COLVIN

IT WAS A breezy day late in July. We had recorded a water temperature of 50 degrees at 75 feet; the ideal temperature for lake trout listed on my preferred temperature list. We began trolling with our baits ticking along the bottom in 75 feet of water in hopes of catching a big lake trout.

My fishing partner was Bill Thompson, a teacher from Flint, Michigan. Little did we suspect what the morning's fishing would lead to.

After 20 minutes of trolling I glanced over to check Bill's Cowbell action and, wham, his rod doubled over from a savage strike.

"Hey, look at that fish jump," Bill remarked, as a re-sounding splat sounded behind the boat.

I turned and saw the spreading rings where a big fish had just jumped. Moments later a huge 15-pound rainbow trout skyrocketed into the air again. It was a splendid sight to see except that Bill's hook was no longer attached to his line. The big trout had snapped the 14-pound-test leader on the strike.

"That fish isn't supposed to be down there," I stated as I checked the water temperature profile we had recorded a few minutes earlier.

Not only was that rainbow down there but so were some of his friends. That morning we landed four rainbows between 4 and 7 pounds and one 10-pound laker.

This episode took place 5 years ago and was responsible for setting me on a line of research which has resulted in a major trout fishing breakthrough in inland lakes.

Nothing I had read could account for the rainbows being at 50 degrees, which was 8 to 10 degrees colder than the rainbow's preferred temperature. I had to find the answer myself. Five years of research and a Bachelor of Science degree in fisheries later, I now have some of the answers. The results of this research will make it possible for you to enjoy the exciting big trout fishing in lakes throughout North America.

Most fishermen have seen the many preferred temperature lists for game fish that are in circulation. None of them would be of much help to the average trout fisherman. It's impossible to give one temperature for a trout species that will work for that species in all lakes.

Certainly each species of trout has a preferred temperature and a good trout fisherman should know what they are. But under most circumstances a trout is resting between feeding periods when it is at its preferred temperature. A fisherman is not seeking resting fish. He is interested in locating feeding fish. So you must know what the trout's main food is in a lake and where and how to find that food.

This new information will revolutionize trout fishing in stratified lakes. That is, lakes which have three thermal

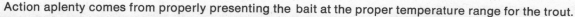

Action aplenty comes from properly presenting the bait at the proper temperature range for the trout.

layers; the epilimnion (warm surface waters), the metalimnion or thermocline (level where the water temperature drops quickly) and the hypolimnion (cold lower waters).

When a trout reaches a size worth catching (3 pounds plus) its main food is small forage fish. If a lake fisherman can locate the trout's bait fish he will also find feeding trout. The key to locating bait fish is water temperature.

This gives the fisherman two temperatures to consider when planning fishing strategy for a lake; the trout's preferred temperature and the bait fish's preferred temperature.

The trout's preferred temperature becomes important when it doesn't coincide with any of the bait fishes temperatures in the lake. In such a case the trout may move to its own preferred temperatures to rest between feeding periods.

The bait fish temperatures offers the fisherman his best chance for success. At times a fisherman will want to fish the trout's preferred temperature for reasons we will discuss later.

To better understand water temperature and its relationship to the various trout we'll list the seven major trout species found in North American lakes, give their temperature and habitat preferences.

RAINBOW TROUT—Rainbows prefer water temperatures between 58 and 61 degrees. They will often suspend above bottom but will also be found on or near bottom.

BROWN TROUT—Brown trout also prefer water temperatures between 58 and 61 degrees and will range near bottom or suspend above it.

LAKE TROUT—Lakers preferred temperature is from 46 to 50 degrees. If this temperature is located conveniently near its food source a lake trout prefers to stay near bottom. It will however suspend when the food source remains away from the bottom.

BROOK TROUT—Brookies prefer water of 56 to 59 degrees and normally stay near bottom when the food source is sufficiently close.

SPLAKE TROUT—The splake is a fish of growing importance in many North American lakes. A hybrid crossed between a lake trout and a brook trout, they are intermediate of their parents and prefer water of 52 to 55 degrees. Likewise they prefer to rest near bottom.

DOLLY VARDEN—The Dolly Varden prefers water of 46 to 50 degrees and will rest near bottom if its food source allows.

CUTTHROAT TROUT—The cutthroat also prefers water temperatures of 46 to 50 degrees and is normally a bottom oriented species.

A segment of the trout population in a lake will be found at all times in their preferred temperatures. These trout are less apt to strike a lure when resting at these temperatures. You need to know what the trout are feeding on and where that food supply is located in a lake.

The following is a list of the major species of bait fish fed on by trout in North American lakes, giving their temperatures and habit preferences along with the trout species that feed on them.

SHINERS—One of the most important bait fish types in many lakes is the large group of shiners. This includes many species, all of which prefer temperatures of 68 to 72 degrees. Shiners generally suspend above the bottom in large schools. During the day, when they are most heavily preyed on by trout, they tend to stay near the lower level of their temperature range and suspend over deeper water (30 feet or so).

In the absence of cold water bait fish both browns and rainbows will prey heavily on shiners. With the presence of a cold water bait fish, shiners become secondary forage for both trout species.

PERCH—Small perch are heavily preyed upon by brown and rainbow trout in the absence of a cold water bait fish. Their temperature preference is the same as the shiners with a preference for staying near the bottom.

CISCO (herrings) & WHITEFISH—This group includes almost all species of cisco and whitefish and will hereon be referred to as cisco. Ciscos are undoubtedly the most important bait fish for trout in North American lakes. A large percentage of the better trout lakes have ciscos. Their temperature preferences are from 52 to 55 degrees.

Ciscos suspend above the bottom in schools and will range throughout the entire area of the lake. All seven species of trout feed heavily on cisco.

KOKANEE SALMON—The western states and a few midwest lakes contain this species which is a major bait fish for trout. The kokanee's habits and preferences are the same as the cisco's. The kokanee is preyed on by all seven species of trout, particularly the larger trophy sized trout.

SMELT—The smelt is a major bait fish in the Great Lakes and some inland lakes. They seek a temperature range of 48 to 52 degrees. Smelt as a rule stay near bottom and all species of trout prey on them.

LAKE CHUB—The lake chub is an important bait fish in many midwestern states and some lakes in the northwestern and northeastern states and throughout Canada. It is primarily a bottom dweller with a temperature preference of 48 to 52 degrees. All species of trout feed on lake chub.

ALEWIVES—An important bait fish in the Great Lakes with a temperature preference of 53 to 55 degrees. Like ciscos, alewives suspend in large schools over all depths. All species of trout feed on alewives.

NINESPINE STICKLEBACK—In many Canadian lakes and some of the northern-most midwestern states, the ninespine stickleback is of importance in a trout's diet. The ninespine is a bottom dwelling fish preferring 48 to 52 degree temperatures. All trout species eat ninespines.

SCULPINS—Two varieties of lake sculpin are important for trout forage. One, the mottled sculpin, is of some importance as a trout forage throughout central Canada, some lakes in the northern midwest states (including the Great Lakes), and some lakes in the northwestern states. The mottled sculpin is a bottom inhabitant preferring water of 48 to 52 degrees in temperature. All species of trout feed on mottled sculpin.

The other variety of lake sculpins include several species and are marked by their deep, cold water habits. Throughout the northern states and much of Canada these cold water species are of some importance and figure somewhat in a trout's diet. Water temperatures of 41 to 45 degrees near bottom is the preferred habitat for these fish.

These cold temperatures narrow the trout predators down to lake trout, splake, Dolly Varden and cutthroat with the lakers as the primary predator.

This covers the major bait fish for trout fishing in lakes. Of course other species of fish are eaten by trout but they are secondary to one or more of the nine species listed here.

The first step is to find out what fish are in the lakes you want to fish. To obtain this information you should write to the governmental agency that handles the fishery in the state or province your lake is located in. Ask them to send you a complete "species content list" of all fish species in your lake, including both game and bait fish, along with general estimates of the size of the population of each species. From this list you should be able to predict at what water temperatures you will find both resting and feeding trout.

Some problems may arise when there are two or more bait fish species present in a lake. To clarify this let's look

An electronic water thermometer, a note book, sonar unit and a knowledge of bait fish temperatures will tune you in to catches of big trout.

at an example.

Suppose your favorite trout lake has the following trout and bait fish species:

Trout Species

rainbow trout	large population
brown trout	small population
lake trout	large population

Bait Fish Species

shiners	large population
perch	large population
cisco	large population
smelt	large population

First of all, when given a choice like this, the majority of trout in the lake will be feeding on cold water bait fish rather than the warm water ones. A few browns and rainbows will be feeding on cisco and/or smelt. That gives two prime temperatures and habitats at which to fish for feeding trout. The point here is the smart fisherman goes prepared to vary his fishing pattern. If you fish suspended at cisco temperature for an hour without catching a trout start fishing on the bottom at the smelt temperature.

The only time you should fish trout at their own temperature is when you have fished the bait fish temperatures thoroughly and haven't had a strike. This would indicate the trout are off their feed and you may pick up the occasional trout fishing at trout temperatures.

All we have discussed until now are preparations you should make at home before going to your lake. Now we'll go into the procedure to follow once you're on the lake ready to set the hooks into a big trout.

Take two things besides your regular fishing gear out on the lake with you; a temperature gauge and a note pad with pencil. An electronic temperature gauge is best. The small thermometer types that are reeled up and down on a fishing line are bothersome and slow to use. Time wasted reeling the thermometer up and down is just that much less time you can spend fishing. Many small inexpensive bulb-type temperature gauges are not reliable in the greater depths.

The serious trout fisherman should consider the cost of an electronic unit as money well-spent. Purchase a model with at least 100 feet of probe wire and make sure the wire is marked at 5-foot intervals. The new types with mechanical counters lack the depth accuracy necessary to the trout fisherman. An error of depth of 1 to 5 feet may completely ruin a day's fishing. You have to be able to pinpoint the proper depth within 2 or 3 feet. Mark the wire yourself on units containing the built in counter.

Once you're on the lake anchor the boat over deeper water (from 40 to 100 feet, depending on the time of the year and the lake). Take temperature readings at 10- and 5-foot intervals until you reach 46 degrees or below. As you read the temperatures record them in your note pad. When you've finished you'll have a temperature profile of the lake for that day.

On larger lakes you should take a new temperature profile every time you move to a different part of the lake. Wind action can make a big difference in a temperature profile from one area to another in large lakes.

With the temperature profile and your species content list you should be able to locate trout in any lake. To make sure you understand it let's set up another example. Suppose that you find the following conditions on your lake.

Temp. Profile	Fish	Habitat
Surface — 72		
10′ — 72		
20′ — 70	shiners and perch	suspended & near bottom
30′ — 68		
40′ — 65		
50′ — 64	resting browns & bows	suspended or near bottom
55′ — 55	cisco	suspended
60′ — 51	smelt	near bottom
65′ — 47		
70′ — 47	resting lakers	near bottom
80′ — 46		

With all of the information compiled in this way it is easy to pinpoint where you would look for the trout. For resting trout we would expect to find browns and rainbows at 52 to 53 feet with the lakers anywhere from 65 to 80 feet. By pinpointing the areas where the trout's forage fish are located we can predict where the feeding trout will be found. Looking at the chart we would predict trout to be feeding on cisco suspended at a depth of 56 to 57 feet with another segment of the trout population feeding on smelt near bottom at about 60 feet and a few rainbows and browns feeding on shiners and perch up at 30 to 35 feet.

Armed with this information you would then systematically fish the bait fish temperatures starting with one of the most likely, either smelt or cisco, and thoroughly working each until you begin catching trout. But remember that when one temperature stops producing, change your technique and fish one of the other temperatures. The versatile trout fisherman is also the most successful trout fisherman.

You now have all the information you need to find the trout in a thermally stratified lake. Fishing for big trout in lakes is an exciting sport and one which has not been heavily exploited. With your knowledge of bait fish temperature fishing you should be able to become one of the few who have mastered this challenging sport.

How to Hire a Fishing Guide

by RICHARD JOHNSON

A good guide knows the habits of trout and he knows the best areas to fish in a lake or stream. Beautiful scenery is just part of the bonus a guide provides. Knowledge of how to take trout consistently is what a sportsman buys when he hires a guide.

THE IMAGE of the professional fishing guide is changing. The leather-lunged guide with a face to match has become a thing of the past. A vocabulary that would put shame to an angry mule skinner has been tempered with newer phrases such as "structure, breakline, deep water sanctuaries and jump baits."

The modern fishing guide is a professional fisherman; he is in tune with the environment, the fish he specializes in catching and he knows how to handle fishermen. Today's guide relies heavily on modern fish-finding instruments such as sonar—either flasher or straight line graphs—and electronic water thermometers. He knows his success in producing fish for clients hinges on his ability to locate them.

A trout guide, especially a *good* trout guide, is as rare as a diamond in a coal pile. His services are in great demand and he demands and receives top prices for a day of his time.

Western trout guides are often much easier to locate than a guide in the East or Midwest States. Guides in the West are often tied in directly with tackle shops in many areas.

A fisherman desiring a guide has only to walk into a good tackle shop in trout country, ask several questions and he's fixed up with the best guide in the area. This is easy and the method most visiting trout fishermen follow.

The western trout guide normally furnishes a canoe or raft if a float trip is in order. Much of the guide business in the West is oriented around a float down one of the better trout streams.

Eastern and midwestern trout fishermen are often puzzled by the seeming lack of good guides on many trout streams. The bulk of these guides operate from their homes and very few are tied up with tackle shops. Word-of-mouth advertising eliminates costly magazine or newspaper advertising and consequently few guides are well known outside their immediate vicinity. This close-mouthed attitude prohibits many prospective trout fishermen from making initial contact with a guide.

Possibly the best solution to this problem is to operate through a booking agent. Agents specializing in outdoor trips know where guides are located and how to get in touch. The sportsman doesn't pay for this service, the guide pays the booking agent a commission. The sportsman just gets good service.

I've had the pleasure of traveling all across North America in search of hot trout action and I'm a firm believer in booking agents. They can ferret out good information and make all the arrangements for a top-notch fishing trip. One of the best firms for arranging fishing trips in the United States and Canada is Michigan Angling Adventures, P.O. Box 165, Clio, Michigan 48420.

They've arranged lake trout, steelhead, arctic char, brown trout and brook trout trips for me and I've never had a bum trip.

What's needed when you book a fishing trip, either with a booking agent or when the arrangements are made yourself? Many things can make or break a trip and the best advice is to plan a trout fishing trip well in advance. A year isn't too much time to plan ahead for a major trip where logistics involve thousands of miles.

I'm so mindful of a middle income friend of mine that had his heart set on making a trip to British Columbia to fish steelhead. He dreamed of the trip for years before he saved enough money to buy the ticket and make arrangements.

Hank (not his real name) decided to try one of the fabled B.C. streams because he heard 30-pound steelhead were caught there. A little checking would have shown that 30-pound steelhead are as scarce as hen's teeth and the odds against him taking a trophy that size were astronomical.

Nevertheless, Hank went off half-cocked, bought his plane

A crackerjack fishing guide was responsible for this fisherman's limit of five big brown trout.

Above—A float trip down a beautiful brook trout stream can produce nice brookies like this one for Tom Gronback, guide from Germfask, Michigan. Below—Guide Emil Dean of Bear Lake, Michigan is a highly sought after trout guide. Here he shows a greedy lake trout that struck two lures at once. A million to one occurrence.

ticket for Vancouver, B. C. and caught the plane. He took his fishing tackle with him, but, he boarded the plane without having contacted anyone on the stream. He had no advance knowledge of stream conditions, availablity of guides or state of the steelhead run. Optimism clouded his judgement.

Hank climbed off the plane at Vancouver, made a series of long distance phone calls and found all the guides in the area were booked solid for a month. The steelhead run was at its peak and professional guides were in great demand. A waiting list of hopeful anglers were standing by hoping someone would get sick or not show up. Hank felt he was above waiting in line for a guide.

A visit to the local bar, two drinks later and Hank had made contact with a guide. This individual proposed the highest going rate for his services, charged an exorbitant price for camping equipment (motels were filled) and wouldn't be ready for two days. My friend spent those days and nights watching sleep robbers on television in a nearby hotel.

The guide finally was ready, took Hank and his money into the bush, made camp and pointed out the river. By this time Hank was chomping at the bit to tie into a steelhead but he didn't know the river, habits of the steelhead and it quickly became apparent the guide didn't know any more about steelhead fishing then he did.

"There's the river," the guide said, "steelhead's in it." With this kind of useless advice Hank flailed the waters to a froth for four days without seeing a steelhead. The guide spent his time relaxing on shore, drinking coffee and reading a pocket novel.

A week later Hank returned home, fishless, broke and entirely disillusioned with guides and steelhead fishing. He vowed never to fish again with a guide and he positively was deadset against trying for steelhead in the future. The trip, a bad dream, cost Hank well over $2000 and ruined his thoughts on fishing for many years to come.

A tall tale? Nothing could be farther from the truth. Incidents such as this are repeated very often across the United States and in Canada. Hank made many mistakes and his lack of foresight cost him a great deal of money.

The first key to having a good trout fishing trip requires pre-planning. Don't enter into a trout fishing trip in foreign waters without giving a lot of thought to the subject and to check ahead.

My friend didn't check ahead to determine the availability of guides. If he'd checked he would have found most guides are booked from year-to-year and a waiting list is made up of hopeful fishermen. The best guides always have a following and the best a visiting fisherman can hope for is a few days of a guide's time.

Hank should have written to the Fish Division in the area he was visiting and asked for assistance in locating a *reliable* guide. Chambers of Commerce are a good bet as are state or provincial Travel Commissions. Most states and provinces have lists of licensed guides or they know of reliable guides in the area.

The next step would have been to write to these guides and inquire as to their availability during the planned fishing time and to ask for a list of references. Ask for both names and addresses of customers that caught their limit and those that caught little or nothing.

Some guides will only give out names of people that caught large numbers of big fish or they'll clue their cousins or father-in-law into being references. These people will always give Joe Guide a glowing reference. I always like to contact people that fished with Joe Guide but were either skunked or only had mediocre success.

If this less-fortunate fishermen gives the guide a solid boost then likely he's your man. Most customers realize a guide can only do so much and if they're happy with a small catch then apparently the guide did a good job. They were just unfortunate enough to not catch fish.

Write or phone several people for a reference as to your proposed trout guide. Try and select fishermen from widely scattered parts of the country. Be sure to include a stamped, self-addressed envelope for a reply. Don't bore the person with a long windy letter about yourself or your fishing exploits. You're imposing on someone for his time. Keep the letter short, simple and to the point. Ask for his honest unbiased opinion of the guide and his services. Was he satisfied and would he recommend you hire him in the future? This can be answered in just a few words and is sufficient to determine whether the guide is usable or not.

Once you've narrowed down the prospective guide then get in touch with him immediately. Don't wait until a month before fishing time. A common complaint among guides is that clients wait until the last minute and then complain because the guide is booked up. A guide is only one man, capable of taking only one party at a time. An early contact is your best hedge against disappointment.

A guide often specializes in only one type of fishing. Float trip specialists often prefer fishermen to fish with spinning tackle. It does little good to bump heads with a guide over fishing techniques. The best advice is to secure a guide that prefers to fish the same way you do.

Some guides furnish all equipment including rods and reels. They know what works best in their area. Mismatched equipment is a common problem with clients. If a guide offers to furnish equipment, use his—it's often better suited to the river or trout lake than anything you can bring.

Some guides are temperamental and others are prima donnas—a good bit like customers. Determine, by letter or phone call, if your prospective guide has any prejudices or taboos about anything. I once knew a client that was rudely dropped by a guide because the sport drank a noon beer with his sandwiches. Another guide I know would strike a client's knuckles with a stick if he touched the drag on a reel while playing a fish. Quirks like this can ruin a trip for a client before it begins. Find out early what kind of a man you're hiring.

The question normally first and foremost in the minds of many sportsmen is: "How much does a guide cost?" This question is best answered by saying it varies: geographic location; going rates; type of trout; fishing hours; demand of the guide; equipment furnished; waters fished; danger to guide, client or tackle; and much more go into determining the going rate for good trout guides.

I've paid as little as $15 per day in Ontario and as high as $100 per day in Michigan for my trout fishing. Western guides often receive from $60 to $80 daily, depending to a great deal on number of people fishing, and the area to be fished. These rates were current during the fall of 1975, but the way inflation keeps spiraling upward, these prices may be obsolete by the time you go fishing.

If I had to select an average wage for a guide it would be somewhere between $70 and $80 per day for either one or two fishermen.

Many fishermen feel these rates are exceptionally high but when one takes into account the shortness of the trout season, wear and tear on tackle, and operating expenses, this figure isn't high at all.

The editor of this book, Dave Richey, is a highly sought after trout guide in Michigan. Dave has to travel long distances to take his clients fishing. Someone has to pay these charges. The day of the underpaid trout guide is long gone. They now can make a comfortable living whereas in bygone days, guides scratched for a living year around.

Many fishermen have a misguided notion that hiring a guide

Above—This guide is also a fisherman and he's shown following the contour of a lake by means of a straight line recording graph. Good guides have all the modern equipment. Below—A guide put this fisherman into a trophy brook trout in the wilds of Quebec. Without a guide the fisherman may never have hooked this 6-pound brook trout.

Hookjawed male brook trout like this represent a catch of a lifetime for most anglers. Good guides are most apt to be able to put an angler into a thrilling catch like this.

is akin to hiring a slave. Few sportsmen realize that what you hire in a guide is his knowledge of local trout conditions and a day of his valuable time. You *do not* hire a packhorse, slave or someone to heap abuse upon.

Guides, by and large, are deeply sensitive people in love with trout fishing and the outdoors. They are better than average fishermen, this is what makes them outstanding guides. Their knowledge of trout and trout habits is outstanding and this is what places the good ones in such high demand.

A competent guide will know when trout are running in the area, where and when the best fishing should occur, what lures or flies work best, best fishing times, isolated locations where fishermen can move away from the crowds and specialized local techniques that pay off with good catches.

Although the client is paying for the guide's time he should listen to reason and follow the advice of a guide. Remember, a guide is the expert in his area and he's had much more experience in taking trout from his waters than you have. A fisherman must have a couple loose boards in his attic to deviate from the advice of his guide. Listen to these pearls of wisdom and have faith in them. Guides want you to catch trout just as badly as you want to. Their continuing reputation hinges on their ability to produce trout.

A guide, on the other hand, has to be receptive to the wishes and desires of his customer. Dave Richey recalls an elderly gentleman he once guided for steelhead. Dave thoroughly explained the fishing technique but the oldtimer wasn't too confident of his ability. He asked for a demonstration.

Dave waded into the river, made several casts and promptly hung a 14-pound steelhead that tailwalked across the river and then headed downstream with his back throwing a spray of water like a rooster tailing speedboat. Dave followed along as fast as he could and landed the big trout after a thrilling battle.

The customer admired the big male and commented, "I didn't believe trout got that big!" The man then flatly refused to fish for steelhead but insisted that Dave fish. He paid a day's guide fee just to watch Dave catch steelhead. He went away from that trip feeling like he'd gotten his money's worth. Dave was tickled at getting paid to do something he thoroughly enjoys.

Many guides simply lose track of the basic fact that part-time or weekend fishermen just do not have the stamina to put in a hard day's fishing. Some guides operate from daylight to dark while others adopt a banker's philosophy and work from 9 until 5 with an hour off for lunch. These factors must be determined long before a client hires a guide. It does little good to assume you'll have 10 or 12 uninterrupted hours on a river or lake and then suddenly find yourself taking a lunch

River guides such as the man in the background
made it possible for this angler to net this large trout.

break 3 hours after you start fishing.

Some guides furnish a shore lunch, others will prepare a shore lunch for an extra fee, some provide sandwiches, and some guides expect to be fed by the customer. Again, check into what is furnished and what to expect. A fisherman used to eating three squares a day will feel like his throat's been cut if he goes an entire day without eating because he thought the guide would furnish a meal.

Some fishermen feel a trout fishing trip won't be a success unless they bring both tackle boxes, several rods and reels and a 20-year assortment of junk. Guides hate to see a dude loaded to the gunwales with useless equipment. I've run across guides that flatly refuse to allow fishermen to bring anything other than personal clothing and a camera. "When I'm trying to net a big trout for a client from my drift boat I don't want to be tripping over his useless crap," said one Oregon guide. Keep equipment to a minimum or better yet, leave it home and use the guide's.

I've yet to find a foolproof way to get around the subject of tipping a guide. The original meaning of TIP was—to insure prompt service. I keep that oldtime meaning in mind when it comes time to settle up with a guide. If I'm impressed with the way he handled himself and me, if he was prompt and courteous, went out of his way to provide me with a good day,

he gets a tip. Ten dollars is usually sufficient.

You'll note the above paragraph made no mention as to whether he produced any trout. A catch of fish is not tantamount to success as many people seem to think.

Fishing is a privilege . . . not a contract for a limit catch of trout. Fishermen hiring a guide should keep that thought in mind. If the guide does the best he can under the circumstances and keeps your personal comfort and well-being in mind at all times, he's entitled to a small gratuity at the end of a long day.

However, if the guide is slack in his duties, rude or arrogant in his behavior towards the client, he doesn't deserve a tip and probably doesn't deserve to be called a guide.

I'm often asked whether a guide should fish alongside his customers or not. I'm a firm believer in fishing guides. They're more in contact through a rod and reel in their hands than if they merely stood by while the customers fished. I'll take a fishing guide any day over one that stands around with his hands in his pockets.

I'm often reminded of the western adage "Treat a guide like your best friend." I've done this over the years and I'm proud of the fact that some of my best friends are fishing guides.

Begin a friendship with a good guide and he'll often show you his best locations and stick with you long after quitting time just to show you a good time.

Float a Western Trout Stream

by KATHLEEN FARMER

RIVERS ENSLAVE the imagination. Visions of adventure, excitement and daring fill the mind when questions about them are pondered. Where does the river come from and where can it take me? What life lurks in its depths? Can man capture wily trout in a sporting manner?

Fundamentally, a river is simply water flowing. Living organisms rely on water to satisfy the basic thirst drive. But a river is more than that. It closely resembles a breathing, conscienceless person. Always changing, never the same, but forever seeking its own ends. Old Man River, powerful, strong and self-centered, engulfs obstacles and sweeps them unwillingly to an unknown destination. In the spring, he bloats, swells, sometimes flooding and drowning. Come winter, he shrinks, tame. He undermines huge chunks of earth and transforms rich soil into mucky river bottom. An irresistible force, he brings out the wanderer, the explorer in the seemingly settled city folk. Hearing the rush, the churning of an angry river, quickens the pulse, sends energy into the arm muscles. "Jump in your canoe and try to conquer me," he seems to dare you, "I bet you can't." A special breed of human can do it. And you are one of them.

Combine the allure of the river with the favorite pastime of trout fishing and you have an unbeatable team. Some say that float-fishing gives an unfair advantage to the fisherman. Cast within centimeters of the shoreline and let the lure dance naturally in the current. Gauge the depth of the hole, reel fast and expect to lose the best fish-attracting flies, spoons and spinners in your tackle box. Those hungry snags are gluttons for the bait-offerings of novice float-fishers.

How to Float a Western River

To float-fish a river, you need a rugged, roomy, easy-to-maneuver canoe, rubber raft or flat-bottomed boat. For a beginner, it is best to hire a fishing guide, who owns and handles a river-fishing craft. A successful guide specializes in one or two 20-mile sections of the river. He float-fishes them daily and knows each hole, snag, bend and calls each trout weighing more than 5 pounds by name. He is a miracle worker to a novice fisherman. He instructs the angler to cast a No. 18 black Midge to that hole, slightly upstream and an inch from a submerged log. Wham! As if the entire scene were rehearsed, a 3-pound brown snarfs down the bait. You can not describe how, but the eight-person rubber raft bounces stationary in the current and before you know it, your fish is netted, the hook is detached from the toothy stubborn lower jaw and you are ready to cast again. The procedure seems almost too easy—too smooth. With the river guide shouldering the responsibilities of boat director and fish locater, you bask in the primitive scenery and sights that only a trout stream can offer. A pair of Canada geese constructing a secluded nest; an osprey circling high and threatening; a beaver slapping his tail loud enough to scare away all the fish within a mile.

Many reputable float-fishing guides advertise in the outdoor magazines. Find one that concentrates on river float-fishing for trout within the covers of *Field & Stream, Sports Afield* or *Outdoor Life* and write to him. Ask specifics, like

price, available lodging or camping and recommended tackle. Most float-fishing outfitters include lunch and transportation to the "put in" spot and from the "take out" destination. Tackle is responsibility of the fisherman. Most trips feature either rubber rafts or flat-bottomed boats. They are stable fishing platforms and anglers have no fear of losing their balance and falling into the torrent. On the other hand, float-fishing from a canoe is like tight-rope walking—frantic and nerve-racking.

A metal frame is attached over the air pontoons of a rubber raft which supports comfortable fighting chairs. The oarsman occupies the center seat, facing the bow. One fisherman sits in the bow chair; the other, behind the oarsman near the stern. Two anglers per boat is the limit. Limited space and the mechanics of positioning the boat to cover good fishing water restricts the number that can be invited aboard. An all-day float with lunch and a guide who manipulates the boat will cost approximately $100 or $50 apiece.

Float-fishing has gained popularity during the past several years. It is considered big business in many circles. The consumer should be careful and he should insist on fair treatment and good service. Before signing up for a float-fishing trip, talk to the outfitter or guide for a few minutes. Ask him about his philosophy of fishing and the policy of releasing fish caught. A river fishing guide is truly the skipper of his ship even if the craft is a mere 15 feet in length. You are dependent on him to point out productive waters and put you in position to cast and reach the holes. Most western rivers are swift. They can speed the angler downstream at a rate of 3 to 10 mph, depending on the time of year and the water depth. Without a conscientious, cooperative guide, you could miss the best holes.

A river can reach breakneck speed during spring run-off. It occurs in April or May when temperatures rise above freezing for extended periods of time. Snow in the surrounding mountains melts and is drawn down into creeks and then rivers by gravity. The avalanche of partially thawed snow carries debris and soil with it. Upon joining the transparent, wintertime river water, the run-off looks like liquid earth. Black, brown or red, the run-off colors the river, increases its volume and force, and makes fishing difficult.

Run-off usually ends sometime in July. If you want to catch fish on the river float, it is best to time the trip before or after heavy water. The outfitter can advise you about this. But exercise caution if he discourages you from fishing during August and September, which are usually outstanding fishing months. Out West, fishing guides often double as big game hunting outfitters during the fall. Many seasons open the end of August or early September. The fishing potential is questionable when the outfitter has his mind on setting up camp for incoming eastern elk hunters.

The fishing philosophy of the river guide is important. Why? A float-fish outfitting business is usually headquartered at a sporting goods or fish tackle shop. Before leaving on the trip, the guide recommends tackle that is locally effective. For example, the Muddler Minnow or silver bladed Mepps Spinner is especially deadly in May before the run-off in the Snake River winding through northwestern Wyoming. Listen to the guides. They float-fish frequently and know what they are talking about.

However, if the guide is a purist fisherman—that is, fishes only with spin gear or fly or bait no matter what the condition or circumstance—he will instruct you only according to his own limited view. If he is a purist fly fisherman, for instance, and you are too, then you and he will most likely see things in the same way and no disagreements will arise. But if you are a bass fisherman from Arkansas and traveled west to catch trout from the Colorado River, you may clash

with the fly-fishing-only guide. He can refuse to allow you to fish with a spoon or insist you release the only fish you caught. What do you do then? I have known fishermen who have left the boat and guide in the middle of a sand bar. They waded the remaining 5 miles to the waiting vehicle, fishing with lures and catching scrappy rainbows.

Many tourist-oriented towns in the West offer day-long fish-floats. Within one hour or two or less from many Western cities, a fishing adventure for trout can begin. Trout streams are scattered throughout the states of Montana, Wyoming, Colorado, Idaho, Washington and Oregon. A fisherman can find one through the Game and Fish Department or by contacting local fishing experts. More preparation is needed to organize a fish-float trip in New Mexico, Arizona, Utah and California. Start months before the vacation and write to the state Game and Fish office for a list of river outfitters.

Do-it-yourself floating can be the ultimate of fishing experiences. Or it can end prematurely and abruptly by a scary dunking in a 40-degree, 7-mph current, dumping fishing gear to the bottom of the stream. Whether the trip is the best or the worst depends on your level of expertise in boat handling, reading rivers and the beforehand knowledge you obtained about the river.

If you know the craft and can induce her to respond quickly without hesitation, then you are 30 percent ready to tackle a river on your own. Can you read rivers? When the river current braids, what ribbon of water should you follow? How important is the tongue of the current? And do you know about the dangers of a "hole," that is, the downstream side of a submerged rock? By observing the stream, can you locate rocks and other hazardous obstacles to avoid. A river changes daily. Natural barricades—such as a huge cottonwood gnawed down by a beaver that blocks the entire channel—are common.

Western rivers are not civilized yet. Some are dammed, yes, but they are fiercer, narrower, more unpredictable than most eastern rivers. Explorers sacrificed years, money and lives trying to find navigable waters in the western frontier. Lewis and Clark wasted time, energy and finances attempting to establish a waterway link, a lifeline, between St. Louis and the unexplored wilderness. But when the rivermen from the East rode the western rivers, they knew they had met their match, a different breed of cat.

A novice do-it-yourself floater would be smart to familiarize himself with a stretch of the river through a guide. The following day, he can challenge it himself. A float-fisher can cover about 20 miles of river per day. Start with a day-long float. Identify a "put in" and a "take out" spot. These should be easily accessible by vehicle. At the put-in site, the water should be relatively slow where you can ease the craft into the stream and load it with supplies. Tie all the gear securely to the boat. Then, if the craft should flip over, the tackle can be salvaged with the boat. Approximately 20-miles or less downstream from "put in," is "take out." This marks the end of the float and should be identifiable from the river. At both the put-in and take-out locations, a vehicle should be parked. Then, where the float terminates, the boat and gear can be packed into the car. After cleaning fish, the last chore of a fish-float is to drive to the put-in point, where the craft was launched, and pick up the second vehicle. This is a matter of strategy and is the most bothersome part of the float.

Where a 2- or 3-day excursion is planned around the river, be certain about camping regulations. In Grand Teton National Park, for instance, camping is not permitted along the river. River rangers patrol regularly during the summer and cite offenders. On the park section of the Snake, only

Shore lunch, featuring "foiled trout" is highlight of western float. Note, plush river boat featuring swivel seats.

one-day floats are sanctioned. Along other fish-float streams, camping is authorized only at designated camp-grounds. This involves extra planning. The floaters should close each day at an organized campsite.

A fish-float river is accessible at convenient points. It has no severe rapids and has soft banks occasionally where an angler can "dock" his boat and fish from shore. While the river may have logs and rocks defying the expertise of the oarsman, it should not be cluttered with these, forcing numerous portages of boat and gear. Portaging is part of the adventure of a back country canoe trip but is unnecessary work for the float-fisherman.

Fishing Techniques

Fishing from a moving craft can be a dizzying sensation at first. Think of sitting in the rumble seat of a Model T chugging along at 10 mph, bouncing, swaying and jerking. Imagine how accurate your casts would be from such a vehicle. This is the problem the angler encounters on a fish-float. And yet casting precision is paramount. Without quick, right-on-the-money casts, you spook wary trout as well as miss many fish-bulging holes. Instead of hooking a trophy, chances are good you will tangle with an endless array of snags. As a result, a frustrating number of lures, flies and bait will be left behind on logs, branches and rocks —everywhere except where you want them to be.

With a good river guide, float-fishing depends on short 40-foot or less casts. To prepare for this type of angling, practice casting from a sitting position to a target about 40 feet away.

Look ahead while floating down the stream. Watch for the best hole in a stretch of water and plan to cast to it. Moving with the current, you will not be able to hit every tempting piece of water. Pick and choose. Be selective. Otherwise, exasperation will set in, flustering your compo-sure and in turn influencing you to overcast and blunder in some other way. Calm, shrewd, careful casters will catch more fish.

Effective gear for float-fishing depends on the river and the condition of the water at the moment. However, be prepared for any type of fishing that you feel will work. Equip yourself with a variety of lures, flies and bait. If one method fails, utilize another. Even though the guide

controls the boat and can suggest fish-producing spots, you are the fisherman. It is up to you to try the local favorites and then to experiment with your own preferences. Who knows, you might teach the outfitter a thing or two about fishing.

One of the best float-fishermen I know is Beau Usher. Living in Santa Fe, he migrates north into Wyoming, Montana and Idaho each spring to sample early season stream trout fishing. Inflating his yolk yellow six-person rubber raft with a hand pump, he smacks his lips anticipat-ing the beer-battered fish fillets that will be cooked over an open fire later on. He is confident and his optimism spills over onto everyone around him. People seem to fish better when they are floating with him. He expects casting perfection. By supreme concentration and determination, they do not disappoint him. No one knows how long he has been around but he says he remembers when 5 pounds was small for a cutthroat.

"Ush," as he calls himself, thinks practice is ". . . hogwash. You're either born with a casting arm or you're not. Don't try to fool anybody with all that practice business. Casting is the best way to learn. If you don't cast on the stream, forget it. Casting on a boat is much different than casting in the backyard at a target, for chriss sake.

"It's real simple. Cast upstream above a hole, far enough so when the bait hits a hole it is down deep where the fish are. Then, start your retrieve. For lures and flies, it is the same. Aim ahead of the hole so the lure can sink down into the hole and the fly can work through the entire hole.

"Don't show off with those gall-durn long casts when you're fly fishing. Keep the line short and cast with little flicks of the rod. So short, in fact, that you can lift the belly of the fly line off the water and dangle the fly in the hole. That is absolutely the best way to handle a fly line on fast moving water. Otherwise, the belly of the fly line gets caught in the current and is pushed out towards the center of the river. This drags the fly downstream. When the fly line needs to be longer or reach where you want it to go, cast downstream. Then, the belly of the line moves with the boat and causes the fly to swirl, natural. As soon as drag occurs, lift the fly off the water surface. Downstream casting is especially effective with the Muddler Minnow."

According to Beau, he has bucked nearly every river in

Western landscape is in evidence along this stretch of North Platte River in Wyoming.

the Rockies, whether it was meant for float-fishing or not. His favorites are the Henry's Fork in Idaho and the Green, North Platte and New Fork in Wyoming. Beau employs whatever he can—bait, lures or flies—to fool trout. The color of the water and how quick the trout respond determine what method he uses. When the water is clear, early and late in the day and of course if there is a hatch out, use flies. The Muddler Minnow is reliable for rainbows, browns and cutthroats. It is a good fly to begin with when a hatch has not yet appeared and there is no natural hint about what the fish are hitting. Brown and black Wooly Worms and streamers, Montana Nymphs and large dry flies late in the afternoon. Cutthroats seem to look for large dry floaters, such as the Humpy and Irresistible. Brook trout are drawn to the red colors. The red-tailed Black Gnat fished wet or dry, red-tailed weighted Nymphs and red-tailed Wooly Worms can be deadly.

For off-color, slightly dingy water and during run-off, bait may be the difference between catching fish and being skunked—"the secret weapon," as Beau calls it. In general, worms, minnows, grasshoppers and hellgramites are the popular choices of trout anglers. Attach a No. 7 split shot to the end of the line. The bait is hooked on a leader, which is tied to the line about a foot above the weight. The dropper rig bounces the split shot along the stream bottom. The bait floats naturally above it in the water. Remember, early in the season, during May and June, fish are lying in deep holes. The bait must be heavy enough to reach them. If nothing happens after a half-hour of casting, put on another split shot. The added weight may be the trick to slay trout.

Rainbows, cutts and brookies like fat, active worms or nightcrawlers. The dropper rig is the most effective way of presenting them to the fish. However, brook trout are especially susceptible to a Colorado spinner bait with a worm. Browns can hardly resist minnows on a plain hook or impaled on a spinner bait rig. With their insatiable

appetite, the bigger the minnow, the better.

Lures are old standbys that seem to catch fish almost any time. Some fish-float rivers have reputations for being spinner streams; others, for being spoon waters. Many fishermen share a similar feeling, favoring either spinners or spoons. Ordinarily, a good spoon is heavier than a spinner and sinks faster and deeper. Some faster rivers are called spoon streams while slower moving rivers or holes are just right for a spinner. In addition, later in the fishing season, in July and August, fish are not as deep as they were earlier. Then a spinner can be most effective.

When the water is slightly off-color, use bright lures, such as, silver, orange and yellow. Do not bother casting lures to shallow water on a fish-float. If any fish are there, they will be small. Concentrate your efforts on deep holes and let the lures sink as deep as possible.

Rainbows and brookies like red-and-white combinations, silver and brass. Small spoons and No. 2 spinners fit their tastes. Browns are bold and prefer their food that way too. Lean towards brass spoons, a sinking minnow imitation and a spinner-rubber minnow combination. In contrast, cutthroats are primarily a spoon fish. Silver and yellow-and-black combinations are the best colors on a float for them. However, a silver bladed spinner has been known to work too.

Float-fishing adds a new dimension to angling. You move with the current and are no longer stationary. The stream sweeps you right into deep holes, right in with the lunkers. Fishing opportunities can last all day. If they are not hitting in one hole, float on to the next 100 downstream.

You are limited no longer. From a fisherman's viewpoint, you are as untethered, as infinite, as you will ever be. Float-fishing a western stream is not simple even with the advantage of mobility but it makes fishing simpler, more elementary and much more exciting.

How to Rig and Fish

Minnows

"YOU'RE NOT going to use *that* for trout?" I said, indicating the huge minnow Ray Gordon was carefully threading on a No. 4 long-shanked Carlisle hook. It was a 2½-inch Flathead, the kind sold in area bait shops as "northern pike size."

"Want big fish, fish big minnows," Ray smiled.

I shook my head, laughed, and slipped a tiny No. 10 shankless gold-plated bait hook lightly through the lips of a 1-inch "trout and panfish size" Emerald Shiner.

"Want trout," I countered, "fish trout-sized bait . . . alive . . . and swimming."

Ray smiled again, shrugged, and went about the ritual of double-hooking the minnow by running the hook through the mouth, out the gills and then into the body beneath the dorsal fin.

It was nearly dusk and the big browns would soon be probing Camp One rapids pool. Perhaps a cruising trophy would be dumb enough to rap a soaking minnow while Ray and I prepared our streamside supper.

Later, about the time the blackened coffee pot belched its first gurgles over the small keyhole fire, and before a healthy dollop of brandy smitten with a mere trace of tannin-dyed river water had slid to the bottom of our stainless steel cups, the trout hit. Man, how it hit!

The first sound was like the slap of an angry beaver's tail. The second, closer, sounded as if someone had whacked a board hard against the water's surface.

The tip of Ray's spinning rod jerked once, twice, and then the handle pulled from under a rock which anchored it inside the gnarled elbow of a cedar root.

Ray lurched from his squatting position near the fire, grabbed the bucking rod, and let the fish whistle line downstream against the lightly set drag.

Again the fish slapped its tail on the surface, not really jumping—browns seldom do—but thrusting hard against the underside of the pool, perhaps to gain leverage for burrowing deep into a favorite sanctuary.

Then, as Ray carefully pumped his fish upstream, the tip of my rod jerked too.

"Hey!" I yelled. "We've got doubles!"

I snatched the rod, reared back and set the hook hard. The light rod bent, kinked back and a 4-inch chub zoomed through the air in a trajectory that splatted it against my forehead. It then ricocheted into a nearby tree where the chub and several feet of line whipped into a monofilament bird's nest of magnificent intricacy.

Danny Kroll, Clintonville, Wisconsin, proves minnow-caught trout average larger than those caught by other methods on Wisconsin's famous Wolf River.

by CHARLES GLASS

Photos and illustration by Walt Sandberg

for Big River Trout

Ray worked his fish slowly to the beach by leading it in a series of figure-eight patterns and finally gilling it as the trout flopped weakly in the shallows. It was a fine 20-inch brown with a sagging belly and red spots on its flanks that were half the size of a dime.

Smiling, he held the huge trout from an extended thumb in a silhouette against the pale light of the early evening sky, and then glanced smugly at the tiny chub still struggling helplessly in the branches overhead.

"Want big trout, fish big minnows," he said.

Calmly, I walked to the fire, picked up my cup, hoisted it and toasted, "Amen!"

I've learned a lot about river fishing for big trout since then. I know they like their food in large chunks and that they're not about to waste energy chasing microscopic organisms all over the river. Instead, larger trout will lay in ambush until a real meal comes along in the form of an unsuspecting laggard minnow.

Results of a study conducted in Michigan indicate that brown trout up to 9 inches in length are insect feeders. But, as they grow larger, they turn to a crayfish and minnow diet. Almost 70 percent of the diets of the largest brown trout were composed of young trout, muddlers, minnows and darters.

A similar study of rainbow trout in Paul Lake, British Columbia (as reported in the excellent book *Through The Fish's Eye* by Mark Sosin and John Clark) showed that during the summer months the diet of rainbows of less than 10 inches consisted of only 6 percent shiners on an average, while those from 10 to 14 inches ate 70 percent shiners, and those larger than 14 inches ingested 94 percent shiners in their diet.

My streamside observations indicate that large brook trout prefer minnows over any other food. The stomach contents of a 12-inch brookie I caught during a high water period last season had gorged on nine minnows, three stonefly nymphs and a miniature crayfish. The brookie was as sag-bellied as a 20-year-old swayback mare when caught but still hungry enough to strike and envelop a rigged minnow.

I also noted that the minnows the fish had stuffed himself with were far larger than those usually classified as trout bait. So I opened his mouth, measured both ways, and discovered that there was room enough to swallow an object the size of a spent .410 shotshell without causing him indigestion.

That's why Ray had been successful at Camp One rapids pool. He'd fished a minnow large enough to entice a big trout.

Ray had something else going for him that night. He had rigged his minnow specifically for river fishing.

Trout hit minnows in a way completely different from other gamefish. Northern, musky, walleye and most panfish will grab a minnow sideways, carry it a considerable distance, pause, leisurely turn the bait and then swallow it head first.

Thus lake anglers usually lip hook the minnow or hook it lightly under the dorsal fin and allow it to swim free. After the strike and initial run, ample time is allowed for the fish to turn the bait and swallow it. Usually, the lake angler will count to 30 after the fish pauses before setting the hook.

Using these tactics on river trout will only result in a hook being stripped clean of bait. Trout in rivers and streams hit right now! A good-sized brookie, brown or rainbow will slam a rigged minnow from any angle, often striking so savagely you won't need to set the hook. That's not to say that river trout aren't discriminating diners—they are. And they possess a unique set of sensory organs that permit them to reject food of doubtful value instantaneously.

But, big trout are predators and will assault their prey swiftly and viciously once they've determined the object of attack is suitable food. This selection and attack process is faster with river trout because they've learned that hesitation means the food will be swept away with the current.

Researchers have proven that trout can detect the vibrations from a swimming minnow up to 20 feet away depending upon the amount of water turbulence in the stream. In fast water and riffles, the detection range is much closer. In slow moving pools or flatwater, it's farther away. And it's probably at its maximum in open lakes or beaver ponds.

Trout can also "taste" a baitfish without actually mouthing or touching it merely by using sensitive organs located on the *outside* of the snout. Other sensory organs allow them to perceive minute variations in waterborne odors. They are also temperature sensitive and can detect changes in water temperatures of as little as 1/5 of a degree.

They have two types of vision cells; one works well in darkness and the other during bright daylight hours. Both are admirably suited to detecting movement.

These exceptional sensory abilities of trout must be circumvented if you're to take trout consistently. Fortunately, fast-moving, turbulent river water decreases their working range. That and the characteristic laziness of large trout when it comes to chasing prey, plus their preference for minnows, dictates the best way to take lunker river trout:

1. Rig a minnow so that it's well hooked and won't be battered off by swift current or by a trout's savage strike.
2. Fish the rigged minnow to imitate a wounded or laggard baitfish that will make an easy meal.
3. Set the hook at precisely the right instant; just before the trout realizes he's grabbed a rigged minnow and before he spits it out. Set the hook as soon as possible after the strike.
4. Play the hooked trout firmly but lightly.

The toughest part of the four rules for an inexperienced minnow fisherman to follow is the timing for hook setting. Veteran anglers often use what might best be called the "drop

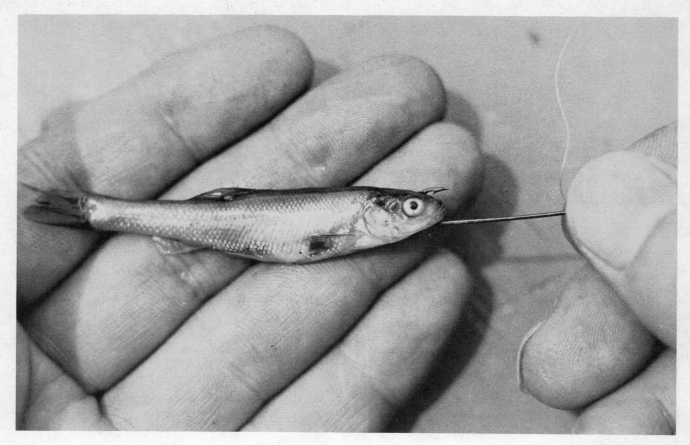

Lip hooking . . .

and strike'' method. Immediately upon feeling the strike, they drop the rod tip to allow the fish time to clamp down on the minnow. Then, in a single fluid motion, they set the hook before the fish has time to reject it. After the hook is set, they lower the rod tip slightly to allow the fish a chance to fight against an arched rod. The reel drag is set as lightly as possible and the fish is controlled by ''feathering'' the spoon with a forefinger.

Proper retrieving is important also. There are almost as many different ways to reel in a minnow rig as there are fishermen. Some of them will work at various times and be non-productive at others.

Once, I was puzzled by the curious actions of a minnow fisherman casting on Wisconsin's Pine River. He would toss the rig at a huge boulder near the far bank, reel like crazy until the end of the line cut the water midway across a fast-flowing run, pause briefly to touch the butt of his rod to his right ear, then proceed with his super-fast retrieve.

After watching him repeat his performance several times curiosity got the better of me and I asked him why he used the novel retrieve.

He smiled sheepishly and explained: ''I caught the biggest trout of my life a few years ago when a mosquito lit on my ear and I stopped reeling long enough to knock it off with the butt of my rod. I've been using the same technique ever since.''

''Caught any more big trout?'' I asked.

''Not a one,'' he admitted.

The secret to fishing a minnow rig properly is not so much how it's brought back but where it's dropped and the kind of water it will be fished through. Generally, you should try to bring it down in pocket water ahead of midstream boulders, near snags and bankside debris, and in the mixing zone edging

fastwater runs and slower sidewater eddies. Then fish it back through deep holes or bubbling runs. Forget the shallows and stagnant slackwater pools.

Usually, the kind of retrieve you use will be determined by the type of river rig you're fishing.

Ray Gordon's double-hooked minnow rig allows him total control. The bait responds to every twitch of the rod tip. It's best fished by quarter-casting upstream and then retrieved with a jerk-jerk-pause, jerk-jerk-pause rhythm. Make the jerks short, about 6 inches and pause just long enough to allow the minnow to drop back in the current. As you pause, reel in the slack line and don't let the rig bounce on the bottom.

The rig works well with any tackle, even with ultra-light spinning gear or fly tackle. Split shot may be added 12 to 18 inches ahead of the minnow for better control in fast water and to get the bait down quickly in deep holes. You can attach a small cork or plastic bubble or bobber ahead of the minnow for buoyancy. Some trout fishermen believe a small spinner blade ahead of the minnow adds to the overall effectiveness.

Many addicted minnow fishermen say the rig works even better if the minnow is sewn on. They knot a No. 6 treble hook or a No. 6 double hook to an 18-inch length of heavy mono-filament leader. They then thread the leader through a large darning needle or a stainless steel surgical needle and run the leader through the minnow from its tail and out through its mouth. The shank of the hook is pulled into the body of the minnow so that only the barb protrudes around the tail. The needle is then slipped off and the rigged leader is tied to a swivel on the fishing line.

Sewn-on minnows are usually too much trouble for most fishermen. But, the bait stays where it's put, and anyone that takes the time to rig up this way for river trout seems to be the

. . . and hooking under the dorsal fin might work on lakes or sluggish rivers . . .

. . . but to take trout in fast water the minnow should be double hooked to stay on.

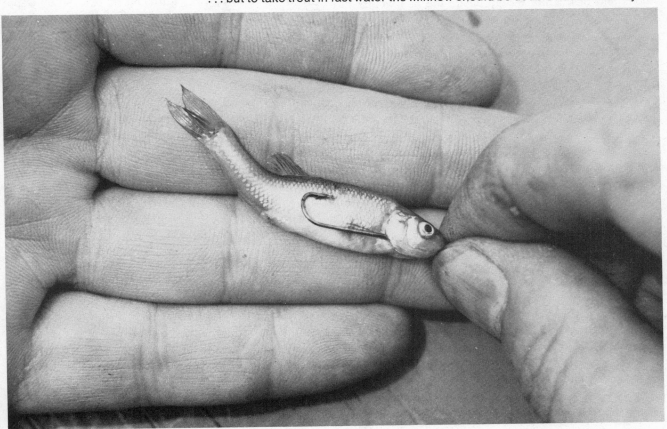

Above—The *Nicki Rig,* one of the few commercial devices that really work, secures the minnow with two hooks and places the weight *inside* the bait where it's less likely to snag.

Below—The "Strip-On," a trolling rig favored by Canadian lake fishermen, works well when fished with spinning gear in fast water, too.

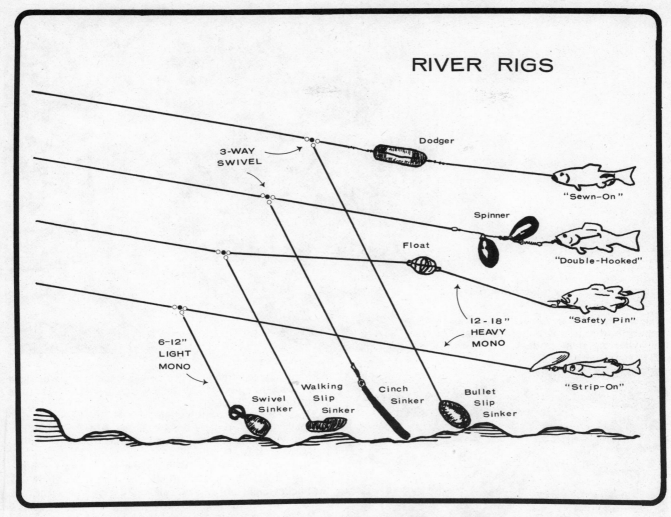

RIVER RIGS

3-WAY SWIVEL

Dodger

"Sewn-On"

Spinner

"Double-Hooked"

Float

"Safety Pin"

12-18" HEAVY MONO

6-12" LIGHT MONO

"Strip-On"

Swivel Sinker

Walking Slip Sinker

Cinch Sinker

Bullet Slip Sinker

River rig components can be mixed or matched to suit fishing conditions on any stream.

same person who creels the largest fish.

Some fishermen opt for the safety-pin hook for rigging minnows. This design is easy to use, but leaves a lot of hardware outside the minnow where a cautious brown trout can spot it. Perhaps that's why I've never had much success using them.

There are a variety of other minnow-holding contraptions on the market that will attract potential minnow fishermen but will seldom lure fish. They exhibit the same disadvantages as the safety-pin hook; too much metal outside where the sensitivities of wily trout can perceive and reject the danger well before a strike is induced.

One commercially available minnow rig that does work is the Nicki-Rig, which is available by mail from Binkelman Tackle, P. O. Box 11522, Milwaukee, WI 53211. The Nicki-Rig uses a unique, oblong, lipped lead sinker that fits *inside* the minnow. The device uses a principle called "sinking buoyancy." With the weight evenly distributed inside the minnow, the bait floats above the bottom in water of any depth or velocity and can be fished to realistically imitate a wounded minnow.

The best known, most widely used and best all-around river rig is the non-snagging set-up built around a three-way swivel and a slip sinker. It's a minnow fishermen's favorite

everywhere in the country and is often named after a highly productive local stream. It's known as the "Wolf River Rig" in Wisconsin and is used for spring walleyes on the same river. Many fishermen leave the rig at home when trout season rolls around but it's a real good bet for river trout.

To make a river rig using a three-way swivel, attach a 6- to 10-inch length of light mono (2- to 4-pound test) to the hanging swivel and a bullet or walking slip sinker of the proper size to the line. The slip sinker will ride over bottom obstructions and the light line allows you to break off the sinker when it does become hung up.

Next, tie a double-hooked, sewn-on or safety-pin rigged minnow and any spinners or floats to the second swivel on a 12- to 18-inch length of heavier mono (12-pound test will do). Tie your fishing line to the remaining swivel and you're ready to go.

The river rig can be fished with spinning tackle in a conventional manner or soaked in a deep hole. By varying the weight of the slip sinker you can use it in any river with enough flow to straighten out the rigged minnow downstream. It works because trout always fin with their heads facing into the current. The river rig lays out an easy target for upstream-facing trout to home in on when they're hungry.

No doubt many seasoned minnow fishermen will disagree

Right—An inexpensive battery-powered aerator can keep minnows lively for up to 48 hours.

Below—Proof that rigged minnows fished to imitate a wounded baitfish can take big river trout.

with the advice given here because all riggings are with dead minnows. They would be absolutely right if the rigs were to be used for lake fishing.

River fishing for trout includes contending with the problem of variable currents. Free-swimming baitfish just can't be placed where the fish are. Rigs using dead minnows allow better control while fishing.

However, even in river fishing, the minnows you rig should be fresh dead. The bloaters, floaters and mushy minnows in the bucket might look like succulent morsels to the fisherman, but if they are long dead they will actually repel trout. Toss a long-dead minnow into a good trout hole and the fish will scatter faster than if you'd introduced a trained otter.

Thus, the real secret to minnow fishing for river trout is keeping the minnows lively until you're ready to string them on a hook.

Galvanized steel or aluminum minnow buckets, the kind with a perforated inner pail fitted within a larger outer bucket, work well if you remember to slosh it up and down every 10 minutes or so.

Better yet are the styrofoam buckets that insulate well enough to keep water cold for several hours and prevent dissolved oxygen from escaping. To increase holding time all you need do is toss in a couple of ice cubes every hour or so.

But, if you're like me, you're going to forget to slosh the bucket and toss the ice cubes in time to save the minnows. Fortunately there are better ways to keep minnows healthy.

One way is to drop a sufficient number of oxygen tablets (available at most bait shops) into the water at regular intervals. But that takes remembering too. And fishermen on long-awaited outings are prone to be poor rememberers.

Instead, use an inexpensive battery-operated aerator—an alkaline D-cell will keep it operating for up to 24 hours. The ultimate in minnow keepers is an aerator that operates on a 6-volt car battery. It will bubble away for a week or more.

So, if you're out to take your fair share of lunker trout this season, fish the rivers and use fresh dead, rigged minnows.

And remember Ray Gordon's quiet admonition: "Want big trout, fish big minnows."

I have and it pays off.

"DOLLY IS NO LADY"

by BILL BROWNING

Dollies have a row of nasty teeth and often cut mono. The gill rakers are also bad and can cut a line if the fish rolls around too much.

STORIES have it that Dolly was a lady character of a Charles Dickens novel who fancied pink-spotted calico. The Dolly I know also wears a pink-spotted cover, was named after Dickens' heroine, but is nothing like a lady. In fact it's a bull-of-a-fish, voracious, dogged and canny. Its bull-like actions have earned it the local name of "bull trout" in many Western areas.

My first encounter with Dolly Varden came several years ago on the Flathead River of northwestern Montana, home of many of these giant brawlers. We were float-fishing for cutthroat in the clear North Fork, a wilderness type, husky river, passing white sandbars in 6-8 feet of water over which small schools of huge dark fish hovered. "Dolly Varden," my guide nodded as he pulled on the oars. "There's a good sandbar in that big hole below. Snap on that big red and white Dardevle and cast it just above and quartering."

The hole was close to a cutbank with overhanging brush and I made a sloppy cast. Retrieving, my lure suddenly stopped. "Hung up on the bottom," I yelled to the guide. "Are you sure?" he laughed. I didn't see anything to laugh at and was losing line fast as we had passed the bar in the swift running river. I could visualize a hard-stretched line cracking with a loud popping spray and another lure gone.

The 12-pound mono stretched, sung, almost pulled me out of the boat, before breaking loose. Instead of drifting downriver the lure moved across the current and revealed a huge body. "Wow!" I yelled. "I'm sure of one thing. I've got a big fish on!"

"I thought so," smiled the guide. "That's the way with a bull trout."

The great fish dogged the bottom often, broke loose, zigzagged, ran for the bank, but yielded very little. My partner reeled in and we sailed downriver, Dolly in tow, passing over bars loaded with Dolly Vardens. After seemingly miles of float I managed to spool enough line to see a vermillion-spotted silver body surfacing and splashing water in a valiant last ditch struggle. The guide's long handled net reached way out and the thrashing 8-pound trophy was ours.

"About average," said the guide. My jaw dropped a foot in surprise. "This is the advance run which will be followed by the really big bulls. They'll run upwards of 20 or more pounds. They come out of the Flathead Lake and are headed for small spawning tributaries near the Canadian border."

It's surprising the variety of waters Dolly Varden use. Basically big water fish, in Montana they are found in lakes over 200 feet deep. The Flathead Lake, for example, is one of the Northwest's largest lakes with a total area of about 200 square miles which the Dollies call home. Come June or with warming waters they run upstream through several big rivers, bucking swift currents, rapids, and natural obstructions to congregate in small, shallow high mountain tributaries of several ranges. Some are only jumping distance wide. Here they spawn and rear the young until time to return to the lakes in September and October.

Enroute from lakes to spawning areas the Dollies are fair game for anglers. Generally local sports eagerly watch the run and a visitor will do well to inquire at a local sports store for best locations. They apparently run over a long period of time, much of which is dependent on water conditions. On the runs they never seem to have much in their stomachs indicating very little feeding. However they will slash out at lures of many shapes, sizes and colors.

Standard color, however, seems to be red and white. Generally the deep running Dollies seem to prefer heavy lures, but will also take large maribou type streamers at times. Big 7- to 8-inch salmon type plugs of orange and red, and white and red seem most popular. These big slow-wobbling plugs, bumping bottom, seem to trigger most strikes, but a 4- to 6-inch spoon will also do the trick.

You should know your quarry's habits and preferences. The best holding waters in rivers are around gravel bars where slow and fast waters meet. I look for choppy pools below gravel bars. Roll the lure over the bar and let it wobble into the chop and often you'll get a flash or a strike. Under and around big brush piles left by high waters and boulders are good spots also. Dollies may be lazy and like slower holding waters but they can stay glued to a sandbar in swift looking water.

Ev Lungren, of West Glacier, used to tell me the best time for running Dolly Varden fishing was from dawn until sunlight hit the water. I proved this strategy one morning. Ev and I made first casts at dawn (4:30 AM) on the main Flathead River. It was chilly and a fog lay just above the treetops, with Glacier Park's jagged mountains silhouetted against the breaking light. We cast for an hour without a hit, moving only a little way to test several holes. I stayed with one run because I liked the way it laid with several currents milling around bars and providing choppy rest stops for any running Dollies. Not a sign of a fish.

The warming sun was rising now and in a half-hour it would hit the water. Where were the Dollies? I took more care in casting now, working out a pattern to cover all good water within reach, drifting the lure into every chop with little jerks of the rod tip for extra lure action. I was just guiding the lure into the last chop when out of the silence the water crashed like an elk hitting the river and spray sailed 2 feet across the surface. A Dolly had taken the high riding spoon near the surface and came right on out in his vicious slash.

Striking hard I put on the pressure but not enough to horse him. He ran me down river stumbling over slick rocks, wading to wader tops through deep holes, getting stuck in deep soft sand, with the fish heading for a big exposed bar. If I could pressure him into the bank side of the bar I could guide him into the still water behind the bar.

Carefully horsing the heavy fish across a fast current I managed to get him to the bar point where the water divided. He thrashed down the outside and wanted to take to the fast deep water. By putting on more pressure I finally got him thrashing across the shallow rocks of the point. On approaching him he sloshed behind the bar and I finally kicked him up the beach among the boulders.

Anyone who says Dollies are not hard fighters has caught very few of them. I have yet to see a docile Dolly. For me they fight to the end with blood in their eye.

The Dolly Varden is a western cousin of the lake trout. native only on the Pacific slopes from the northern California coast to Alaska, and inland to the Rockies. Commercial salmon fishermen of the coast felt a threat from the Dolly Varden years ago and successfully initiated a bounty on them,

Anyone who says Dollies are not hard fighters has caught very few of them. They fight to the end with blood in their eye.

thus creating a bad image for a fine fish. They do like to eat fish eggs (and thus grow big in the process) but so do trout and many other species. Dollies prefer small fish, roe and other meat. Even marshmallows, corn and pickles! A friend once caught a Dolly with a baby mink in his gullet. I saw a 7-pounder with seven long baitfish in his gullet, and with the tail of one sticking out his throat. That fish fell for a big red and white marabou streamer.

The Dolly is not a true trout; rather, like the brook and lake trout it is a char, cousin to the Arctic species. Big of head, long of body, muscular and trim, the Dolly is nevertheless very good to eat. Delicious, in fact, any way you want to prepare them. I like mine smoked, baked or home canned.

"Some people still look down their noses at the Dolly Varden," said Ev, "but there are some anglers here who specialize on them, following them in all kinds of waters."

One Polson shoemaker I know made charts on the water conditions, wind direction, temperatures and food in their stomachs, whenever he caught Dollies. Over the years it took him to exact spots of best fishing and he could almost predict his catch. Others simply take it as it comes and often go fishless, or by accident run into a good school of Dollies when they're feeding. This man, however, liked to cast from shore, while others were out trolling. His theory was that at certain times Dollies laid under a school of kokanee salmon or cutthroat and waited for weaklings to drop down to them. Under this condition he would cast beyond a ledge of the lake, let the red and white spoon flutter down to depths, then slowly jerk and retrieve upwards to shore. His success was phenomenal.

Dollies are first of all meat eaters. Gamefish bait is forbidden by law in Montana but sculpin or other dead fish may be used effectively. I know one angler who uses squawfish or suckers 9-10 inches long, harnessed in a homemade rig, with the nose cut off to bleed, and, drifted or trolled, depending whether he is fishing a river or lake. Others use cut sucker meat or even raw beef. I like lure action best but probably catch fewer fish than the meat fishermen. I've tested many bait fishing techniques and do know they work.

Dollies, like other trout, will select resting spots behind boulders or below a falls. Climb a tree or high bank to spot them but don't show yourself or allow your shadow to fall on the water. Then try drifting a lure or bait past their holding spot.

Above—It's very hard to hold a fighting Dolly with one hand and net him with a too-small net—you've got the water pressure and a tough quarry and size alone makes it very difficult to land.

Right—A western cousin to the lake trout, the Dolly is native only on the Pacific slopes from the northern California coast to Alaska and inland to the Rockies.

You don't want light tackle for Dolly Vardens. For heavy salmon plugs you need to use a stiff rod with heavy line. Locate a gravel bar or hole with varying currents around them and make long casts, allow the plug to wobble slowly downriver with just enough pressure to keep the lure active and under control. It's a killer technique for big ones at times.

An excellent time to float a Dolly river is during their run up or downriver (spring and fall). Explore every likely hole at bankside or around gravel bars. Then stop at likely looking spots and stay with an area for an hour or more. Persistence often pays off. You may fish a hole for an hour without a strike, when suddenly you'll land a bull of immense proportions. There are several theories about these. The Dolly is in the hole and not feeding or for some unknown reason he gets tired of the lure persistently passing him and madly tries to put an end to it; or perhaps the hole is barren for a while and then a Dolly moves into it and likes the offering.

One of the very best times to fish Dollies in the big Flathead or Swan Lakes is just before or after the run. About the middle of October, when kokanee are spawning and snagging for

The Dolly Varden is not a true trout; rather, like the brook and lake trout it is a char, cousin to the Arctic species. Big of head, long of body, muscular and trim, the Dolly is nevertheless very good to eat.

Once you get Dolly Varden fever it becomes an obsession. To jump from fishing for small, delicate trout into a brawling 8- to 10-pound Dolly is to find a fitting, fighting quarry.

them is in process, the Dollies have returned for the winter and deep trolling with great bottom-bumping plugs is a top method. Now they're after kokanee or cutthroat, stashing away fat for the winter, and go on a feeding spree. Troll out from or around points on the shoreline in fairly shallow water and you may pick up several giant Dollies in a day's fishing. Odds are great you'll also hang a huge lake trout or good cutthroat as a bonus.

One October I was with Bill Remaley, of Big Fork, when we caught a 20-pound lake trout, several 3- to 5-pound cutthroats, and about seven big Dollies in half a day. The Dollies were by far the most exciting. We kept only what the law allowed. Here, the law prohibits taking Dollies *under* 18 inches. Now that's a good size fish in anybody's backyard.

For trolling under this condition you should have heavy gear, including a big, long-handled net. Be prepared for cold weather and to stay several days. Close-by motels and restaurants are available; ramps for your boat, and parks for camping. Cloudy days are fine, but windy days—zilch.

Several good Dolly lakes are found in Glacier National Park, and other area lakes and reservoirs, including the huge Hungry Horse Reservoir where they run up the South Fork of the Flathead into tiny wilderness streams.

On a Boy Scout Explorers trip in the Bob Marshall Wilderness I once saw a scout take a 6-pound Dolly from a stream no deeper than his ankles. It was the talk of the camp and a delicious change of menu for several hungry kids.

Dollies have a row of nasty teeth and often cut the mono unless you use heavier tippets. I often use 8-pound mono line on a spin reel but add a 12-pound tippet. His gill rakers are also bad and can cut the line if he rolls around too much. Many sportsmen like deep sea tackle, wire or lead lines, etc., when trolling. I usually use a lighter casting outfit even for trolling. Handled with care, playing the quarry and given plenty of time, I have more fun and get more time to study the Dolly's habits.

Some fishermen use a gaff to land a large Dolly although most fishermen use big, long-handled nets when fishing from boats. If banks are low, or a gravel bar is handy, I like to beach them because it's very hard to hold a fighting Dolly with one hand and net him with a too-small net. You've got the water pressure and a tough quarry and size alone makes them very difficult to land.

Once you get Dolly Varden fever it becomes an obsession. To jump from fishing for small, delicate trout into a brawling 8- to 10-pound Dolly is to find a fitting, fighting quarry. Some deplore its underwater fights, preferring aerial acrobats of a rainbow. Fighting a really big fish, slugging it out around boulders, buried tree trunks, brush piles and heavy currents will soon get into your blood. And the size alone will thrill you to pieces.

I remember one Dolly that made a believer out of me. We were on the Middle Fork of the Flathead, just under Glacier Park, deep in a canyon, with perfect bull holes interlaced with sparkling white water rapids. A bald eagle circled the escarpments, and a nanny goat and her kid were skirting the yellow rim, knocking down rocks and dust, when I was jerked back to fishing. My line and lure had hung up. After my first encounter I always strike hard at any hangup and sure enough steel bit into a tough jaw and I was into a fighting bull. Dave Thompson, of West Glacier Mercantile, was just landing a beautiful 11-pound, vermillion-spotted Dolly as I glanced his way. I had my hands full and was too busy to admire it.

Sloshing downstream I yelled, "Here we go again, Dave!" My 8-pound line was singing through heavy whitewater currents and seemed like a spider web as I anticipated a parting of company. Not so! The Dolly dogged into a slow pool, sulked, then when I added extra pressure he raced downstream.

I was worn almost to exhaustion from splashing along the bankside waters; my breath coming in short bursts and my heart pounding from the exertion. I heard Dave yell and advise there was a good sandbar just below the bend.

I finally beached a sparkling, pink polka-dotted Dolly on the fine white sandy beach. Breathing hard, I fell exhausted between the Dolly and the green water, and draped my arms around it, partly to rest tired muscles, partly in glory of a victorious moment.

Dave came stumbling around the bend, his Dolly's tail dragging water. "Are you alright, Bill?" he asked anxiously. "Yeah, Dave. I'm worn out but couldn't feel better. Weigh him up for me will you?"

Dave laid his fish in the soft sand, and lipped my Dolly on the scales. Then he hefted the two side-by-side. "You won't believe this, Bill, but we've got a perfect match. Your Dolly and mine are both exactly 11 pounds even."

I grinned sheepishly. "Sorry I couldn't do better, Dave, but I couldn't handle a bigger one. Dolly Varden just don't act like ladies."

The beauty of trout water is half the fun of fishing.

NO MATTER how long I live, I'll never forget my first trout.

It happened more than 60 years ago, when I was a boy on the farm in southern Michigan, possessed of the lore common to country boyhood in that day and place.

I had learned to fish as soon as I could hold a cane pole, in a slow-currented creek where sunfish, rock bass and bullheads shared the deep holes with big watersnakes. I learned to swim in that same creek, heedless of the bloodsuckers that teemed in the soft black muck of the bottom.

Then we moved to another farm, and there was a lake at the back of it, and I graduated to bluegills and bass and now and then a northern pike.

But trout? They were the stuff of which dreams are made. The nearest trout country was more than a hundred miles to the north, and that meant it might as well have been on the moon so far as I was concerned.

However, we had in our neighborhood a man who did not belong in the farmlands. He worked a few acres of unproductive land in the summer. From fall to spring he trapped muskrats, skunks and what mink were available, and hunted rabbits, foxes and grouse. Whatever he did was done unobtrusively, with the craft of the born outdoorsman.

His method of fox hunting told a great deal about him. Red foxes were scarce then in that part of the country. He would start out in the morning on a new fall of snow and walk until he found a fox track. Sometimes he walked all day and failed. But once a track was found, he followed it until he jumped the fox and got a shot. No dog, no hunting partner. Man against animal, single-handed, indomitable.

Now and then he invited me along on a hunt. Those were red-letter days. And one spring, to my astonishment, he asked me to go with him trout fishing.

He took me to a cold, spring-fed stream that wandered through a tamarack bog, a place I'm sure fewer than half a dozen people knew about, and from a pool I could have jumped across I took a brook trout 7 inches long.

To my eyes it was a fish set with rubies, and the beauty of its mottled back, streamlined shape and white-bordered fins was staggering.

I went home that day with five or six like it. Mother fried them in home-churned butter, in a black iron skillet, and I learned that trout are as extraordinary on the table as they are beautiful. I have been a trout fisherman most of the years since.

I suppose the pleasure of any fishing experience can best be measured by the length of time it lingers in memory, and if that is true then some of my best have had little or nothing to do with catching trout.

I remembered an opening day on Michigan's Little Manistee many years ago, when conditions were as perfect as they ever get to be. Marsh marigolds were blooming in yellow clumps at the water's edge where the current was slack, birch and alder catkins stirred in a warm breeze. I was tired of winter. I waded in and felt the push and tug of current against my legs and listened to the river's song as it swirled around snags and sunken stumps, and drank the heady wine of spring in the finest fashion known to man. I remember a ruffed grouse that drummed in the woods, the muffled thunder of his wings starting with slow beats but blurring swiftly into an explosive roar. And in the blue vault of sky overhead a jacksnipe winnowed tirelessly, the faint far off sound coming to earth like ghost music.

Did I catch anything that day? I no longer know.

The Bonus Pleasures of Trout Fishing

by BEN EAST

This young man is getting an early start on trout. A reasonable facsimile of the author many years ago on his first trout trip.

Then there was another opening that I remember fully as well. I camped in a tent with two partners that time. There was snow on the ground, ice formed on our water bucket, and until noon our lines turned stiff as iron in the guides. That time I know I took no trout. But, it was the first day of the season, after a long winter, and I reveled in it. In retrospect, even the discomfort was fun.

I recall a 100-mile drive home from the western Michigan trout country to Grand Rapids, where I was living at the time, on a warm rainy evening in May, when every roadside pond was pulsating with the sweet and birdlike trilling of thousands of treefrogs and the wet air smelled of the incense of spring. Again, I no longer remember how many trout I had in my fern-lined creel.

But I don't want to create the impression that I don't enjoy catching fish when I go fishing. I relish that as much as any man, and some of my trips I recall just as vividly for what I caught.

There were, for example, the native cutthroats in a remote pool on the South Fork of the Flathead in Montana's Bob Marshall Wilderness. The river moved through the hole at a leisurely pace and the water was cold and clean, with a hint of green in the deep holes. I found a place where cutthroats were loitering in the shelter of an undercut bank, and started tempting them. Of all the things I offered, they liked best a big mayfly that had proven itself many times on Michigan streams when the mayfly hatch was on.

It was a dry pattern, but they would not come up for it, so I let it sink down to where they were, and the entire school slashed at it so eagerly that I had to twitch it out of their reach until one of the size I wanted came along.

There was another pool I'll never forget, on a small brush-bordered creek in the roadless wilderness of what is now the Isle Royale National Park. To fish that place I had to poke my rod through the brush and let a worm down to the water on 2 or 3 feet of line. But it was worth it. I took almost a dozen brook trout there, from 8 to 10 inches, dark from the dark, shaded water, one of the most beautiful catches I have ever made.

There are few things that can befall a trout fisherman more rewarding than to find and fish virgin water, where he can be reasonably sure no angler has been before him. It doesn't happen often, but it has been my good fortune to find such a place on two or three occasions.

The first time was in the roadless bush of Ontario's Algoma country, north of Sault Ste. Marie. I was a guest of my friend Spence Postal at his fishing camp 60-odd miles up the Algoma Central Railroad from the Soo.

The mixed freight and passenger train that then ran three times a week would stop at any milepost to unload or pick up fishermen and their gear. From the railroad we traveled by canoe and portage along a sluggish stream and across a couple of small lakes to the camp. Much of the nearby country was unfished.

Toward the end of May, when the last snowbanks were melting in the bottoms of the ravines and trailing arbutus was blooming in sunny places, and before the blackflies came out, Spence and I left the camp with a canoe, our fishing gear, and enough grub for 3 or 4 days, and headed for a lake he had fished with one of his guides the summer before. He had warned me the trip would be no pushover, and it wasn't.

The previous year he and the guide had taken 14 trout, the big squaretail speckles of the Algoma bush. So far as

A silently gliding canoe, two friends and the wind in the trees. These are bonus pleasures of trout fishing.

Spence knew, they were the only fish that had ever been caught in that lake. But he was to be proven wrong, for on our trip we found a rusted pocketknife on an island. Presumably it had been dropped by a prospector passing through, maybe 20 years before, and in all likelihood he had caught a couple of trout for his supper.

But that's close enough to unfished water to satisfy me.

Spence and I camped the first night at a place called Dead Man's Falls, on the outlet of the lake we were headed for. The next morning there were long streamers of ice on the cedars that overhung the falls.

We paddled up the creek that morning and carried the canoe along the foot of a high ledge just below the lake, and then we saw blue water sparkling through the trees ahead and dark old pines leaning out from the shore. That's a sight, coming at the end of a portage in to an unknown place, that I rate as close to paradise as anything a man will ever see on this earth.

The fishing that day was as fast as I have ever had. We were using night crawlers, with spinners ahead, and big trout simply wouldn't leave 'em alone. Spence had rigged up a bait rod. I insisted on staying with the flyrod that has killed good fish for me over half the continent.

The trout came out of rock lairs 15 or 20 feet down, and half the time we could see them streaking through the clear green water before they hit. None of them were less than 15 inches long, most were 18 or over. They struck like famished wolves and fought like caged tigers, and there was enough excitement in one of them to last a man a year.

More than once Spence and I had two on at the same time. We landed a dozen in an hour, kept two for our noon meal— with bread and strawberry jam and the strong black tea of the bush—and released the rest very gently without lifting them from the water.

Do you wonder that I remembered that trip?

Then there were the unfished streams that ran into the salt water of James Bay, along the Quebec side. I fished them almost 40 years ago, but they are etched as sharply in my memory today as if it had been only last summer.

I was a member of a party of sportsmen cruising north into Hudson Bay from Moose Factory, aboard a free trader's weather-beaten schooner. We were the first such group to travel along that coast, and the country was virgin, peopled only by scattered trading posts and the nomadic Crees who summered there and trapped over a vast hinterland of rugged wilderness in the winter.

The coast was uncharted, and the smaller streams, at the mouths of which we anchored and camped, were not even named on our maps.

The character of the country had changed drastically as we sailed north from the mouth of the Moose River. We had left the last trees behind, the tallest brush was arctic willow that grew no higher than a man's knees, and the rolling, rocky barrens were carpeted with moss into which we sank ankle-deep at each step. For the 10 days we camped there we carried our tent poles with us and combed the beach for driftwood for campfires and cooking.

The roving Crees, traveling by canoe along the coast, were accustomed to taking what trout they wanted from those streams. But they used nets and fished only the first pool or two above the sea. A net strung there at the turn of the tide would take enough fish to fill a drying rack, and no Cree was interested in hiking inland along the stream a mile or so when that was not necessary, nor did he care about fishing with a rod and catching one trout at a time.

The rivers came down across the barrens in short reaches of fast water with small ponds between. Once we had put three or four of those ponds behind us, we could safely as-

The Arctic peace and quiet of a Quebec trout stream is worth the trip.

sume that no one had ever wet a line ahead of us. This was trouting adventure at its best.

The fish were squaretails, 15 to 22 inches long, but they were totally lacking in the wariness of normal trout. They came of countless generations that had not seen flies or spinners or hooks, and they were no harder to deceive than bluegills in a millpond.

I watched one member of our party, fishing with two wet flies, take doubles three times in 15 minutes. And in one place where fast water ran silk-smooth in a deep rock chute, I decided to try an experiment. I tore a narrow ribbon from a red bandanna, knotted it around the shank of a bare hook and gave it to the current. An 18-inch trout knifed up from the shadows and struck as eagerly as if it had been a perfectly dressed Coachman.

One thing alone limited our fishing in those streams. That was the quantity of trout we could eat. There were 18 in our party, including guides, our skipper and the Eskimo pilot and Cree deckhand. We lived mainly on trout for weeks, since we had no facilities aboard the schooner for carrying fresh meat. Eighteen people can consume a lot of speckled trout, eating them three times a day as we did, but we made it a rule to catch no more than we could use and time after time, under that rule, we quit when the fishing was at its best.

That summer cruise was a wonderful one, and nothing about it was more enjoyable than the ready-to-strike, hard-fighting square-tails of those faroff streams.

Of such stuff is trout fishing compounded, and its most lasting memories built in the hearts and minds of its followers.

SINCE EARLY morning, when we had lashed heavy loads onto the pack horses Gene Wade had led our pack string steadily upward into the Beartooth Primitive Area just northeast of Yellowstone National Park. Even though it was July a light frost had covered the corral area and the breath of the horses was white against the thin mountain atmosphere.

For the first hour or so after finally getting underway, the well marked trail led through dense evergreen forests, now and then interrupted by open meadows. The horses moved quickly without urging. Gradually the meadows grew larger, the tall trees gradually disappeared, giving way to more stunted timber blown into grotesque shapes by mountain winds. The changing environment was awesome to see.

Bisecting one of the larger grassy meadows and undercutting the banks was an alcohol-clear, ice-cold stream. Gene found a riffle shallow enough for the animals to ford belly deep and in mid-stream I noticed foot-long trout darting away from under the horses' feet. Upstream other trout were dimpling the river to where it resembled raindrops falling on the surface. I had a terrible urge to dismount and start fishing.

"Forget those," the outfitter commented drily, "because they're small. We'll find more and much bigger trout where we're headed."

The rest of that ride into a lonely wilderness country was one which nobody in the group would soon forget. Now on the edge of timberline and winding well above it, the trail

Pack Your Way to Trout

by ERWIN A. BAUER

Pack string heads out and up into Beartooth Primitive Area trout country. Gene Wade leads pack horses, anglers follow.

disappeared at times over bare granite outcroppings and under lingering snowfields, and we had to find our way by instinct and frequently by consulting a U.S. Geological Survey topo map of the Beartooths. At times riding either wasn't possible or very safe and we had to dismount to lead the horses around the steepest, sheerest places. We stopped occasionally to rest and "blow" the horses. Newcomers in our party to the 9,000-foot altitude felt slightly light-headed.

"We've got to clear that next ridge," Gene pointed ahead, "and then drop down into Jorden Lake where we'll camp."

After another tedious, slow, switchbacking climb, we reached that ridge and from that point looked down on one of the most magnificent scenes a traveler will ever see in the Rocky Mountains, a region which is full of awesome beauty.

Just below was the azure, heart-shaped Jorden bordered on one side by cliff-like banks onto which the winter's snow was still piled deep. On the opposite side fresh green grass meadows went directly to the water's edge. As we watched, a moose strolled across the meadow and a pair of ravens circled overhead. A feeder stream coming from a whole chain of lakes well above Jorden, rushed down over waterfalls and cascades to empty into Jorden, forming a small, many-pronged delta. Beyond that the lake was suddenly very deep, as we could tell by the darker color of the water. It practically spelled "T-R-O-U-T" in capital letters.

"We'll camp in that grassy spot," Gene said, "and use it as our headquarters."

Nowadays remote fishing holes which are rarely fished from one year to the next are scarce indeed. Modern transportation makes it possible for anglers to go almost anywhere anytime. But here, a day's ride from the Cooke City to Red Lodge, Montana, highway, was no sign whatsoever that humans had ever even seen or visited the place. No sign existed of human presence or development; not even a footprint marred the spot. No wonder we hurriedly spurred the horses down the steep and sometimes slippery trail to our campsite at the bottom. But, setting up tents was forgotten temporarily as pack horses were unloaded in a hurry so that all hands could quickly set up fishing tackle. My gear was put together with five thumbs on each hand. I always get the jitters when fishing new trout water.

What followed during the next few days should happen

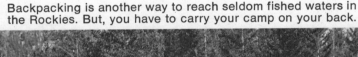

Backpacking is another way to reach seldom fished waters in the Rockies. But, you have to carry your camp on your back.

Pause on the trail in the Beartooths for lunch.
There is no heavy fishing pressure here.

to every serious trout fisherman before he hangs up his rod for keeps.

I needed only one cast near the stream mouth to hook a trout. I saw the flash of a foot-long cutthroat before it struck—and almost reacted too soon. But the fish caught my spinner anyway and during the next few minutes my light spinning rod was dancing. Before the fish was flopping out on the bank, someone near me also had a hard strike.

No serious fisherman would forget what happened at Jorden Lake that day. A multitude of cutthroat trout, some weighing up to 3 pounds, had concentrated in the current around the inlet. Catching them was about as difficult and as complicated as getting a small lure in water. It was a brand of trout fishing which can only occur nowadays in extremely remote waters of our western mountains. But we found even faster fishing by hiking out to other alpine lakes, especially to one called Butte, in the watershed all around us.

Although that incident actually happened several summers ago in a distant part of the Shoshone National Forest, such fishing still exists in many areas of the Rocky Mountains from the Mexican border north to the Yukon. In fact it just may be the best angling for wild trout left anywhere in America. But how does the average or typical sportsman enjoy such fishing, which, of course, is far from paved highways and heavy angling pressure?

The answer is to go on foot—a horse's or your own. The latter, backpacking, is the cheapest and simplest. It is also the toughest because a fisherman must carry everything he needs (camping gear, all food, as well as tackle), often for two or three or more days just to reach fishing country. The alternative is to take a pack trip; to let horses do the hard work.

Packtripping is almost as old as civilization on earth—or at least as old as man's association with beasts of burden. A good bit of the world was first explored by pack trippers and the American West was initially invaded by the pack trains of trappers, prospectors and the U.S. Cavalry. Although the horseless carriage long ago replaced horses elsewhere, horses and mules are still kings of the western mountains—and nowhere are animals so important for getting hunters and fishermen into the promised lands.

A pack trip can be organized for any duration from a weekend to several weeks and for any number of fishermen. What happens is as follows: fishermen ride out on saddle horses and enough gear to be self-sufficient for the entire venture is carried along on pack horses. Each trip is led by one or more guides or outfitters—this staff depending on the size of the party, the distance to be traveled and possibly on the previous experience of the riders.

One qualified outfitter is capable of leading a party of up to six. An extra horse wrangler or cook may be necessary to handle larger groups. The larger the party and/or the fewer hired hands, the less expensive a trip will be. However we'll discuss these costs later on.

Professional pack trip outfitters exist in all the Rocky Mountain states and provinces. Some are full-time caterers to sportsmen and even transport their pack strings from place to place to coincide with the seasons. Most however are ranchers who do pack tripping on a part-time basis—usually because they savor getting out into the mountains as much as the profit. There are good outfitters and bad ones, but fortunately the latter seldom stay in business very long.

How do you make contact with a qualified outfitter? One good place to start is in the where-to-go section of *Outdoor Life*. Many of the best men advertise here and all welcome inquiries. In many states, pack-trip operators and guides are licensed and a letter to the state's fish and game

Rainbow jumps on end of light spinning tackle in Banff National Park.

Below—Typical scene of mountain trout fishing, above timberline and at the edge of it. Adventuresome anglers can have lakes like these to themselves. Right—Fat skillet-size cutthroat caught by Peggy Bauer where a small feeder stream enters a mountain lake.

department, or to the state tourist bureau, will produce a list of all who are accredited. Also a number of national organizations sponsor many trail rides (pack trips) every summer and it is also a good idea to contact them. A list of these groups would include The Wilderness Society, 4260 S. Evans Ave., Denver, Colorado 80222; Sierra Club, Mills Building, San Francisco; American Forestry Association, Washington, D.C.; Trail Riders of the Canadian Rockies, Warner & Mackenzie, Box 448, Banff, Alberta; Hiland Guide Service, c/o Postmaster, Cooke City, Montana; L.D. Frome, Frome Outfitters, Afton, Wyoming 83010. It is good advice to book any trip as early as possible, perhaps even a year in advance.

Unless other arrangements are made, the outfitter furnishes everything except the fisherman's personal gear. That would include all livestock, saddles and tacking, tents, camp gear and food. It would not include sleeping bag and mattress, toilet items, clothing or fishing tackle.

Let's consider here what every fisherman should take along. First the tackle: one light spinning rod and one fly rod in a durable tube case should cover virtually every situation. Most of the fishing is in moderately deep lakes, rather than in streams, so spinning is the best bet in most situations. I always carry along a good selection of small spoons and spinners in ⅛- to ¼-ounce sizes. I prefer 4-pound-test monofilament line and see no need for anything beyond 6-pound test.

My favorite mountain fly rod is an 8-footer and among all flies, nymphs (sizes 8, 10 and 12) are invariably the best producers, probably because many alpine lakes contain large populations of tiny freshwater shrimp. Occasionally dry flies or streamers will pay off. Some good patterns to carry are the Muddler Minnow, Light Cahill, Joe's Hopper and Adams.

Sometimes just as valuable as tackle, and perhaps more so, is a light inflatable boat or raft which can be packed onto a horse. This will help a person reach waters beyond casting distance from shore. A floater bubble will accomplish the same thing as a raft.

Even in midsummer, the weather at high altitude can be changeable, unpredictable and offer great fluctuations in temperature. The best advice therefore is to be prepared both for very mild, pleasant days as well as for cold ones. A two-piece foul-weather suit with parka hood can be worth its weight in gold and so can a supply of good insect repellent. At times mosquitoes can fairly swarm around the best fishing lakes.

A warm sleeping bag is also important, although no more so than a 3-inch thick polyurethane foam mattress pad. A good night's sleep can be doubly welcome after a day of hiking or climbing. A packtripping fisherman may also want to consider some of the following items: camera and film to spare, low rubber boots (waders are normally too bulky for this type of angling), a small rucksack for carrying tackle and cameras, a light landing net, a multi-pocketed fishing vest, belt knife, broad-brimmed western hat and sunglasses.

For an outdoorsman unfamiliar with the Rocky Mountain region, the most bewildering decision may be where to go on that first trip because there certainly are many choices—in fact far too many to attempt listing them all here. Perhaps Montana contains the most remote mountain lakes in which the trout fishing ranges from good to excellent.

The Beartooth Primitive Area alone, which is just northeast of Yellowstone Park, boasts nearly 200 lakes (some of which never see an angler in a season's time) which in total contain several species of trout. Access to this region begins at Cooke City. Other outstanding areas

Deep snow blocks further travel into the mountains by jeep. From this point anglers must don backpacks to fishing waters.

in Montana are the Spanish Peaks, the Lincoln-Scapegoat Wilderness, Absaroka Wilderness, the Pioneer Mountains (access from Canyon Creek Ranch near Melrose), Bob Marshall Wilderness and Glacier National Park.

A partial list of Wyoming's best areas would have to include the Jim Bridger Wilderness, the Wind River Indian Reservation and the proposed Gros Ventre Wilderness. In Idaho, there is great back-country angling in the Selway Bitterroot country, and through the Salmon, Sawtooth, Clearwater and Challis National Forests. New Mexico's best mountain fishing is hidden deep in the Gila Wilderness (Mogollon Mountains) and an excellent, although little-known region of lakes is high atop Utah's Uinta Mountains. Productive water exists in Colorado's San Juan Rio Grande Wilderness.

In Canada, Banff, Jasper, Yoho and Kootenay National Parks all offer fishing which is far from the beaten tracks. So do Mt. Assiniboine and Wells Gray provincial parks, both in British Columbia.

A mountain packtripper is likely to encounter any of the trouts, plus (rarely) grayling, found elsewhere in North America. But the bulk of the fishing is provided by the black spotted cutthroat and the eastern brook trout. Cutthroats seem to thrive best and grow fastest in this lofty alpine environment. Brooks also do fairly well, but in places where natural spawning takes place, they have a tendency to over-populate lakes and become stunted. Rainbow-cutthroat hybrids do better than true rainbows—

and I've found these hybrids to be especially plentiful in Montana's Pioneer Range.

Brown trout tend to do poorly when released in most mountain regions. Goldens imported long ago from the High Sierra, furnish some scattered good fishing in the Bridger Wilderness and in the Beartooths. At times they hybridize with rainbows and grow to surprising size. But keep in mind that none of these high mountain lakes contained trout originally; rather all have been stocked and maintained by various state and federal government agencies. The original stocking of fry or fingerlings may have been done by airplane, by helicopter, via containers lashed onto pack horses, or simply by carrying fish alive from one lake to the next nearest one. Natural reproduction occurs in some waters while others must be restocked at regular intervals.

A pack trip is not an inexpensive undertaking. Any good outfitter has a considerable capital investment both in horses (which he must feed the year around) and saddlery—and this fact accounts for much of the cost. However, a pack trip need not be out of the question. The most economical way is to join one of the group trips already mentioned. Although the number of packtrippers in one group may number as many as 2 dozen, this very fact reduces the cost to as low as $25 per person for a 10-day trip. Because these trips invariably go into some of the most spectacular regions of this continent—usually where wildlife is abundant—these must be considered among the best bargains of all in outdoor

Mountain trout fishermen, no matter whether hiking or riding, encounter much wildlife such as (here) a bull elk on a cold morning.

holidays. I have been on a number of Wilderness Society and Trail Riders of the Canadian Rockies trips; without exception the food, the saddle stock, in fact the entire package has been very,very good.

Smaller "custom" trips are certain to be more expensive, perhaps as much as $50 per individual per day for short trips. However even the costs of these can be pared substantially if the packtrippers are experienced enough to pitch in with such chores as cooking, wrangling, saddling and packing up the horses. For many anglers, this type of participation makes the trip all the more memorable. Kids particularly enjoy it.

There is always much more to a western pack trip than just the fishing. To begin, there is no better way to completely escape the ordinary and to explore a precious part of America which still remains unspoiled and undeveloped. The water is usually pure enough so that you can pause beside any lake or brook for a cool drink. And the clear mountain atmosphere is in sharp, wonderful contrast to what we breathe in most cities nowadays. Next consider also the wildlife and the wildflowers. Summertime—the best fishing season—is also the period when a hundred species of alpine wildflowers cover the meadows and lake shores in a profusion which one must see to believe. Whole mountainsides may be colored a solid blue, scarlet or yellow, or a combination of these for weeks on end.

Few pack trips ever end without seeing elk, moose, mule deer, sheep, bears or perhaps all of these. I have had moose come right into camp and have watched them swim across the same lake in which I was fishing. Small game is usually easy to see. Canada jays steal food from camp and marmots whistle at camping anglers from their rock pile dwellings nearby. All these are priceless ingredients which lowland anglers seldom can enjoy.

Perhaps you are wondering if you are physically fit to make a pack trip? The answer, briefly, is probably yes.

Age, riding experience and physical condition are important of course. But not critically so. I can recall one pack trip to Alberta in which one rider was an 80-year old grandmother and she got along very well. Outfitters always select gentle, steady, dependable horses for guests. Before beginning a pack trip, it *is* wise to do as much hiking or bicycling as possible—beforehand—and if a stable is handy nearby, to do some riding as well. Riding requires use of some muscles not otherwise tested.

Not every moment of every pack trip is entirely enjoyable. Keep that in mind. There will be times and instances, as everywhere, when trout are not striking. Fatigue and saddle soreness are also realities, especially early in the trip, but they soon vanish. Figure also on sudden drenchings, squalls, balky horses and other minor inconveniences. But these soon—invariably—seem unimportant. Even saddle soreness takes on a bittersweet quality at the end of a day amid America's most magnificent scenery.

Summed up: a summertime pack trip can be the highlight of any fishing season—or even of any trout fishing career.

Quartet of fine cutthroat trout taken on Montana pack trip. Cutts seem to thrive better than other species in alpine waters.

THE GREAT LAKES —A BROWN TROUT

BONANZA

by DAVID RICHEY

Wading and casting the shorelines produced this 17-pound, 11-ounce trophy brown trout for John Duffy. He had deserted shoreline to himself.

THE FIRST blush of pink tinged the eastern skyline as John Duffy and I wheeled out of the Frankfort, Michigan harbor and began a southerly cruise down Lake Michigan in search of trophy brown trout.

Gulls wheeled and cried overhead as we cruised at half-throttle looking for the jumping, splashing action of early morning browns feeding on alewives and smelt. "They're around here somewhere," John said enthusiastically, "it's just a matter of time until we find them."

It took an hour to locate the trout but suddenly the water boiled ahead of the boat as a frantic alewife skipped into the air ahead of a broad-shouldered brown. Seconds later another brown bulged the surface and 20 yards off our stern a silver colored brown with large black Xs drilled into the air in a savage display of raw power.

John is a charter boat captain with a daily job of taking fishermen out for salmon and lake trout, and a personal obsession with catching big brown trout, and he is an excitable fisherman. He grabbed my arm and squealed, "Here they are! Man, look at 'em! LOOK AT THAT!" A brown, fully 15 pounds, had just surfaced within netting distance of the boat and gobbled down a hapless minnow.

We started letting out our lines behind the boat, a rhinestone spoon on one line and a silver wobbling plug on the other. We worked in and out of the cruising browns at a slow trolling speed and had strike after strike.

I was John's guest so he gave me first crack and a feisty 8-pounder grabbed the spoon before it wobbled 50 yards and began boring off for Wisconsin. My reel was equipped with 6-pound monofilament so it took a bit of playing before the fish was slid into the cooler.

We were rinsing the slime off the net when John's rod began a slow steady screech before building up to a high-pitched whine as a big brown headed downlake. John grabbed the rod, jabbed the hooks of the silver plug home and hung on.

"He's taking all my line," he yelped, as mono melted off the spool at an increasing rate. I wheeled the small boat around and we slowly moved down onto the wallowing trout. As we approached, the fish dashed away from the boat and smashed into the air with small droplets of water spraying from wide spread gills. "He's 20 pounds!" John gulped, line again peeling off his ultra-light spinning reel. The whippy rod

Browns enter some of the smallest tributaries during spawning time.

tip was bent over in a throbbing arc as the fish headed for the bottom.

The brown settled down to a bulldogging battle beneath the boat. John pressured the fish as much as he dared but it was 15 minutes before the fish could be worked toward the surface. Exactly 30 minutes after the strike John wormed the brown to the surface and I slid the net under 18 pounds of tired trout.

We finished the day with seven browns; the smallest was the first fish I caught and the largest was John's 18-pounder. The average was close to 10 pounds each and we'd each lost a couple of other fish.

The fascinating thing about this day, other than the large size of the fish we caught, was that we were the only boat on the lake after browns. Several boats passed us on their way out to the lake trout grounds but no one fished inshore for the brown trout bonanza that was available. Literally hundreds of trophy brown trout had been boiling the surface off Frankfort and not a fisherman was after them.

What's the reason? It's simple. Fishermen in the Midwest just didn't know the browns were there. Michigan has been planting large numbers of brown trout in Lakes Michigan and Huron since 1970 and these plantings began bearing fruit during 1974.

True, some browns had been taken incidental to lake trout and salmon fishing, especially in Lake Michigan, but never with any consistency. Nineteen seventy-four was the first year sportsmen could go fishing and say that brown trout was their goal. And fishermen had their choice of fishing either the Lake Michigan shoreline along the entire length of the Lower Peninsula, across the Straits of Mackinac along the northern shoreline of Lake Michigan, or in several excellent locations along the Lake Huron shoreline—both in Michigan and Ontario. Wisconsin has some truly fantastic brown trout fishing along their Lake Michigan shoreline and especially in the Door Peninsula.

It took dedicated fishermen like Captain John Duffy of Midland, Michigan to work out the specialized techniques to consistently catch these potbellied browns. Many fishermen found that trolling with heavy line right behind cannonballs (like you'd fish for salmon and lake trout) just wouldn't produce any strikes from trophy browns.

Fishermen would find the browns rolling on the surface (from a distance they look like spawning carp), but when their boat would pass over the feeding fish, the rolling porpoising pattern would quit . . . or move to a different area. The fish couldn't stand being trolled over constantly with lures following close behind the turbulent throb of the props or the disturbing humming noise produced by downrigger cable wires.

John finally figured the fish had to be spooky from all the commotion. He began fishing with line testing 6 pounds or less and began catching fish. His catch ratio really soared when he began trolling at least 125 to 150 yards behind the boat. Lures fished within 50 yards of the boat will catch the odd brown, but lures twinkling along way behind the boat produce many times more strikes.

This long-lining makes for thrilling fishing because often you'll see a brown vault into the air, turn and nudge your buddy and say, "Did you see that?" About the same time the rod tip will snap down and a greyhounding brown will start snatching yards of line off the reel.

Brown trout are shoal fish and are commonly found in 10 to 25 feet of water. They prefer a water temperature of 55 to 60 degrees and will feed actively all day long as long as they aren't disturbed.

Favorite locations are along quick dropoffs close to shore, near river or creek mouths, points or areas of rocks and small boulders. A dull overcast day will usually produce fewer fish than bright sunny days. A hot muggy day, with no wind, is

John Duffy poses with a heavy 18-pound brown that put up a tremendous battle on light tackle.

best. Rolling fish can be spotted from a mile away and once they are located, it's just a matter of following the accepted methods of fishing.

Three methods produce the bulk of the browns from Lakes Huron and Michigan. Two involve trolling and the other is wading and casting along the shoreline.

Wading and casting into rocky areas is one of the hottest methods of taking the edge off a long winter's fishing appetite. Browns are often found close to shore from April through June and the wading caster can often pick up a limit catch without getting into water over his hips.

Small spoons in silver, silver-blue or silver-orange are used on 6-pound monofilament with a light action spinning outfit. I'd suggest using either a ⅜- or ¼-ounce spoon and cast as far out as possible and retrieve just fast enough to bring out the wobble. Fan casts out in all directions as you wade. Make four or five casts from one location and then wade down the shoreline 20 feet and repeat the fan-shaped casting pattern.

Mid-April finds smelt running into rivers in northern Michigan and this is the key to begin wading the rivermouths and adjacent shorelines. Silver spoons that imitate smelt produce savage strikes.

The ardent brown trout fisherman keeps his eyes peeled to the TV weather map. When offshore winds blow for a day or more, browns will move in onto the beaches in a feeding spree. I picked up a 13½-pounder while fishing in the foam off Alpena after a 2-day blow kept the cold water close to shore. Boat fishermen trolling offshore were fishing too deep. They

didn't know that browns will often work into 3 feet of water during cold water periods.

Although I enjoy working the surf and pounding casts out to protruding rocks in hope of catching a shore-bound brown, I also enjoy trolling.

Brown trout trolling is an uncrowded fishery because many fishermen simply won't try fishing with light line. They are afraid of not being able to "horse" a big fish in. It takes a tremendously large amount of line to stop a truly big brown. Claude Nensewitz of Alpena found that out when he landed the old Michigan state record brown from Thunder Bay near Alpena. The 27¾-pound fish sizzled out 350 yards of 8-pound-test mono before he could be stopped. John Duffy has had big browns take out over 300 yards of 6-pound line before he could get his boat turned around and overtake them.

A downrigger fishery has developed for browns in Lake Huron that rivals anything the Great Lakes salmon has offered. Fishermen in Thunder Bay have found that temperature conscious browns often go to depths of 30 to 60 feet which necessitates either using downriggers or staying home. The question remained as to how they could still long-line and use the downrigger to keep the lure traveling at the proper depth.

Downrigger releases are available that allow the fisherman to run their lures back any distance they desire behind the boat. These enterprising fishermen attach their lures to a 6- or 8-pound line and allow the forward speed of the boat to take out at least 125 yards of line. The fishing line was then attached to the downrigger release, the cannonball and lure

Claude Nensewitz right with his 27-pound, 12-ounce brown taken from Michigan's Thunder Bay. This fish sizzled off over 300 yards of line before Claude could bring the fish under control.

lowered to the proper depth and they begin trolling. When a brown strikes, the line is pulled free from the release and the battle is on.

John uses a different method because he finds most of his brown trout fishing to be in shallower water and he feels that foraging trout will come up some distance to slam a lure passing over their heads.

He trolls a flat line of 6-pound test with absolutely no weight on it. A Sugar Spoon or silver Flatfish is attached to the tiniest snap swivel available. This prevents any twisting of his line. The lures are run out 150 yards and John measures this by counting the number of pulls from the bail of his spinning reel to the large gathering guide on his rod. He knows just how many pulls it takes to put his lure back the required distance. It's time-consuming to measure line out this way when trout are biting but it pays to follow his rules. No one in Michigan catches more giant brown trout than he does.

A slow trolling speed is needed and this shallow water fishing necessitates the use of a small boat. Large cabin cruisers produce too much noise and vibration and seem to scatter the overly-cautious brown trout.

There is more to trolling than merely pulling a plug or spoon behind the boat. "The savvy brown trout fisherman knows his fish is spooky so he'll do anything to keep from making noise and to present his lure in a manner that makes the brown think he's about to scoff down an easy meal," says Duffy.

This means a slow zig-zag trolling pattern. John starts trolling in 12 feet of water, cruises slowly out into 20 feet and then angles back into shallower water. This keeps the lures constantly passing through unfished and untraveled water. A

brown may be following close behind the lure and a sudden change in direction may be all it takes to trigger the strike reflex.

Another trick that pays off for trollers is to alternate the zig-zag course with short bursts of speed. A 10-foot burst of speed will change the action of the lure drastically and a brown may think it is an injured alewife in its final death throes.

Another technique John uses is to fish around large clusters of rocks or boulders on the lake bottom. He's found that browns seek out the shade and ambush sites that this type of bottom cover affords. He trolls as close to the rocks as possible or motors upwind and winddrifts downwind and casts with small spoons on ultralight spinning tackle. Strikes are often visible to the casting angler on a silent downwind drift.

Pier fishermen get a crack at the browns during April and May when the fish move shoreward after spawning smelt and alewives. Casting with small spoons or spinners or bottom fishing with spawn bags or nightcrawlers are steady producers.

Just how plentiful are brown trout in Lakes Huron and Michigan? The answer came from Lud Frankenberger, fish biologist for the Michigan Department of Natural Resources in Lansing. "Brown trout fishing really hit its stride in 1974 with more large browns taken than during any time in the past. We were on the verge of giving up on the planting program because anglers seemed either disinterested or totally unaware of the large numbers of fish available.

"We've planted several million brown trout in Lakes Michigan and Huron since 1970 and the outlook for the coming years is very good indeed. Browns are available in many locations and there are several hotspots that fishermen haven't found out about yet."

As an example, Lake Michigan received a total of 1,225,119 browns in 1973 while Lake Huron received a smaller planting of 485,000 fish. These fish were lunker 8- to 15-pounders by the summer and fall of 1975. Fish from earlier plantings (1971 and 1972) probably showed up as fish the size of Nensewitz's Thunder Bay brown. These fish show an inclination toward getting almost as big around the belly as they are long. I've caught browns 23 inches long and 19 inches in girth that weighed over 13 pounds.

Brown trout in Michigan waters show a definite tendency toward straying. Many Michigan fish, for instance, are showing up in the creels of Ontario fishermen, especially in the Georgian Bay area of Lake Huron.

Five years of intensive plantings by Michigan has pointed the way to several exceptional fishing hotspots for browns. These areas have unlimited fishing potential, harbor large numbers of big fish and are capable of supporting a large intensive brown trout fishery.

Thunder Bay, on Lake Huron near Alpena, has to rate as a top hotspot. Brown trout have been planted here for years and an excellent fishery has developed for boat fishermen in Thunder Bay, nearby Squaw Bay and in the vicinity of Sulphur Island. Night fishermen pick up feeding browns during the summer by wading the shallows off Partridge Point south of Alpena. The bulk of boat fishermen troll the Thermocline (look for 55- to 60-degree water) with silver-blue spoons.

Tawas Bay, also on Lake Huron, is a real sleeper for browns. Big fish have been taken here by salmon fishermen but they seem to be keeping a good thing quiet.

The Thumb area, around Grindstone City-Port Austin-Harbor Beach, is a natural hotspot for Lake Huron browns. Cool clear water, large rocks and boulders and abundant feed make this an untapped fishery. No one fishes the area except for a brief flurry during the fall spawning run. The area is full of fish, totally unfished and easily accessible to either boaters or wading fishermen. Sixty thousand browns were planted at these sites during 1972 and 1973.

The Hessel-Cedarville area in northern Lake Huron received a plant of 20,000 browns in 1973, which should produce excellent fishing for fishermen willing to explore a desolate shoreline in search of trophy browns.

The Detroit and St. Clair Rivers near Detroit each received a shot of 25,000 browns in 1974 and they added action of a new caliber for downstate fishermen.

Lake Michigan had so many hotspots in 1975 that it's hard to name them all. It goes without saying that the entire shoreline of Lake Michigan, from the Indiana border north along the entire coastline of the Lower Peninsula, and in scattered locations in the Upper Peninsula were hot.

For openers, a hotspot that has been overlooked is Little Bay De Noc in the Upper Peninsula. This seldom fished body of water received a tremendous dose of browns in 1971 when the DNR dumped in 446,000 fish. A subsequent plant of 30,000 went in 1972 and 40,000 in 1973. A small plant of 15,000 fish went into the Bay in 1974 so fish of all age classes are available in sizes up to 25 pounds plus. Little Bay De Noc is definitely underfished.

The Little Traverse Bay area near Petoskey and Harbor Springs is another sleeper. A large plant of 267,000 browns were planted at Harbor Springs in '73.

Another coming hotspot is the West Arm of Grand Traverse Bay near Traverse City. A healthy slug of 272,000 fish were planted in 1973 and an additional dose of 25,000 in 1974 which adds up to some exciting fishing in this largely protected body of water. Fishermen can safely fish Grand Traverse Bay when the rest of Lake Michigan is a seething mass of flying spume and 10-foot-high whitecaps.

A wealth of brown trout fishing awaits fishermen farther south in the White Lake-Holland-South Haven areas. Each of these fine ports have had large numbers of browns planted and no one seems to know they're there. The southern portion of Lake Michigan will produce excellent brown fishing earlier in the spring because the water will warm up before the more northerly areas.

Much of Ontario's brown trout fishery exists near river mouths as the browns work inshore to feed on forage fish. Browns are taken with some consistency near the following river mouths: Sydenham, Saugeen, Bighead and Nottawasaga. This is largely an unknown fishery in Ontario but indications are that the runs are building in size and more rivers are attracting brown trout.

Last July I was fishing with John near Traverse City for browns. We had five fish aboard in the 10-pound class when we happened onto a lucky fisherman with a bowed rod and a rampaging fish on his line.

We laid back, satisfied with our catch, and watched the battle which lasted for 10 minutes. The man, obviously a novice, finally worked the fish close to the boat after two breathtaking jumps. He scooped the fish into the boat, unhooked it and held it up for us to see. "What a steelhead," he yelled. We looked at each other and went over for a closer look. It was a silver colored brown of 13 pounds. It took a bit of talking on our part to convince him his catch was actually a brown trout. His reaction summed up the existing fishery in both Lake Huron and Michigan:

"I've fished off and on in Michigan all my life and I didn't know browns existed in the Great Lakes. That fish fought as hard and jumped higher than anything I've ever caught before. If I'd known browns existed in the large numbers you say are available, I'd been fishing for them instead of salmon and lake trout."

Anyone that's sampled the brown trout bonanza of Michigan's Great Lakes waters would surely agree with that statement.

James Moore (right) and the author, David Richey, teamed up to land this big Wisconsin brown trout.

How to Choose Proper Fly Tackle

by WENDELL THOMAS

IN FLY CASTING, the weight of the line is being cast just as the lure provides this momentum in spin or bait casting. The leader and fly are merely pulled along by the weight of the fly line. Thus the weight of a fly line should "balance" with the designed action of the fly rod to achieve smooth, straight and accurate casts. It has been said you might choose a proper line for the fishing you plan to do, and then select a rod which presents the fly well and permits control of the line while the fly is being fished.

A fly tackle dealer I know will spend hours assisting an angler who wants to purchase a quality fly fishing outfit. He goes out on the lawn with the customer who casts with several weights of lines using rods suitable for the fishing to be done. Though rod manufacturers mark a recommended line weight on a rod near the handle, a line which is a size heavier, or one a size lighter, may be needed. If the majority of fishing is to be with short casts to 30 feet, the heavier line will bring out the action in a rod.

Should the angler wish to make mostly longer casts, a line one size lighter than marked on the rod will put an effective weight of line working in the air. Beyond this generality, different anglers may find casting more comfortable and achieve better results with a particular line (on the same rod). As this fly tackle dealer says, "No two casters, like no two golfers, have the same swing."

Ideally, you should cast with several lines before purchasing any tackle. This is especially helpful when putting together your first fly outfit, which usually is a basic line and rod for a variety of trout fishing situations. If it is necessary to purchase the rod, try several different line weights using a friend's lines. This may help you determine which one will be best for your purposes. When a line casts parallel on both front and back cast and the outfit feels comfortable to cast with, this gear will fish well on the water.

With the quality of modern lines and rods, a variety of matched combinations are capable of giving top performance in the same fishing situation. Even in choosing a basic outfit for most of your fishing, the deciding factor may be personal preference.

Fly lines are designated by numbers according to weight. The number indicates the weight in grains of the first 30 feet. The smaller the number, the lighter the line; the larger the number the heavier the line.

For trout fishing, lines of 3, 4 and 5 weights arbitrarily can be called *light*. They are most often fished when delicacy is needed as in low, clear water, and with the smallest up to size 12 (and sometimes larger) flies. Lines of 6 and 7 weight are *medium* and probably the most common fly lines for basic trout rods. When you want to cast consistently with large and wind-resistant flies to trout a long distance off, a *heavy* line of 8 or 9 weight will handle the bulky feathers. Keep in mind that the three divisions don't necessarily limit the lines to those described uses but merely give an idea of their common uses.

The shape of a fly line plays an important part in presentation of a fly. Though the three basic fly line shapes all weigh the same for the same weight line, the distribution of weight along each line is different. Thus a No. 6 weight level, double-tapered, or weight-forward tapered line each will seem to cast differently on the same rod. And each will present a fly differently.

A level line is okay if you don't need delicacy, as in streamer fishing. Its chief attraction is that the level line costs less than half the price of quality tapered lines.

A double-tapered line is thickest in the middle, and tapers to both ends. It is designed for delicate presentation with a fly and will "paint" lightly onto the water. It's also the best line for roll casting.

The level and double-tapered lines have the advantage of each being two lines in one. When the casting end becomes

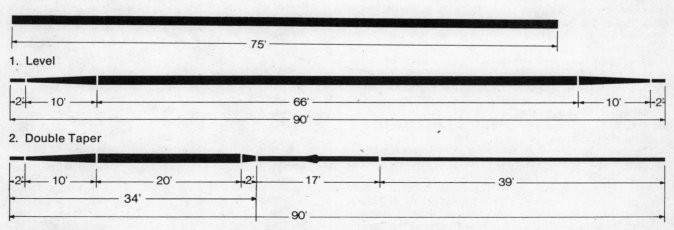

1. Level

2. Double Taper

3. Weight Forward

How to Identify Fly Lines

Letters and numbers are used to simplify the identification of fly lines and are found on line boxes and labels that come with the line.

The first letter or letters gives the line's shape:
L—level line
DT—double tapered line
WF—weight forward tapered line

The number designating the weight of the line is printed in the middle:
6, 8, etc.

The last letter indicates the line's floating characteristics:
F—floating line
S—sinking line

A typical line identification tells the shape, the weight, and whether it is a floating or sinking line, as this:
WF-6-F (weight forward, 6 weight, floating fly line)

worn, simply reverse the line on the reel.

Even a beginning fly fisher will appreciate the ease in casting a weight-forward tapered fly line. This line is thickest toward the front of the line, a design for casting wind-resistant flies and for longer casts. The modern weight-forward lines have longer (more gradual) tapers and also will present a small fly with delicacy. Just finish the cast a foot above the water so the line drops lightly to the surface.

I'd recommend getting a quality weight-forward fly line. Never compromise on the fly line for your first outfit. If need be, buy a quality line and spend less on the rod. Top quality tapered lines cost as much as $15 or $20, and the price is worth this if you are serious about fly fishing.

Generally, longer fly rods of 8½ to 9 feet are designed for heavy lines of 8 or 9 weight. A few rods up to 9 feet especially for large, heavy waters and lunker inland trout and steelhead will cast a 10-weight.

For most stream fishing, you won't want a line heavier than a No. 8. One can be fished with some delicacy as well as for long casts with big flies. I've used an 8½-foot rod and No. 8 line with midge flies for long casts on flat water, and often do so for short casts when wind makes this outfit the easiest one for me to fish with. However, most of the time such gear is preferred for large flies and tackle control where the fish run large.

Many anglers learn to fly fish with an 8- or 8½-foot rod weighing about 5 ounces and carrying a 7-weight line. Such an outfit will do well for almost every trout fishing situation.

Selecting a balanced fly fishing outfit that's right for the fishing and is comfortable to use is easier today with advances in construction of equipment. A 7½-foot rod for a 6-weight floating fly line is a basic outfit for most trout fishing.

For bulky flies such as large dry flies and bucktails or streamers and longer casts over wide waters, an 8-weight line (floating or sinking as needed), a rod with backbone of 8 to 8½ feet, will do the job. A single-action fly reel is handy for several reasons. One, its revolving spool will let trout such as this lunker brownie run out lots of line. Two, carry an extra spool, which will snap quickly into reel frame and thus permit changeover to floating or sinking line as needed. For such fishing, which includes large trout and steelhead, get a reel with capacity for at least 100 yards of backing behind the fly line. A backing of 20-pound dacron line is excellent, as this material won't stretch much.

My basic stream rod is a 7½-footer which weighs less than 4 ounces. One season I used a 7-weight line, the next a 5-weight line, and now I fish a 6-weight line. My point here is that the line I became used to over time seemed to handle the most comfortably, though all fish well on this rod. Personal preference isn't the only reason why I call this my basic outfit. It'll cast accurately on short pop-casts, make the standard 20- to 35-footers which catch the most trout in the greatest number of fishing situations, and even toss a fly 60 feet or a bit farther without difficulty. With this gear I can fish midges, wind-resistant dry flies, and streamers or bucktails.

Today there's a trend to shorter rods, and many anglers, whether or not they started with a longer rod, develop a liking for rods in the 6-foot range. After a few seasons with a long rod, one friend decided he liked the short-cast and small-fly brand of fishing enough to purchase a 6-footer of 2 ounces. (Most rods in this length range carry 4, 5 or 6 lines.) My favorite rod for low, clear water and finicky trout which want small flies is a mere 5-foot, 1½-ounce wand.

You need exact timing in casting with a short rod. I think of my forearm as an extension of the rod. This extra "rod length" adds casting ease. Keeping my casting wrist rigid, I begin each casting motion (whether fore or back cast) from the shoulder and, with the lower arm as another part of the rod, bend my elbow as the fulcrum as though it were the handle of the rod. Short rods are not trick or toy rods;

they are practical fishing tools. They give some anglers more enjoyment and will actually play out a fish more readily than heavier tackle—if you are proficient in their use.

There's little margin for error in fishing with a small rod whereas a longer rod will compensate for less-than-perfect casts in medium-distance work. As one engineer states, "One man's willowy wand may be another man's baseball bat, even under identical angling conditions."

Let me illustrate how different approaches to angling on the same stream and personal preference can result in very different tackle being used. The stream averages 10 to 30 feet wide with one stretch nearly 70 feet across, as it traverses open meadow and then bushy-banked woods. I usually fish in an upstream approach by alternately walking the bank and wading.

My casts mostly are upstream ahead of me. With a rod no longer than a 6-footer my casts can reach nearly every pocket or rising fish, even in the bushy areas. A short rod takes up less space and the line can be worked through or around holes in the foliage.

Another angler has fished the stream successfully in this way sticking mostly to open areas and he uses an 8½-foot fly rod and flies I also prefer here. The only advantage of his long rod is when he can stay back on the bank and dapple a short line over the grassy stream edge.

A third man who fishes this stream is a wet-fly specialist, and he likes to work downstream. He prefers an 8-foot rod, which is an aid as he frequently roll-casts. The long rod

Light fly rods of 1½ to 2½ ounces, 5 to 6½ feet in length, balancing with lightweight No. 3 to No. 5 lines, are the favorites of an increasing number of trout anglers. In low waters on large rivers and mostly on small streams, they deliver small flies with delicacy to fastidious trout. A short rod tires a fish rather quickly and, where practical, it has opened up brushy pockets for the moderately skilled caster which previously were inaccessible with longer rods.

gives him control when swinging a sunken fly across current below him. It is a light rod with a sensitive tip and a light fly line, both of which instantly telegraph the often light take of a trout to a nymph. The limber rod which carries a light line minimizes surface disturbance.

Rod "action" is basically the resilience or spring in a rod. This is a determining factor in which lines will cast well with the rod. Action also is important in the fishing. A rod with a "softer" action and a sensitive tip is favored by many anglers who want to be able to present and "feel" the drift of a small wet fly. A rod with a stiffer, springy action which has a sensitive tip is more versatile and has a faster casting cycle. This snappy-casting action permits use of some wind-resistant and larger flies and for fishing in winds. These two brief remarks are by no means complete descriptions of rod actions; there are many rod actions, and each rod seems to be different. (Sometimes two similar rods have a different "feel" in the casting!) An angler should pay close attention to the action which will give the best performance for his fishing. For example, a rod for tossing large flies beyond 40 feet for large trout should have plenty of backbone in the butt—both for pushing out those flies, and to enable the angler to set a big hook into the hard mouth of a trophy trout.

The length of a rod is a factor in your ability to fish certain waters. A rod which is too short may mean that heavy waters will drag the line around, and you won't be able to achieve a presentation which catches fish. The tackle should make fishing easier and efficient, not more difficult. The rod should be an aid in controlling presentation of the fly even *after* it is in the water. A rod which gives you control of the line will make mending line a simple technique, and a wrist-flip so the rod arcs in a semi-circle will belly the line either up or downstream to a longer natural drift of the fly. You'll be able to add action such as twitching or darting the fly. And to repeat, a rod that works for one angler may not be adequate for another fisherman.

For a long time I did all my trout fishing with a glass rod which cost $10 at a discount counter. Today, quality brand-name glass rods cost from under $20 to more than $40, with a few going for twice that amount. A glass fly rod is a durable rod for a beginner and the choice of many experts.

Bamboo gives a fly caster a smooth "feel" which many say isn't found in any other rod. Bamboo rods generally are priced around $100 to $300.

The newer graphite rods are light, strong and someday may compete with glass as the most popular fly rod material. Most run in the $100 or higher price range. A graphite rod will cast a lighter line than other rods of the same weight, and tests show an average caster may achieve a longer cast than with rods of other material.

A long cast with a light line and a delicate presentation may mean catching more trout from a lake. Besides reducing line disturbance on the water, a light line makes it easier to lift the line off the water to hook a fish. I have fished crystal clear mountain lakes where cutthroat trout ran 6 to 14 inches and I needed a 12-foot leader tapering to a 5X tippet and small fly to interest them to strike. An 8-weight fly line was too heavy and by the time a light nip at the fly reached my rod tip, the fish was usually gone. I just couldn't get that weighty fly line tight in time, even when trolling slowly with oars lashed to my inflatable nylon two-man raft. I switched to a 6-weight line and began hooking most of the striking trout.

Where trout are deep in lakes, streams or heavy-flowing rivers, getting a fly down deep requires a sinking line. Lines are sold which sink at various rates. For deep-down fishing, a fast-sinking line puts a fly near or on bottom the quickest. Though in a transparent lake a longer leader may be necessary, in a moving flow use a short leader so the fly works near bottom. A 7-foot leader is the longest I use, and I prefer a 5-footer.

Some entire lines sink. Others have only the front portion weighted to sink. These are excellent for a natural presenta-tion where the fish aren't too deep in a lake and for shallower streams. A line with a 20-foot fast-sinking front end, and the remainder a floater, will allow you to mend the floating portion. For shallow-fishing with a sunken fly, only the front 10 feet or so of the line is designed to sink.

Most trout fishermen prefer a single-action reel that balances with the rod in casting. Line spools can be snapped in and out, so that in a few seconds the changeover can be made from a floating to a sinking line. Carry extra line spools in your vest.

A single-action reel should have enough backing for the time you tie into a lunker. My first whopper rainbow on a fly struck on a short cast, and in seconds it ran out the 90-plus feet of fly line, and another 50 yards of backing. My backing is 20-pound dacron. This material doesn't stretch much, and I like it for this purpose. Backing behind the fly line also enables the reel to be filled within ¼-inch or so of the spool.

Most trout fishing may consist of trying to catch that 1-pounder a short cast away, but it's a reassuring feeling to have at least a hundred yards of backing when one day the line begins melting off the reel. When you hook that fish, plenty of credit must surely go to having balanced fly tackle which functions for the fishing you are doing at the time.

Float trips are becoming more popular, and you need a rod with backbone and a reasonably stiff tip to pot-shot casts to pockets with no wasted time. This is because the boat moves rather quickly along past the trout lairs. Photo shows the famous AuSable River Boat, used by skilled boatsmen as sometimes a one-man operation, on Michigan's AuSable River. My choice for such waters, or a rapid Western river, is an 8-foot rod with enough stiffness to put the fly out on the productive water as quickly as possible (a soft action rod means a slower casting cycle, with the result the fly spends more time in the air).

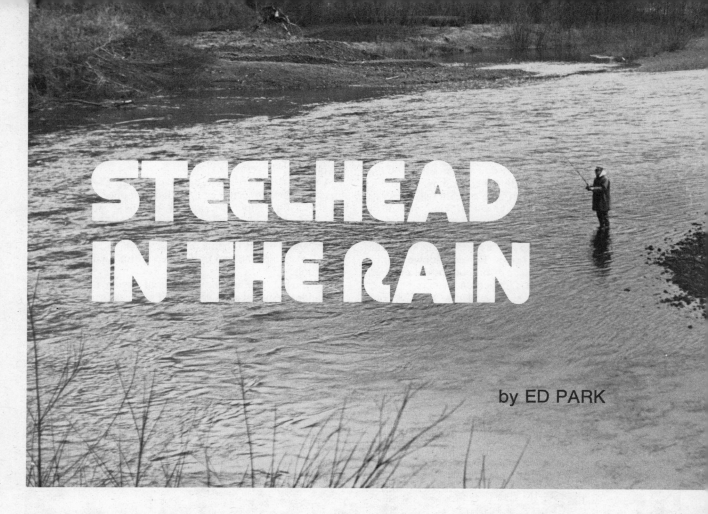

STEELHEAD IN THE RAIN

by ED PARK

WE'D BEEN standing since dawn, the three of us, like grim scarecrows attempting to protect the river from the incessant rain that seemed to increase with every passing hour. Few words were spoken and the main sounds were the gurgling of the mighty Nestucca at our feet and the constant staccato beat of rain on waterproof hats, coats and ponchos. Expressions were blank and sullen.

Now and then one scarecrow would abandon his streamside vigil and slog to the smoldering warming-fire, to stir up both that fire and his own circulation, to rub cold-numbed hands before him and to cast beseeching eyes skyward through the downpour, toward the steel-gray sky.

Less frequently the three of us would gather, by some unspoken agreement, to stand in mutual sodden misery, silent except for the offer of, "coffee?"

The hot cup did double duty—warming our insides as well as the hands—but it did little to dispel the apparent gloom of the scene, or help the aching shoulders that had been held hunched for so long.

Suddenly Lew dropped his cup to the gravel bar and ran to his rod—now jerking and thrashing in its holder at water's edge. He grabbed it from the holder and reefed back on it hard—once, twice, three times!

"Fish on!" he sang out, and all at once the cold, the wetness, the miserable gloom of that morning, were forgotten by the magic of the greatest gamefish of them all—the steelhead!

Bob and I reeled in quickly to get out of the way and then began lending verbal encouragement to Lew. The mighty brute on Lew's line had taken out a quick 60 yards or so in one powerful, swift run back toward the salt. Lew had let him run, holding his rod high but applying no pressure other than the loosely-set drag of his reel.

At the end of that run the steelie, bright silver and sparkling with gems of water, shattered the river's surface to dance in the air—shaking, twisting, trying his best to throw that annoying hook.

But the hook held through that jump, and two more, so the steelie decided to try running—taking away the few yards Lew had managed to pick up, plus another 30 or 40. Lew let him go, knowing his line's strength did not match the power of a fresh-from-the-sea steelhead in a slugging match. He'd have to let the fish spend his initial strength on runs and jumps—and a light drag. Lew's turn would come in the long run, in the final test of endurance of fish versus fiberglass and nylon.

As the fish powered off line, Lew worked his way downstream along the gravel bar, now holding the brute when he could, but letting him run when he wanted. The pool was long; there was little danger of losing him to the fast water below.

Long minutes later the battle began to turn with Lew slowly beginning to take in line. Eventually Lew worked the fish back upriver and we all got a good, close look at nearly 20 pounds of fighting fish.

But the fish got a good look at us also, evidently didn't like what he saw, and found hidden strength for another run.

Again he terminated the run with a spectacular aerial display and "terminated" was the right word, for in mid-air the hook flipped loose and was tossed, with disgusting accuracy, right back at Lew's feet. His fish, the only hook-up we'd had in 5 hours of standing in the rain, was gone.

Was it now a time for remorse, a returning to the sullen mood around the fire? A time to bitch and moan, to gripe

The winter steelhead fisherman is a special breed, seemingly putting as many obstacles in his path to success as he can. Winter rivers are high and cold. He attacks such rivers with determination and dedication—and he catches fish.

Four steelhead—the object of the miserable hours in the rain.

and complain and cuss the weather, the river and these blasted fish?

No.

Sure, it was a time for consolations, for the loss of that beauty, but it was also a time for celebration, for Lew had sampled the best part of a winter steelhead trip—having a fish on. It might have been a bit nicer if he'd managed to land it—but then, knowing Lew, he'd have released it anyway—but he'd had one on, and that is an experience rarely equaled anywhere in the world of angling.

Lew had experienced once again the strength, speed and sheer power of a big steelhead. He had felt the brute force of a long run and had thrilled to the spectacular jumps. He had finally turned the fish, seen the battle swing his way, and even had the fish, nearly beaten, to our feet. He had savored the best, so the ultimate loss was not that important.

Losing that one fish was not a tragedy for Lew Dyer, nor would it have been for Bob Simpson or myself, for each of us have caught hundreds—and we expect to catch hundreds more. But we also know that many other anglers go days, weeks—yes, even years—without even so much as hooking a steelhead, let alone landing one.

Obviously some anglers do the right thing; and just as obviously, some other anglers are doing all the wrong things. Sure, there's a certain amount of luck in hooking or landing a tough winter steelhead, fresh into a river from the nearby ocean, but there has been too much written about the mystic qualities of this fish, and not enough about the practical aspects.

If you are a beginning winter steelheader—or possibly a frustrated veteran with lots of hours, but few fish—you can probably use a few words of encouragement. I've read too many articles that state that steelhead fishing, in any form and in any season, is something that is reserved for the chosen few—not for the general masses.

This might be true, but only if you'll acknowledge that anyone can become a part of that select group, with a little study and determination.

To begin with, you need to try a good steelhead river. Knowing where to go though is not enough, for you need to know when to be there. You can fish the finest steelhead river in the world, but do it at the wrong time, and you'll end up with nothing.

In Oregon, many fine rivers will have steelhead runs all winter long, depending on the particular weather conditions. The Nehalem, Kilchis, Wilson, Salmon, Siletz, Yaquina, Alsea, Yachats, Umpqua, Coos, Coquille, Elk and Chetco are some than can have fish most anytime from fall until spring.

From November to January, try the North Fork Nehalem, Little Nestucca, Siuslaw or Rogue. From December to January, try the Nestucca or the Sixes. The Tillamook is usually good from December through February. January is the month to fish the Winchuck, while January and February you ought to try the Necanicum, Trask, and Smith. February is usually a good month on the Miami and Pistol.

In Washington, the all-winter streams are the Dungeness, Hoh, Sol Duc, Pilchuck, Skykomish and Wynooche. In December good success can usually be found on the Cowlitz, Humptulips, Snohomish, East Fork Lewis, Bogachiel, Chehalis, Elochoman, Naselle, Willapa, Lyre and Columbia. January is top month for the Nooksack, and North Fork Stillaquamish.

The Skagit, Toutle, Kalama, Snoqualmie and Washoughal can be hot in December or January. February is usually the top month on the Satsop.

From February on into spring you could do well on the Elwha, Grays, Queets and the Quinault and, sometimes, the Toutle.

For Northern California, the Mad River can turn out steelhead all winter, with the Klamath being hot from August into November. The Eel is a November river while the Van Duzen is good from November through January. The

Ed Park with a steelhead taken on the John Day River near Kimberly, Oregon.

Smith is usually best in December and January while the Mattole is best in January and February.

There are dozens of other fine winter steelhead rivers in British Columbia, but this will be covered in another article elsewhere in this book.

Just knowing the months to be on a particular river is not the entire answer, for day-to-day and week-to-week weather will make the essential difference between good and bad luck.

Steelhead are migratory, hatching in fresh water and going to sea to spend most of their lives in the salt. When they return to their natal river to spawn, their movements are determined largely by river conditions—the conditions of the water.

If the water level is too low, the fish will not enter the stream nor move upstream from deep holding pools. It takes some new water, a freshet, to get fish moving. This is why an experienced steelheader will wait until there has been a storm to dump new water in the river's drainage.

This new water, if it isn't too much, will get the fish moving into and up the rivers. If the rain is too great—as so frequently happens in our coastal areas—the rivers will rise, out of shape, and be unfishable. The fish will be there, and moving, but the rivers will be high and muddy.

If the river is high and muddy, the only thing the angler can do is wait for it to lower and clear. This is where a knowledge of several rivers is vital because some clear much faster than others. Usually a small short stream will clear much more quickly than one of the larger ones. It can be only a matter of hours for a small stream to go from worthless to ideal.

There is much advice floating around on which gear to use. Some recommend pretty heavy tackle while others seem to favor much lighter stuff. There's a lot of personal opinion here with a great deal of variation.

Most steelheaders seem to favor a rod that is of medium

Bob Gabriel after winter steelhead on Oregon's John Day River.

Author Park with a small John Day River steelhead taken with spinning gear.

action and 7½ to 8½ feet in length. Some favor spinning reels, while others feel you have more control with a bait-casting reel. As you become experienced you'll find there are times when one will outfish the other and vice versa.

The weight line you use will also depend on opinion and water conditions. Heavy water, heavy fish call for heavy line. For low, clear water you'll have to go to lighter mono. I've used all weights from 2- on up to about 17-pound, depending on the situation. Eight-, 10- or 12-pound test lines would be good places to start.

Terminal tackle, and the selection of such, is a multi-million dollar business. Vast sums are spent by manufacturers, trying to convince the angler that his particular piece of wood, metal and plastic is *the* best for everything. It's a difficult choice.

If you want to fish bait, nothing can top fresh salmon eggs. For that matter, I'd wager that eggs catch more steelhead than any other bait, lure or fly. But anglers are funny, and some refuse to use bait. Others don't like bait because the steelhead tends to pick it up gently. Other times you just can't seem to find bait at any price.

Top lures include the wobbling spoons—such as the Fat Max, Krocodile and Birdie—or the spinners such as the Metric, Tee-spoon and Sneak.

Many favor merely a small piece of brightly colored yarn and have the fish to prove this is a good lure.

Of all the artificial lures, probably the most popular are those that resemble a cluster of natural eggs—those hunks of plastic known by such names as the Steely-Bob, Gooey-Bob or Egg-Drifters.

As a general rule, the lower and clearer the water is, the smaller the size of bait or lure. For heavier, darker water, go to a larger lure.

Color is again a matter of opinion, though red is the top color in its various forms. Some days a chartreuse, silver, gold, or other colored lure will be the answer, but the only

Above—One of the choicest ways to prepare steelhead is with a small electric smoke-house. Left—Most fishermen favor a rod of medium action and 7½ to 8½ feet in length.

way to find out is to try them.

There is much mystery written into the fishing of lures or bait, but the basic need is to get deep. There are many ways of rigging up your lead, using dropper lines with pencil lead, or surgical tubing, and so on. Try one method, improve on it to fit your own methods of fishing, and continue to experiment. One angler will favor one method; another angler will favor another. They'll both be hooking steelhead.

As a general statement, there are two methods of fishing for steelhead with bait or lures—drifting and plunking. Plunking is easiest to describe because it consists of rigging up with heavy enough lead to hold your lure or bait in one spot. You then sit and wait, and hope a steelhead will move within range and take the bait.

Drifting covers more water and is the favored method of most steelheaders. This consists of using just enough weight to get your lure or bait down near the bottom, but not enough to anchor it. The best amount of lead is the amount that just bounces along the bottom, touching often. You then know you are deep enough.

For drifting, I prefer a three-way swivel. One loop is tied to the main line which goes to the rod. The opposite loop is tied to the leader, which will vary from about 12 to 24 inches. The third loop has a short length of line tied to it, always making sure it is lighter in strength than your main line or leader. Over this dropper line I slip a hollow pencil lead and crimp it in place with pliers.

In use, as the lead bumps along the bottom, it will hang up frequently. In pulling it loose, you'll probably lose only the lead which is simple and easy to replace.

Others use a similar set-up, using surgical tubing instead of a dropper line to hold the lead. It's up to you.

The proper depth to fish a steelhead lure or bait is just off bottom. Your lead, or the lure, ought to bounce along touching bottom now and then. The steelhead will be hugging the bottom so your lure will have the best opportunity to be seen and taken if it's scratching along the gravel.

Since you're fishing along the bottom you can expect to lose a lot of gear. There's an old saying, in reference to winter steelhead fishing, that if you aren't losing gear, you aren't fishing right.

The winter steelhead fly fisherman is a special breed, seemingly putting as many obstacles in his path to success as he can. Winter rivers are high and cold. He attacks such rivers with fly rod, sinking line and colorful steelhead flies. And he catches fish.

Fly fishing for winter steelhead is not for the beginner fisherman. Begin steelhead fly fishing in the summer. Begin winter steelhead fishing with bait or lures. Combine the two only when you have much experience, and much patience.

Last winter I went winter steelhead fishing with Jim Teeny of Portland. Jim is the inventor and manufacturer of the famed Teeny Nymph, a deadly fly for all kinds of fishing, especially trout.

We fished the Lewis River of Washington, but conditions were lousy, with the river up and rain falling steadily. Nobody on the river was catching a thing. It was a great day to stay home and watch football.

But Jim and I went and we fished hard. I got skunked with my regular spinning outfit and lures. But I didn't feel badly because we heard of only four or five fish being caught on the river that day but two of those fish were taken by Teeny and his nymphs.

The last piece of gear I'd like to mention is rain clothing. There is no way a consistent winter steelheader is going to keep dry. The Pacific Coast is one of the wettest places on earth, and nowhere is it wetter than on a steelhead river. It can rain, it can pour, it can drizzle and drip. Now and then the sun must shine but I haven't seen it yet. I must have missed that day.

So go prepared with adequate, comfortable rain gear—and a change of clothes back in the car. Steelhead rivers can be miserable places for those not prepared.

So if winter steelheading is done in such lousy weather, for a tempermental fish that frequents rivers that are often unfishable, why bother to go out there, stand in the rain, and fish?

The answer is something that is hard to describe, but once you've tied into a powerful brute of a fish, weighing an average of about 8 pounds and going on up to well over 20, and felt its dynamic runs and seen its spectacular jumps—you'll know why.

There is no finer, no stronger, no more colorful gamefish than the steelhead, and he reaches his zenith during the depths of winter in the rain-soaked rivers of the Pacific Northwest.

A History of U.S. Trout Fishing

by MARK C. DILTS

TRYING TO pinpoint exactly when trout fishing became a popular American sport is like trying to convince your wife you need another new fishing rod to add to your present collection—it ain't easy!

Actually, hook and line trout fishing was rather slow in spreading across this new land. The settlers had little extra time for such frivolities. They found making a new home and living for themselves and their families took all of their time and energy. If there was a need to take fish for food it was done in a simple straight-forward manner, and little time was wasted with hook and line when a spear could be quickly fashioned or a net was handy.

While the settlers may have ignored the sporting aspect of taking fish, the country was not lacking in angling opportunities. As a matter of fact, fish were so abundant in New England streams that farm laborers often stipulated that they would not be fed more than one fish dinner per week before they would agree to work on a farm. Similarly, factory workers, along one of the better New England salmon streams, refused to carry on their duties until they were assured that they would not be served fish more than twice a week.

There was an inkling that sport fishing might come to this country when, in 1614, Captain John Smith visited New England and recorded in his journal: ''What pleasure can be more than to recreate themselves before their owne doores, in their owne boates, upon the Sea, where man, woman, and childe, with a small hooke and line by angling, may take diverse sorts of excellent fish, at their pleasure?''

A relatively tiny handful of people may have engaged in sport fishing during those early years, but it wasn't until the mid-1700s when it became a popular sport for early Americans. During this time, fishing clubs began springing up among the northeastern states. However, these clubs were more social than sporting in nature and members could hardly be classed as being dedicated anglers.

This Little Betsie River fisherman didn't burden himself with any extra fishing gear back in 1898.

Most early trout planting was done by individuals and organizations such as the Elk Rapids, Michigan, Rod and Gun Club shown here planting trout in Yuba Creek, in 1902.

The establishment of fishing clubs, however, marked the beginning of a more leisurely style of living and signaled a budding interest in sport fishing in America. Even so, the development of angling knowledge and technique was slow and made little progress until the first part of the 1880s. Even then, relatively few American sportsmen were attracted to the sport until the 1840s and 1850s.

It must be remembered that the equipment and technique, used by this country's earliest anglers, originated in England where the primary fish was the brown trout and not the brookie—a white-finned trout of our eastern streams whose feeding habits and whims were entirely different. New lessons had to be learned and tackle modified before American trout fishing truly became an American sport.

In the early 1800s, there were two methods of sport fishing—bait and fly. The latter method was confined to the use of wet flies, since dry fly fishing wasn't introduced to America until the latter half of the century. Techniques posed little problem since the brook trout of wilderness streams readily came to almost any offering that happened to suit their fancy. If it represented food, the eastern brook trout fed readily and was easily caught by anglers.

Fishing techniques and tackle improved as more and more sportsmen took to streams and lakes. As civilization spread across the land, industrialization and deforestation began taking a toll on the brook trout and their habitat. By the 1850s, salmon had disappeared from southern New England streams and brookies were being depleted from the more accessible waters.

Despite this forewarning of impending doom for brook

trout, fishing was so great it would boggle the mind of many of today's brush-busting brook trout fishermen. An account of a fishing trip made by the Oquossoc Angling Association to northern Maine, in June, 1869, was recorded in a little-known book entitled, *Brook Trout Fishing*.

The gentlemen of the fishing association told of fishing Maine's fabulous Rangeley Lakes and of their fantastic catches of trout. Six-pound brook trout were said to be a common occurrence while an occasional 9-pounder was brought to net.

Official records kept at the turn of the century bear witness to the truthfulness of the statements of the angling association members. The records reveal that numerous brook trout, in the 9- to 11-pound bracket, were caught in Moosehead and Rangeley Lakes of Maine.

Although the brook trout is a fish of the East, its original habitat extended south through the Alleghenies to northern Georgia, north through Ungava and into Hudson Bay, and west from Labrador to Saskatchewan. The fish originally was not found west of the Mississippi River, with the exception of Iowa.

Good squaretail fishing wasn't limited to the northeastern states. Excellent fishing was also found in northern Minnesota, Wisconsin and Michigan.

William B. Mershon, a prominent Michigan sportsman at the turn of the 20th century, wrote in his book, *Recollections of My Fifty Years Hunting and Fishing*, of a five-day fishing trip on Michigan's Black River.

"There were seven in the party. The total catch was 346 brook trout and 46 grayling. The largest trout was 16 inches

The typical wilderness trout fishing camp consisted of a tent, bunks,
cook stove and table, all brought to the site by horse and wagon.

and the largest grayling 14½ inches.''

In another passage, Mershon wrote of taking 25-30 trout a
day from the North Branch of Michigan's famous AuSable
River, in 1902.

"On the 10th (May) it snowed all morning, but Morely and I
took 49 fish in the snowstorm. There were eight in the party
for the four days fishing; took 400 fish, all with the fly."

When speaking of excellent brook trout fishing, one should
never forget the superb squaretail fishing of the Canadian
provinces; the world record brook trout of 14½ pounds was
caught in Ontario's Nipigon River, in 1916.

As the brook trout declined, a substitute was waiting to fill
the void left in the nation's eastern waters. The rainbow trout,
whose original range was the Pacific slope of the Sierras, from
California to Alaska, was introduced to eastern streams by
the United States Fish Commission in 1880. Seth Green, an
early fish culturist, had brought some adult rainbows to his
Caledonia, New York ponds and bred them several years
earlier.

About the same time (1877), Frank N. Clark, of Northville,
Michigan, a member of the U. S. Fish Commission, went to
California and returned with over 125 rainbows measuring 5
to 7 inches in length. While most of the fish were retained as
brood stock at the Northville hatchery, about 25 of the small
rainbows were planted in the Rogue River near the hatchery.
This was probably the first planting of rainbow trout in waters
east of the Mississippi River.

During the early days of fish propagation, rainbows were
planted in streams in the Alleghenies, the Ozarks, New England and Michigan. Now, due to their eggs being easily trans-

ported, rainbows are found in most states except for some of
the southern ones bordering the Gulf.

The rainbow was disliked by many fish culturists because
their eggs were not readily impregnated which caused additional work. But the fishermen loved them. Rainbows readily
rose to the fly and bait fishermen found they could be taken
using a variety of natural baits. In addition, 'bows grew faster
and larger than brook trout. A 4-year-old stream fish could
measure 20 inches and weigh 4 pounds and a lake-bound fish
of similar length and age could tip the scales at 8 pounds or
more.

The rainbow was a dream fish for many anglers. He furnished unexcelled excitement because he rarely took lures
half-heartedly. Most of the time the battle was joined by a
slashing strike followed immediately by an aerial display
which sent blood coursing through the veins of the lucky
angler.

"The rainbow is, without doubt, one of the most muscular
and resourceful of fishes for its size, rising freely to the
artificial fly, leaping on slack line, and fighting literally to the
death,'' wrote William C. Harris, noted author and fisherman, in 1902. "They made on my rod in the wild waters of the
state of Washington as sturdy a fight as the steelhead and a
greater one than the cutthroat or the Montana grayling,
coming frequently into the air and making longer and stronger
surges than the brook beauty of our Eastern mountain
streams.''

While the New England states had some difficulty retaining
the rainbow in some of their smaller streams because of its
desire to seek bigger water, other states seemed to have less

The gentlemen fishers of the late 1800s often went astream dressed in their tweed suits and bowler derbies.

trouble and the rainbow became firmly established.

By the late 1800s, rainbows were well situated in Michigan's AuSable and Pere Marquette rivers; numerous lakes and the Platte River of Colorado; the Ozark regions of Missouri and Arkansas; numerous streams and their tributaries in Iowa; the Jack River of eastern Tennessee and various streams of North Carolina, as well as the Green River of Virginia and streams of Maryland, Maine, Wisconsin and Pennsylvania. This was in addition to the hundreds of rivers and streams of California, Oregon and Washington which was the original home of this flashy fighter.

"One year ago last fall, I had a camp on the AuSable River for the purpose of getting a stock of brook trout eggs and upward of 10,000 spawners were secured," wrote Frank Clark, superintendent of U.S.F.C. stations in Michigan, "and at each haul we would catch from 500 to 2,000 rainbow trout which were hatched out the spring before. In the AuSable, the presence of rainbow trout in large numbers has evidently been established."

As the brook trout populations declined and rainbows were being welcomed as a fine addition to the American trout fishing scene, the brown trout was introduced to the nation's trout fishermen.

In the winter of 1882-83, Fred Mather, a nationally known fish culturist, received a personal present of approximately 100,000 brown trout eggs from Baron von Behr, president of the German Fishery Association. Since the Long Island hatchery, which Mather had been appointed to manage, was not prepared to receive the eggs, part of them were sent to Caledonia, New York, while the balance was sent to Michi-

gan. The Michigan eggs were hatched and the resulting fry were planted in the state's Pere Marquette River—the first major American river to receive such an honor.

The brown trout turned out to be a favorite of the country's fish culturists and they began a nationwide stocking program. By 1900, brown trout had been planted in 38 states and the massive stocking program resulted in a brown trout population explosion.

Fishermen, who were used to catching the more gullible brook and rainbow trout, were unwilling to admit that they were having difficulty catching the more wary browns and were up in arms over this "spotted carp" being planted in their favorite trout streams. They criticized it as being poor table fare and, when small trout were found in its stomach, they called it a "cannibal" and claimed it was eating all the other trout.

A total of 1,747,000 brown trout had been planted in Michigan alone by the end of 1896. But, despite the brown trout success, the political clout of America's trout fishermen was being felt by fish commissions across the land.

The Michigan Fish Commission, in 1897, appraised the brown trout as being: ". . . inferior in every respect to either the brook or rainbow trout, with few exceptions. This verdict is in harmony with the verdict of the anglers and epicures everywhere. The stock of adult brown trout has therefore been turned adrift and no further distribution will be made."

And, while numerous other states agreed with the Michigan philosophy of banning brown trout, Mather forcefully defended the fish he was responsible for introducing to American fishermen.

This string of 54 trout made a typical picture
of the early American fisherman and his catch.

"Some anglers have objected to the introduction of brown trout in our streams because they grow too fast and might eventually kill out our native fish. To this I say: 'Let 'em do it if they can, and the fittest will survive.' The chubs, dace, pike, bass and other fishes have worked this game for centuries before a white angler wet a line in an American trout stream, and here we are! A trout is a cannibal when he gets to be 3 years old, whether he is a native American or an adopted citizen, and it is only a question of which fish matures in the shortest time for the angler."

Despite Mather's defense of the brown, it was more than a decade before some of the states returned to a brown trout stocking program. But it took even a longer period of time for the German immigrant to be fully accepted by the American trout fishing fraternity. However, once its good qualities became appreciated by fishermen, and the various fish commissions became free to use the fish to its full potential, it truly became the savior of trout fishing in many American streams.

The nation's "progress" was taking a heavy toll on trout habitat by the late 1800s. Railroads were opening new pathways into the wilderness and civilization, with its penchant for industrialization, was following close behind.

The lumberman's saw and ax cleared the riverbanks. Towns and factories used the streams as handy sewage drains while the farmer's plow destroyed tiny tributaries. The brook trout retreated to the headwaters and, in many cases, still could not escape the heat, silt and sewage and they were doomed.

Near the turn of this century, the *New York Tribune* wrote a scathing editorial entitled "Sewage Reform":

"The same law that governs Piper's Brook should be applied to the Passaic River and to every river and brook in the land. There is no more precious gift of nature than pure water. It is abundantly given in this part of the world in springs and streams. It is intolerable that men should defile and destroy it simply through laziness or shiftlessness or through pecuniary meanness. Every community and every individual establishment should be compelled to dispose of its unclean refuse in a manner not injurious to its neighbors."

Few people listened and the brook trout's habitat continued to decline until, today, one must travel to Labrador, northern Quebec or Manitoba to catch big brook trout.

What about the rainbow? Well, luckily, he survived the onslaught of our maniacal yearning for growth and is still found in abundance in many of the streams of his original habitat and where he was planted. Everything considered, fishing for the acrobatic rainbow is probably better today than it was at the beginning of the century.

And the brown trout? He's doing just fine, thank you. Today he is the predominant fish caught by America's trout fisherman and is being caught in ever-increasing numbers and size. While the world's record of 39½ pounds, set in 1866, still stands, the American record is being broken repeatedly until it now stands at a whopping 31 pounds, 12 ounces.

And what about our trout fishing history? If history teaches us anything it is to think fondly of the past, appreciate the present and look forward to the future. Our country's trout fishing history makes no exception to this rule. So, go fishing when you can—it can only get better in the years ahead.

HOW TO CON TROUT WITH CORN

by GEORGE RICHEY

Above—The author checks his graph to locate the drop-off where browns and rainbows congregate for after-dark feeding activities. Below—Harold Persails nets a 6-pound brown for author. Note Coleman lantern hanging over the gunwale.

"**GEORGE,** look at all the boats. We must have picked the right night," said Larry. As we unloaded the 14-foot boat, Larry Jacobson and Marv Whitcomb listened to the chatter from the other boats on the lake that were corn fishing for trout.

All the boats were catching rainbow and brown trout. Every 2 or 3 minutes someone would holler they had a fish on.

We loaded the boat, hooked up the sonar unit and motored slowly toward deeper water. We cruised to a stop in 20 feet of water, took a water temperature reading in search of the 61 degree level rainbow and browns thrive in. The temperature we wanted was down 17 feet.

After taking the lake's temperature we moved back toward the nearest dropoff that fell into 17 feet of water and carefully anchored both ends of the boat so it wouldn't blow around in the brisk summer breeze.

We fastened the lantern brackets to the sides of the boat and placed the Coleman lanterns so they shone brightly over both gunwales of the boat. Larry was the first one to lower his corn baited hook over the side and immediately hooked a rainbow.

"Boy, on this light line, these trout fight like tigers," Larry said. I netted his fish and it weighed a chunky 1½ pounds. Marv and I quickly put our two lines over the side and promptly hung silvery browns, beautiful fish with large black "X" marks dotting their gleaming sides.

The action slowed after several minutes so I broadcast a handful of whole kernel corn over each side of the boat. I told Larry and Marv to raise their lines from the bottom and slowly let them sink again under tension. Trout often hit corn as it drifts toward bottom.

Marv was next to get in on the action. His bait didn't reach the sandy bottom before the largest fish of the night hit.

As Marv hooked his fish it started running toward the bow of the boat. He had to lean hard on the rainbow to turn it away from the anchor line. The spunky fish crashed out of the water, did a splashy cartwheel and jumped again a foot in the air next to the boat. The acrobatics tired the trout and it tried one last half-hearted run for freedom before Marv could turn it back toward the waiting net.

Marv's fish was a fat 3½-pound rainbow, all silvery except for a faint pink stripe down its flank. Rainbows like this aren't unusual when you lantern-fish after dark. We greeted the pink sky of dawn with a combination of nine rainbows and browns and this action happened only 40 miles from home. There are countless trout lakes around the United States that lie close to home for fishermen and which would be likely candidates for after dark fishing with whole kernel corn.

Most fishermen use at least two lanterns when they corn con trout and some use as many as four; one on the front, one on the stern and one or two over each side of the boat. The theory is the bright lights after dark attract flying insects, which in turn attract baitfish, which brings lunker trout on the run. They find the corn irresistible and begin active feeding. Sooner or later the angler will be into fish.

I prefer using three lanterns, but I add aluminum foil to the inside of the globe facing the boat. This reflects light away from the boat and places the maximum illumination on the water. This has two advantages; one is the light doesn't get in your eyes as you watch for a bite and it also keeps many moths and mosquitoes away from the boat.

I've seen serious after-dark trout fishermen line the bottom and sides of their boat with aluminum foil to further reflect light from the lanterns. They report excellent results from the added reflection.

A list of lakes planted with trout can be obtained from the Department of Natural Resources (DNR) in any trout area. This is a good place to start in selecting a potential fishing site. These lists are usually free for the asking.

Most trout lakes are planted yearly, normally in the spring, but not all trout taken are freshly released ''planters.''

Many fish caught are hold-overs from the previous year's planting. I've heard of trout taken on corn that ran up to 8 or 9 pounds. These trout are usually hold-overs such as the 3½-pound rainbow that Marv caught which was mentioned earlier.

Occasionally the Fisheries Division will plant lakes with brood stock from the trout hatcheries. These brood fish are often in the 6- to 8-pound class. One of these lunkers is sure to perk up the spirits of any corn fisherman that hooks into him after the sun goes down.

We use 4- to 6-pound line with a sinker just heavy enough to take it to the bottom. I tie a small three-way swivel about 18 inches up from the sinker and a dropper line about 8 or 10 inches long from the swivel and on the end of the dropper I tie a No. 12 hook.

I usually try to ''chum'' the trout in close to the boat. We use cream style corn for ''chumming'' because this has a desirable milking effect. As it sinks, it releases juice and odor that spreads out in the water and attracts trout. A tablespoon is used to ladle out the cream corn.

You can use too much corn in the chumming process and it has two distinct disadvantages; one is you will actually be feeding the fish when all you want is to attract them to your boat. Secondly, too much corn constitutes littering and this has to be avoided at all costs. Use just enough to get the trout coming to the immediate fishing area.

Bury the hook in one or two whole kernels of corn. Occasionally we'll use a double hook rig with one swivel 18 inches up from the sinker and another swivel 36 inches from the sinker. Never use droppers longer than 10 inches. We've found that it pays to squeeze the corn kernels slightly so just a bit of corn oozes out of the bottom of the kernel. This adds to the effectiveness of the bait.

If corn doesn't do the trick, with occasional chumming, try the double hook rig and place a kernel of corn on the bottom hook and a night crawler or worm on the upper hook. Every now and then single salmon eggs will also work. Salmon eggs will milk and release desirable juice into the water. Cheese or garlic flavored eggs are deadly, although corn is normally the steadier producer.

Trout will usually move up from deeper water to the drop-offs at dusk. Some nights they won't show up until 11 or 12 o'clock although early evening migrations from deepwater to the breaklines are the rule.

A sonar unit will speed up locating drop-offs, although I've had pretty fair luck by just going out to the crowd of lights and anchoring near the other boats. Most fishermen know where the trout hit the drop-offs to feed and they find hot fishing night after night in the same spots.

When anchoring make sure you don't bang the anchors against the side of the boat. Ease them down so you don't spook the fish.

Light line and small hooks means you have to watch closely so that when the trout bites you'll be able to set the hook quickly. Lip hooked fish can be released if they are undersized although this method seldom takes many small trout.

Trout seldom hit corn hard. Many times the tip of the rod barely moves on the light take. I've seen bobbers used that were barely large enough to keep bait and sinker from pulling them beneath the surface. When the bobber begins to quiver, no matter how lightly, set the hook.

The best bobbers are either painted with a luminous paint or plain white in color. Quill bobbers are very sensitive and work well. Another good bet for detecting strikes are the spring rod bobbers that are used on the end of ice fishing rods.

The best corn-conning time seems to be from Memorial Day through Labor Day. Night fishing slows down after Labor Day due to the cooling off of the water.

The best night we've had was last July when my wife Jean, my brother Dave and I went to a lake near home. We arrived just as the frogs began their dusk serenade and we had the boat in the water, rods rigged and the can of corn open before the moon came up.

We found a drop-off in 24 feet of water, located the proper water temperature and anchored quietly.

This was my wife's first trip for after-dark trout and she wasn't really sure of what to expect.

She lowered her first line to where it hovered just off bottom and was putting her second line down when I looked and her first rod was jumping. I hollered ''Jean, grab your rod!''

She set the hook and that was the start of all the excitement. By the time she got that rainbow to the boat Dave and I were hooked into jumping fish. We boated four rainbow and three browns in the brief 15-minute flurry of action.

There was a lull in the action so I ladled a tablespoon of creamed corn out on each side of the boat and off the stern. I brought up both lines and rebaited with fresh whole kernel corn. I advised Jean and Dave that many times after chumming it's wise to add fresh bait to the hooks. This usually starts the trout biting again.

Ten minutes after chumming Jean landed a 4-pound rainbow. After a spirited battle, I chummed again while she admired her fish before putting it in the cooler.

Within the next hour we hooked over 20 bows and browns and landed eight fish. Each of us had our limit of five trout before midnight. Dave caught a 4-pound rainbow and Jean's

There are countless trout lakes around that lie close to home for fishermen and which would be likely candidates for after dark fishing with whole kernel corn.

Close-up of hook baited
with two kernels of corn.

largest was her 3½-pounder, her largest to date. I scored with a hefty 6-pound brown.

All you need for after-dark trout fishing is two to four white gas or propane lanterns and brackets to hold the lanterns over the sides of the boat. Aluminum foil to reflect the light, rod holders if desired, and a can of corn completes your list of equipment. Insect repellent is a must for nighttime trout fishermen.

Make sure the brackets prevent the lanterns from dipping too low or they may wind up in the water. I've used an oar propped under a boat seat to hold my lanterns out of the water. The best brackets are commercially made from heavy gauge wire and attached with a thumb screw to the boat's gunwales.

Trout will occasionally be suspended off bottom, so if there isn't any bottom action after fishing for a few minutes, try chumming a handful or tablespoon of corn out each side of the boat. Then raise the bait up a foot or two. Raise the bait several inches every few minutes and the trout will often follow the bait up and take it 3 or 4 feet off the bottom.

Points that jut out into the lake with sharp drop-offs on either side are always a good bet along with the sharper drop-offs along shore. Edges of deepwater weed beds or submerged islands are good spots to try.

We've often had excellent success fishing points when everyone else is fishing the drop-offs. I'd much rather fish the points anyway.

Try to anchor off the end of the point and cast off either side of the point into deeper water.

Allow the bait to sink to the bottom and slowly crawl it back beneath the boat. If there aren't any hits as you work it back, try letting the bait hang directly below the boat near the bottom and jig it very slightly. Trout will follow it in and strike as it is jigged gently beneath the boat.

This method covers a larger portion of the lake's depths than does anchoring the boat off of a drop-off. It is advisable to allow the bait to stay at a certain level for several minutes while crawling it in off a point before moving it to a shallower level.

This method covers the greatest amount of area for the corn fisherman. Anytime you have to cast, such as when fishing off a point, use a soft lob cast. If you don't you may cast the bait off in the dark without knowing it.

Fishing with corn is quite productive, whether it is after-dark on lakes or daylight fishing in rivers for steelhead or brown trout. It is just a matter of using the proper techniques. Corn, as bait, is very adaptable.

A river I used to fish was closed for many years to trout spawn or salmon egg fishing. My brother and I have caught many steelhead and browns by simply chumming a hole or deep run with corn. We'd put two kernels of corn on a gold No. 6 Eagle Claw hook and bounce it slowly along the bottom.

We once fished this particular river and we'd taken several steelhead and lost two others. Nearby fishermen saw our bait and they thought we were using illegal salmon eggs. They called the conservation officer to investigate two suspicious fishermen and he witnessed us landing another steelhead.

He hustled over and asked to see what we were using for bait. "You know, that's the first time I've seen corn used for bait," he said. He told us that corn was a good imitation of single salmon eggs and was entirely legal in every state he knew of. We ended up the day with an 8-pound steelhead as our largest.

When fishing corn in rivers for steelhead or brown trout, be careful that you don't chum too much in a run or drift as there are usually only a couple of fish present in each drift. You want to attract the trout—not feed them.

Look for a smooth flow of water near the tail end of a hole that has some cover available. If the run has a log jam at the side of it with deep water in the hole, the steelhead will usually lie in the run near cover toward the shallow end of the run. The browns will usually be in the hole or the upper end of the run near the hole. The edges of the swirling eddy water are hotspots for both browns and steelhead.

If you aren't occasionally hung up on the bottom then you aren't fishing the corn properly.

Both river fishing or after-dark lantern fishing for trout is fun and a productive way to fish. I prefer the lake fishing as I have to work during the day and often my only time to fish is after dark.

The thing I like about fishing with corn after dark for trout is it is a relaxing atmosphere, everything is quiet and I enjoy the silence. About the only noise is an occasional splash from a silvery trout as it battles for freedom under the liquid glow of a summer moon.

Trophies Off the Beaten Trail

by JACK ANDERSON

Richard Smith of Marquette, Michigan, shows a 3½-pound brook trout, the result of canoeing back in from easily accessible places.

"FISH ON!" partner Eric Putnam warned as a 5-pound steelhead sliced from the river and began dancing in mid-air.

"Keep your rod high," I encouraged as I tried to horse my spinner out of his way. Trout and salmon fishermen in southern Michigan's St. Joseph River have enough problems with the rock-strewn bottom and don't need nuisance competition from other anglers.

Eric kept the pressure on his steelie which quickly tired in the swift current. He nursed his prize to shore, a bright orange sponge tuft, meant to resemble a cluster of salmon eggs, sticking above the trout's upper jaw.

"That sure beats yesterday's bummer," Eric remarked as I slipped his trophy deep into the net's security. "The best idea we've had all weekend was to move downstream."

The day before, Good Friday, was spent in a futile effort to catch steelhead whose spring runs are fast making the St. Joe one of the Midwest's top trout rivers. Apparently, the good news that spawning steelhead were in the river had spread since I counted 47 boats strung along 2 miles of river from the launching facility at Berrien Springs.

The fish were in the river to spawn, but it's my guess that all those boats racing up and down had pretty well scattered the fish and frightened them into not biting. Many of us went fishless that day. After 10 hours of it, we lost our desire to return the next morning and instead were fortunate enough to find an abandoned farm where the back 40 lay along the river. We saw only two other fishing parties all day and turned what could have been a bad memory into a successful fishing weekend.

After chasing trout for many years, I've decided that the "Some fishermen have all the luck" theory just isn't true. There are many other factors involved. In addition to being in the right place at the right time (luck), patience, knowledge of the quarry, and experience are all ingredients that help separate successful trout anglers from those less fortunate.

Fishermen I know that are consistently fortunate in filling their creels have at least one other personality trait in common—a determination to find the best fishing spots away from heavily used areas.

The typical trout fisherman is no different from most other anglers. He's content to share a crowded pool since half the reason he went fishing in the first place was to socialize. He likes to park his car at public fishing access points and generally won't be found more than ¼-mile from the nearest bridge, grocery store or restaurant.

The untested hotspot back in the woods will remain untested by him even though he knows he'd like to try it. The venture would require too much extra equipment, he reasons, making a long hike or portage too difficult. Besides, he's been out of shape for so long he no longer knows his tolerance for physical endurance and, because of the high rate of heart disease in this country, is afraid to test his stamina. He assures himself that the fish probably wouldn't be biting anyway and if he really wanted trophy trout, it would be easier overall and certainly more fun to run up to Canada where everyone knows the big ones are.

On the other hand, the angler with the full creel might very well have hiked or paddled in to less crowded places on any well known stream where fishing pressure is intense.

Most trout rivers in America, with the possible exception of some wilderness or western mountain streams, have high use areas. Bridges, launching sites, dams, boat liveries, and

This trophy steelhead wasn't caught near a bridge or public landing where most fishermen congregate. Getting to less crowded fishing spots might take some effort but is worth the chance to catch a trophy trout.

parks are all places where anglers congregate. Even though the fishing might remain unusually good, the big, trophy trout are picked off early or are spooked out to more remote stretches.

Many of this country's most famous trout rivers, like Michigan's AuSable, the Madison River in Montana, and the Beaverkill in New York, receive intense fishing pressure during the long open seasons. Each of these rivers, and probably your own favorite trout stream, contains trophy, tacklebusting trout that are just a short distance from convenience areas.

A float trip downstream, where a portage or two might be necessary on smaller rivers, could put you into little known pools where monster trout lurk.

A cross country hike from some point on the state highway might mean a couple miles of busting through puckerbrush, but is well worth the effort if you can find a piece of private stream where the only competition is an otter or two.

Half the reason I go trouting is to get away from the daily competitive grind and into myself by way of quiet reverie. I can't find peace and solitude while standing in an easily accessible stretch of river and trying to cast to a popular pool with a dozen other guys.

The popular spots all have their best angles of approach and some trout anglers, being me-firsters at heart, vie for the pole position. When I think of the near fights caused by overanxi-

ous anglers who have trespassed over imaginary river boundary lines, I can't help remember why I decided to either get away from crowds or give up the sport. If you, too, have lost big fish due to fouled lines with other fishermen or nearly had your ear lobe ripped off by a neighbor's faulty backcast, you know what I'm talking about.

Michigan's Big Creek, one of the AuSable's feeder streams, is a 10- or 12-foot wide river which has native trout of its own, but occasionally big browns, rainbows, and brookies move in from the big river a couple of miles downstream. Near the town of Luzerne, Big Creek is blocked by a small dam which forms a small, deep pool below. Buster browns up to 8½ pounds have been caught in the 8-foot deep hole, which is about twice the size of a two-car garage. The fishing pressure here, only a block from the highway, is unbelievably intense. The only thing of value I've ever been able to catch other than an occasional 12-inch brown or rainbow, is other fishermen's tackle, snagged from the bottom of the boulder-laden pool.

Over the years I've never been able to fish this pool alone. I've come in early morning when fog shrouded the pool and have had to jockey for a parking spot. I've returned as late as 11:00 PM only to be greeted with flashlight beams upon approaching the river.

Finally I gave it up. Securing a county map and making sure the gas tank on my car wasn't too low, I began checking out back roads for a different access. I reasoned that some of those fish could clear the dam; besides, there should be natives upstream.

In a couple of hours I was able to make my way down unused logging trails to within 100 yards of the 5- or 6-foot wide stream. I've since caught 12-inch brook trout and

A 2-mile cross country hike was the only effort that produced this handsome catch of rainbows.

The brown trout is a shy and elusive quarry. When fishing pressure increases, browns move in to more remote stretches of streams.

browns up to 15 inches from the upper reaches of Big Creek. Only once have I seen another angler and he was looking for a way back to the mainstream. He was lost.

Each time I drive past the popular pool hotspot and see cars lining both sides of the highway, I think what a sucker I was for not heading out on my own earlier.

The use of state highway maps or county road maps will help get you in where the big ones are and the crowds aren't. These maps are usually free by writing to the respective seats of government and asking for a copy. Local Chambers of Commerce sometimes publish tourist's maps also.

Circle the typical high use areas—you don't have to be familiar with the region to spot bridges, public access points, etc.—and then look for other means of access. Is there a railroad grade, for example, that crosses the river or stream at some less publicized point? What about back country roads, fire lanes, or power company rights of way? A little backroads cruising could turn up an abandoned farm or friendly rancher who might agree to let someone cross his fence if only he was asked.

Some maps, especially county editions, shade in public land which helps the unfamiliar angler to keep from trespassing. Most public libraries have an excellent collection of state and county maps. Is there a better way to spend a winter evening than systematically plotting your plans for the spring trout opener?

What about the water between bridges which are handy put-in and take-out spots for river floaters? I was once able, a few years ago, to fish the Madison River near McAllister, Montana. With the help of a partner, we parked one car downstream and put in our boat near the Madison Dam. Stopping and fishing likely looking places several times got us into some good brown trout fishing.

On another fishing trip my brother and I were able to catch some dandy 2-pound rainbows from the Beaverkill River in the Catskills of New York state. The reputation of the Beaverkill preceded itself but being from Michigan, we knew nothing about the river except what we'd heard and read. While staying over in Rockland one night, I picked up an issue of the county weekly and discovered that local anglers were doing well using mayflies on rainbows.

That put trout fishing on our minds and so the next morning found us wading the Beaverkill in a likely looking spot near the road. We caught nothing and gave it up as a lost cause about mid-morning, deciding to continue our trip north into Canada. Later, I told a gas station attendant of our disappointment at not being able to catch a trout from the famed river.

As he returned my change, he leaned over the car door and said in a low voice, "You fellows want some trout, hey?"

We assured him we did. Pulling a small notebook with a smudged cover from his greasy overalls, he went on, "You boys were fishing in the wrong places today. All the big trout were caught out of there weeks ago. Let me show you where to go." He then drew a backroads map, showing us an accessible, but not well-known way, to get into the 'Kill.

That evening we stopped by the filling station to thank him and offer him some of our fat, fresh-caught rainbows. "Those are the ones I meant," he admired, adding, "I'm glad you boys are from out of state."

Such lucky breaks are rare. Getting a successful trout angler to divulge his favorite fishing spots is about as hard as getting a termite to attack a plastic log. We've never been able to get back to the Beaverkill but I'll forever be indebted to this man who showed us the way to a couple of hours of unforgettable fishing.

Whether or not you pass on out-of-the-way hotspots is up to you, but I've found that most trout fishermen are about as closed-mouthed as a teenager with braces and protect their secret trout grounds with the spirit of a mother bear with cubs.

I'll never forget the time Jack Cournyer of Mio, Michigan, took me out one moonless night to try for browns on the famous AuSable. Jack is a life-long resident of the area and has known the AuSable intimately for many years. During the summer he spends more time chasing brown and rainbow trout than he does in his own bed.

The AuSable is a deep, fast stream with unpredictable log obstructions, swirls and eddies that make night fishing from a canoe particularly hazardous. Jack waited until after dark and then took me down several backroads and then back upriver to his favorite haunts which he usually fishes alone. I carried only my camera since it is difficult to river fish two lines from a canoe in the middle of the night.

I doubt if I could have found my way back into these little known spots again even in daytime but Jack talked about blindfolding me anyway. If I had agreed, I think he would have done it.

Every serious trout angler should read Ernest Hemingway's "Big Two-Hearted River," the story of why a young Michigan man leaves the city to fish undisturbed in wilderness of this Upper Peninsula stream.

Like most anglers, Hemingway wasn't about to divulge the true secret of one of his favorite trout rivers. Recent evidence shows the story probably occurred on the Fox River, a lesser known stream, also in the same area. The Fox is just as accessible and the fishing excellent but most people would rather gather where the action is supposed to be.

Sometimes good fishing sites on popular rivers are right under the unsuspecting angler's nose. Pete Jones, a friend and avid trout fisherman, once had a favorite, little known spot on the Sturgeon River in Michigan's northern Lower Peninsula. The Sturgeon receives heavy fishing pressure for 6 months of the year, beginning with spring-run steelhead and ending with a second spawning migration of these sleek, silvery fish in the fall. In between lies some choice brown trout fishing.

My friend knows the river well, having fished it for over 20 years. One of his favorite spots was right off heavily travelled Old U. S. 27 near the town of Wolverine. Several times each year he would pull off the busy highway and park his car between two towering pines whose skirt-like lower branches concealed the car from a casual roadside view. Trout fishing was usually good and the roar of this swift river was loud enough to drown out the drone of traffic 100 yards away. Over the years he's snaked enough trophy trout from this river to make anyone's den a point of conversation. Again, this just points out the validity of seeking out trout hotspots well away from the hustle and bustle of the ordinary trout fisherman.

The smart trout fisherman will always pack angling gear whenever he journeys into unfamiliar areas. A person never knows when he'll have an opportunity to test some little known hotspot on an otherwise heavily fished river.

While travelling through Utah with a friend native to the state, my brother once had a chance to sample some great rainbow trout fishing in the Green River near the town of that name. Many Utahans fish the Green and do well, even in the more accessible places, but only my brother's friend and perhaps a handful of others, knew that 3-pound 'bows could be taken regularly from this site a short way from the highway.

Trout are where you find them, but as fishing pressure increases on popular U.S. rivers, more and more anglers are discovering that the really big ones are away from the easily accessible places.

Your next trophy trout might well come from a spot off the beaten trail.

These four handsome brown trout came from remote spots of the popular AuSable River in Michigan.

Western Flies for Eastern Trout

by DAN ABRAMS

AT 8:00 P.M. the temperature was still hanging at a hot 86 degrees. The sultry overcast of that August evening seemed to have everything locked into a state of lethargy.

Overhead, a lone crow lazily rowed his wings through the humidity as he headed for his evening roost. The summer-low waters of the North Fork of Redbank Creek at Brookville, Pennsylvania, edged along sluggishly—almost reluctantly. It was sure a far cry from the full, vibrant flow which coursed between these banks in early May when the trout had risen eagerly to high-riding Hendricksons.

Once in a while a rather large, dusky caddis fly buzzed aborning from the slow current directly in front of me. There were too few to be honestly called a full-blown "hatch," but maybe enough to touch off the feed glands in a nearby trout.

After 2 hours of steady but fruitless casting, I hunkered down on a streamside log to rest a while. A caddis was floating a few inches from the far bank, and just as the gray-tan fly unfurled its tentlike wings to launch itself clear of the water, it disappeared in a dainty slurp.

While frantically searching for a caddis imitation among the

Royal Humpy (left) and Humpy (right). Two high floating flies often used to suggest an airborne caddis fly.

disorderly array of feathered barbs in one of my fly boxes, I spotted a rather heavily-hackled, gray fly I had purchased while on a fishing vacation in which I had sampled some of the fine Rocky Mountain trout streams of our western states.

"Why not," I thought. "A fly like this served me well during a heavy caddis hatch on Henry's Fork of the Snake River in Idaho. Maybe a Humpy would do the trick on this Pennsylvania brown."

Called a Humpy by some and a Goofus Bug by others, this fly is constructed by tying a small bunch of deer or elk hair on top of a hook, wrapping the thread firmly over the hair back toward the bend, then folding the hair back toward the eye of the hook, forming a hump-like body. The color of the tying thread determines the color of the belly of the fly. Red and yellow are the favorite colors. The tips of the hair form the wings of the fly. For fishing the heavy currents of western streams, the Humpy is rather thickly hackled. It floats like a cork, and has proved to be an effective pattern, even when casting over some rather choosy fish.

I laid out a cast, three-quartering it upstream so the Humpy would float right over the spot where the trout had risen. As it drifted into his dining room, there was no hesitation on the part of the fish. With a businesslike rise, he slurped in the fly just as he had the naturals. Despite the summer-warmed stream, the 13-inch brown gave a good account of himself before coming to net.

Before leaving the North Fork of Redbank Creek, I missed two strikes and landed another brownie slightly smaller than the first while fishing the Humpy. Altogether it was a satisfying evening considering the circumstances.

Out west there is much discussion about what insect a Humpy represents. The concensus of opinion among knowledgeable fishermen seems to be that it suggests a caddis just as it becomes airborne, buzzing just above the surface of the flies. It can be constructed with either deer or elk hair body and wings or it can be tied with a deer hair body and white calf tail wings.

This latter is the result of crossing a standard Humpy with a Royal Wulff, and it is a fine rough water fly. It has the advantage of being highly visible to the fisherman (something I appreciate, since my vision at late evening isn't all it used to be).

For eastern trout, I have found that Humpies tied in sizes 12 to 18 work best. This pattern in sizes 16 to 18 works well even in stretches of quiet water. When fishing the Humpy, don't hesitate to give it an occasional twitch during the drift (moving the fly about an inch per twitch). The caddis is an active fly on the surface, so it is natural to impart a little action to your artificial. Even while casting No. 12 Humpies, I lean toward the use of a finer leader tippit than usual (never larger than 4X, and more often a 5X), so that the fly can easily swing and move in the current, giving it a lifelike float.

This experience with one western fly got me to wondering if there were other patterns usually associated with Rocky Mountain fishing which might do a good job in fooling eastern fish.

In my fly box I came across two other caddis patterns popular in some parts of the West. The first is the Troth Elk Hair Caddis which is tied with a slim brown body, ribbed with fine gold wire, wrapped with brown hackle the length of the body (palmer style) and finished off with a light elk hair overwing. By varying the color of the body and elk hair one can imitate the local natural caddis flies which come in a wide variety of hues.

The Colorado King is a caddis dry fly pattern which is tied with a forked tail (to give the fly balance and support), a body dubbed with cream, gray, or brown material, has grizzly or brown body hackle wrapped palmer style and is topped with a deer hair overwing.

Because both patterns incorporate the hollow hair of deer or elk, they are excellent floaters. They are just the ticket for the rough water dry fly fishing conditions which you often encounter on eastern streams.

The caddis fly should receive more attention than it does by

water. I'm convinced these Pennsylvania trout felt the same way about it.

Some types of caddis take to the air very quickly after swimming to the surface during their "hatching" stage while others drift in the surface film for several seconds. The ones hatching in the North Fork that evening got off the surface without much hesitation. In fact, the naturals were all in the process of taking to the air when the trout intercepted them. This is probably the reason the Humpy was rather effective on that occasion.

Since then, I have used a Humpy with great success in casting to the fish of several trout streams in the eastern states. Its capacity to float from sun-up until noon endears it to the hearts of anglers who like to fish broken water with dry

fly fishermen who have been deep-hooked by the traditions rooted in mayfly imitation. Because the caddis is more tolerant than the mayfly to the acid conditions and pollution present in many streams, it is now a very important part of the trout's diet all over the United States. These western patterns are useful additions to your inventory of other caddis flies.

My fly box also contains a Whitlock Sculpin which I decided to try in some of the streams of our Mid-Atlantic states. This streamer has a clipped deer hair head giving it a slight resemblance to the well-known Muddler Minnow. The Whitlock Sculpin is a great imitation of the bottom dwelling sculpin

minnows which are found in the streams and rivers all over the United States.

Not long ago, I had the opportunity to fish with Dave Whitlock for three days and he talked at length about his baby, the Whitlock Sculpin Minnow. Dave pointed out that most people don't fish this streamer in the most effective manner. He has found this pattern produces best when it is tied rather heavily-weighted, fished with a quick-sinking fly line, and retrieved very s-l-o-w-l-y along the bottom of the stream. He said ''it's a bear to cast and it takes the patience of Job to work that slow retrieve, but if all this is done properly, it will sure take fish!''

I like to fish the Whitlock Sculpin by casting it slightly upstream or directly across the stream, letting it sink deeply and giving it an occasional twitch to keep it somewhat broadside to the current. When it reaches the end of the drift, retrieve it deep and slowly for quite a distance before making another cast.

For large streams, early spring fishing and after-dark angling, you would do well to give the Whitlock Sculpin a serious try.

The Wooly Worm is a fly used in many parts of the country, but when tied in larger sizes it certainly enjoys its greatest

Above—Troth's Elk Hair Caddis (left) and Bodmer's Colorado King. Two western caddis imitations which have done well in eastern waters, too.
Right—Whitlock Sculpin. Fine imitation of the ubiquitous sculpin found in streams all over North America.
Below—Wooly Worm: A versatile tie that has proved itself in a variety of situations.

popularity among the fishermen of the western states. Longtime residents near Yellowstone National Park would confirm the observation that the Wooly Worm has accounted for more trout taken from the streams and lakes of Yellowstone than the next several most popular patterns combined.

It does the job on eastern fish, too! Tied in various color combinations and sizes, it is said to suggest a nymph, a caterpillar, a stubby baitfish, a fresh water shrimp, a soggy mouse, and who knows what else. This versatile tie can be fished on the surface or on the bottom and it is one of the buggiest looking concoctions ever dragged through the water. Although some say it is impossible to fish a Wooly Worm incorrectly, it is more effective when you give your presentation more than a passing thought.

When the pine worms, inchworms and other green worms are dropping from trees along the stream, tie a green-bodied Wooly Worm on a light wire hook and fish it in the surface film or just an inch or two below the surface. Use a floating line on these occasions. When fishing broken water, it sometimes pays to grease your leader to within 6 inches of the fly to keep it riding high.

When using Wooly Worms to suggest other caterpillars, imitate the color of the natural at hand. Depending on the type of water you fish, tie them either weighted or unweighted. As a general rule, use weighted Woolies in deep runs and the unweighted ones in the shallower or slower stretches.

When a natural worm or caterpillar falls into the water, they hit with a "splat." If the trout ignore your Wooly Worm, try casting it in a way to make it land with a soft "splat." On some days this really gets the attention of the trout just as if a dinner gong had been sounded.

It is a terrific fly for lakes and ponds, but here most anglers tend to retrieve it too quickly. Some like to trail a Wooly Worm behind a small spinner when fishing it in lakes, but my druthers lean toward fishing it without extra hardware. The important thing to remember is to employ a leisurely retrieve when casting in still water.

I have a friend who really goes to extremes on this matter. Using a sinking fly line and weighted Wooly Worm, he waits as long as 2 or 3 minutes after each cast before starting to retrieve. By then, the fly has settled to the bottom and his

on these occasions. The Montana Nymph, Troth Terrible Stonefly Nymph, and the Schwiebert nymphs (described in *Nymphs*) are all good suggestive patterns of those large eastern stoneflies.

Fish these nymphs near bottom. A split shot or two about 10 inches in front of the fly will help keep the nymph bouncing and rolling just above the bottom of the stream. Be alert when the nymph reaches the end of its drift and the current swings the fly toward the surface. Trout often hit these "escaping" nymphs with a vengeance. Also, use these to fish the pocket water behind large rocks in fast runs. Fish often lie there waiting for the current to wash food their way.

Where regulations permit it and circumstances warrant it, angling for large brown trout after dark adds an exciting dimension to your fishing experience. Nocturnal fishing by knowledgeable anglers has resulted in some very large trout taken from streams that other fishermen swore were barren of fish. I have used some large western dry fly patterns for this kind of fishing with outstanding success.

A few suggestions about fishing in streams at night are in order at this point. First of all, become familiar with the water you intend to fish during the daylight hours before you go blundering into the stream after dark. A wading staff to check

Left—Troth's Terrible Stonefly Nymph (left) and Montana Nymph (right). Two western stonefly nymph patterns which have taken a good number of eastern trout.
Below—Bucktail Caddis (left) and Bird's Stonefly Dry (right). Two large dry fly patterns which do well on large brown trout after dark.

slow retrieve keeps it inching along just above the rocks or weeds.

I just don't have that kind of patience. Each time we go out, I outcast my fishing buddy 10 to one. But I should also point out that he outfishes me by about a 10 to one margin.

Digging further into my box of flies which at one time were exclusively reserved for use on western fishing trips, I have discovered others which have had moments of effectiveness on trout swimming east of the Mississippi River.

A Black Montana Nymph or some other big, ugly western stonefly nymph has proved to be just the ticket for trout during the high water days of the early season. Many eastern fishermen are not aware of the fact that some of the fine trout streams of New York and Pennsylvania have a fair population of large stoneflies. In his comprehensive book, *Nymphs*, Ernest Schwiebert points out that most of these large dark stonefly nymphs emerge at night or just at daylight in eastern waters.

Some of the typically western stonefly patterns work well

Opposite page—This fisherman is working his way into position to cover a nice trout with a western fly.

Above—Dr. David Rose casting a western trout fly on a typical eastern stream.

water depth is a handy item. To step unexpectedly into a sudden drop off can be embarrassingly uncomfortable at best, and fatally dangerous in some cases. Plan your wading and casting strategy while it is light. Know where you can safely wade and where you can cast to avoid those streamside branches and bushes which eagerly wait to grab your line and fly.

Secondly, rig your gear before going near the water. Do not use that flashlight once you reach the stream unless absolutely necessary. Rig up at the car.

Know where the large fish might be found. Big brown trout get paunchy because they utilize good cover. Look for under-cut banks, overhanging brush, deep pools and large rocks in deep, heavy runs which hide big browns during the daylight hours. But these large brownies often move out and feed in surprisingly shallow water under the cover of darkness.

The techniques of nocturnal fishing are a little different than your daylight style. Generally it is better to use a shorter

cast than you would during the day. Keep that line under control.

Use your ears. Splashy rises and surface disturbances often pinpoint a big trout chasing minnows in the shallows or taking something on the surface. When large brown trout are on a feeding prowl, they usually are looking for a real mouthful. This is where some traditional western patterns come in.

If you are using a streamer, the Whitlock Sculpin mentioned earlier makes an ideal pattern to entice the big fellows.

Three other western flies are just the ticket if you intend to fish on the surface. One is the Bucktail Caddis dry fly. In larger sizes, it is used to imitate stoneflies rather than caddis in the Rocky Mountains. It is tied with an orange floss body, brown body hackling tied palmer style and elk, deer or bucktail overwing.

Two other good patterns are the Bird's Stonefly (dry) and big bushy Sofa Pillows. They can be ordered from most mail order catalogs featuring western patterns.

These flies do an effective job on night-feeding giant browns. The trout probably mistake them for a small mouse, a grasshopper which fell off its streamside perch, a moth, or some other juicy morsel.

When you hear a fish rise, cast to the sound and listen for another disturbance which might indicate a take of your imitation. Lift the rod tip at the slightest suspicion of a hit. If he's on—good luck! Even with a heavy tippet I manage to lose more of these lunkers than I land.

Some of the patterns I have mentioned are not total strangers to eastern fishermen and eastern waters, but they certainly have become closely identified with the West in recent years. Under some circumstances these flies might scare the living bejabbers out of many self-respecting eastern trout. But there are other conditions when East does meet West and these Rocky Mountain patterns have proved to be real killers on eastern fish.

I'm not about to suggest you discard your fly box full of traditionally eastern patterns in favor of these western ties. My fishing vest is still full of boxes jammed with Quill Gordons, Light Cahills, Jassids, Hendricksons, Dun Variants, etc., and I will continue to use them for eastern trout much of the time.

But I am suggesting that we don't lock our thinking into one narrow track to the extent that we cannot open our minds to other possibilities. Don't discount the potential effectiveness of western flies (or other regional patterns) for eastern fish without giving them an honest try. Many of them work and work well indeed!

We still don't have all the answers to the question about what drives a trout to strike at one fly or lure while ignoring others. So, keep an open mind and never be afraid to experiment. Who knows, you might discover the hottest fly of the year for your favorite stream might be some pattern developed in Idaho, Argentina or New Zealand.

Above—Highly oxygenated stretches of water below white water are excellent spots to fish.

Below—The author landing an energetic brown trout on the Brodheads Creek in Pennsylvania.

Canada's Big Brook Trout Waters

by JOHN DAVEY

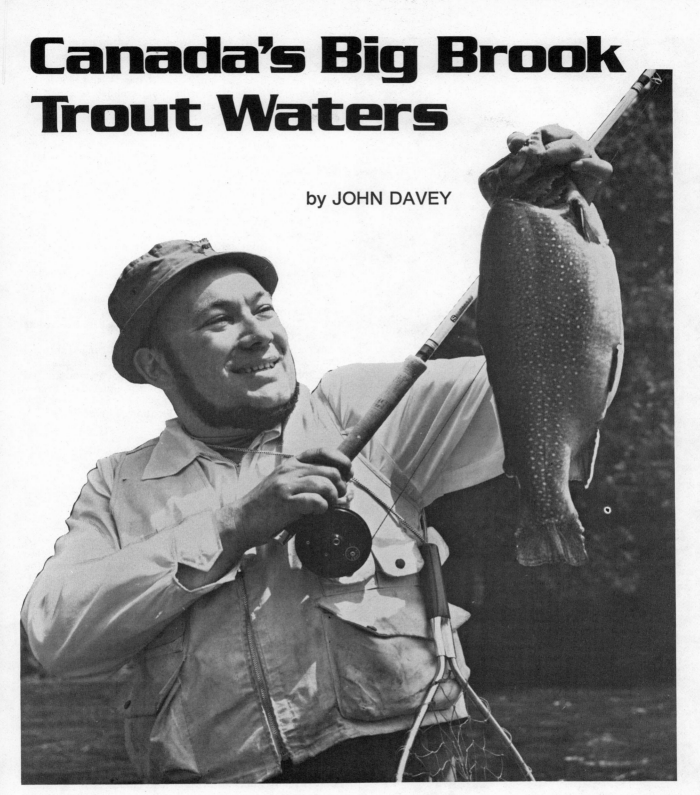

THE WATERS of Quebec's Kaniapiskau River rushed downstream around husky boulders, bounced through a flat shallow stretch and then widened out slightly before sliding into the next riffle.

My guide Pat Cleary of Club Chambeaux positioned the canoe so I could cover the pocket water below the boulders. I flicked cast after cast with spinners and small spoons into the pocket before I saw a swirl of white-edged fins and a savage strike bounced the rod butt hard against the palm of my hand.

I jabbed the rod tip up to set the hook and a square-tailed brook trout twisted downstream along the edge of the white water, my drag buzzing in pain and me yelling at Pat to get the canoe in motion.

The canoe sluiced sideways through the white water and quickly caught up with the headstrong speck. The fish stayed

Ray Gilbert gills a big brookie caught on the Groundhog River. The big fish hit a Comet fly.

deep and jerked my rod tip around for 5 minutes before trying one last run upstream around a ragged edged rock. I lifted my line over the rock, applied extra pressure—as much as my 6-pound mono would stand—and slowly the brookie drifted away from the rock, crabbed sideways for an instant in the fast water, and then drifted down into the waiting net.

Pat swung the heavy chested brookie into the canoe. A male, bedecked in the fall spawning colors, weighing between 4 and 5 pounds, it was a solid 22 inches in length. The white piping along the leading edges of the fins set off the raw beauty of the heavy vermiculated back and the broad square tail. Tiny spots of red were surrounded by pale blue halos. A golden glow of reds, pinks and oranges caressed the belly of this beautiful trout. Big brook trout are the dream of almost every trout fisherman and nothing in the world of trout can surpass a male brook trout dressed up in his spawning clothes.

Canada has the locks on big brook trout in North America. Although some good brookie fishing can be found in the mainland U.S., it generally is for smaller native brookies that may run up to 14 inches. Seldom is a larger brook trout taken. The odd really big speck may come from a remote lake but these are rare indeed.

My trip to Club Chambeaux had been arranged through Quebec Eskimo Indian Outfitters in Rawdon, Quebec. I'd been told that 6-pound specks were not uncommon and I'd be able to catch many trout in the 3- to 5-pound class. Brookies of this size are pretty scarce anywhere and it takes diligent searching to turn up good locations where consistently lunker brook can be caught.

It goes without saying that many new and untried brook trout hotspots are awaiting exploration in the Canada bush. Outfitters and float plane bases know of some of the hotspots but new areas are there if a fisherman is willing to take a chance on meeting failure. I've tried it in a few lakes and met with success on a couple and also have flown in to lakes to find them brim-full with undersized and stunted brookies.

The best Canadian bush lakes for brook trout are generally those that contain only brookies and those in limited supply. Larger concentrations of trout in a lake decrease the amount of food available and consequently only the smallest number of trout can attain any size. I'd rather fish all day for one or two strikes and one lunker brook trout than to catch fish consistently all day and have them undersized or stunted.

That was the way my trip to Club Chambeaux proved. I caught three or four fish daily in the 2- to 5-pound class and occasionally I creeled a smaller 12-inch fish. We kept some of the smaller fish for shore lunches on the Kaniapiskau and released all but a couple of the trophy trout. Fishermen, in near virgin waters, have an obligation to themselves, other fishermen and the big brook trout to keep only one or two trophies and release all the others.

The bulk of North America's trophy brook trout fishing extends from Labrador on the east, across the near-Arctic reaches of northern Quebec, Ontario, Manitoba, Saskatchewan and Alberta. This is land of spruce, caribou moss, cold Arctic evenings and warm days with clouds of blood sucking mosquitoes for company. Evenings are a beautiful outdoor experience when the shimmering beauty of the northern lights are accompanied by plaintive howls of wolves. A wild, beautifully rugged land is the last frontier for big brookies.

Many of the rivers flowing north into Ungava Bay or into Hudson's Bay have runs of sea trout—huge ocean roaming brook trout that return to their natal streams to spawn. I've seen big sea run trout in September while I've been caribou

A fly-in trip is often the best way to get to quality brook trout.

hunting that would make any trout fisherman's heart skip a couple beats.

I managed to wrestle a chunky 5-pounder from the Tunulik River, in northern Quebec near Fort Chimo, once while fishing Arctic char. The big brookie was visible much of the time and it took concentrated casting efforts with a streamer before the fish would take. I beached and released several smaller sea run brookies in the 2-pound class. I did see one brook trout, easily 10 pounds, try repeatedly to scale thundering Tunulik Falls in order to reach the spawning grounds far upstream. As far as I know, he never made it.

One of the most productive spots of all time has been the Gods River-Gods Lake area in northern Manitoba. This remote area is reached only by plane flights originating in either Winnipeg, Manitoba or one of the smaller seaplane bases located in the north.

This area is singularly beautiful, rugged and productive. Single hook regulations are in effect on this river where long stretches of broken water form countless hiding places for big trout.

Additional information on the Gods River country can be obtained by contacting Manitoba Department of Tourism, 200 Vaughn St., Winnipeg, Manitoba.

Contact Canadian Government Office of Tourism, Ottawa, Ontario K1A 0H6 for fishing information anywhere in Canada. They have a wealth of information on trout fishing available and will be able to assist fishermen in determining where to go.

Ontario has several hotspots for big brook trout that have been overlooked by many fishermen. The Nipigon River is famous for having produced the world record brook trout. Other famous Ontario brook trout rivers are the Sutton and Albany. Unknown to many brook trout chasers are the Groundhog River north of Hearst and the Fawn River about 300 miles north of Sioux Lookout—big trout and a conspicuous lack of fishing pressure.

Record brook trout? Nobody knows but 4- to 6-pound brookies are possible and larger fish could be located. These rivers are for the fisherman willing to explore new water and try various methods to determine whether the fishing can be consistent or not.

Lake Nipigon, although heavily fished, probably has some of the biggest brookies left in Ontario. I've seen good stringers of fish averaging 5 and 6 pounds come from this lake. The lunker 7- to 10-pound fish are very scarce and only a handful of fish of this size will come from Ontario waters yearly.

Blue Lake west of Temiscaming, Quebec, still in Ontario waters, and Mashagama Lake north of Thessalon are probably two extraordinary brook trout lakes. Big brookies have been taken from Blue and Mashagama over the years and fishermen have a better than even chance of taking a trophy fish here.

Fishermen seeking brook trout information from Ontario should contact Sport Fisheries Branch, Ministry of Natural Resources, Parliament Buildings, Toronto M7A 1W3.

My favorite brook trout waters are in northern Quebec. I've fished some unnamed lakes 300 miles from Ottawa that are literally crawling with brookies in the 4- to 8-pound class. A friend of mine wrestled an 11-pound, 4-ounce brookie from an unnamed lake. Asked where the lake was, he shrugged and answered, "North of Ottawa." That, my friends, takes in a large chunk of spruce rimmed lakes and rivers.

My largest brook trout scaled an even 6½ pounds and fell to a well placed Dardevle. The lake, so small you have to hike overland for 3 miles, doesn't show on even the smallest contour maps. I managed to catch and release four others one day and all were over 4 pounds. Recently I went back and beaver cuttings had flooded one end of the lake and opened up the other end. The brookies were gone.

Quebec fishing information can be obtained by writing Ministry of Tourism, Fish and Game, Place de la Capitale, 150 Blvd. St. Cyrille E., Quebec City, P. Q. G1R 4Y1. Or contact Quebec Eskimo Indian Outfitters, P. O. Box 520, Rawdon, Quebec for information concerning the Kaniapiskau River.

The Minipi River watershed and Lake Ann Marie in Labrador may be *the* place to go for a shot at a record fish. Fish from this watershed are known to be the fastest growing brook trout in North America. Many trout have been found to increase their weight by a pound a year from the Minipi area.

Flyfishing only is the name of the game in the Minipi River area. Local lodge owners prevail upon sportsmen to keep only one trophy fish and return the others to the water. This type of philosophy will help insure future generations of sportsmen the opportunity to do battle with a white finned brookie.

There are several other hotspots for Labrador-Newfoundland brook trout fishing. For more information contact Department of Tourism, Confederation Building, St. John's, Newfoundland or Northern Labrador Camps (Minipi River), P. O. Box 8, Northwest River, Labrador.

The Far West has a touch of brook trout fishing that has been touched on by some of the outdoor magazines. Pine Lake in Wood Buffalo National Park, Alberta is home to some deep dwelling brook trout of enormous sizes.

Pine Lake is stocked with brook trout on a regular basis. Some brook trout in the 7- and 8-pound class have been taken from Pine and fishermen have located giant fish assumed to be of world record caliber.

This lake is located inside Wood Buffalo National Park and a special season license is needed. The lake can be driven to on the MacKenzie Highway via Fort Smith, Northwest Territories. Fort Smith lies right on the border between Alberta and Northwest Territories on Highway 5.

Additional information on Pine Lake can be obtained by writing Division of Fish & Wildlife, Natural Resources Building, Edmonton, Alberta T5K 2E1 or Superintendent, Wood Buffalo National Park, Fort Smith, Northwest Territories.

Knowing where brook trout reside is only part of the battle. You must still be able to catch them and therein lies the challenge.

Brook trout can be the most naive fish at times and the most bullheaded stubborn trout at others. I've seen times when schools of good sized specks would follow a lure for long distances just like a cantankerous musky and then sink to bottom without striking. A change of lure or lure color would result in another follow and another rejection. This maddening behavior can go on for days on end before the fish decide to strike. No one knows whether they follow out of boredom or whether they are feeding on something else and are merely curious.

All the follows and fishless days are forgotten when big specks go on the feed. I've watched half-acre patches of water churned to foam when brookies move into the shallows to feed. At times like this they are easily caught.

The largest brook trout grow that way due to a very rich diet and favorable water temperatures. Some of the trophy lakes I've fished are rich in freshwater shrimp and this diet results in pinkish-red flesh and trout almost as big around as they are long. These pot-bellied brookies are usually the largest specimens in an area and they grow to such chunky sizes by unlimited feeding.

Above— Pat Madigan unhooks a 5½-pound Quebec brook trout. Right—This angler reaches out for a big brookie from Quebec's Kaniapiskau River.

Fishing techniques vary considerably from river to lake. Many fishermen report excellent success on rivers with flies. Gods River and the Minipi are just two examples of this. Brightly colored wet flies and streamers are standard.

I've used steelhead flies such as the Skykomish Sunrise, Orange Comet, Golden Demon, Mickey Finn or any other brightly colored fly. Brookies seem to be attracted to the colors as much as the action of the fly.

Flies must be fished near the bottom and near some type of cover. Brook trout favor rocky areas and quiet slack-water areas just off the main current. Most of the strikes on flies will come as the fly swings around at the end of a drift. Try jiggling the fly after it completes its drift. This sometimes provokes a strike.

Rivers and lakes where spinning lures can be used show a decided preference for either Mepps spinners or small spoons such as the Devle Dog. The lure should be fished behind rocks or in deep pools along the edges of the current in a river. Brook trout often lay right at the edge of a rushing torrent of whitewater. Here they find easy picking from food washing downstream.

Lake fishing can be easy or difficult, depending on time of year and the lake. Many times brookies are in shallow water for a 2-week period after the ice goes out and then they go deep. I've picked up some brookies trolling in 25 to 30 feet of water.

An angler with an electronic water thermometer can home in on the 58-degree-water specks prefer during summer months. The fish will often be found in a compact school at a certain level. Once located, a good catch can occur.

I like ice-out fishing for quick action. Big slab-sided specks are in the shallows and you can often see the strike. In lakes conducive to the sport, I much prefer wading the shallows and casting. Not many Canadian lakes lend themselves to this type of sport. A sharp dropoff often occurs near shore and this precludes any but the shallowest wading.

The best bet is to quietly row an aluminum boat or canoe paralleling the dropoff. Stay outside of the shallows and cast in. I prefer a small wobbling spoon for this type of work. Copper colored spoons often produce exceptionally well in tannin-dyed waters.

Pay particular attention to fishing sharp points and quick rocky dropoffs. Experiment heavily with lure retrieves. One time I fished an unnamed trout lake and the only retrieve that worked was a cast, let it sink for a slow one-two-three count, give it a jerk for action, reel up the slack and repeat the sinking count again. The specks would strike just as I reeled up the slack line and as it settled. Nothing savage for strikes—the fish were just there. One scaled just an ounce over 6 pounds.

Trolling is an excellent method of taking brook trout from inland lakes. I like to troll a fairly long line behind the boat and I never use over 6-pound monofilament. Big brookies may be cannibals and they may have the reputation for being dumb but I treat 'em like other trophy trout; use the lightest possible tackle, keep the lure away from the boat and handle hooked fish gently.

One of my favorite trolling lures is a Williams Wobbler with the hooks removed. I attach a 12-inch length of mono and a small (No. 8) treble hook. Bait the hook with a nightcrawler and troll this behind the boat. Pump the rod tip occasionally to make the lure dart and weave. The 'crawler will be swinging along behind the lure and specks seem to really go for this combination.

Trophy brook trout are a very rare fish. Brookies cannot compete with other trout and survive to large sizes. They are a fish of northern waters, far removed from the pollution problems and people pressures of civilization. I hope I'll always be able to go to Canada and find an area where red-bellied brook trout fin lazily in rivers and lakes. Much more than that, I hope that fishing continues so my children will be able to enjoy remote areas as much as I have.

Our Favorite Fish Recipes

by THE AUTHORS

Charcoal broiled trout with wild rice stuffing is food fit for a king. Expose stuffing by carefully slicing along the lateral line of the trout.
(Walt Sandberg photo)

ALL SPECIES of trout represent the most delicately flavored fish available to sportsmen for home cooking, canning, shore lunches or cold snacks.

Since trout are so delicately flavored it doesn't take much to ruin some mighty fine eating. Proper steps must be taken to insure that the flavor is preserved from the time the trout leaves the lake or stream until it is prepared for the table.

Many trout, especially larger specimens, tend to be fatty and rather soft fleshed. The matter of only a few minutes time in warm weather or warm water can ruin a trout for eating.

The best precaution for keeping trout cool and fresh is to place them *on* ice. The fish should be dispatched promptly after landing and picture taking and then immediately placed in a chest type cooler. Be sure all ice water is drained out and lay the trout on the ice in a straight position. Curled or kinked trout, once cooled on ice, are devils to clean.

A trout should be cleaned as quickly as possible after landing to insure retaining its full flavor. The longer a trout nestles on ice, in a willow creel, or in the water, the less taste he'll have at meal time.

For smaller trout we prefer to gut and gill the fish and to leave the heads on. A decapitated trout may look slightly more appetizing in the frying pan but one with its head still attached is easier to cook and eat.

All entrails and gills should be removed and the stomach cavity rinsed with clean clear water and wiped dry with toweling. Make sure all of the so-called "blood vein" is removed during the cleaning process.

Larger trout, unless they are to be baked, are better filleted, skinned and boned. This removes all excess fat and leaves nothing but the finest portions of the fish. Fillets should be rinsed in cold water and refrigerated for use on the same day or promptly frozen for eating at a later date.

We'd like to point out one method of freezing trout that has proven to provide excellent eating. We save the quart and half-gallon paper milk containers, rinse them out thoroughly, cut the tops off and place fillets inside. Fill the containers up with water and freeze. Small trout will fit nicely in the quart containers while the larger fish go in the half-gallon sizes. Trout frozen in this manner are just as tasty in 6 months as when they were placed in the freezer.

Trout can be double wrapped in freezer paper if they are to be eaten within a week's time. Anything longer than this reduces the eventual taste of the trout. Fish that are to be kept for a long time should be frozen in clean water.

Before we delve into our favorite recipes, allow us to leave you with one final tip: *Do not overcook trout.* This merely ruins the taste of the fish because all the natural juices have been cooked out. Allow trout to be served fairly moist and flaky and you'll enjoy your trout eating much more.

BARBECUED TROUT

Ingredients:

1 to 1½ pounds of trout per person. Filleted and boned with skin left on.

1 Large bottle of Open Pit barbecue sauce

Minimum of 1 pound butter (not margarine)

1 can warm Budweiser beer for each jar of barbecue sauce
1 teaspoon garlic salt
2 tablespoons lemon juice per bottle of sauce
Salt and pepper to taste

Ready a glowing bed of charcoal while the barbecue sauce is prepared. Once the coals burn down lower the grill until it rests just above the heat. Cover the grill with Reynolds Wrap. Dip the fillets into the barbecue sauce and place skin side down onto the grill. As the surface barbecue sauce glazes (10- to 15-minutes) slide a spatula between the skin and meat and turn the fillet over onto the skin. Salt and pepper the fillets as they are being cooked. Baste the newly exposed flesh with barbecue sauce, salt and pepper and cook until done. Try adding Worcestershire or smoky barbecue sauce for a different taste treat.

George Richey

BEER BATTER BINGO

Fillet trout, size doesn't matter. Add two cups of Bisquick to a shallow pan. Add enough beer to the Bisquick to make a pancake-like batter. Add salt and pepper and one well-beaten egg to the batter. Salt and pepper the fillets to taste.

Add 2 inches of vegetable oil or Planter's Peanut Oil to a deep fry pan. Heat until it is crackling hot. Plenty of oil insures a crisp brown crust. Add fillets to the hot grease after they've been coated thoroughly with the batter. Cook about 5 minutes per side or until the fillets take on a delicious golden brown crust. The meat should be flaky and moist. Prevent overcooking. Serve piping hot with streamside watercress, steaming biscuits and mugs full of frigid beer.

Charles J. Farmer

POCONO MOUNTAINS BREAKFAST TROUT

Save one or two breakfast sized trout per person. Keep cool or refrigerated at night. Coat the small trout with flour, salt and pepper to taste and fry in butter over a hot fire. Serve with hot coffee and biscuits smothered in honey. Simple but good.

S. R. Slaymaker II

TANGY TROUT

Cut a 3- to 6-pound trout into 1-inch steaks. Lay the pieces in a shallow pan early in the day and pour lemon juice over them. The lemon juice needn't cover the pieces entirely but they should be turned occasionally while soaking. Refrigerate at least 2 hours.

Mix a batter from two large eggs, 1½ cups of evaporated milk and 1 teaspoon each of salt and pepper (add more of each for larger sized fish).

Remove the trout from the refrigerator and dip into the batter. Carefully coat each piece with finely crushed bread crumbs. Deep fry for about 7 minutes or until a deep, golden brown. The lemon juice adds a slightly tangy flavor to the trout. No tartar sauce is needed with this recipe.

Thomas E. Huggler

POACHED TROUT IN WINE

Nestle one 2-pound trout in a bed of aluminum foil. Bathe the trout with ½-cup dry, pink or white wine (rosé or chablis is my favorite). Place two pads of butter inside the cavity, two on top of the fish and season to taste. Garnish with sliced tomato, sliced green pepper and sautéed mushrooms (morels are best).

Seal the package and fork the top of the foil to allow for escaping steam. Bury the trout in coals and cook for approximately 20 minutes (more or less depending on heat). The

A husky brown trout such as this must be properly cared for to insure being fit for table use. Prompt cleaning and icing is important to insure full flavor.

Left—Pan fried potatoes and trout are the makings of a great shore lunch.

Below—David Richey, editor of TROUT FISHERMEN'S DIGEST, prepares scrumptious eating by cooking trout in a fish boil. The finished product tastes just like lobster. Delicious!

Left—Guide Charley Hamelin of Branson's Lodge on Great Bear Lake knows what pleases the appetite of hungry fishermen. Here he prepares a shorelunch of pan fried lake trout cooked slowly in butter.

This backpacker's meal of fresh-caught trout panfried over embers is mouth watering indeed. *(Walt Sandberg photo)*

fish will be done when the flesh is very moist yet flakes free of the bone when teased with a fork.

Norman Strung

GREAT LAKES FISH BOIL

One pound of steaked lake trout, steelhead or brown trout per person. Leave skin on the steaks. One whole peeled onion per person is optional. Two cups salt and drawn butter, parsley and lemon complete the list of ingredients. A Leyse 12½-quart Trout Kettle is needed for proper fish boiling.

Heat potatoes in 8 quarts of water and bring to a boil. Cover with the kettle vents open. When water begins to boil add 1 cup salt and onions. Timing begins when water starts to boil again. Boil potatoes for 20 minutes. Regulate the heat to produce a steady roll action boil with the kettle vents open.

After the potatoes have boiled place the fish steaks in a basket and lower into the boiling water above the potatoes. Add 1 cup salt, cover and boil the fish for about 12 minutes. Spear a potato with a fork to check for softness. The fish is cooked when it can be flaked with a fork. Make sure the water doesn't lose its rolling while the fish and potatoes are cooking, otherwise they may absorb some of the salt. Remove the fish, drain off the potato water and serve with drawn butter, parsley and lemon. Coleslaw, pickles, garlic bread, sour cream and pie add delightful touches to a fish boil. Any potatoes left over should be saved for a breakfast of American Fries.

David Richey

TO POACH A CUTTHROAT

Fillet cutthroats and cut fillets into serving portions. Fill a roasting pan with about 2 quarts of water. Add a dash of lemon; chopped celery; grated onion; 2 drops olive oil; and salt and pepper and bring the water to a boil.

Add the fillets, reduce the heat to simmer and cook about 20 minutes or until the fish flakes easily with a fork. Cool the trout, remove it from its stock and drain on paper toweling. Place in refrigerator until cold. Serve with leaves of fresh lime or any commercially prepared fish sauce. This recipe makes a tremendous appetizer before the main course or as a complete meal in itself when served with young, tender dandelion shoots or sautéed, fresh woodland morel mushrooms. A chilled white wine compliments the poaching feast.

Kathleen Farmer

STUFFED GRILLED TROUT

Ingredients:
One 6-ounce box Uncle Ben's Brown & Wild Rice
One 6-ounce box Uncle Ben's Long Grain & Wild Rice
½-pound wild rice
One 6-inch length hard Polish sausage, diced

Foil fish with vegetables is a delicacy when cooked slowly over charcoal. *(Walt Sandberg photo)*

One small onion, chopped
Two chopped celery stalks
One small chopped green pepper
½-lemon, grated
One 4-ounce can mushroom pieces
Two teaspoons parsley flakes

Prepare rice according to directions and combine in a large mixing bowl and allow to cool. Fry the diced sausage. Sauté chopped onion, celery and green pepper in sausage drippings. Add mushrooms and grated lemon and combine with the rice and mix well.

Wipe the body cavity of a large trout dry and dust lightly with salt and pepper on both inside and outside. Make a ball of aluminum foil and pack inside mouth and gill cavity. String heavy thread on a large sharp darning needle. Begin stuffing body cavity and sew as the cavity is filled up. Begin stuffing at the tail end and work toward the head. Use double thread and tie firmly around the head. The stuffed trout is ready for the grill. Extra stuffing can be heated and served as a side dish or frozen for later use.

Lay the stuffed trout on a sheet of heavy duty aluminum foil. Place belly up at least 6 inches above the coals on the grill. Wedge sides of fish to hold in an upright position with the back toward the coals. *Do not* grill on the sides. Allow 45 minutes per pound grilling time. Meat is done when a finger can be pushed into the meat near the backbone and the finger leaves an indentation.

Garnish the trout with endive sprigs, parsley, carrot curls, lemon and orange slices or olives. For an added decorative touch, place a brightly colored lure or fly in the corner of the mouth before serving. To serve, slit the side of the fish to expose stuffing. Spoon a serving of stuffing with each piece of trout. This makes fantastic eating.

Walt Sandberg

NEXT-DAY TROUT

Broil trout or fast smoke-cook them over the coals of a hardwood fire. A home smoker will do fine.

Refrigerate the trout in a closed plastic container where they'll last for several weeks depending on the amount of smoking.

When ready to eat, mix mayonnaise and mustard in a bowl to make a spicy but smooth sauce. Break the trout from the bone and place the pieces onto a bed of lettuce. Squeeze fresh lemon or lime over the trout. Dip the pieces into the sauce and eat cold in company with very frosty, dry white wine or beer.

Jerry Gibbs

FOIL TROUT WITH VEGETABLES

Place single layers of filleted trout (1 pound per person) on a large piece of heavy duty aluminum foil. Cover with a couple tablespoons of cooking oil per package. Place a layer of chopped celery, green pepper, onions, and thin slices of tomatoes across the top of the fillet. Salt and pepper to taste and add 2 teaspoons of butter or tabasco sauce

Trout, stuffed with wild rice, is shown being sewed closed with darning needle and thread. *(Walt Sandberg photo)*

for extra seasoning. Fold the foil to seal in the juices. Punch several holes in the top of the foil to allow steam to escape. Cook over a medium-hot charcoal grill for about 30 minutes. This is a quick tasty method of preparing trout and vegetables together that doesn't leave a lot of dirty dishes for the cook to clean up later.

John Davey

PICKLED TROUT

Cut about 10 pounds of trout into individual serving portions. Wash in cold water, drain and cover thoroughly with fine salt. Rinse the salt off after ½-hour and simmer the trout until done. Place the warm fish in a crock and cover with a spiced vinegar sauce made from the following ingredients:

1 quart distilled vinegar
1 quart water
½-cup olive oil
1 cup sliced onions
1 tablespoon white pepper
1 tablespoon mustard seed
½-tablespoon bay leaves
½-tablespoon cloves
1 tablespoon black peppers

Cook the onions in olive oil until they are soft and yellow. Add the rest of the ingredients and simmer gently for 45 minutes. Allow the sauce to cool and pour over the fish until all pieces are completely covered. Allow to stand in the pickling solution for 24 hours before eating. This makes a delicious cold snack.

Richard Johnson

DEEP FRYED TROUT

Select a minimum of 1 pound of filleted, skinned and boned brook, brown, cutthroat, rainbow or lake trout per person. Other ingredients are one box of Golden Dipt seafood coating mixture, salt and pepper and one large bottle Planter's Peanut Oil.

Cut the filleted pieces into 1-inch square cubes and pat dry with paper toweling. Salt and pepper each fish cube to taste. Place the fish in a small plastic bag containing Golden Dipt and shake until all sides are thoroughly covered. Fill an electric fry pan with peanut oil and heat until the oil smokes slightly. Back the heat off just a little (about 400 degrees is about right). Use enough oil to completely submerge the fish. Cook until golden brown. Small pieces like this are two-bite size and cook within 5 minutes. Serve with baked beans, french fries and cold slaw.

Rich Lawrence

Cooking fish can be a rewarding experience for trout fishermen whether they do it in the comfort of a well equipped kitchen or over an open fire. Nothing can top the taste of a properly cooked fresh-caught trout.

Try one of these trout recipes for a taste treat you won't soon forget.

Cutthroats—Big Game Fish of the West

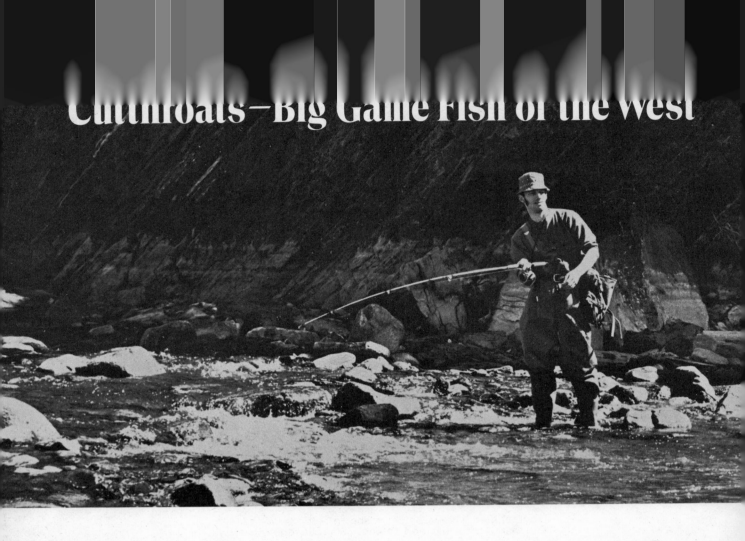

THE WORLD record cutthroat trout was caught by John Skimmerhorn in 1925 from Pyramid Lake in Nevada. The fish weighed 41 pounds and measured 39 inches in length. This fact supports the title of the article. Cutthroats are the big game fish of the West. Big in size, without a doubt. But even "bigger" in popularity.

The cutthroat is native to the West and it is not found in any significant numbers in waters east of the Rocky Mountains. The fish has a wider natural range than other trout. It can be found from northern Mexico to southern Alaska. Generally speaking, good cutthroat fishing can be found in Idaho, Utah, Montana, Wyoming, Oregon, Nevada, New Mexico, California, Colorado and the Canadian provinces of Alberta and British Columbia. Some of the most famous cutthroat waters are in Wyoming and Colorado and even under the influence of increasing fishing pressure and encroaching "progress" some waters have held their own.

Possibly the two most well-known cutthroat fisheries are the Snake River and Yellowstone Lake in northwestern Wyoming. Without supplemental stocking, those two waters have produced quality "wild" trout fishing for quite a spell. Yellowstone Lake, in Yellowstone National Park, could very well have the best cutthroat fishing in the United States. However, a new regulation initiated by the National Park Service for Yellowstone Lake requires that anglers return all cutthroats to the water that are 13 inches or *larger*. Supposedly the basis for such a ruling is that the larger fish are the spawners and that releasing them will prevent those fish from being harvested. Most fishery biologists agree however, that when trout reach spawning age and size their days are numbered anyway. And spawners are especially vulnerable to unhooking and handling by anglers in the releasing process.

Having fished Yellowstone Lake thoroughly with good, consistent success, I can only say that most fish caught average 17 to 19 inches with slender bodies and heads too big for those bodies. Yes, there is definite evidence of stunting and need of *more* harvest of larger fish. All of which contradicts the reasoning behind the new Park Service ruling.

That portion of the Snake River north and south of the town of Jackson Hole, Wyoming once produced the finest fishing imaginable. The river still produces fair to good angling success. But the Army Corps of Engineers has done its part to hurt the fishing. To protect valuable, private bottomland along the river, the Corps built and maintains dikes along the river. The dikes have shut off feeder streams that were once used for spawning by cutthroats. The channelization effect caused by the dikes has also washed away protective islands and peninsulas that once held valuable trout resting and feeding areas. Unfortunately the end of diking is not in sight and at this writing more dikes are planned for the Snake and more spawning areas will be eliminated.

Not all is gloomy for cutthroat anglers however. State Game and Fish Departments have worked reasonably hard to maintain "pure" cutthroat strains in native waters. Strict regulations against "importing" and using minnows not native to those cutthroat waters are enforced. And exotic

by CHARLES J. FARMER

Betty Price lands "average-sized" Yellowstone Lake cutthroat of 19 inches.

species like rainbows, browns and brookies have been prohibited from mixing with cutthroats. It has been found that other trout species tend to dominate and eventually wipe out native cutthroat populations. And in the past, some conservation agencies have made the serious mistake of indiscriminate and thoughtless stocking programs. Today however, the remaining pure strain cutthroat fisheries are carefully guarded for the most part.

Techniques for River Cutthroats

If, by some strange reason, I was obliged to choose two months of the year to concentrate on river cutthroats, May and August would be my choices. Why?

May *can* be a magic month in the West. For anglers, myself included, it is that delicious time before heavy run-off when fish and fishermen alike feel the first soothing rays of spring. Cutthroats are hungry.

In August, the rivers have usually recuperated from the annual infection of high, cocoa-colored water. Streams are clear and at moderate level. Not too clear or too low. Insect hatches are in full swing and summer weather is as stable as it will ever be. Fly fishing is at its peak.

I used to recommend September and October as the best months for stream cutthroats but now I feel the majority of anglers spook more fish than they catch in ultra-clear, puddle-deep waters. Granted, fall fishing can be pleasant and rewarding but August is the best in the West.

There's a good variety of small, wadable streams to choose

Cutthroats are notorious "ice out" feeders. An open patch of water, usually in a cove, draws hungry fish and casting from shore to open water gets results.

from in the spring, but efforts should be concentrated mainly below riffles in deep holes. May water temperatures keep cutts congregated at those spots. Work the lairs with fast sinking spinners or spoons. Cutthroats are partial to silver bladed spinners in the No. 1 or 2 sizes. Spoons, 2 to 3 inches long, should be as heavy as possible. If they can't be worked deep, they won't work. Silver and brass works well. But old time "cutters" will tell you that nothing beats yellow spoons with black dots for May fish. And I agree.

The best way to fish for spring cutthroats is to float for them. I like a rubber boat best for early season. It keeps me going at a fishable pace and lessens the chance of a spring swim that could literally shock the life out of a fisherman.

Guides in the Jackson Hole area say that the fishermen who consistently put their baits within a foot of the bank will catch the most fish. Nothing could be truer. The red-throated trout hangs tight to the bank in holes below riffles; in back eddies and under protruding logs and rocks.

There are three successful ways to fish for early trout. The bait method features dead minnows, nightcrawlers or worms dangled enticingly from a dropper rig. Tie a loop in the end of the line. To this loop, clamp a heavy enough split shot so the bait can be fished along the bottom of deep holes. About a foot above the shot, tie a dropper (with a slightly stiffer monofilament) about 7 inches long. Number 8 or 10 bait hooks are about the right size. Tie the hook to the dropper.

The dropper rig is ideal for floating and correctly working deep holes. Cast about 10 feet ahead (or upstream) of the hole as you float. Keep the line tight and allow shot and bait to bounce along the bottom. Hold the bait deep through the length of the hole and your chances are excellent of picking up a fish. You will encounter plenty of snags when bottom fishing

River floating is often best technique, but casters must get baits within a foot of bank and obstructions.

Author feels that May and August are the best months to concentrate on river cutthroats.

Best fly fishing for cutthroats is in August in the Rockies.

Open coves in May can prove to be hotspots.

the proper way but chances are you will lose only the split shot.

As far as the effectiveness of certain types of bait go, I can only say that cutthroat streams vary, with worms producing best in some and minnows in others. Do some experimenting on your own. If the water is slightly off-color and rising and the dropper rig is not working, tie a spinner-bait rig directly to your line. Silver spinners with red beads will often draw cutthroats to the bait in high, cloudy water.

A good, floating rig for minnows consists of two hooks—the smaller (about a No. 12) lead hook goes through the minnow's snout and the larger (No. 8 or 10) is hooked just below the dorsal fin. This arrangement keeps the bait on in heavy water and hooks ''tail-biters.''

When using garden worms or nightcrawlers, thread the hook once through the collar. Water current will give a worm hooked in this manner a natural, inviting appearance.

When fly fishing, there are two consistent ways of taking May cutts. One of them, ironically, consists of delicate dry fly techniques. And the other makes use of fast sinking caddis and stonefly imitation nymphs.

There are often good ''snowfly'' hatches on the water in May. The warmest part of the day, usually from noon until three, often produces the best hatches of these tiny, ⅛-inch long, black insects. An imitation that works with regularity during the hatch is a Black Midge tied on a Mustad 7957B hook in sizes ranging from 18 to 22. The body of the fly is make from three strands of black ostrich herl and the hackle is black neck. A simple pattern to tie, the Black Midge is dynamite in May.

Nymphs, such as caddis and stonefly imitations can be weighted or fished with fast-sinking fly lines. The best looking nymph patterns in the world won't work in May unless they are fished near the bottom.

When lure fishing, cast upstream of the hole, count to three and retrieve the lure about midway through deep water. Successful early season cutthroaters fish spoons and spinners as deep as they can through a hole and in back eddies. There are

Surface feeding cutts are easily put down on calm lake water. A small boat or canoe for working the coves makes for fine fishing.

Above and left—The cutthroat is native to the West—it's not found in any significant numbers east of the Rocky Mountains.

Below—Cutthroat fly tiers specialize in weighted stonefly nymphs for spring.

times when a split shot or two above the lure will be needed to take it deep.

Lake Fishing Techniques

Cutthroats are notorious "ice out" feeders. If a fisherman can time his action right, usually in May and June in the Rocky Mountain states, the hottest fishing of the season can be enjoyed. Good timing is vital for the success of an early season trip.

From the first football field-size hole in the ice to an open "pond" of water, the cutthroat feeding switch is usually turned on. I never cease to be amazed how an open patch of water, usually in a cove, can turn out so many fish. Uncovering the ice lid does the job. Cutts usually lay thick in open areas. Casting from shore to open water gets results. And sliding a lure off the ice into open water; letting it sink to the bottom and retrieving with a rapid, jerking motion is a consistent producer.

As the ice recedes and the open patch gets bigger, cutthroat fishermen follow the ice in a canoe or small boat. Action remains hot with yellow-black combination spoons, fished deep, working best. When ice disappears from a cove or inlet, the action often ceases as abruptly as if someone had thrown a switch. Cutthroats move out of the coves and scatter into deeper waters. Feeder stream spawning, feed, sunlight and oxygen draws them in open water coves in the first place.

After the May-June ice-out surge fishing drops off somewhat. Trollers, using "pop-gear," "cow-bells" or "Christmas lights" (a long, relatively heavy string of spinners, flashers and beads to which a lure or bait is attached), continue to get results off points and drop-offs. Shore casters have scattered results using still fishing methods with worms, cheese and marshmallows.

From mid-July to October fishing usually picks up again. I concentrate on late afternoon and early evening fishing in the coves. Good hatches of mayflies and mosquitoes come off the quiet water in the coves and a fly fisherman can do well.

Surface feeding cutts are easily put down on calm lake water so long fly rod casts or spin fishing with fly and bubble usually get best results. A small boat or canoe for working the coves makes for fine fishing. And walking and wading the coves can also be effective.

When using a bubble with spin gear, tie on a 4-pound, 12-foot leader below the bubble. The longer leader will be harder to cast than shorter ones, but it often makes the difference in a good, fly presentation. Fill the bubble with enough water weight to reach feeding fish and experiment with slow, jerky, fast and stop-and-go retrieves.

Good fly patterns for summer cove fishing are brown No. 12 and 14 Wooly Worms; No. 16 and 18 gray and black gnats and mosquitoes; No. 16 brown and black midges; mayfly imitations; grasshopper patterns (in August), fresh water shrimp and nymph imitations.

As cooler weather sets in and hatches start thinning out in September, switch to silver, brass and yellow-black combination spoons. Work deep coves and gravel bars off the points. In October, drift fishing a nightcrawler behind a spinner-bait rig is a good way to stock up on some big fish for the long winter ahead.

I have yet to catch a cutt through the ice. They are relatively dormant under the ice, although I'm sure a few fish have fallen to winter tactics.

The cutthroat is a real cowboy. He likes the West and its deep, pure lakes and streams. Some call him finicky . . . temperamental, which he is at times. But Rocky Mountaineers are proud of their native. And those anglers east of the rockies seem to admire the spirit of that western roughneck.

Spin fishermen do well with spoons and spinners worked deep.

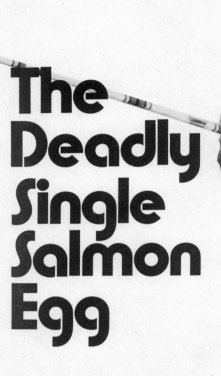

The Deadly Single Salmon Egg

by STEVE WILSON

A FLAT pale-yellow sun hung low and sullen in the October sky as Gary Marshall and I joined the line of rivermouth fishermen off Michigan's Thompson Creek. Twenty-five men, women and children stood shoulder to shoulder in knee-deep water and cast to the mouth of the yard-wide stream.

Gary nodded recognition to a familiar face as we baited up with his processed single salmon eggs. He chummed a small handful of eggs 10 yards out in the hole, gave them time to settle and made his first cast. There were muted mutterings up and down the line about the slow fishing.

I followed Gary's example and my single salmon egg made a dainty dimple on Lake Michigan's surface as the bait plopped into the water. Ten seconds later, an unseen fish scooped the egg off bottom, felt the pin-prick of a No. 14 single hook and raced south across the lake's surface with his back out of water.

Six-pound mono melted off my spool as the fish made a panicked sprint for freedom. The 100-yard dash ended with a tumbling gill-rattling leap that revealed a broad gleaming flank. A shorter run parallel to shore forced me to stumble down the shoreline in an attempt to stay in contact with the headstrong fish.

Twenty minutes later and a ¼-mile down the shoreline, I slid the net under a mint silver 9-pound rainbow. Gary had landed two smaller fish, a 6-pound rainbow and an 8-pound brown, while I tussled with my first rivermouth rainbow. It was an exciting introduction to the thrilling Great Lakes sport of rivermouth fishing with single salmon eggs. We finished the day with nine fish and a mixed bag of steelhead (rainbow trout) and brown trout.

Single egg fishing at river mouths is a relatively new sport in the Great Lakes area and so far too few anglers have learned just how productive and thrilling the sport can be. Catching trout from a rivermouth hole can be a demanding sport in which proper fishing techniques are extremely important.

Baitfishing is by far the most productive fishing technique for trout during the October through December and April and May months. The premise is that trout will be feeding

This fisherman scored on a big brown trout by fishing along the shoreline. Gorgeous browns like this big male are commonplace catches for single egg fishermen.

Rivermouths such as this are great gathering spots for trout during spring and fall months.

on free-drifting eggs from fall spawning coho and chinook salmon or spring spawning steelhead. Single salmon eggs is the preferred bait during this period since it most closely matches what the fish are actively feeding on.

Gary Marshall of East Lansing, Michigan is the producer of a brand of salmon eggs called Egg Eze. He markets eggs in various colors, odors and consistencies to match the fishing conditions. Another large producer of single eggs is Uncle Josh.

Favorite colors of eggs are natural (clear), red, orange, yellow, pink, brown and orangish-brown. Odors play an important role in single-egg fishing because feeding trout and salmon home in on strange smells. Garlic and cheese flavored eggs are steady producers.

Rivermouth fishermen commonly select dark colored eggs on dark days or when fishing dirty water (after a rain or wind storm) and clear or brightly colored eggs on bright clear days. A natural colored egg is a good choice when fishing calm waters. Fluorescent colored or red eggs are good on overcast days.

Single salmon eggs must possess a good milking action in the water. Once the egg is pierced by the hook it should slowly release a steady stream of natural or artificial (such as garlic or cheese) juice and odor into the water which will attract feeding fish. This juice, odor and color combination is the key to successful single egg fishing. Eggs should be changed every 3 or 4 minutes and fresh eggs kept on the hook at all times. It takes only 4 or 5 minutes for an egg to completely milk out.

Much of the skill in single-egg rivermouth fishing lies in

This angler has found hot trout action in the fast water where it empties into the lake.

one's ability to read the water. A rivermouth will have one hotspot where rainbows, browns, and lake trout pile up before migrating upstream. Some rivers, such as Thompson Creek, have such a small trickle of water flowing that the current isn't strong enough to cut a noticeable hole where the river enters the lake. In areas such as this the fish may be found anywhere nearby although trout will often congregate within 200 or 300 yards of the river mouth.

Rivermouth fishing attracts the gregarious type of fisherman with many women and children joining the men, especially on weekends. Find a hot rivermouth and you'll find fishermen stacked in as thickly as hatchery trout at feeding time. This is normally the easiest method of determining where to fish. Politely elbow your way into the line, cast out with an eye to avoiding your neighbor's line

and you're in business. Rivermouth fishermen have come to accept close fishing conditions and consider it part of the game.

A lucky fisherman, upon hooking a trout or salmon, yells "Fish on!" and nearby fishermen will reel in to give him a chance to land his fish. Etiquette demands you try to work your trout away from the fishing line which will allow others a chance to fish while you play your catch.

Isolated rivermouths (there are many around the Great Lakes) are often better fish producers than the more noted areas merely because they do not receive the concentrated fishing pressure.

A location is found at every rivermouth where the river current mixes with the incoming wave action of the lake and creates either a small rip or a deep hole. Holes are more

Dusk is a great time for the single egg fisherman to catch trout.

prevalent at mouths of larger rivers, while rips occur only where violent wave action confronts the river current.

The mixing action of river and lake water can be turbulent and trout and salmon will seldom lie in such heavy water. Look next to the rip for quiet eddies where twisting currents wash drifting salmon eggs around before they settle to the bottom. Look for pockets of eddy water on both sides of a rip or along the edges of the river current. Small areas of quiet water, near the river flow, often harbor trout or pre-spawning salmon and are great spots to fish.

Some rivermouths have distinct holes or pools where out-flowing river currents empty into the lake. A sharp dropoff into deep water is usually located nearby and the edges of these dropoffs are hot-spots to fish. Trout will lie along the edges of dropoffs and pick off free-drifting eggs as they wash over the sand or gravel bar and into deep water.

Finding the exact place where trout lay off a rivermouth can present an exciting challenge to a fisherman. Many rivermouths change daily due to wind and wave conditions and this factor must be dealt with. I've watched Gary Marshall study a rivermouth, the outflowing current and the lake's wave action for 10 or 15 minutes before he selects the hottest location. He's seldom wrong in his choice of where to fish.

"I look for fairly deep water, about 5 to 8 feet, just off the main flow of river current. Trout and salmon will not lie in the full thrust of the current but will take up feeding stations in quieter water. Look for quiet swirling eddies and pockets of slow moving water where the river current will carry food to the waiting fish," Marshall said.

Migrating trout will often follow a shoreline as they move toward a rivermouth to feed. This feeding migration route and depth is important for fishermen to consider if actual rivermouth fishing isn't producing.

These fish will follow a shoreline in 5 to 10 feet of water and this route will parallel the first minor dropoff into deep water. Locate the first dropoff and cruising trout will normally be found somewhere along the ledge. Once the proper depth has been found, cast bait or lures into the area and keep trying new spots. The fish are constantly moving and if you can determine which direction they are heading, it is possible to catch a fish, stringer it quickly, move on down the shoreline and intercept the migrating school several times before they spook into deeper water.

Rivermouth fishermen often select long buggy-whip rods (8½ to 11 feet) to help cushion the shock of large fish on light line. Four- to 6-pound mono is entirely adequate for big trout as long as the reel has a smooth nonstick drag system and a large line capacity to cope with headlong runs of 100 to 200 yards.

Two methods of rivermouth fishing produce and both involve bait fishing. Possibly the most effective method is the moving bait technique. All bait fishing is done with a No. 12 or 14 single hook knotted to the light line. Use just enough split shot (one or two BB-size shot) to take the single eggs to bottom. Long distance casts aren't needed and the majority of fish will be caught within 10 yards of the angler.

One or two single salmon eggs are rolled onto the hook. Do not hook the eggs through the "eye" or they will milk out quickly. If the hook is very small use only one egg and completely immerse the hook in the egg. An alternative is to slide the first egg up the hook shank and onto the line before sliding a second egg into position on the hook. There are times when two eggs will out-perform a single egg.

Lob cast the egg-baited hook out in a smooth overhand or sidearm cast and allow it to sink to bottom. This is where learning how to read the rivermouth pays off in knowing where to cast. Slowly raise the rod tip and gently inch the

Right—Two big rainbows and a heavily spotted brown trout made quite a catch for this fisherman.

Below—Favorite egg colors are natural (clear), red, orange, yellow, pink, brown and orangish-brown. Odors play an important role in single-egg fishing with garlic and cheese flavored eggs as steady producers.

egg toward you. Don't hurry the retrieve. Drop the rod tip and reel up slack line and then inch the egg again with a gentle lift of the rod tip.

Move the bait about 6 inches each time and then allow it to lie motionless on bottom for several seconds. Steelhead and brown trout will normally savage the bait although they will occasionally just mouth the eggs gently.

Still fishing with eggs is the most common method seen at rivermouths as anglers stand knee-deep to hip-deep in cold autumn water and wait for cruising fish to come to them. The same tackle, with one exception, is used and the eggs are allowed to remain motionless on the lake's bottom. This technique involves the use of a very small egg sinker, a small barrel swivel and the hook. The line from the rod is placed through the sinker and tied to one end of the swivel. The swivel prevents line twist and keeps the sinker from sliding down onto the hook. An 18-inch leader is tied to the other end of the swivel and down to the hook.

The stillfisherman lob casts his bait out as far as possible —while still paying attention to fish holding spots in the rivermouth, and keeps a tight line as the bait settles to bottom. Some fishermen use sandspikes with rodholders to

Much of the skill in single-egg rivermouth fishing lies in one's ability to read the water.

hold one egg-baited hook while they cast with another rod.

A stillfisherman will take the anti-reverse off his spinning reel and this allows the fish to pick up the bait and swim off without feeling any resistance. The line flows off the reel and through the egg sinker without any telltale drag.

A trick some fishermen use is to wrap a small rubber band around the rod handle above the reel. Once the bait is in the proper location they reel up slack line, open the bail and lightly place a loop of monofilament under the rubber band. A fish will grab the bait, pull the loop out of the rubber band and swim off to feed on the eggs. This gives the angler enough slack line to reach his rod, close the bail and set the hook.

Chumming is an effective method when rivermouth fishing to bring trout and salmon to your area. Many fishermen feel that chumming involves tossing out large amounts of salmon eggs. This type of chumming defeats your purpose. Throw just enough eggs (a ½-dozen is plenty) to stimulate the fish's feeding reaction. Give chummed eggs plenty of time to drift to bottom and attract cruising fish. In clear water you can often spot trout and salmon flashing as they dart in for a free meal.

Cast in the immediate vicinity of the chummed eggs and chances are good a fish will be there to suck in your offering. Chumming is usually done about once every 15 or 20 minutes or whenever the fishing action slows down.

Migrating trout can often be pinpointed because of their tendency to porpoise as they move up and down the shoreline. Anglers alert to this habit can often intercept a school of moving fish as it homes in on the rivermouth.

Michigan has a host of rivermouths that annually attract hordes of trout and salmon during the fall and early winter months of October through December. The Upper Peninsula has several hotspots such as Thompson Creek and the Manistique River near Manistique, Carp River near St. Ignace, Cedar River and Ford River near Escanaba, Two Hearted River north of Newberry, and the Presque Isle River near Ironwood.

The Lower Peninsula attracts schools of fish to both Lake Michigan and Lake Huron rivermouths. Hotspots are: Ocqueoc River near Rogers City, Thunder Bay River near Alpena, AuSable River at Oscoda, Tawas River at Tawas City, East Branch of the AuGres River near Alabaster, and harbor mouths at Caseville, Grindstone City, Port Hope, Harbor Beach and Port Sanilac, all along the Lake Huron shoreline.

Lake Michigan rivermouth hotspots are: Bear River at Petoskey, the outlet of Lake Charlevoix at Charlevoix, Elk River at Elk Rapids, Boardman River at Traverse City, Platte River near Honor, Betsie River near Elberta, Manistee River at Manistee, Muskegon River at Muskegon, Pere Marquette River at Ludington, Black River at South Haven and the St. Joseph River at Benton Harbor-St. Joseph.

Many areas of Wisconsin and Minnesota host excellent rivermouth fishing where single-egg fishermen can find hot action. The best advice would be to check with your local Department of Natural Resources for a list of hot rivermouths.

Rivermouth fishing is the hottest new sport available to Great Lakes fishermen. Nowhere else can a fisherman take his choice of either fishing in seclusion or standing shoulder to shoulder with other fishermen and catch a mixed bag of trout and salmon.

The fishing is hot and promises to be hotter this fall as more trout and salmon are planted in Michigan waters. Maybe I'll see you in some remote rivermouth. If I do, I hope you've got a big bend in your rod and are willing to share your rivermouth with a friend.

Tennessee's Three Routes to Trout

by H. LEA LAWRENCE

LESS THAN A mile above Chilhowee Shoals Landing on the Little Tennessee River is a brown trout that is longer than your leg.

This sounds like an ordinary "lunker tale" at the outset, so just to take it out of that category right away, let's add another segment.

In the general vicinity of this fish, there are several more browns that have hip-to-toe proportions. There is no way to know how many more of the huge fish populate the entire 33-mile free-flowing portion of the river.

There's no doubt that this is a spectacular introduction to trout fishing in Tennessee, but it's a valid indication that there's something worthwhile seeking in the state's waters. What you've read so far is only a small (how about "big?") example of the offering. There are three routes to trout in the state; this is just the beginning.

Since the Little Tennessee—called the "Little T" by those who fish it—is on your mind, I'll start with it, because this one river has enough trout potential to drive any angler wild. Too, there's a particular reason why it should be at the top of your list.

The section of the Little T that extends from Chilhowee Dam to its confluence with the Tennessee River is the most sensational big trout water in the eastern United States. It is a good-size river, perfect for float fishing, and it has a fantastically large population of brown and rainbow trout. I've mentioned big browns, but there are also rainbows in the Little T that range up toward the 15-pound level. Fish between the 5- and 10-pound mark aren't at all uncommon; in fact, the locals don't bother bragging about trout this size.

From a fisherman's standpoint, the river provides a setting where any kind of tackle can be employed, all the way from ultra-light fly rods and spinning gear to heavy casting tackle with floating-diving plugs with three sets of treble hooks. A tiny dry fly is just as much at home.

By the same token, because the water level fluctuates due to generating schedules at the upstream dams, there are times when a fly fisherman can wade and cast to pools that are bigger than a football field. An evening hatch on one of these expanses of water resembles the same effect produced by a summer shower. When the water level is up, casting from a boat can be equally as exciting.

You do not want to put off fishing the Little T, however, because unless congressional action intervenes, a Tennessee Valley Authority dam will impound the full length of this river—all 33 miles—and it will be lost forever. This is scheduled to take place within the next couple of years, at which time this fabulous stretch of water will be transformed into another warm water impoundment, and a place of the sort that fulfills trout fishermen's dreams will become only a memory.

The thing to remember, though, is that it isn't gone yet, so

Float fishing in the Little T puts an angler within reach of the trophy trout this fabulous river holds.

here's how to take advantage of the opportunity:

U.S. 129, which branches off U.S. 411 South of Maryville, is the best route to the upper reaches. Full float trip facilities are available at Chilhowee Shoals Landing, and there are also sites for tent campers and RVs there. Grocery stores in the vicinity handle all normal supplies. Motel accommodations are limited, but there are plenty along U.S. 411, and there are excellent restaurants there, too.

Suggestion: The most satisfying way to fish the Little T is to float from Chilhowee Shoals to the U.S. 411 bridge, a trip that requires less than half a day if the normal generating schedule is in effect; if the water is off, it will take longer. Boat and motor rentals are available, as well as a pick-up service. Guides can be obtained, although an experienced boater will have no difficulty navigating the river.

As terrific as the Little T is, it is only one of the tailwaters in Tennessee that produce trophy fish; in fact, there are enough others in the eastern part of the state alone to keep an angler busy for a long time.

For example, the Hiwassee River, which is South from the Little T, and which is also crossed by U.S. 411, is a magnificent stretch of water that provides top brown and rainbow fishing. It also affords the same type scenic beauty, but while it can be floated when the water level is high, low water makes it tougher and trickier. This same condition, though, is what makes it an ideal fly fishing stream, and those who prefer this kind of action will find the Hiwassee thrilling, to say the least.

Several float trip facilities are located on the Hiwassee, and there are good accommodations in the area, particularly in Cleveland, which is only a few miles distant.

The state's oldest tailwater, the Clinch River below Norris Dam, remains a favorite spot, and one which continues to produce hefty rainbows. The Clinch isn't a good float stream; in fact, it can be very dangerous at times of high water, but fly rodders and spin casters can enjoy some exciting sport in the first several miles of river below the dam.

Access to this tailwater is best accomplished by exiting from I-75 at Lake City. This town makes a good place for fishermen to stay, since it has high quality accommodations and restaurants. Too, information on the tailwater can be readily obtained at the local sporting goods stores.

In the northern part of East Tennessee, the tailwaters of South Holston Lake are a fine trout fishery that offer approximately 20 miles of challenging and minimally-utilized water. Like the Hiwassee, the South Holston tailwater isn't floatable except under certain conditions.

There are some bragging-size browns and rainbows in this water, and once away from the dam itself, where access to the river is easy, there are lengths of the stream that give a fisherman all of the elbow room he could desire.

A secondary road from Bluff City on U.S. 19E between Johnson City and Bristol is the best route to the dam, and this road follows the river's course most of the way. Either Johnson City or Bristol are good base headquarters.

There is also trout fishing below Fort Patrick Henry Dam on the South Holston. This is the next impoundment below South Holston, and it is accessible from U.S. 23 near Kingsport. To date, results from this fishery haven't been on the level of those in the previously mentioned tailwaters, but this could improve in time.

Middle Tennessee's Dale Hollow tailwater on the Obey River has been well-known for a long time, since the former North American brown trout record was established there,

Fisherman nets a big rainbow in the Little Tennessee River below Chilhowee Dam.

This nice rainbow came from below Center Hill Dam, one of the state's most productive tailwaters.

and it is still a recommended location, even though the impoundment of the new Cordell Hull Lake on the Cumberland River has changed the conditions there to some extent. At full pool, Cordell Hull backs up almost to Dale Hollow Dam, so the free-flowing portion of the river has been lost; however, the trout are still numerous there, and lunker browns and rainbows continue to be taken—The Dale Hollow tailwater is near the town of Celina·on State Highway 53.

Another U.S. Corps tailwater area lies slightly southwest—Center Hill—and it is one of the most productive in the state next to the Little T. Rainbows and browns are the fare, and 6- to 8-pound fish are often taken. As with all tailwaters, water fluctuation can have a great deal to do with fishing conditions and methods.

The lengthy stretch of the Caney Fork River below Center Hill isn't a recommended float stream, since the narrow valley through which it flows causes the fluctuation level to be severe at points. Water can rise very rapidly in this river, and the results can be dangerous to even experienced boaters.

Both Smithville and Carthage are reasonably close to this tailwater, and both have high quality motels and restaurants. There are also several resorts around Center Hill Lake that can be considered. Out-of-state fishermen will find I-40 the most simple reference point in terms of access to this fishery.

Two other "younger" tailwaters in the mid-state region are well worth thinking about, since results from these places have been sufficiently impressive to indicate great potential.

One of these is the Cordell Hull tailwater near Carthage, and the other is the Tim's Ford tailwater near Tullahoma, and they are on the Cumberland and Elk rivers respectively. Actually, because of their recent entry into the picture, the pressure is likely to be less than at some of the other places, and both hold trout that you wouldn't hesitate to have hanging on the wall. The Carthage exit from I-40 will take you to Cordell Hull Dam; the Manchester exit from I-24 between Murfreesboro and Chattanooga will head you toward Tim's Ford Dam.

One thing worth considering: With three tailwaters—Dale Hollow, Center Hill and Cordell Hull—in one general vicinity, a trip can include some time on all of them, and this would provide an experience of memorable quality!

If the tailwaters seem like an extensive offering, the "biggie category"—streams—will be stunning! In this department you will find a great deal more than you can handle, but you will have a selection of a sensational sort.

The mountain region of eastern Tennessee from the Virginia line all the way South to the Georgia boundary is in the hands of the U.S. Forest Service and the National Park Service, and within this vast expanse are trout streams too numerous to list. The Forest Service portion is classed as the Cherokee Wildlife Management Area, and it is jointly handled by this agency and the Tennessee Wildlife Resources Agency. Some of the streams within the area require permits to fish, while others do not; also, regulations specifying seasons and days on which some of the streams can be fished apply, so it is best to obtain current information on all such waters from: Tennessee Wildlife Resources Agency, P.O. Box 40747, Ellington Agricultural Center, Nashville, Tennessee 37204.

The Great Smoky Mountains National Park affords some of the finest back country trout fishing to be found anywhere for fishermen who don't mind trekking back into the head-waters to reach it. All streams within the park—which includes many on the North Carolina side—can be fished with a license from either state, so there's a lot of territory to consider. Too, there are waters in the park which are classified as sport fishing streams on which no trout less than 12 inches in length can be retained, and there are special children's fishing streams. Except in the latter, artificial flies and lures having one single hook only are permitted.

Information on regulations applying to park streams can be obtained from: Superintendent, Great Smoky Mountains National Park, Gatlinburg, Tennessee 37738.

The U.S. Forest Service and National Park waters are by no means the entire picture, however, because there is quality trout fishing available in Tennessee as far west as Kentucky Lake. Some of these waters are put-and-take fisheries, but there are some where natural reproduction occurs—and there are many where the carry-over fish keep getting bigger and bigger. One such stream I know, and a rather small one at that, has produced brown trout upwards of 8 pounds year after year, and these are fish that have grown to this size.

Presently, there are around 60 streams in 33 counties that are stocked annually by the TWRA, and this number doesn't reflect the total number of streams which actually contain trout that are present due to either natural reproduction or stockings in previous years. A list of the streams stocked can be obtained from the previously noted TWRA address, and it can be very beneficial to those not familiar with the state.

The tailwaters and streams take care of two of the "three routes to trout," and the last one to come isn't necessarily the least in terms of opportunity.

Since some of the lakes in Tennessee are classed as either "cool water" or "cold water" impoundments, several of these have been developed as top-flight fisheries, and there is one in particular that will be of particular interest.

Watauga Lake in the extreme northeastern part of the state has a kaleidoscopic variety of cold water species, and if there is such a thing as an overlooked bonanza, this impoundment fills the bill precisely. Consider this:

There are rainbows, browns, kamloops, ohrids (an exotic trout), cutthroats, kokanee and coho salmon in Watauga, yet the fishing pressure is unbelievably low. This is amazing in itself, but in addition, the lake is mountain-ringed, scenically gorgeous, and practically undeveloped around the shorelines. Only one full-facility resort exists—Watauga Lakeshores—and the marina at this location, along with Fish Springs Dock, are the only ones on the main body of the lake.

The reasons? Because of its isolated location, it is consistently passed by, and since a majority of the anglers heading south are looking for bass, they are aimed at the better-publicized spots. Trout fishermen shouldn't make this mistake.

Watauga lies adjacent to U.S. 321 northeast from Elizabethton, and while the limited accommodations have already been mentioned, tent campers and RV campers have several well-developed U.S. Forest Service campgrounds on the east side of the lake to choose from.

OK, Watauga is a "sleeper," but in explaining all about it, I haven't meant to under-rate the other trout lakes, because all of them must be classed as "first rate" in anybody's book. Each of these impoundments produce lunker trout—both rainbow and brown—and they attract fishermen familiar with the tactics necessary to take fish in lakes. This know-how, along with the proper gear, makes the difference.

This 26 lb. 2 oz. brown was taken from the Dale Hollow tailwater and was the former North American record.

Deep trolling is the favorite method for the trout in the lakes, and for the most part, lead core lines are used. This is a satisfactory approach, but anglers who have experience with the rigs used in the West for lake fish may have an edge that will put them well ahead of local fishermen. The use of downriggers has just been introduced with impressive results, since in combination with depth finders, stratified fish can be located and fished for in a precise manner.

The other trout method is fishing at night under lanterns, and at certain seasons, this is a highly productive approach. May and June are considered the best time by many fishermen, but fish are taken all through the summer and into the fall this way.

Since the locations of each have been given in describing the tailwaters, the remaining top lakes for trout are: South Holston, Dale Hollow, Chilhowee and Cordell Hull.

Non-resident annual fishing licenses cost $12 in Tennessee, with a 10-day license available at $5, and a 3-day license at $3. A $3 trout license is also required.

TROUT WATER ECOLOGY

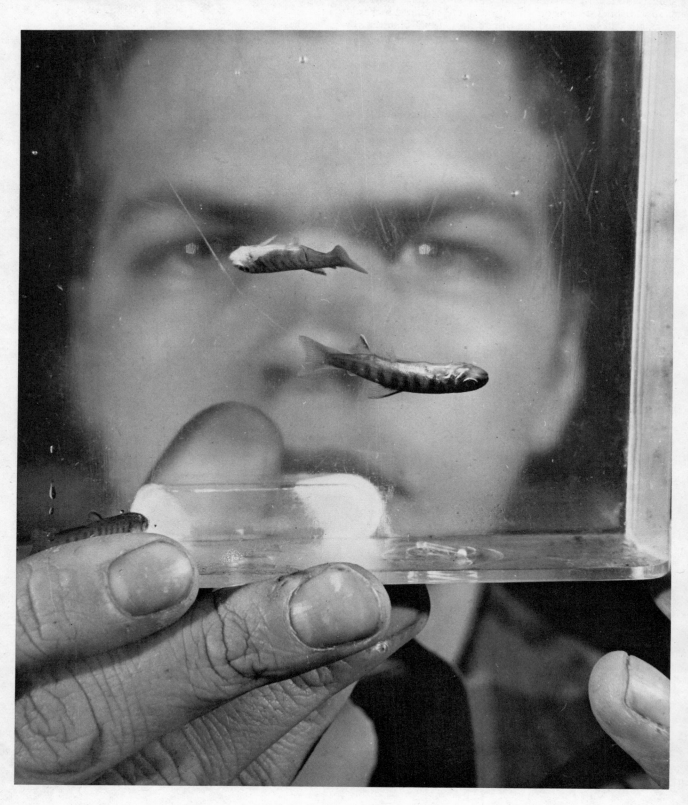

by THOMAS E. HUGGLER

WHEN THE AVERAGE person thinks of ideal trout waters, he usually pictures gin clear streams and lakes where cold, clean waters lap wilderness shores far from the supermarket society and its polluting ways.

Pollution levels and water clarity are only two indicators as to how good the fishing might be in a particular stream or lake. We seldom give a thought to the many variables that can make or break trout water.

Predators and diseases, geologic age, water temperature, oxygen saturation level, nutrient level, bottom composition, and turbidity are several important factors that regulate trout welfare. These ingredients vary from stream to stream, lake to lake, and probably no two bodies of trout water are exactly the same in respect to the above factors or to their relative populations of trout.

The successful trout angler should know something about these limiting conditions and how they affect the quality of the streams and lakes he fishes.

Predators and Diseases

Mergansers, herons, water ouzels, eagles, ospreys, mink, otter, and larger fish prey on wild trout, but not to the great extent that many people believe. As will be seen, man poses a far greater threat to trout than do natural enemies.

Trout require clean water and quality living conditions and, consequently, are usually disease-free. Sometimes trout (especially steelhead) will suffer from fungi growths if protective mucus is rubbed from the body. This problem may happen during mating or migration but usually occurs with improper handling of caught fish that are to be released during hatchery egg-taking procedures.

Another problem that American trout are being exposed to is whirling disease which has long been established in Europe. Whirling disease is caused by a protozoan parasite that attacks the central nervous system of fingerling trout under 3 inches in length. First discovered in this country in Pennsylvania in 1956, whirling disease spread to the eastern states and by the mid-1960s was evident in Ohio and Michigan.

The disease can be a serious hatchery problem where maintenance of sanitary conditions is difficult and trout are raised under confinement. The problem is not a serious one at this time in the wild although wild trout may be carriers of the disease.

In the spring of 1975, Michigan Dept. of Natural Resources (DNR) biologists found evidence of whirling disease in the Sturgeon River Rearing Station near Wolverine. Eradication of the disease in the natural environment is impossible, the DNR has found, and to avoid the spread of whirling disease to Michigan streams, the agency destroyed 2.5 million salmon and trout and closed the Sturgeon River facility indefinitely. Whirling disease could spread

Opposite page—A Michigan DNR fish biologist examines chinook fry, dying from exposure to DDT. DDT and other pesticides do not decompose and can remain in the environment, affecting the future of trout for many years.

Geologic Age

Like people, lakes are born, grow old and die. Lakes age over thousands of years due to enrichment of the waters with nutrients. Most North American lakes were carved from the ground by huge, slow-moving glaciers that inched southward, the last one about 10,000 to 15,000 years ago. The cold, deep waters were sterile at birth, but gradually, due to the constant leaching of nutrients from erosion and a warming climate, saw the introduction of plant life.

Spreading plant life, from the shallow shorelines to deeper water, encouraged the growth of animal organisms such as plankton and insects and gave off oxygen which helped support fish populations like lake trout. Aquatic plants increase and die in young lakes. As the lake matures, organic deposits begin to pile up on the bottom, making the lake warm and shallow. This process of organic decay uses increasing amounts of precious oxygen which eventually suffocates animal life. The lake then becomes a marsh and dies.

Man's activities, such as farming and manufacturing, add excessive nutrients in the form of fertilizers and waste discharges to some lakes and accelerate this process of eutrophication (the enrichment of water with nutrients). In populous areas these nutrients sometimes age a lake as much in 20 years as nature would in 1,000 years.

Rivers constantly change too. Mature ones can be identified by their fairly fixed current rates, predictable temperatures and rates of erosion, depending on the seasons. Too-close tillage of the soil near stream banks, timber cutting and thermal and waste discharges are some of the ways in which man accelerates change and tampers with natural stream evolution.

Trout are the most delicate of fresh water fish, and an abundance of trout indicates a clean environment as well as a maturing body of water in terms of geologic age.

Temperature

Although little scientific knowledge is available on how temperature affects the over-all life of a stream or lake, it is known that most trout would live well at about 60 degrees Fahrenheit. There is really no optimum temperature for all trout since lake trout prefer water temperatures in the 50- to 55-degree range while browns and rainbows do nicely at 60-65 degrees. Brookies and cutthroats like the colder headwaters of streams and lakes and prefer temperatures of 55-60 degrees.

Trout feed more heavily in warmer temperatures and fish generally grow larger. The reason is that temperatures are warmer downstream from lakes or stream origins which are often spring-fed. Food growth is poor in the colder, semi-sterile upper reaches, and the trout are usually stunted. Downstream there is more food, warmer temperatures, and more willingness to feed.

Some streams' temperatures can fluctuate 15 degrees from day to day. The hot, dog days of late July or early August can warm streams to the point that trout flee their favorite lairs to cooler temperatures upstream or even downstream where there might be better shade and cooler water from tributaries or springs. Maximum summer temperatures occur in late afternoon one or two days each season following a succession of hot days. Luckily for trout the natural evaporation of water makes temperatures go down after the sun sets, giving the fish temporary relief from the heat.

Lakes can also warm to such a point that trout seek cooler layers near the bottom. Brown trout have been known to rest

on the bottom of lakes and not feed at all during hot spells, and some streams experience a "temperature run" of fish that flee warm lake waters.

Thermal discharges from industrial plants can also change water temperatures in localized areas although it's not often a serious environmental problem. It could become troublesome in the future as this nation seeks additional power.

Thermal pollution, as it is popularly known, is the addition of heat to water which upsets the balance of nature and may be injurious to plant and animal life. Seventy percent of the thermal pollution in the United States comes from the generation of electrical power with steel making, paper making and other industries responsible for the rest.

There are some beneficial aspects to thermal discharges; it warms local waters and attracts some species of forage fish. Trout follow the bait fish and this provides excellent early spring and late fall fishing. In northern states where water temperatures may fluctuate from 32 to 80 degrees seasonally the discharge may not be harmful. Too much heat too soon can kill trout and can directly alter reproductive habits, rates of metabolism, feeding, growth and respiration, as well as migration patterns.

Thermal pollution can indirectly affect fish by decreasing the capacity for water to hold oxygen as it gets warmer and by decreasing the trout's resistance to toxicants. Also, the use of chlorine to kill plant growth in the plant's plumbing can endanger fish while other trout may be drawn into the protective gates and destroyed by the turbines when cooling water is forced in to help run the operation.

Oxygen Levels

One property of water is that it can hold gases in solution and cold water can hold more saturated oxygen than warm water. The degree of oxygen available in solution is usually expressed in parts-per-million (ppm).

Trout require oxygen at the rate of 10 ppm or twice that of warm water fish species. Sixty degree water will hold

Above—Water pollution comes in many forms, most of them manmade. We have a responsibility to keep quality trout waters as unchanged as possible and an obligation to clean up the messes we've already created. Below— Algae buildup and weed growth on lakes in the summer can be controlled with herbicides but the chemicals may also be injurious to trout.

oxygen at 10 ppm which is about 80 percent saturation. A temperature of 50 degrees will hold oxygen at 11 ppm, a temperature of 70 degrees—9 ppm and so on. Therefore, the colder the water, the greater the oxygen saturation, and so temperature and oxygen level are closely linked.

There are other factors, such as atmospheric pressure, that help determine the amount of oxygen in solution available for trout. An abundance of aquatic plants will insure a healthy oxygen supply since plants take carbon dioxide from the atmosphere in the manufacture of their food and give off oxygen. Lakes young in geologic time are sometimes devoid of plant life and fish. High mountain lakes in western states are often ice-locked and snow-covered for several months of the year. The available plant life does not receive the sun's light and therefore cannot manufacture its own food. Plants die, the lakes cease to produce oxygen, and trout succumb to oxygen starvation.

The amount of oxygen consuming material and organisms also helps determine the oxygen supply. The decomposition process of organic materials such as phosphates and sewage requires huge amounts of oxygen. Streams too rich in these organic waste materials rob oxygen from trout and other organisms.

Some kind of turbulence is necessary to properly mix oxygen into solution with water. Wave action in lakes and current speed, rapids, and waterfalls in rivers help the aeration process and ensure an adequate oxygen supply.

Nutrient Levels and Growth

Biologists and ecologists speak of the term "ecosystem," which is how living and non-living portions of environment

The construction of fish ladders on trout and salmon rivers is an important environmental consideration since they aid the fish in their upstream spawning migrations.

affect each other physically. How temperature and oxygen work together to influence the welfare of trout has already been observed. Nutrient levels and the growth of nutrients is another important part of the trout's ecosystem.

Nutrients such as phosphorus, nitrogen, and trace elements are essential to the continued growth of plants which produce the oxygen that all living organisms require. A supply of plants also insures a supply of insects, which, in one form of development or another, make up most trout diets. Nutrients get into trout habitat in two ways. As plant life in a stream or lake decays, the decomposition process enriches the habitat with nutrients. These nutrients, in turn, help nurture the growth of new plants which produce more oxygen and shelter for fish.

Nutrients also enter bodies of water through erosion of surrounding land. This erosion process may be due to the natural geographic contours of the land, the soil substance, amount of rainfall, etc., but may also be man-induced, especially where deforestation and heavy tillage of the soil has occurred. In addition to destroying shade trees, which help keep summer water temperatures down, the cutting of forests weakens the soil's resistance to erosion.

A lack of nutrients means a loss of food supply in a trout stream or lake and the results is often mature, stunted fish, such as small brookies found in the headwaters of streams. Lakes that are old in a geologic sense but produce little food are called oligotrophic. Trout that inhabit oligotrophic lakes are slow-moving and generally not plentiful unless connecting rivers produce food and forage fish. Many Canadian trout lakes are oligotrophic and since the trout are not as readily renewable as similar species in warmer climates, great care should be taken to insure an orderly harvest.

Bottom Composition

The type of bottom in trout streams and lakes is a critical environmental condition since it is directly related to the quantity of insect life upon which trout feed. Also, bottom composition tells something about maturity and corresponding plant growth and nutrient level, as well as water clarity and rate of flow.

The erosion process that is constantly occurring may or may not be beneficial to trout waters, depending upon the amount and rate of nutrients leached from the soil. Like all other quality trout water conditions, the optimum degree of erosion is always a delicate one and rarely constant for any period of time.

Too much erosion, for example, can choke the plant and animal life of a stream or lake through silt deposition on the bottom which builds up over years. In streams, gravel stretches necessary for spawning are sometimes obliterated under tons of silt. This silt in both lakes and streams also effectively cuts off sunlight—necessary for food manufacture.

On Idaho's Bear River 10,000,000 tons of sand silt was deposited from poor agricultural practices in the years 1910-1950. This silt covered the natural bottom to a depth of 5 feet and more, suffocating all life in the substratum. Below the source of erosion for more than 40 miles downstream the only living bottom-dwelling organisms were found on rocks above the silt line.

In Wisconsin, tests show that a cornfield growing on a 20 degree slope loses 630 pounds of organic material, 38 pounds of nitrogen and 1.8 pounds of phosphorus annually. Most of this eroded material finds its way into lakes and rivers where it helps smother bottom life.

Any cross section of a stream will show different current speeds which help determine bottom composition. Stream currents are usually swiftest in the middle and slowest along

Industrially flanked Rouge River, principal tributary of the Detroit River, was Michigan's black eye and one of the Midwest's most polluted waterways. Now, thanks to tough state laws and a massive cleanup campaign, salmon and steelhead trout will run these rivers in the near future.

the sides with corresponding silt and mud deposits along the edges. Streams having current velocities of 4 feet per second usually run over a bedrock bottom while current speeds of under 1 foot per second are usually over sand, silt, or even mud bottoms if the current is barely visible.

Insect larvae by species inhabit stream bottoms according to the type of composition. Since most trout take 80 to 90 percent of their food underwater, bottom composition is a highly critical food supply factor.

Turbidity

Sometimes eroded materials remain in suspension as fine particles and thus cut off the availability of light penetration. Transparent water is important for proper food growth. This is why the bulk of food produced is in the clearer, shallow shorelines of lakes and in shallow riffle areas of streams.

Industrial operations that spew waste materials into trout waters greatly increase turbidity. Discharges from slaughterhouses, mining, glass sand, tannery, milk, oil, canning, lumbering, smelting, and pulp operations often remain in suspension for long periods, especially in rivers with strong currents, and thus dirty the water. The turbidities eventually settle out in a lake or slow-moving section of stream and gradually alter the bottom composition through deposition. If the bottom sediments from industrial wastes are particularly heavy, the result is sludge formation.

Water Pollution

In recent years environmental pollution and careful use of our natural resources has received a tremendous amount of attention. Legislation and governmental monitoring across the country is making it increasingly difficult for people and industries to misuse our natural resources. Massive educational efforts both in and out of the classroom are underway to teach Americans the importance of conservation practices. Overall, millions of dollars are being spent annually by private and public interests to clean up the messes we've already created.

All of these efforts are for good reason since natural resources such as water are not renewable. Directly or indirectly the source of our water supply is precipitation from clouds where evaporation and condensation has already occurred. Most of this rainfall is not available to recharge the ground water supply since it is lost to runoff, evaporation, and demands of plant life.

There are two types of manmade pollution in trout streams and lakes—toxic and non-toxic. Non-toxic pollutants are organic wastes such as sewage that are dumped into water. As we have seen, a certain amount of organic pollution, such as the leaching of nutrients from the soil or the introduction of phosphates from detergents, can be beneficial to a stream that has a low capacity for generating food. Too much organic pollution, though, consumes the oxygen supply in the process of decomposition, may distort the water's transparency, increase temperature, build up deposits on the bottom, and eventually age a lake or stream at an accelerating rate.

Chemical toxic pollution is perhaps more serious because it can destroy quality trout water faster and has much longer lasting effects. Pesticides often used to control mosquitoes

As our most delicate freshwater fish, trout require a clean, unpolluted environment such as the northern Michigan lake that produced these rainbows.

and other insects, algae and weed growths, sea lampreys, and rough fish species may also kill trout or alter their basic functions in undesirable ways. An example of the toxicity of some of these chemicals is the pesticide Endrin. One-half pound of Endrin released in 120,000,000 gallons of water has been shown to kill most fish.

Mercury, DDT, and the newer PCB's are other toxic pollutants that are dangerous and do not readily decompose. The PCB's (polychlorinated biphenyls used in the manufacture of oil derivatives and other industrial components) are extremely hardy in that they require a temperature of 2,000 degrees Fahrenheit to destroy. One of the reasons for the planting of Great Lakes salmon and trout was to restore good fishing with edible species, but the constant threat of toxic pollutants remains.

As this country increasingly depends upon oil and petroleum products, the threat of oil pollution remains high. Spilled oil on streams and lakes covers the water's surface, preventing the free exchanges of gases and thus shuts off the oxygen supply to trout.

Another serious pollution problem is agricultural runoff produced by rains that wash farmlands. Wastes from animal feed lots and other pesticides and herbicides used to aid the farmers' crops can easily wash into trout streams. Also, irrigated water that is continually reused may leach through the soil, collecting salts and minerals which become concentrated as the water is recycled.

Mining wastes in western trout streams have been known to destroy bottom organisms with their abrasive and smothering action. The outflow from unsealed, abandoned coal mines in some eastern areas can cause sulfuric acid to form. Acid mine drainage in weak solutions may not kill trout but can surpress their reproductive cycle.

One of the country's most serious pollution problems is occurring in the iron ore country of Minnesota. The separation of iron ore from taconite, through a combined magnetic and grinding operation, results in particles of worthless residue called tailings. For years the dumping of taconite tailings in unpolluted Lake Superior was widespread, but today all the mining operations except one have converted to on-shore, closed-cycle systems for the disposal of residues.

The battle with Reserve Mining Company of Silver Bay, Minnesota, is currently locked up in the courts. According to a recent article in *Field & Stream,* evidence was presented to show that the company was dumping 67,000 tons of tailings daily into Lake Superior. Taken together, the some 200 rivers and streams that surround Lake Superior put only 20 percent of this total daily into the entire lake as solids.

Continued safeguards by way of laws and conservation must be established to protect the quality environmental conditions that we know trout need to survive.

The search for the perfect trout stream or lake may very well be a mythical search when one considers all the precise conditions that these fish require to live. The ecosystem that trout share is very delicate and easily subject to change. We have a responsibility to effect change in quality trout habitat as little as possible and an obligation to restore that which has already suffered from our influence.

The future of mankind, as well as trout, depends upon clean water and its wise use.

The Great Lakes Steelhead

by PETE JONES

THE STEELHEAD is a will-o-the-wisp character, here today and gone tomorrow, and this characteristic typifies fishing in Great Lakes waters. The beginning steelhead fisherman quickly learns a hole containing fish today may be empty of fish tomorrow. An anadromous species of fish, the steelhead always seems to be in a state of migration, even when found in the open water of the Great Lakes.

Strangely enough, steelhead fishing in the Great Lakes and tributary waters has been going on for 75 years or more but the heydays occurred in the 1940s and early 1950s until the sea lamprey made its presence felt. By the mid-50s, steelhead fishing was on its way downhill and little seemed possible to salvage a once great fishery.

After many years of trial and error with lamprey weirs on spawning streams, an effective lampricide dealt a lethal blow to much of the lampreys spawning in Great Lakes tributaries. By the mid-1960s, midwest states such as Michigan were undertaking massive planting programs of steelhead to fill an empty hole in their fishery plans.

By 1967 and 1968 massive runs of steelhead were homing in on many Lake Michigan tributary streams in Michigan. The Little Manistee River in Michigan became the "in" place to

be if you were an avid steelheader. Other streams up and down the Lake Michigan shoreline swelled during spring and fall months with huge runs of large steelhead. Many oldtimers, used to the runs of the glory days in the 40s, said they'd never seen so many steelhead and such large fish.

By the late 60s steelhead were averaging 11 pounds and many fish were topping the 19- and 20-pound mark. Michigan's current steelhead record is a whopping 26-pound 8-ounce fish.

Bolstered by Michigan's success, other Great Lakes states jumped on the bandwagon. Wisconsin annually plants close to a half-million steelhead yearly in Lake Michigan waters. Minnesota is undergoing a stream barrier removal project on many rivers in hopes of opening up many more miles of spawning water to Lake Superior fish.

Ontario has a tremendous steelhead fishery along the North Shore of Lake Superior as well as the Georgian Bay portion of Lake Huron. They have a limited stocking program in certain areas as well as excellent natural reproduction. Some Ontario-caught fish are strays from Michigan plantings.

The bulk of the Great Lakes steelhead fishing revolves

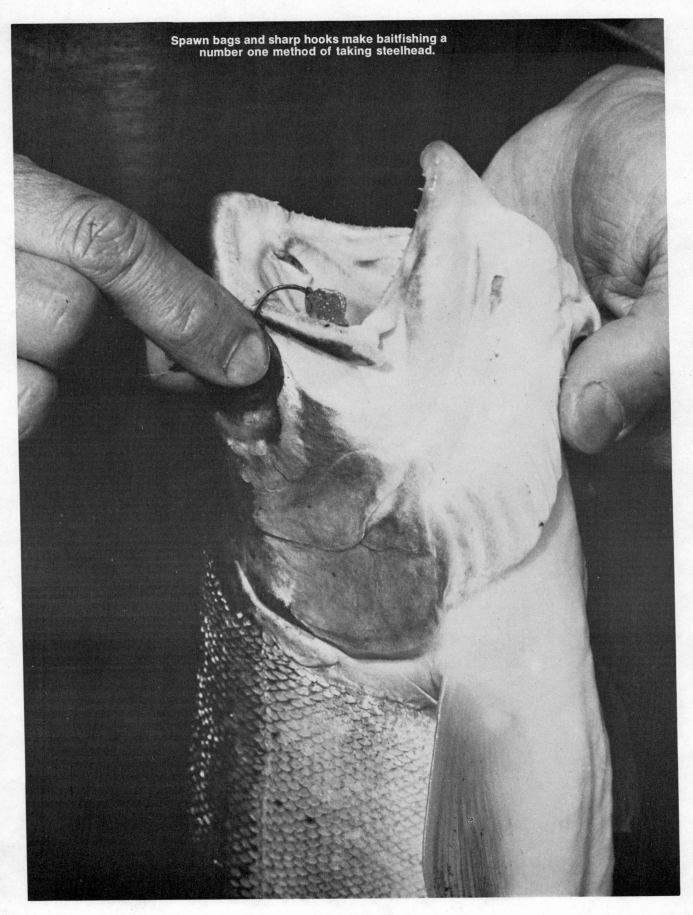

Spawn bags and sharp hooks make baitfishing a number one method of taking steelhead.

around the three upper Great Lakes—Superior, Michigan and Huron. A smattering of steelhead fishing exists in Lakes Erie and Ontario but the runs are small and the fishery relatively undeveloped in comparison with that found farther west.

There are many different methods of taking steelhead but most anglers will agree that bait fishing is the number one method.

This fisherman nailed an 11-pound steelhead on a Mepps spinner and, lacking a net, gilled it.

Baitfishing undoubtedly takes more steelhead from a river than all other methods combined. The list of natural baits that will sucker a steelhead are endless. I've used corn, salmon eggs, chunks of raw spawn, nightcrawlers, wigglers, minnows and even taken a few on commercially packed "stink" bait such as used by catfish fishermen.

The same type of drift fisherman that uses live or processed bait will also resort to lures that imitate the spawn steelhead are accustomed to striking. Imitation spawn lures such as Okie Drifter, Cherry Bobbers, Cherry Drifters, Gooey Bobs, Egg Drifter, Spin N Glo and others are deadly at times. These lures come in a variety of shapes and sizes and the best results normally occur when using small sizes in clear water and larger sizes in dirtier water. One of the hottest colors at this writing is chartreuse with red spots. Steelhead hammer this color lure at any time.

Baitfishing is normally done with a spinning rod and reel. A 7½- to 9-foot medium-action spinning stick is best when coupled with an open-faced spinning reel. Select a reel with a smooth trouble-free drag system. Most bait fishermen stock their reels with mono testing from 6 to 15 pounds depending on water clarity, the river being fished, and any obstacles that may be encountered if a fish is hooked.

Once steelhead begin their upstream migrations for spawning they can be found laying in relatively predictable locations in almost any river. Expert steelhead fishermen have learned to read a river and can usually tell within a few feet where a steelhead will pause for a rest.

Deep holes often harbor steelhead but these are not the fish that will actively strike. Steelies in deep holes are primarily resting fish.

The tail end of a pool or hole where the water begins to quicken before rushing over the shallows is often one of the hottest places for steelhead. The fish will lie in this 4- to 8-foot water at the tail of a hole and these steelhead are often the best strikers.

Obstructions have a fascination for steelhead. They'll be found loitering in front of or behind boulders, rocks, logs, pilings, stumps or brush piles. If the water isn't too savage, steelhead will often lie next to these obstructions and take advantage of the cushioning effect of the water bouncing off the boulder or stump.

Another hotspot is the extreme top end of a hole. Steelies often lie just to one side of the inrushing current and scoop up goodies without having to fight the full thrust of the current.

This brings up an excellent point about holding water for steelhead: they will seldom fight the full force of the current. Look for swirls or eddy water off the mainstream as being hotspots for steelies. They just won't be found facing into heavy current because they must face a further upstream migration and have to conserve their energy for traveling and spawning.

There are several methods of presenting live bait or imitation bait to steelhead in these positions. The favorite method is the across and slightly upstream method of casting. It is essential to attach enough weight in the form of split shot to a line to take the bait to the bottom. The best presentation is to have the bait bounce downstream along the bottom at approximately the same speed as the current. Too much weight causes the bait to stop while too little weight will cause the bait to lift off the bottom and swing by far over the heads of steelhead.

Aim the cast so it lands far enough upstream from the suspected steelhead holding spot so it will be bouncing along bottom when it invades the fish's sanctuary. As the bait and split shot hits the water, allow it to sink and then reel just enough to keep the shot tapping along bottom. Keep the line tight and occasionally lift slightly on the rod tip to work the

Bard McClanahan nets a big Manistee River steelhead for Jim Bennett while Captain Emil Dean watches the action.

bait over underwater obstructions.

Steelhead normally strike bait very softly. It's generally a soft tapping sensation. Many times the drifting bait will just go slack as a fish picks it up. Set the hook anytime the constant tapping is interrupted. Steelhead often strike imitation baits much harder.

Some steelhead fishermen increase their odds when using lures like the Okie Drifter by adding salmon eggs, a spawn bag or a piece of brightly colored yarn.

Bait fishermen should present their bait from every conceivable angle in order to be sure they've offered the bait to a steelhead. At times, in certain locations, only a bait presented from a specific angle will produce a strike.

There is one technique that can aid a baitfishing steelhead fisherman—chumming. The occasional chumming of several salmon eggs into a hole before fishing often spells the difference between taking a rambunctious steelhead or merely spending a day on the river.

Baitfishing produces well off many of the rivermouths along the Great Lakes. If a stream receives a run of steelhead then the rivermouth is normally a good place to fish. Rivers attracting runs of salmon during fall months are often the hotspots since steelhead will lie just off the rivermouths and gobble up free-drifting salmon eggs that drift down from above.

Steelheaders that ply the rivermouths are a gregarious lot. Men, women and children stand shoulder-to-shoulder and fish the open water where the current from the river meets the incoming waves of the lake. This mixing action can produce some outstanding steelhead fishing. Single salmon eggs are normally the best bet and this spectacular sport will be covered elsewhere in the book.

One of the most productive methods of steelhead fishing is practiced by Emil Dean of Bear Lake, Michigan. Emil plys his trade on the Big Manistee River and he uses a technique called "drop back fishing."

This method involves the use of light action baitcasting rods and reels stocked with 20- or 30-pound braided Dacron. Two lures do the bulk of the duty; a Flatfish (U-20 size) for slow water conditions and a Tadpolly for higher water.

The lure is released behind the boat with the rod tip held low to the water. Approximately 10 yards of line is initially released and then thumb pressure is applied to the spool of the reel. This halts the downstream flow of line and the plug begins to wiggle toward the bottom.

After the lure wiggles for up to a ½-minute another 3 or 4 feet of line is released. Thumb pressure is applied again and the lure shimmies in a new spot. This procedure is followed until the lures work completely through a drift. Normally three fishermen fish at the same time, one off each side and the third man straight down the middle behind the boat.

I fished one day with Emil and dark winter snow clouds swirled down from the north, obliterated our vision and made a day on the river all but impossible for fishing. If it hadn't been for Emil's heated river boat we'd probably froze to death.

Action had been slow, it usually is during mid-winter, but along about two in the afternoon the sun peeked through for 15 minutes. The sun had just come out when I had a tremendous yank on my Flatfish and 50 yards behind the boat a big steelhead corkscrewed halfway out of the water before piling back with a helluva splash.

"I'll get my lure in," Emil hollered, as I bent to the task of trying to keep the steelhead out of a treetop. Emil's lure was almost back to the boat when a steelhead knifed up off bottom and smashed his bait.

My fish decided to stay downstream and slug it out while Emil's tried vainly to swim upstream around the anchor cable.

Emil leaned hard on the fish and it somersaulted out next to the boat and landed with a hefty splash behind the motor.

We spent the next 10 minutes passing rods back and forth as one fish crossed one line and the other tried to play catch-up with his wildly running partner. Finally Emil's fish, a scrappy 10-pounder, succumbed to his heavy-handed rod pressure and came to the net. I scooped the fish up one-handed while my fish made another determined downstream run.

Emil raised the anchor and we drifted downstream toward my fish. I'd steered it out and around the treetop and it now lay wallowing on the surface like a gleaming silver torpedo. One brief spurt upstream and the fish drifted back on the surface, completely tired out. Emil tucked the 15-pounder into the net and we had a nifty double header.

The strange thing about the dropback fishing method is it very seldom produces small steelhead. I'd say the average weight would be 10 or 11 pounds and 20-pounders aren't unheard of. Emil's top steelhead is a 21-pound 1-ounce male taken on the spring spawning run.

Trolling is another method that hangs big steelhead for Great Lakes fishermen. Much of the trolling is done either off rivermouths that attract runs of steelhead or in inland lakes where steelhead must pass through on their way upstream to spawn. Michigan has a number of these inland lakes along the western side of the state.

Baitcasting or spinning tackle is used and monofilament testing 10 or 12 pounds is adequate providing the angler will play the hooked steelhead in a cautious manner. Many steelhead taken by trolling will weigh in excess of 15 pounds.

An X-4, X-5 or U-20 Flatfish in silver, orange with black stripe, gray pearl, silver with pink spots or yellow with red spots works well. A very slow trolling speed is necessary. Some oldtime steelheaders row their steelhead boats in order to achieve the slow trolling speed necessary.

A minimum of 75 to 100 yards of line should be released behind the boat. Trollers normally troll a slow deliberate zigzag pattern with occasional speed ups and slowing down periods. Steelhead strike the lures ferociously.

Another strictly Great Lakes method of steelhead fishing revolves around the use of a flyrod and a spinner. A fairly stiff action flyrod in the 8- to 8½-foot class is used. A sturdy fly reel and level flyline is used with a 6-foot leader of level 15-pound monofilament. A small copper Colorado spinner is knotted to the leader. The angler stalks the river banks in search of spawning steelhead—polarized sunglasses aid in spotting resting fish in deep water or on the spawning beds.

Once the fish are spotted the fisherman eases into the river downstream from the steelies and slowly wades upstream until he's in casting position directly behind the fish. He quickly reads the river current and depth and casts the spinner upstream past the steelhead.

The spinner is allowed to sink to the bottom and is gently drawn downstream with the rod tip. As the spinner reaches the fish the angler speeds up the retrieves which forces the spinner to lift off bottom with a madly whirling blade. The steelhead often strike out of anger.

Many times the steelhead will part and allow the spinner to drift between them. Once the spinner passes the fish, the angler lifts the spinner from the water in a soft sidearm lob cast, allows the line and spinner to straighten out to the side of him and quickly lays the lure back into the same spot. On-

the-mark casting accuracy and quick, repetitious casts are the keys to making this method produce.

Fishermen that fish the spawning beds take only male fish and never catch the female. Knowledgeable anglers can tell the difference between male and female steelhead and they know that several males can often be taken from along the side of one female. Besides, one male can fertilize a great many steelhead eggs.

Steelhead fishing is definitely on the upswing around the Great Lakes. It would be an impossibility to list all the hotspots in the three western Great Lakes states and Ontario so I'll cover those spots I've fished and know to be exceptionally productive at various times of the year.

The topic of Michigan steelhead fishing hotspots could cover a chapter of this book by itself. Lower Michigan hotspots would be St. Joseph, Grand, Muskegon, White, Sauble, Pentwater, Little Manistee, Big Manistee, Betsie, Platte, Boardman and Elk Rivers along the Lake Michigan side.

The Lake Huron side of the Lower Peninsula hosts the Thunder Bay, Ocqueoc, AuSable, Tawas, and East Branch of the Augres.

Lake Superior streams that are good would be the Two Hearted, Anna, Mosquito, Misery, Huron, Chocolay, Middle Branch of the Ontonagon and the Presque Isle.

Excellent trolling can be had in Pentwater, Pere Marquette, Muskegon and Manistee Lakes.

Wisconsin steelhead fishing is primarily an open water fishery in Lake Michigan. Steelhead are taken off the shoreline at all times of the year from Milwaukee north to the tip of the Door County Peninsula. I especially like the areas around Jacksonport and Bailey's Harbor.

Stream fishing for steelhead in Wisconsin is something that occurs only when water conditions make a run possible. Many times either insufficient flow or too-warm water prevent the steelhead from ascending the streams.

Minnesota has quite a few steelhead streams entering the north shore of Lake Superior from Duluth north. The Knife River, just outside Duluth, is one of the most famous Minnesota rivers. Further north I've fished the Stewart, Lester, Reservation, Temperance, and Baptism Rivers. All these rivers, except the Knife, are short streams with upstream barriers to migration. Many average much less than a mile in length although some excellent rivermouth fishing can be found in Lake Superior itself.

Ontario has some of the most virgin steelhead fishing still to be found in the Great Lakes. Many of the rivers flowing into Lake Superior, from Sault Ste. Marie west to Thunder Bay, are relatively untouched as far as steelhead fishing goes.

I highly recommend the Michipicoten, Old Woman, Agawa and Montreal Rivers which lie east of the town of Wawa. Queen's Highway 17 traverses this area and numerous other smaller less-well-known streams are available.

Lake Huron's Georgian Bay area has some excellent steelhead streams such as the Nottawasaga, Saugeen, Sydenham, Pottawatomi, Bighead, Pretty and Beaver Rivers.

Everything about steelhead fishing in the Great Lakes area is big including the size of the fish, the quality of the runs and no one can deny that it's big business. Steelhead fishing has come a long way since the bottom-floor days of the mid 1960s.

And I'm glad. I don't know of any fish, size-for-size or pound-for-pound, that can outscrap a steelhead fresh in from the Great Lakes.

Emil Dean grins over a husky 14-pound steelhead taken from the St. Joseph River.

Bait Fishing for Stream Trout

by JERRY GIBBS

THE RIVER fairly smoked with rain. It had started suddenly with heavy drops that bored holes in the quiet surface, and now as far as we could see a silvery spray extended down the course of the summer-low Esopus. Phil Jensen and I squeaked back in waders to the car.

"What do you want to do?" he asked.

"We still have some sandwiches and coffee," I said. "Let's kill time and see what happens."

The downpour tapered off, then stopped almost as quickly as it had begun soon after we had drained the vacuum bottle. The river looked higher and was definitely colored now. I began rummaging in the gear chest in back of the car. I found an old Shakespeare 1810 closed face spinning reel that hangs down from the rod grip like a fly reel. I put it on my long fly rod and strung up, tying on a No. 8 bait-holder hook. From the ice chest I removed a small waterproof container.

"You're not..." Phil started in.

"I am," I said. "With the kind of luck we've had so far today, I'm not going to let this opportunity go by."

We sloshed through little rivulets that were draining brown into the river. The container held damp moss and smallish earthworms.

Phil waded in and began to toss a small streamer. I walked downstream from his position. Several large dead trees jutted out into the water here, and the current broke around them and carved into the bank. Now New York's Esopus is known for its good rainbows, especially in the spring, but the river also harbors some excellent hard-to-catch brown trout. In half an hour I nailed two good ones casting upstream with the unweighted bait, getting the drift just right down along and under the banks and around the trees. Phil came over to take a look.

"All right," he said. "I'm not that stubborn. You want to give me a couple spare worms from that box before the water goes down again?"

"Another purist down the tube," I laughed.

Conditions such as those under which Phil and I had been fishing—low clear water and hot temperatures suddenly tempered by a strong rain—are almost a sure bet to get sulky trout feeding; and they are just one of the many situations tailored for bait fishing.

I'll go on record as preferring to use artificials—especially flies—for most of my trout angling, but there are times when the man-made baits are going to take a far back seat to the natural stuff.

The very largest, thus cannibalistic, trout want more to eat than small mayflys over the long haul of things, and if you fish a wide variety of waters and are out for the big ones, the use of natural baits is bound to increase your odds for success.

Many anglers scorn the use of natural baits because they feel that trout taken on such offerings are bound to be deeply hooked and thus there will be no chance for their survival should you wish to release them. This is just not so. A skillful natural bait fisherman can usually set the hook with exactly the right timing to avoid this problem. Lest the flies-only angler persist in an overly superior attitude, let it be known that wets and nymphs can and have caused the demise of

Above—Big native brook trout like this Pennsylvania beauty are not expected near large population centers. Natural bait is the sure temptation to bring them from deep holes. A worm took this one and his twin in a short period during the early part of the season.

This 23-inch stream trout fell for worm draped on wobbler drifted and jigged past tiny, seemingly unlikely pocket cut into bank during high water conditions.

Joe Peters used a grub to nail this still-thrashing rainbow from a small urban stream. Light natural baits like grubs, crickets, grasshoppers are easily cast with a fly rod.

many a trout which has gorged upon the deeply sunken flies. Experienced biologists will tell you the same thing. A treble-hooked lure is probably the most difficult device from which to free a trout without seriously injuring him.

Fishing with natural bait for stream trout is a particular art which, in some cases, is as exacting as the finest far-off fly fishing. Learning to fish trout through the use of the naturals in medium and smaller waters is an ideal way to begin understanding both the fish and stream angling. There are several reasons. The novice stands a good chance of catching at least one or two fish during a given session—especially important for youngsters. While using natural baits, it is often possible to bring the most stubborn fish visibly from their hiding places. You get to see where the trout hide and you also get to see how they attack the bait. Using natural bait you learn faster about midstream trout lies because more fish will roll, if nothing else, as the bait passes than would do so on incorrectly presented artificials. And, you also develop a sensitive touch when using deeply sunken baits. This exacting touch is important for later stream fishing with nymphs and for the times you'll want to work the big steelhead rivers with eggs, bouncing spoons or deep-working flies.

Let's take a look at some of the top natural baits and how to use them. The common worm has probably started more fishermen on a career of stream trout fishing than any other natural bait. I prefer small worms or bits of large ones for brook and brown trout. In medium to fairly large rivers, worms are most effective in spring, in summer after rains (or after the water rises due to pumping operations), and then again just before the cold weather sets in. Normally I hook a worm only once through the middle leaving the two ends to wiggle freely. In spring, however, gobs of worms are often more productive.

I work worm "balls" made of several hooked crawlers in slow water sections out of the main current, back in slough mouths, on flooded banks and eddies. Lethargic in the cold early season, stream trout seek the easiest holding places. They will not expend much energy chasing small tidbits. An obvious easy stomachful such as my nearly stationary worm hunks are gently scooped up. You must be prepared to strike at each tightening of your line. If the bait becomes absolutely dead in the water, raise it ever so gently from time to time to get it slowly moving. A short line is in order here, and no long casts are required. A spinning outfit is ideal for this kind of fishing.

In spring the beginning trout angler can gain some excellent experience by fishing the smallish streams that often see little pressure during the season. Using single worm baits the best method is to work the banks both upstream and down as streamside conditions dictate. You'll learn how to carefully stalk your quarry, how to keep out of sight, and the reason for wearing dull clothing. The medium to slower water sections should be your first targets as a novice. After gaining more skill try the pockets in the fast water sections, as well as the riffle water. Using fly or spinning tackle cast your worm upstream beyond the obvious holding places. You're after accurate placement here rather than long casts. Take in line and raise the rod tip as your worm bounces and rolls back downstream. This must be done to keep out slack in order to detect a pickup by the fish. Once a fish takes, if your line is fairly taut, lower the tip a fraction of an inch, pause for a milli-second, then hit with a short not-too-strong upward flick of your wrist.

This procedure is the only big difference between fly fishing and fishing with worms upstream. With both methods you must continually follow the movement of the lure by pointing your rod tip at it.

I prefer not to use any weight if possible. Lead will cause

Rigged minnow cast with light spinning gear into bank undercut nailed this big brown trout which author nets.

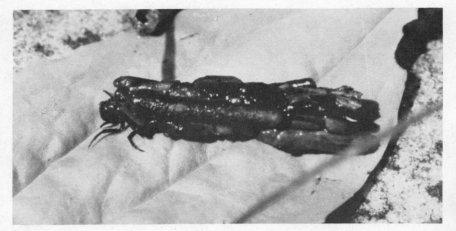

Left—The caddis, here just emerging from his casing is an excellent natural bait. The larvae, to be fished, must be removed from their tiny gravel cocoons that appear as humps fastened to the undersides of stream rocks.

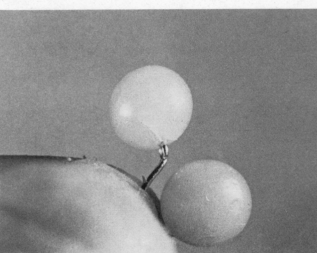

Above—Double salmon egg rig will be completed when bottom egg is rolled up slightly and upper egg is pushed down on hook eye. Note short shank egg hook being used.

Below—For finicky fish, bright hook eye and entire hook should be embedded in single egg. Eye is pushed in with tip of toothpick or similar instrument.

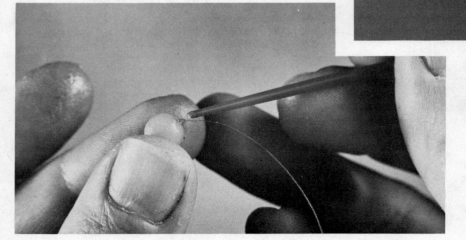

Above—Salt water fish roe can be used as effective fresh water bait. Used simply draped on hook it will stay on through careful gentle casts and last for several drifts.

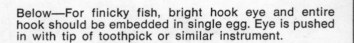

Joe Peters works grubs around edge of fast water. Small streams and bait teach anglers about trout fast.

your bait to drift at a slower rate than the current. This can appear unnatural to fish. In bigger water, however, the addition of clip-on weight either on a monofilament dropper extending from the leader or on the main leader itself, may be necessary.

Small stream fish usually attack worms as well as other natural bait, willingly and ferociously. Freestone wilderness or mountain streams are not very fertile and the fish take every opportunity to put on fat. When you move to larger water, you'll often have to work harder.

I know some areas where big browns lurk at rivermouths. Where the river empties into a lake, they'll hang, moving slightly upstream to feed on stray rainbow spawn in spring. Worms will also take them at these times. In autumn, when browns and brook trout are preparing to spawn, natural baits are excellent choices and the worm is one of the best.

Small minnows, live and dead, are one of my favorite baits for browns and rainbows. Live minnows carried in a little chest can are one of the most effective baits for wading anglers on many of the big rainbow streams I fish. The minnow is hooked once through the back or through the lips. The tackle used consists of long old-fashioned river rods in the 12-foot class. The live bait is dipped into likely pockets and either kept on the surface to flutter or allowed to swim down slightly. Other techniques include swinging the minnow up current and allowing it to drift freely through a glide. The bait usually is not strong enough to swim back up current. Anglers who use this method exclusively take fish when others are hooking none.

Dead sewn minnows or bottle-preserved minnows are top brown trout bait. I use these on a conventional 8-foot fly rod or spinning gear. Using a No. 6 or 8 thin wire snelled Aberdeen hook you can rig the smaller minnows by hooking the eye of the snell into a baiting needle. Run the snell through the vent and body then out the mouth through the upper lip. Pull the hook up close so the bend and barb protrude from the

vent. For larger minnows the technique is more complicated. The snell is sewn in and out beneath the skin on one side of the minnow. Start close to the tail then come out moving along the lateral line toward the minnow's head. Now bring the snell outside along the belly and insert the needle beneath the head. Run the needle straight up so the snell comes out at the top of the head. Now bring the snell around under the bait's "chin" and sew through the bottom jaw and out the mouth. When you tighten up on the snell the minnow should curve and the hook should ride along one side of the minnow near the tail. If you use spinning gear you must tie in a swivel about 18 inches up your line. This sewn minnow rig is excellent when cast in the deep water areas favored by big browns. You can work it around big deadfalls, undercut banks and in pools.

The technique to use is to allow the bait to settle deep then jig it up with easy wrist movements. The bait will dart, spin very slowly, and arch down again as a dying minnow would act. Don't try this with anything lighter than 4-pound tippet or even 6 if you are not skilled in handling large fish on light tackle.

Steelheaders know the effectiveness of fish eggs on big lake or river-run rainbows. The angler fishing streams for resident trout in spring or fall can also put eggs to good use. They'll take all trout. Fishermen who take Pacific salmon both in the far West and the Midwest know that chinook or coho eggs are excellent bait. They save their salmon roe for trout fishing. The eggs may be used plain or tied up in mesh net bags about the size of a marble in diameter. But don't neglect the commercially bottled individual eggs for use on fussy trout. Many anglers become frustrated trying to cast these eggs some distance. The eggs regularly fly from the hook. The secret is to know your water then stalk close so that only short casts—30 feet and under—are needed. Buy those individual eggs that are marked "firm" or "for stream use." They'll stay on the hook longer. Make sure you use the special short shank (usually gold finish) salmon egg hooks. Change your bait after

Right and below—Charles Szeglin fishes worm baits in small stream around bridge supports, and in larger water.

every few casts and never leave an egg on longer than five minutes. Beyond that time it loses its effectiveness.

Coastal anglers know that the tiny salt water grass shrimp is extremely effective on all trout in nearby streams and ponds. The bait is easily transportable in sawdust or in moist seaweed, but it must be kept cool. Inland, tiny fresh water amphipods—scuds—are quite shrimplike in nature and heavily consumed by trout east to west. There are also small true freshwater shrimp which are also eaten by trout. Some of these little creatures may be gathered from thick vegetation. They can be used hooked on small hooks—Nos. 16 to 18 are about right. Some anglers who keep their trout find freshly devoured scuds or shrimp in the stomachs of their quarry. Usually these are too soft, but sometimes they may be used for bait.

I know some Colorado trout anglers who successfully use both fish eggs and genuine insects in the good fast nymph waters. They employ tiny three-way swivels such as those used by some midwestern steelheaders. One eye holds a light 8-inch section of low-test mono plus lead weight. One eye is connected to the leader tippet. The line is tied to the third eye.

The baits are short-cast up-stream or quartering across and up. There must be enough weight to bring the bait to the bottom. Now here's where the skill comes in. The rig bumps along the bottom and sometimes hangs up. If you do not keep a tight line by the time you raise the rig from its snag there will be no time to strike should the fouling object on the bottom in fact be a fish. This is very much like steelheading. Here the waters are swift and usually white. Everything happens fast. What are some of the natural insect baits used for such angling? The answer is nymphs.

Trout feed on the nymphal forms of insect life all season. Usually they are able to obtain these creatures when they are metamorphizing into adults and rising to the surface. When nymphs are dislodged from beneath rocks and are floating free you can bet trout do not waste time in gobbling them. Some of the top nymphal creatures to consider are these: caddis worms, stonefly nymphs, hellgrammites, damselfly

Author landed this good rainbow on white grub in slow water section of agricultural belt river.

nymphs and dragonfly nymphs. All can be used as bait using hooks proportionate to the size of the nymph or worm. I suggest bait holder type hooks when possible.

You can collect this natural bait by overturning stones in the shallows just out of the strong main current. In fairly deep water you should have a partner standing just downstream of the rocks you turn. Equip him with a 2-foot square piece of netting tacked to two sticks which he holds in either hand. Washed-down nymphs will collect in the mesh. Keep the insects in ventilated containers containing damp vegetation. The caddis worms will regularly be found in cocoons made of silt, sticks and gravel. They stick fairly hard to the rocks and must be plucked off. You should remove the caddis worms from their cocoons for use.

The caddis worm and most nymphs may be hooked from the head end, out through the tail end. Make sure the barb protrudes to help hold the bait if your hooks are not bait holder type. You should hook big hellgrammites—often called nippers for what they can do to unwary anglers' fingers—through the collar just behind the head. The bait lives longer this way and the legs wiggle to attract fish. I hook the largest stoneflys through the head end, but let the abdominal section hang free.

These baits are best worked without weight when possible. The technique requires very light monofilament plus a clear teardrop-shaped or round casting bobber if you are using spinning gear. Attach the casting bobber about 2 feet from the hook and bait. Use the upstream or quartering presentation and keep a fairly short line. With fly gear you'll need a leader no shorter than 10 feet. Grease the top section of the leader so it will float with the line. How much leader must sink depends, of course, on the water depth. Use an easy lobbing cast. Fast fore-and-aft casting will throw the bait from the hook.

You must watch your line or flyleader like a hawk. A strike is signaled when the greased, floating leader section makes a slight forward movement while the rest of the line is still coming down toward you. With the spinning tackle, the casting bobber will pause slightly and possibly twitch or move forward. Strike then or it will be too late. Anglers who use fly gear and who cannot master the ability of detecting the slight forward movement of leader can put on a strike indicator—a small bit of cork with a matchstick stop—on the butt section of their leaders. Paint the indicator a bright fluorescent orange or red the better to see it.

In deeper, faster water you'll have to use weight or sinking lines or wire incorporated into the monofilament leader. These things all make detecting the take more difficult.

In midsummer don't fail to enjoy the pleasures of drifting crickets and especially grasshoppers—the medium size yellow ones—for trout. It's hard to beat standing hip deep in chill water on those thick hazy days, sending a kicking hopper down along a lovely meadow stream and watching the water explode to froth as a good fish suddenly comes tight against your line. And don't ignore the oddball baits such as tiny pink marshmallows that give an egg impression, or bread or cheese or salamanders. I like the little red wood newts for brook fishing, and garden or lawn grubs make good bait too.

A tip worthwhile remembering if you are using spinners or streamer flies with little luck, is to tip these lures with bits of worms, minnows, fish belly or fish eggs. The results are frequently fantastic.

An enterprising angler can discover new baits and ways to use them if he works at it, and working at bait fishing for stream trout will make you infinitely wiser to the ways of these fish.

If you're learning about trout via the natural bait method, and find yourself eating some flack from artificial lure fishermen who look down upon on what they may term inferior angling methods, ask them how they got started in this sport. Or remind them of the words of famed British trout and salmon angler John E. Hutton—straight from the land of the dry-fly-only mentality:

"Let the angler beware of becoming a 'purist': one who fatuously declares there is only one way in which to catch a fish . . . their inhibition discloses a one-way unimaginative mind whose narrow outlook causes them to lose a lot of fun . . ."

181

How to Find and Take Trout Close to Home

by WALT SANDBERG

A COMMON complaint among serious-minded trout fishermen today is that all the good streams are so overcrowded that trout fishing isn't much fun anymore. And when you do manage to elbow your way to a likely pool, they say, the meager catch will be sponge-fleshed hatchery fish with about as much fight as a winter-sluggish salamander.

Still, many anglers take native trout consistently from the unlikeliest places and vow that trout fishing is as good today as it was decades ago. Usually, they're the Old Timers with a thorough knowledge of an area. Over the years they've learned, mostly by accident, the locations of secluded streams and hidden trout haunts that are often within earshot of stocked stream fishermen.

But every area in the U.S. has trout streams and even if you're a newcomer lacking an Old Timer's knowledge, you should be able to find a good stream or two within a reasonable distance of home.

How close to home can you expect to find one of these overlooked trout streams? I once found one only 50 yards from my front door!

It was nearly dusk on a warm July evening when Wayne Doucha, my across-the-road neighbor of nearly 8 years, smugly watched as I pulled into the driveway after an unsuccessful trip to a favorite trout stream 125 miles away. The weather had been downright miserable and the fish off their feed.

"How'd you do?" Wayne needled.

I merely grimaced in reply.

"You should have stayed home," he smiled, rocking back on his heels with his arms clasped behind his back.

"Oh?" I said. "At least I got some exercise."

"Yes," he laughed. "While I took it easy in my backyard and caught trout, too."

He pulled his hands from behind his back and thrust out twin 13-inch brown trout. They were brightly hued and shiny, obviously freshly caught.

"Whose trout pond did you poach to get those?" I grunted suspiciously.

"They came from our creek," he said, pointing to the brooklet that tumbled along the roadway separating our suburban homes.

"Sure they did," I scoffed. I had crossed that tiny creek several hundred times in the past 8 years. It was spring-fed and a good gathering ground for watercress but only a handspan across in most places and not very deep.

"Come on," he said, "I'll show you the secret."

In the gathering darkness we walked a few yards upstream of his driveway culvert, to where the stream meandered through a cedar-choked lowland, and watched as dark shapes darted from under the banks to feed in mid-stream on a tiny, white freshwater shrimp. They were trout all right. No question of it.

We probed under the banks with a long stick and found that some holes undercut the streamside by three feet and were relatively deep; ideal trout hides. The fish holed up in them during daylight hours to avoid overhead predation and ventured into the stream only at twilight. That's why we hadn't noticed them before.

You won't often stumble across a new trout stream quite that easily, of course. Most will take a good deal of exploring to find.

But it isn't necessary to stay with the Old Timer's hit-or-miss methods that take away valuable fishing time. Instead, use a streamfinding kit—maps, aerial photos, compass and stream thermometer—to classify streams fast.

The basics of a good streamfinding kit are U.S. Geological Survey maps of the area you want to fish. Each state is covered by a series of maps or "quadrangles." They're inexpensive and will help you locate streams, spring holes, beaver ponds, and lakes.

Maps covering the states west of the Mississippi River, including Alaska, Hawaii, Louisiana, and Minnesota, may be ordered from the Denver Distribution Center, U.S. Geological Survey, Federal Center, Denver, CO 80225.

For states east of the Mississippi River, order maps from the Distribution Section, U.S. Geological Survey, 1200 South Eads St., Arlington, VA 22202.

Before ordering a specific map, write for a free "index" map of your state, then select the maps you'll need from the index. It's a good idea, too, to request a free copy of the folder which describes maps, map symbols, and map use.

Useful, too, are the official highway maps of your state. They show all the roads in a county, section, or highway district. Most states publish them and they're available at low cost by writing the State Department of Transportation in the State Capitol.

To supplement the topographic maps and the highway maps, the "guide" maps and brochures published by tourist bureaus, chambers of commerce, resorts, and conservation clubs, are sometimes of value. They will show hiking, snowmobiling, and cross-country skiing trails that won't be found on the others.

One recently completed recreational trail that I first spotted on a tourist bureau guidemap, saved me a half-hour of tough, cross-country hiking to a little-known trout stream close to my home.

But the ultimate "map" to place in your streamfinding kit is an aerial photo. They're available in several scales and sizes from the U.S. Department of Agriculture. For information on how to get them for states west of the Mississippi River, write U.S.D.A., Aerial Photography Division, Western Laboratory, 2505 Parley's Way, Salt Lake City, UT 84109. For states east of the Mississippi, write U.S.D.A., Photography Division, Eastern Laboratory, 45 South French Broad Avenue, Asheville, N.C. 28801.

◀ This easily assembled streamfinder's kit contains all you'll need to find trout close to home: maps of all kinds, aerial photos, compass, stream thermometer, and ultra-light spinning gear.

When the stream thermometer registers about 60 degrees, you've found a trout stream.

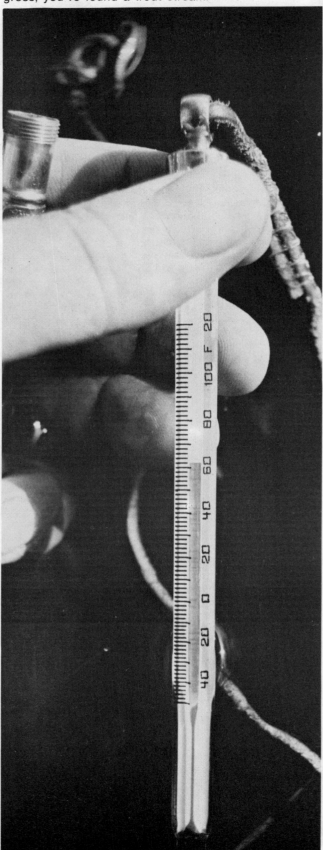

The aerial photos, used in conjunction with the other maps, will help you find hard-to-reach beaver ponds, spring holes, and portions of streams that might not show up clearly on the others. Aerial photos make it easier to determine the location of swamps, ridgelines, and various types of vegetation in relation to the stream.

Another good addition to the streamfinding kit are old plat maps, the older the better. Copies of these are sometimes available at the Register of Deeds office in the county seat of your area. Use them to spot abandoned railroad grades, bridges and highway crossings, washed out dams, and old logging roads; anything that can make the way in easier or the fishing better once you get there.

After you've assembled the various maps, the next step in streamfinding is to decide where to go. If you know the area well, you already have a pretty good feel for which hidden streams have potential. But if you're in unfamiliar territory, where do you start?

One way is to get a list of recently stocked streams. Fish and game departments in most states have them. If a ready-made list isn't available ask the local warden or the manager of the nearest fish hatchery. Usually, they will be happy to give you all the information you need.

Stocked streams, of course, are proven trout habitat. You might not want to fish them but their upstream portions and tributaries might be just the off-the-beaten path trout water you're looking for. So locate them on your maps, find the stocking points, then mark likely headwaters and feeder streams.

Another way to classify which streams have potential as trout producers is to talk with the Old Timers who no longer fish but still enjoy the sport. Usually, they'll be happy to tell you where all the best fishing "used to be."

Don't discount their stories. Many of these areas still produce fish but are too out-of-the-way to attract all but the hardiest of modern trouter.

Better still, take an Old Timer on a nostalgic tour of his old haunts. You'll enjoy it and so will he.

Once, when driving a back road with an elderly trout fisherman who suffered from arthritis and was no longer able to fish his favorite bush country streams, he asked me to stop the car at a roadside, then pointed out a high ridge that snaked off into the timber.

"Beaver pond in there," he said succinctly, "took many a trout out of it. But that was 30 years ago."

I perked up, of course.

"Boy! Did I hit 'em one day," he mused. "All 12 inches and better. You could take as many trout as you could carry out in those days, so I shucked my shirt and used it as a sack. The mosquitos just about ate me alive by the time I got out to the Model A."

I made a mental note of the location and checked the topographic map as soon as I got home. A thin, blue line squiggled within three-quarters of a mile of the road. And a check of the aerial photo showed a slight widening of the stream with marshy lowland all around. Perhaps the beaver pond, or its replacement, was still there.

A week or two later I walked the ridgeline in and found the remnants of the pond without difficulty. And I found a stream channel no more than a yardstick across and silted shut in most places. A bittern gulped at me from a hummock of tall reeds and a kingfisher family swooped overhead, patrolling the stream. Red-wing blackbirds cackled from their perches on fluffy, year-old cattail and dragonflies flitted here and there on the hot afternoon breeze.

A pleasant walk, I thought to myself, but obviously there will be no trout today.

Then, as I turned to scale the ridgeline, a slight twist of

the wind brought the sound of rushing water from upstream.

"Might as well check it out," I said aloud, as solitary fishermen are wont to do when they know there is no one around to hear them.

Ten minutes of hard brush-busting later I found the source: A *new* beaver pond, no more than 2 or 3 years old.

I waded in and the first cast with my favorite lure, a No. 2 gold Mepps Spinner, brought a slashing strike. Moments later I had a fine, 9-inch brook trout cooling in my canvas bag.

An hour later, I had my limit of 10 fish, all brookies, the largest a 10-inch male. He, and two, 9-inch beauties, went to the Old Timer who'd pointed out the hidden stream. He was delighted with them and vicariously hooked and fought each strike with me, when I brought them to his door that night.

Once you've assembled the maps for your streamfinding kit, and have also gathered the tips and information necessary to make them useful, you can do most of the work of stream classification and selection on the kitchen table.

First, locate the streams you want to try on the maps and aerial photos. Eliminate those streams or portions of streams that run through urban areas, agricultural feedlots, parks, and industrialized areas. Then mark the locations of the remaining selected streams on the topographic map with an indelible ink marking pen. (Red is the best contrast color.)

Note the nearest access points to the portion of stream you want to cover. Mark them, too.

Next, check the tourist maps for new and shorter routes; and the old plat maps for remnants of stream structures that might mean good fish hides or for abandoned right-of-ways that might make easier walking.

Then check the aerial photos for swamps, thick brush, or other obstacles that might make the going harder.

By now, if you've done your homework, you'll have a good idea of the route. But to save time later, write in the compass bearings; predetermining where you're going to go can save a lot of headaches in the field.

A compass, of course, is an important part of the streamfinding kit. Much of the best fishing isn't at access points. It's cross country. And even if the way in is short, noting the bearings on the map and using a compass once you're in the field will save needless wandering.

I've learned to include a third item—a stream thermometer—in my streamfinding kit after a tip from an area game warden a couple of years back. He suggested there were trout in a small creek that coursed along a country road near a crossroads village and then flowed into a larger river. The trout, he said, hid out in the headwaters of the stream during warm weather.

I did my kitchen table homework, found the stream on the map, but when I drove the country road I found nothing but a mushy wallow. The waters there didn't even have a flow!

The walk up to where the fishing was supposed to be looked formidable. A dense maze of alder brush and willows interspersed with stinging nettle and briars. And all of it growing from marshy hummocks surrounded by muck, the kind that is nearly impossible to trudge through without ripping waders to confetti on hidden snags or pulling boots

The streamfinding fisherman's only companions will be an osprey or a dappled fawn at streamside. (Olive Glasgow photos)

Left—Upstream portions or tributaries of stocked streams might be just the off-the-beaten path trout water you're looking for. Above—Wayne Doucha prefers tote-in waders and landing net for small stream fishing.

off your feet with every step.

But a hot tip on a possible unknown trout stream was good enough for me, so I battled the willows.

Finally, I found a hole. Dozens of casts failed to produce a strike. No sign of a trout.

Then I found another hole, and another. I fished them all carefully. Not a strike!

Dusk came down hard before I found the hole my warden friend had been telling me about. The first flip of a night-crawler brought a resounding strike and I was fast to one of those brookies that seems to head for bottom before you can set the hook, and, instead, gets his own hooks set in bottom. Long minutes later I pumped him to the surface and beached him gently on his side; a 14-inch male with the start of a hooked underjaw and flesh the color of an October sunset.

I took two more nice brook trout from that hard-found pool before night came down, and I've taken many more from it and another hole farther upstream since that day.

For it was only later that I learned the fish held in those two pools—among dozens of others that look just like them—because spring seeps feed trout-tempered waters into them year around.

Now I find similar pools easily by simply dipping in a stream thermometer rather than wasting time flaying the

waters to a froth only to come up fishless.

Brown trout and rainbow trout seem to prefer water temperatures of 61 degrees. Brook trout seem to prefer 58 degrees. That's when they feed best.

All three species will tolerate water temperatures in the range of 48 to 68 degrees but they feed actively, grow faster, and fight better only when stream temperatures are within 5 degrees, either way, of their preferred ideal.

So it's easier to classify streams, or portions of streams, as trout water with a stream thermometer. If the stretch you've selected registers higher than 68 degrees, it's unlikely it will contain trout.

But before you scratch this "possible" off your list, take stream temperature readings at several other locations upstream and down. Trout will congregate in astonishing numbers in spring-fed holes of the right water temperature. Find the proper temperature and you'll take fish from the unlikeliest places.

Once you know where to find the hidden streams near your home there's still two nearly-insurmountable problems that streamfinders face—brush and bugs.

Bugs can be handled with large gobs of insect repellent and headnets. Brush is another matter. It's there, clutching at you all the time.

One way to beat it is to strip yourself of the usual para-

Above—Six native brookies testify to the success of diligent stream-finding. Right—Steve Reckner prefers to leave troublesome, brush-clutching gear at home and wade wet.

phernalia of the Abercrombie & Fitch trout fishermen—waders, nets, wading staffs, even bulky wicker creels. These accoutrements, although absolutely necessary for trout fishing enjoyment on larger streams, have no place in the tangled, brush-choked sidepockets where native trout abound.

Your waders are better left at home: Wade wet. A pair of rubber-soled canvas sneakers will grip the rocks as well.

And the walnut-handled landing net that snags even on the most hairlike of twigs to rebound into the back of your head on its springy, rubber lanyard—leave that at home. Beach 'em, or tire them well and slip a finger through a gill.

And the wicker creel, the most notorious of brush-clutchers, leave it behind. A plastic bag will do, a chunk of denim trouser leg sewn up on one end and hitched around a shoulder with a length of clothesline rope is better, and a hard canvas creel-bag that cools and breathes when wetted is better still.

You might consider leaving your prize flyrod at home, too. Most small streams are a fly fisherman's nightmare. Insect hatches are usually sparse. Nor is there room for a proper backcast.

Still, one of the best streamfinders I know always carries in a stiff, 9-foot flyrod. His theory is that you can use it to drop a bait into a likely hole without spooking the quarry.

I've tried it. And after futilely fencing brush like some demented backwoods Don Quixote, I've decided it isn't worth the effort. At least, not for me.

Another good streamfinder I know takes the opposite approach. He uses a short, 2-foot spin casting outfit that was originally designed for ice fishing. And he has this pokerlike wand strung with 12-pound-test mono. His idea is that you hit 'em fast and horse 'em out.

I've tried that set-up, too. It solves the long-rod-catching-in-the-brush problem but it isn't sporting nor does it have the reach you'll often need.

My favorite small-stream outfit is a 5½-foot ultralight spinning rod, miniature open-face reel, and 4-pound mono.

The combination is short enough to snake through the brushiest tangles, strong enough to keep even trophy stream trout from tearing-off out-of-control, affords reasonable reach, and is great fun to fish with.

Is streamfinding worth all this effort?

You bet it is!

Use a streamfinding kit to pinpoint a little-known trout stream close to home and you'll share it only with an osprey, sometimes a dappled fawn at streamside, occasionally an otter, kingfisher, or an eagle, but never with another angler.

And you'll take trout. Native trout that fight like tethered submarines and taste, panfried in butter, like a little bit of heaven.

Build a Trout Fishing Library

by DAVID RICHEY

TROUT FISHING has its roots buried deep in angling literature. Without books, written by knowledgeable fishermen, anglers today might still be in the dark ages of fishing.

It's been said that books were written to be read and this is doubly true of books written for fishermen. There are many classics and near-classics on today's book shelves and these books are meant to be read and read again.

I'm in the fortunate position of being a book reviewer. I review about a dozen outdoor-oriented books monthly and out of this number there occasionally emerges only one or two destined for greatness. Books, to impress me, must be both informative and entertaining. I can obtain little satisfaction from a book that merely entertains. It's got to have some substance; something that either teaches me something about my sport or teaches and entertains at the same time. Unfortunately, few books can accomplish this task.

The subject of trout is broad indeed and many books have been written on the subject. Many books give just partial coverage to the subject of trout while others give it the red carpet treatment.

The following will be a compilation of books I've found particularly useful in both informing and entertaining me. All deal either wholly or in part with the subject of trout. All have either taught me something I didn't know or have made me feel like I'm on a trout stream or lake. In either case, the authors did the job for which they were striving; they entertained and/or informed.

I'm a student of good angling writing and I've found it impossible to place any trout fishing writer above Roderick Haig-Brown of British Columbia. Crown Publishers has elected to reprint Haig-Brown's memorable works *Fishermen's Spring, Fishermen's Summer, Fishermen's Fall* and *Fishermen's Winter*. These books have become known as classics in angling literature. The four books take the fisherman through all phases of the year and trout fishing figures prominently in all books. I've got a complete collection of Haig-Brown titles and I treasure them dearly. This is a writer in tune with trout fishing, the environment and with what it takes to make a winter-bound angler feel feverish and eager for spring. I highly recommend these titles.

Crown Publishers has gathered together the works of another extremely gifted writer in Robert Traver. Crown has published *Trout Magic,* a book destined to fame just as *Trout Madness* achieved. Traver is a talented writer and his warm humor and amusing anecdotes make any reader eager to seek secluded beaver ponds or backwoods streams where native brook trout are numerous and willing to come to the fly. *Trout Magic* is an excellent book to read anytime.

Joe Brooks penned *Trout Fishing* for Harper & Row back in 1972 and this book is a tribute to a dedicated trout fisherman. This book contains trout fishing wisdom not found in many books and the angling public should be forever happy Joe Brooks authored the book before his death. This book covers all facets of trout fishing from tackle to tactics. Well worth purchasing.

Getting Hooked on Fishing by Knap & Richey (Pagurian Press) is a pretty basic fishing book. Three chapters set this book a notch above others; it contains well-written chapters on downrigger, temperature and sonar fishing. These subjects have never been covered in such depth. Fishermen interested in learning how to fish with downriggers or according to water temperature would be well advised to buy the book. Other chapters give detailed instructions on how to catch trout in lakes and streams.

It goes without saying that DBI Books' *Fishermen's Digest* has a wealth of trout fishing information gathered by famed book author Erwin A. Bauer. Bauer has a knack for putting excellent trout fishing stories in various editions of *Fishermen's Digest* and he features trout stories from all over North America. Each trout story fills the bill on informing and entertaining.

Anyone interested in instructing their youngsters would be well advised to purchase a copy of *Teaching Your Children to Fish* by Jack Fallon (Winchester Press). The author gently guides the parent through the comical—sometimes tragic—process of teaching youngsters how to catch fish. A parent can easily adapt his philosophy to deal with trout fishing. This is a complete and informative book on the subject and one that should grace any reader's bookshelf—especially if he has children.

Nighttime is when big trout feed heavily and a book has been authored by Jim Bashline titled *Night Fishing For Trout.* Freshet Press is the publisher and it stands as the only book I know of dealing strictly with how to fish at night for trout. Bashline covers tackle, methods of presentation, flies, wading techniques and feeding habits of trout after dark. Any trout fisherman with a yen for hanging a big trout on his den wall should read this book and practice what Bashline preaches. He's an expert on nighttime trout fishing.

Selective Trout is a Crown Publishers title that swept the world of trout fishing like wildfire several years ago. Authors Swisher and Richards startled trout fishermen with their new "no hackle dry flies." This revolutionary new concept of fly fishing for selective trout has opened up an entirely new world to trout fishermen. The drawings and photos represent some of the best insect imitations I've ever seen. This book, if it's not a classic already, will surely become one in years to come.

Trout Streams by Needham (Winchester Press) is a classic work on the subject which was recently updated and revised. It gives the reader a look at a trout stream and the life in it. A good, fairly comprehensive and scientific book on the subject.

Ray Ovington's *Tactics on Trout* (Alfred A. Knopf) leads the trout fisherman by his rod hand through many classic trout fishing situations. Easy to understand diagrams and drawings teach the fisherman how to best cover typical lies on almost any trout stream. A different approach to tactics.

A book I've found immensely useful is Kreh & Sosin's *Practical Fishing Knots* (Crown). This book taught me about knots I'd never dreamed existed. I've tried many and found they offer much to the world of trout fishing. Clear photographs and line drawings illustrate this book and lead the fisherman, step-by-step, through even the most intricate knots. Breaking strength of each knot is listed which I found very informative. Many of the newer knots are much stronger than the old favorites.

Possibly one of the finest angling books available is *McClane's New Standard Fishing Encyclopedia & International Angling Guide.* This hefty volume by Holt, Rinehart & Winston covers all aspects of fishing but there is some very good information on the various species of trout and trout fishing. Color plates of trout flies and trout makes this a dandy book for reference. Highly recommended.

The soon to be published book titled *The Complete Steelheader* by David Richey (Stackpole) is the most up-to-date book on this mighty migrant from the Pacific Ocean and the Great Lakes. All the newest techniques of steelhead fishing are spelled out in easy to follow chapters. Learn all about bait fishing, fly fishing, trolling and assorted tricks of the trade that make this sport so appealing to both West Coast and Midwest anglers. The most complete and detailed book on the subject. A welcome addition to any angler's bookshelf.

Art Flick's Master Fly Tying Guide by Crown hosts a world of flies—dries, wets, nymphs, midges, no-hackles, and streamers—for the serious trout fisherman. A host of fly tying greats such as Ernest Schwiebert, Lefty Kreh, Carl Richards, Dave Whitlock and others describe how they tie various flies. A very informative book for trout fishermen.

Campground Cooking by Charles and Kathleen Farmer (DBI Books) will tell even the most novice cook how to prepare trout they've caught. A variety of cooking experts divulge their favorite methods of cooking trout in this fascinating book. Scanning its pages for the umpteenth time, I find myself getting hungry for trout cooked around a campfire.

Fly Fishing the Lakes by Rex Gerlach (Winchester Press) is a good example of a book being written to fill a much needed gap. This book offers some much needed information on how to fly fish a lake for trout. Learn how a lake's environment is important to the angler, how to fish the various types of flies, how to hook and land a fish and much more. A solid "how to" book on angling.

Peter Barrett's *In Search of Trout* (Prentice Hall) is a book I've enjoyed reading several times. It deals primarily with fly fishing for trout but also contains some good information on bait fishing. The amusing anecdotes make the book both interesting and fun to read.

Dana Lamb's exquisite *Green Highlanders and Pink Ladies* (Barre Publishers) is a tiny book written by a master fly fisherman and master story teller. This is a book to be read just before bed or while you toast in front of a winter's fire. Lamb has the knack of putting the reader right into his short stories. I love his books.

Kamloops by Steve Raymond (Winchester Press) is a definitive book written about this trout of the West. The Kamloops grows to large sizes and is fairly regional in nature. The author studies the fish and presents a thorough and scholarly look at a little known fish.

There are many other books available dealing wholly or partially with trout and/or trout fishing. I've covered some of the newer books that trout fishermen should read and enjoy.

A trout library is a thing of beauty—something to be savored and indulged in whenever possible. Good books on trout fishing never lose their value. If anything, they increase in value as years go by.

TROPHIES AT NIGHT

by JIM BASHLINE

THE BIGGEST brown trout are caught at night. Well, maybe not the record fish because they're mostly accidents . . . but consistently, the really super-size wall hangers usually fall to some die-hard who happens to be out there trying when the big browns decide to do some feeding.

In streams that are affected severely by summertime temperatures, the reason becomes quite obvious. Surface temperatures frequently rise into the low 70s in many eastern and midwestern trout waters and trout are not anxious to take a warm bath. They find undercut banks and submerged hiding places to get away from the hot water. When evening approaches, they begin to move around a bit, out into the shallows where insects, minnows and crustaceans are easy pickin's.

Large brown trout have also become accustomed to seeing the man-silhouette along the water's edge during the daylight hours and—call it "brains" or instinct—they soon discover

that being abroad in the daytime is not good for their health.

There is also an abundance of food at night. Junebugs, moths, crayfish and numerous night flying insects including some of the larger mayflies are out and about at night. It's much easier for the big fish to take up a feeding position at the tail end of a deep pool and wait for something edible to drift by.

In the far western streams of the United States, there is somewhat less night fishing done than in the East or Midwest. The cooler water temperatures allow the fish more daylight feeding time . . . and there is much less fishing pressure. But even in the more remote locations, there are still individual brown trout who are quite simply, night feeders. They prefer to dine at a more refined hour and only they know exactly why. Available food, water temperature, fishing pressure, water chemistry are all possible factors. But there is also a mysterious X factor that has never been fully explained. The same thing happens during the daylight. We have all (those of us who have fly fished for trout) been on a stream when everything seemed to be perfect but nothing happened. There

This angler belly lifts a chunky brown trout from a Pennsylvania stream. Properly presented flies after dark fool big trout.

were flies on the water, the water temperature hung at 59 or 60 degrees, trout were in evidence but they would not rise or take any of our offerings. Then suddenly, as if someone threw a switch, they began to feed. It was just like a signal had been given. In concert, the fish came to the surface and just about everything that was offered in the shape of a dry fly was eagerly sucked in.

Precisely the same thing can happen at night. Sometimes, that wild feeding spell takes place just as the sun goes down. At other times it won't occur until an hour or two after total darkness sets in. Still again, it might not start until midnight or later. A lot of answers come to mind. Changing water temperature is certainly one of them and so is availability of food. John Alden Knight said it was the moon and its relative position to the earth that triggered the feeding spree and he may well have been right.

I must admit that I have never caught or seen caught, a really big trout on a bright moonlit night. I have seen some big rainbows and browns come out of deep lakes on bright nights but never a fly-caught fish in moving water. Oh sure, the little

stocked trout will hammer most anything at anytime but even they become more selective on bright nights.

Okay, what's the best time to go night fishing for trout? Ideally, it should be on a moonless night that features a mild west wind. It would help matters tremendously if the barometer was on the rise and a nice sunset wouldn't hurt anything either. My diary indicates that handsome sunsets usually mean good night fishing. Don't ask me to explain why . . . they just do.

Surface activity before darkness doesn't necessarily mean that the night fishing will be good. I've had some excellent before-dark dry-fly fishing and then been skunked after dark. Just the reverse can happen as well. That peculiar X factor is the thing. Big trout on most waters are not active surface feeders (although there are some notable exceptions. Pennsylvania's Letort is one). They are usually looking for a more substantial meal. Crayfish, minnows, small mice and anything that moves is fair prey to a big brown.

But even the food angle is suspicious. I have performed autopsies on dozens of large, night-caught brown trout and more often than not, they had nothing or very little in their stomachs. It seems like they might have struck my fly for the sheer hell of it.

For those unfamiliar with night fishing for trout as it is practiced in the eastern part of the U.S., let me quickly point

Left—The author ties up his leader and two flies for nightfishing. It's best to do this before full dark sets in.

Below and below left—Jim Bashline shows his hand retrieve method. A light action rod and hip boots are all that's needed for night fishing.

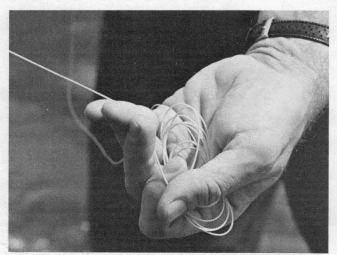

Below—Many fishermen get the "feel" of the water by fishing down through it before dark. It will be more familiar after the sun goes down.

out that there are more fish taken on flies than on anything else. This is because more night fishermen are using flies but mostly because they are more effective on most nights. There are exceptions to this too but year in and year out, the angler casting a pair of No. 6 wet flies will hang more big fish than will the bait fisherman or lure user.

I had the privilege of fishing with some of the masters of the night fishing game. They were the cadre of dedicated night flyers who worked the streams of northcentral Pennsylvania when I was a fuzzy chinned kid. Their usual armament consisted of a trio of flies. The two droppers were tied on about 24 inches apart. The old way was to use a level leader into which

four loops had been tied. All wet flies were snelled then. A sometimes not-too-secure arrangement but it did make for speed in changing flies. In later years, after the advent of monofilament, the regulars switched to eyed flies with droppers fashioned by extending one end of a blood knot. I still use this system and it works well. If you tie loops well, there is nothing wrong with using snelled flies. They are much easier to change after dark.

The tail end of a familiar pool is the best place to begin a night fishing career. During the heat of the day, the large fish will stay in the protective depths of the pool. As night time progresses they will move to the tail end of the "slick" water

A big Nebraska brown trout fell to this angler after darkness spread across the Snake River. Lunker browns like this are more commonly caught at night than any other time.

Twelve-inch brookies like this are fun to catch after dark.

and there, the fly caster can get in his deadly work. You may or may not see some surface rises in the slick water but chances are, you will see a looping swirl as a big trout takes up his watching station or darts after a minnow or roots around for a back-peddling crayfish.

Cast your string of flies 10 to 12 feet above the end of the slick (or the spot you saw the fish surface) and allow the flies to drift without any motion. A dead drift is the proper nomenclature. If this doesn't produce a strike in five or six casts, apply a bit of jiggling action to the flies. The best trick is to cause the top dropper or "hand" fly to tickle the surface. This will frequently bring a strike and if it does, it will be a spectacular one. The same technique can be employed with two flies. Incidentally, two flies will work about as well on small to medium rivers. The three-fly rig will simply cover more water and give the fish a three-way choice.

In very still pools and ponds, it may be necessary to allow the flies to sink to the bottom or nearly so. Then, the best way to impart action is via the hand-twist method. This means coiling the fly line loosely in the hand and stacking it up shuttle fashion for the next cast.

The easiest part of fly fishing after dark for trout is the strike. Most of the time, the take will be solid and positive. Trout don't usually piddle and peck at the big night flies. When they decide to inhale it they do just that and your reaction is ordinarily vigorous to say the least. For this reason, the night fly leader can be reasonably stout. Four pieces of mono, say 20, 15, 12 and 8, will do nicely. You can go down to six if you wish but trout are not notoriously leader shy at night. The heavier leader is also an advantage in playing and landing the fish. Unless you are totally familiar with the pool, you won't know exactly where every snag is located. Fight the fish hard and "lay the wood" to him. It's more fun that way and besides if you wish to release the fish he'll be in better condition than one that has been fondled to death with a 6 X tippet.

In shallow lakes where brookies and rainbows may be found, night fishing works also. A pair of wets trolled from a canoe or slowly putting boat equipped with an electric trolling motor, is highly productive at times. All trout will hit at night . . . it's just that the browns seem especially susceptible to the nocturnal stuff.

The fly patterns that have taken trout at night are many and varied. However, 30 years of chasing fish after dark have brought me to some rather ordinary patterns as my favorites. The three all-time-great night patterns in the eastern U.S. are: the Governor, Professor and the Silver Doctor. Old patterns to be sure, but a bit bizarre when we consider what sophisticated brown trout are supposed to take. The iridescence of the peacock body on the Governor has long been a proven trout getter. The flashy, silver body of the Silver Doctor may suggest an escaping minnow but what of the yellow bodied Professor? I suppose it's just a democratic suggestion of a lot of bugs . . . at any rate it works. So do the Hardy's Favorite, a salmon tied Jock Scott and a host of other odd looking flies.

Night flies in general should be tied fat and succulent on a No. 6 or 8 hook. At times, I have used smaller and larger flies but 8s and 6s are my favorite sizes with the 6 getting the edge on most waters.

Just after a rain, if the water doesn't become too cloudy, a worked minnow, rigged on a wire trace or a loosely hooked night crawler will also produce big browns at night. Night cruising trout have been caught on every sort of creeping, crawling thing but the all-time best night bait for trout has got to be a small crayfish that has just shucked its shell. There are few trophy browns who can resist a look at a tail-hooked crayfish worked slowly across a shallow bar. The little ones about 3 inches long are just right.

In deeper rivers and ponds, spinning lures and small surface plugs will also entice brown trout at times. However, the over-powering splash will usually spook trout in shallow water so I much prefer the flies in these locations.

With the big trout's liking for small minnows, it would seem that streamer flies would work well at night. In most cases they don't. Lord knows I've thrown a thousand different streamers at night feeding trout with very little success. The standard wet fly configuration seems to work much better. Trout in lakes and ponds may hit streamers better at night when trolled, but my experience is rather limited here.

If you do get hooked on the night fishing bug, my sympathies. Your fishing buddies will forsake you (most of them), your wife will threaten divorce and strange dogs will bark at you. But it's fun and the best way I know of to hang a bragging size brown trout.

Dusk is the magic time to be on a stream for big trout.

Lake Trout —King of the Clan

by DAVID RICHEY

TROUT FISHERMEN'S DIGEST editor David Richey grins happily over a 26-pound lake trout from Great Bear Lake in the Northwest Territories.

GREG MEADOW'S ultra-light spinning rod was bowed over in a tight curve and the drag on his reel was howling as a Great Bear Lake laker hummed off hard earned yards of his 6-pound line.

"Look at him go!" Greg hollered. The fish continued to peel off line as it worked its way toward deeper water. "I can't stop him," Greg howled, "I can see the spool."

Our Cree guide, Charley Hamelin—a seasoned veteran guide at 22 years of age—quickly spun the light aluminum boat around and we followed Greg's fish.

Greg's arm was spinning like a top as he crowded spare line back onto the spool. Soon Charley had us positioned directly above the fish and Greg leaned into the lake trout.

Several lunging rushes later the laker turned on his side and slid toward the surface and Charley's waiting net. We exchanged congratulations as Charley weighed out a whopping 23-pounder. Greg massaged the stiffness from his wrist and we headed back for a hotspot we'd located in front of Branson's Lodge.

Ten minutes later the wobble of my spoon stopped and a deep throbbing headshake came from 30 yards astern. A laker had taken the large yellow and red diamonded Dardevle and was shaking its head trying to work out the barbs of the treble hook.

I slammed the baitcasting rod back and firmly anchored the hooks. My rod tip jerked strongly toward the stern as the lake trout sounded for deep water. I forced the rod tip high and the lake trout slammed it down again. The second time the rod was yanked, it broke—just below the ferrule.

I yelled at Charley to back me up as I cranked frantically to recover some line. The rod tip was pointing directly down the line toward the fish and only a couple of fibers held it together. I was reduced to fighting a big laker with just my rod's bottom guide and the reel. This was going to take some doing.

The lake trout, once it eased into 30 feet of water, sulked heavily on bottom and moved very little. My rod was useless for pressuring the fish into action. I began trying to lift the fish off bottom inches at a time.

The trout would come up a foot or two and then angle back towards bottom. This back and forth charade went on for close to 10 minutes before I could feel the laker easing toward the surface. I reeled slowly, kept a tight line and didn't apply any pressure.

When the trout was about 20 feet below the boat I could see him rolling and thrashing in the crystal clear water. He looked as long as an oar.

Charley was standing by with the net while Greg stood on the bow shooting pictures. The laker kept coming in, rolling in the line and swapping end for end. But he never made another attempt to head for bottom.

He surfaced 10 feet from the boat and I simply reeled him the last few feet across the surface and into Charley's net. I tossed the busted rod in the bottom of the boat and gave him a hand lifting my prize into the boat. He popped the needle on the scales down to 26 pounds, not bad for a busted-rod fish.

Lake trout are considered to be the king of the clan—the tackle busting variety that grows to fantastic weights in many places. Needless to say, Great Bear Lake in the Northwest Territories reigns as *the* place to go for lunker lake trout. Branson's Lodge, my favorite on this huge ocean-like lake, holds four world records including the lake trout, lake whitefish, arctic char and grayling.

Lake trout in Great Bear range in size from young 3- and 4-pounders up to the mythical fish scaling over 100 pounds. The record lake trout weighed over 60 pounds and yearly visitors to the lake tell stories of spotting lake trout almost

Greg Meadows sweeps a lunker lake trout into the boat.

as long as the boat they're fishing from. Taking into account a bit of excitement and exaggeration, a lake trout half the length of a boat is one big fish.

The fact of the matter is that these lakes in the north country have a huge number of large lake trout but the supply is not inexhaustible. The things that keep lakes such as Great Bear producing lunkers year after year is their relative inaccessibility and the fact that the government places restrictions on openings of new camps and further restrictions on the number of camp guests each lodge may have yearly.

Since the lakes are so huge, only the smallest areas can be covered by fishermen. Hopefully, this will always remain so and our children and grandchildren may enjoy top notch fishing in the north.

Trolling is the best method of making connections with Great Bear lake trout. I've found the Dardevle to be the hottest spoon on the lake for trolling. Red and white or yellow with five red diamonds are the two best colors.

No weight is needed on the line for trolling in Great Bear because the lakers are near the surface at all times. We were able to fish 18 hours a day and we'd often see lake trout cruising or breaking the surface at midnight. Without a watch you'd never know what time it was because during early July the darkness is never complete. A fisherman could conceivably fish 24 hours a day if his body could stand the constant strain.

We found that pumping the rod tip would give the lures a bit extra action and lake trout often clobbered the spoon as it dropped back after being pumped.

Casting the shallows in bays was an excellent method of catching lake trout. Most of these fish ranged from 5 to 15 pounds and it wasn't uncommon at all to hook and land 50 fish a day per person. Many fishermen, myself included, took to pinching down the barbs on the spoons. This facilitated easier removal of the hooks.

One of the angling thrills I place at the top of my list is the sight of 30 or 40 lake trout converging on a spoon at one time. It's unnerving to watch lakers peel off, like miniature fighter bombers, and converge en masse on a lure. It becomes a trick trying to steer the spoon away from a small fish and into the maw of a larger one. This happened every day at Great Bear Lake.

Not all of Canada's lunker lake trout water lies in the Northwest Territories although Great Slave Lake is another top producer of jumbo trout.

Lake Athabasca in far northern Saskatchewan is world famous for producing big lake trout. Anglers visiting this lake just after ice out are often treated to spectacular lake trout fishing in the shallows.

Sport-caught lakers have scaled 50 pounds or better at Athabasca and netters have taken fish close to 100 pounds. An angler stands an excellent chance of landing a mounting size fish.

Manitoba has some excellent lake trout fishing and Lake Athapapuskow (Athapap) once held the world's record lake trout. Giant lakers are still entered yearly in the Manitoba Master Angler award program.

Lake Athapap lies between The Pas and Flin Flon in northern Manitoba and several commercial lodges and fishing camps are located on the lake. Thirty- to 35-pound lakers come from Athapap every year and June or July seem to be the best months.

Athapap is easily accessible by road and consequently gets heavy fishing pressure. Another hot lake trout lake in the same vicinity is Atimeg Lake just north of The Pas.

Many lakes in the Far North have lake trout and at this writing there are a goodly number that have never been fished extensively. I do a great deal of exporatory fishing in northern Canada and I've talked to many bush pilots that tell of gem-like lakes nestled in the mountains or far back in the bush with huge schools of big lake trout. Much of this country hasn't been tapped yet for its partial yield of lake trout.

As sportsmen push further and further into the bush in search of hot new fishing spots, more and more lake trout holes will open up. Some may possibly make anything that we know of now look ridiculous in comparison.

Anyone with a yen for travel and hot fishing action normally considers a trip to Canada or to one of the hot Arctic lakes already described.

Many fishermen do not have the financial means with which to pursue a trip that costs well over a thousand bucks. For them a lake trout trip can revolve around Great Lakes lake trout; not the huge trophy fish commonly associated with a lake like Great Bear but hard fighting lake trout from 6 to 20 pounds. The average Great Lakes lake trout is commonly pulling the peg down to about 8 pounds and 15-pounders are a daily occurrence. Twenty-pounders are still somewhat of a rarity, but well within the realm of possibility.

There's no denying the fact that Arctic lake trout can often be caught off the lodge dock, from the floats of a Cessna or Beaver seaplane, or by casting indiscriminately from shore in almost any location.

Such catches are unheard of in the Great Lakes, but there are times during spring and fall when lakers are in shallow water and can be caught casting from shore, pier or a small boat. True, you'll seldom hear the hyena-like yodeling of a loon, but the lake trout are there and they're getting bigger every year.

Prime lake trout country in the Great Lakes is limited at this time to Lakes Michigan and Superior. Some plants have been made in Lake Huron, but so far a fishery hasn't developed.

Lake Superior is the traditional trolling grounds in the Midwest for lakers and this has recently been disputed by Lake Michigan. Fishermen in Michigan, Wisconsin and Indiana are currently enjoying some of the best laker fishing imaginable during open water months. Lake Superior, although once the kingpin of lake trout fishing, now is decidedly in second place behind her second cousin.

Black River harbor, in the far western Upper Peninsula, is probably the best bet on Lake Superior for a chance at an over-20-pound lake trout. Lakers, locally called "fats," are taken off this port north of Ironwood every summer and many of the fish are oldtimers ranging from 20 to 25 pounds. These are the largest lake trout taken from the Great Lakes.

Unfortunately, some illegal gill netting by whites and Indians alike, is currently wreaking havoc on Lake Superior's lake trout population in certain areas. The fish are there, but indiscriminate gill netting is taking the trout off the shoals and in deep water. A sad but true commentary on the times.

Lake Michigan, a huge inland sea, is host to a catch of thousands of lake trout yearly. Planting figures remain steady but the lake trout, often called the "bread and butter" fish of charter boat skippers, is becoming overharvested in certain areas.

Michigan fisheries officials are trying to spread fishing pressure around the state so trout populations can rebound in some popular spots. Grand Traverse Bay at Traverse City is a classic example: Protected on three sides by land, Grand Traverse Bay is a haven for fishermen whenever Lake Michigan kicks up. It takes a hell of a strong north wind to make the Bay unfishable. Fishermen know this and flock to

L. Williams caught this huge lake trout trolling a Williams Wabler in Great Slave Lake.

Above—Lake Superior still produces the occasional big lake trout for Ontario fishermen. Below—Quebec is becoming famous for producing some big lake trout like these.

the area whenever fishing conditions are impossible elsewhere. Consequently, fishing pressure at this popular port is very heavy, fish catches on the whole are down, and many fishermen are wondering why.

The best bet now is to look into fishing in some of the other hotspots up and down the Lake Michigan shoreline. Plantings are very high in the southern part of the lake. South Haven in southwestern lower Michigan produces an extremely healthy catch of big lake trout every year. This is a consistent fishery with flat level bottom which makes for easy fishing. I've fished South Haven for years and have never been skunked for lake trout. Too many people pass it up because they are oriented to "up north."

One of the most popular Michigan ports in terms of fisherman attraction (lake trout) is Manistee. It hosts an excellent marina and the laker fishing is nothing short of fantastic during June and July. Sure, lake trout can be caught during the other openwater months but those are the peak times. Catches run to 15 fish per charter boat (with four or five customers aboard) on almost every charter that goes out. The Michigan limit is three lake trout per fisherman in possession.

Other excellent ports for lake trout fishing in Michigan would be Elk Rapids, Leland, Frankfort, Ludington, Pentwater, Muskegon and Benton Harbor-St. Joseph.

Indiana hosts some top-notch spring lake trout fishing as soon as the ice goes out and up until June. A resurgence occurs during the cooler fall months. The bulk of the fishing occurs off Michigan City where charter boats and private fishermen vie for limit catches of fish.

Illinois has some lake trout fishing early in the spring while the water is cold. Diversey Harbor and Waukegan are two favorite ports in the Chicago area and laker fishing often takes place within sight of the skyscrapers of the Loop. Once the water warms up the lake trout tend to move out, either up the Wisconsin shoreline or up into Michigan water.

Wisconsin has a lake trout fishery that rivals that of Michigan. There are certain areas where limit catches of lake trout are a daily occurrence and where 15-pound lakers are commonplace and no one raises an eyebrow until a 17- or 18-pounder hits the deck.

The ports of Milwaukee, Sheboygan, Manitowoc and Sturgeon Bay are centers of lake trout activity. I personally can well remember a trip out of Bailey's Harbor with charter boat skipper Jerry Cefalu.

Accompanying me was fish manager Lee Kernen of Green Bay. Jerry had invited us along for a trip and asked how much time we had and how many lake trout we wanted to catch. We told him a couple of hours and we didn't care how many fish, just so we had enough trout for a fish boil.

We ran out from Bailey's Harbor for about 15-minutes and Jerry shut the engines down to trolling speed. "We're over a submerged reef," he advised us. He set the four lines and we began trolling.

I was watching Jerry's graph when we went over the underwater hump. Lake trout marks showed on top and all sides. The first pass netted us three strikes and one fish—a creamy spotted 11-pounder.

Four more passes and we had six fish in the box and many strikes. Lee boated the top fish—a chunky 16-pounder. The others averaged 10 or 11 pounds. We'd had several strikes and hung fish for an instant before losing them.

I like the area around the Door Peninsula for lake trout. Washington Island, at the tip of Door County, is a good spot for lake trout as is certain areas at the northern end of Green Bay. Lake trout average quite large in this area and the fishing pressure isn't nearly as heavy as in the more southerly waters.

A happy fisherman poses with his catch taken at Great Bear Lake.

One area in Wisconsin's portion of Lake Superior stands out head and shoulders above the rest and that is the famed Apostle Islands. A group of a dozen or so islands, the Apostles are noted for dishing up big lake trout. It used to be a favored trolling grounds for the old time laker fishermen and, since the resurgence of good lake trout fishing in some parts of Lake Superior, many people are flocking to the docks at Bayfield for another shot at the Islands.

Trolling is the primary method of catching Great Lakes lake trout and this is normally accomplished in two manners —with downrigger or by trolling with wire line. There seems to be a personality conflict between wire-pullers and downriggers fishermen and this can best be explained by their methods of fishing. The downrigger fisherman is fishing almost directly beneath his boat and can make quick positive turns to port or starboard. The wire line fisherman has as much as 400 feet of wire strung out behind his boat. The two often tangle and the mess can be a calamity.

Downrigger fishermen use a variety of lures and attractors to bring lake trout in. The favorite of many fishermen is the Herring Dodger and Barber fly. Trolling flies are long affairs with a mylar body for extra flash at great depths, a hair wing of blue, green or yellow, and a stout hook to hold a lake trout once it's hooked.

Another excellent combination is a Cowbell and almost anything behind it. My most productive lures are Andy Reekers, Tadpollys, Dardevles, Fire Plugs, Flutter Spoons, Bayou Specials and almost anything else at any given time that seems to be producing.

There are times when trolling a lure with an attractor pays off big and other times the fisherman must troll the lure "clean"—without an attractor. The downrigger fisherman can usually stagger his lines and include some with an attractor and some without.

The wire line fisherman normally uses an attractor. A Cowbell is generally accepted as best. Two schools of thought come to mind in regard to the lure. Many fishermen opt for a lure such as a spoon and they chug their lines to give the spoon action.

The other wireliner uses a Cowbell and sewed-on minnow. The same type of hookup is used as described elsewhere in this book on trolling inland lakes for trout. The only significant difference is the lake trout fishermen uses a larger minnow. I've gone along the beaches, early in the morning, and picked up fresh-dead alewives in the 3- to 5-inch size. They are deadly for lake trout.

The wire line fisherman fishes the bottom area exclusively and a large percentage of the time that's where the lakers are congregated. But not always. Many times lake trout will suspend themselves below a school of alewives. A good many lake trout fishermen merely locate schools of alewives and fish near these forage fish. They know lake trout will be somewhere near.

Lake trout are fun to catch and nothing can match the bullheaded battle of a big laker on light line. I thrill to the first glimpse of the opalescence glow of a laker coming up from deep water; the creamy white spots that sparkle when the fish comes from the water and the fine eating the fish graces the table with.

Lake trout fishing is certainly fun whether you're tied into a lunker on Great Bear Lake or a 10-pounder on Lake Michigan. Either way, you've got a handful of excitement.

Float a Lazy River

by JOHN EIS
Photos and illustration by Walt Sandberg

ED ROMANSKI leisurely paddled the 15-foot aluminum canoe downstream with the current until we were opposite a spring seep gently sluicing from the sedge meadows bordering north-central Wisconsin's Red River. One tug on a slip knot dropped the bleach bottle drag anchor and we glided to a stop within easy casting range of the pocket water downstream of the spring.

The Red, like many lazy trout rivers, is a transition stream—a hybrid. Because of the encroachment of man, the river is maturing as a trout stream and fast becoming smallmouth bass habitat. Here, under a fierce August sun, the water is tannin-dyed and sluggish; flowing listlessly like thin maple syrup and appearing fishless.

Nearby, a kingfisher plummeted from its perch atop the skeleton-like spire of an ancient tamarack tree. The bird screeched to a stop at the water's surface, snapped up a tiny fish, and zoomed skyward again in a single, fluid motion.

"Is that the reason local fishermen call this *Chub Creek*?" I asked.

"Could be," Ed smiled. "But those who call it that are wading fishermen. They don't know how to find trout this time of the year."

We popped open icy cans of beer from the styrofoam cooler and sat silently and watched the placid stream. Soon a soft swirl appeared at regular intervals downstream from the flowing spring. Perhaps it was a trout.

"You're up," Ed said, indicating the rise with the wave of a paddle. "Drop your fly on that rock, then flick it off into the foam."

I overcast on the first try and the tiny Green Jassid tangled in a clump of blueberry brush several feet inland.

Ed looked exasperated:

"Bring your rod tip up hard and high to break it off," he ordered. "Make sure the line flies directly back at us. We don't want to spook the fish."

My second cast was as ineptly thrown as the first but more accurate. The fly curled down to settle on the rock precisely over the foam. I twitched the rod, the fly tumbled off, and *Slur-whompt!* the fish took it savagely and quickly before it hit the water.

A handful of minutes later, a tired 13-inch brown trout came to the gunwale of the canoe in a series of slow, grudging circles. He was deep-bodied and colorful, with a scar across his snout and a tattered caudal fin.

"Some chub!" I commented, trying to conceal my glee. "Who said the Red doesn't hold trout this time of year?"

"A wading fisherman might," Ed grinned," and he'd probably have good reason. No brush-buster I know could have spotted that trickle of springwater as easily as we did from mid-river."

Since then, I've caught many larger trout while float fishing more highly publicized trout rivers in the U.S. and Canada. But that 13-inch introduction to the pleasures of float fishing the slow, lazy streams remains bright and vivid in my mind. And I clearly recall, Ed had a terse explanation of why it pays to fish the transition streams in preference to the brawling white-water rivers with better reputations as trout water.

"There's a simple secret to taking trout every time out," he said. "Keep your lure in the water, working, in places that hold big trout. Float fishing gets you to the best trout hides faster. And you're guaranteed more lure-in-the-water time. A wading fisherman on the same stretch of stream wastes too much time on activities that don't produce trout."

"Yes," I agreed, "activities like bug-slapping, brush-busting, hole-hopping, and wringing-out after a spill."

"Exactly," Ed laughed.

Float fishing for trout, whether by canoe, inflatable boat,

Slow stretches of idyllic tranquility . . .

. . . a "wet wading" excursion to test likeliest holes . . .

rubber raft, cartopper, or flat-bottomed jon-boat, is outdoor adventure in its purest form. It takes you to the hidden holes between the pathways that are trodden deep in both directions of every access point.

Indeed, only a few hundred yards upstream or down of a roadside parking area, float fishermen will often find virgin fishing. Shorebound anglers usually don't go that far because they're frazzled-out before they get there. Most are beyond the reach of the 4-wheel drive crowd, too. So the trophy trout that defend the choicest holes have become less wary for their inexperience and easier to catch. And their younger, smaller cousins are less wary still. Probe such hidden places on a quiet float trip and you'll find hot trout action that will amaze you by its intensity.

Sooner or later, of course, most dedicated trout anglers will realize that those virgin in-between areas can only be reached by float fishing. So they buy or borrow a suitable craft, load it with gear, and head for the nearest Blue Ribbon trout stream with high hopes. More often than not they'll come back with memories of an enjoyable scenic trip and also with a disappointing creel.

Why?

According to fisheries biologists, the noted Blue Ribbon streams are so classified because they "flow in a high gradient favoring trout." Translated, that means whitewater: Series-after-series of rapids, occasionally impassable waterfalls, and always several back-breaking portages. Float fish such water and you'll need to spend most of your time controlling the craft. There will be little time left for actual fishing.

Instead, select the laziest nearby stream that harbors trout, even if it isn't noted as classic trout water. Fish it s-l-o-w-l-y. And you'll take trout. On many slackwater trout streams, too, you'll find a bonus—the exciting, hard-fighting, smallmouth bass.

Generally, float fishing will be most enjoyed if there are only two fishermen per craft. The stern man should be responsible for paddling and guiding while the bow man does the fishing. Change places every ½-hour or at predetermined points along the river and each will have a chance at hot trout

. . . an uninteresting and unproductive stop at a potential "Lunker Log" . . .

. . . casting to the pockets of downstream rocks well before you get there and spook the fish . . .

action intermingled with periods of stream study and scenery-watching. Creels can be increased, too, if the stern man acts as the rise-spotter and directs the bow man precisely where to cast.

If both occupants try to fish and also work to control the craft, the usual result is neither fish nor fun. Share responsibility and you won't need to spend a lot of valuable fishing time paddling back upstream to retrieve snagged lures, jockeying the craft away from hang-ups, or disengaging craft, gear and fishermen from streamside brush. Try it otherwise and less than an hour after you slip the craft into the water you'll find even your best friend has turned into a reasonable facsimile of Count Dracula, craving your blood.

Another sure way to make a leisurely float fishing trip a real nightmare is to turn it into a Grand Prix of river running. Float easy, paddle slowly, stop often. Use your craft primarily for transportation and do most of your fishing by wading or while at anchor. Fish each hole thoroughly and then move on. You'll have more fun and take more trout.

It pays to fish from a slow moving craft only when you can't reach likely spots any other way, or when you don't know the water. Then, probe for fish by floating to the side of the stream that looks the least "fishy" and quarter-cast upstream and across to the better looking side. Floating mid-stream and casting alternately to either side will disturb wary trout well before you're within casting range. Neither will a trolled lure take trout. The disturbance caused by the craft passing overhead will move them out long before your lure reaches the hot spot.

But normal river flow always scours a good trout hole at the outside bend. Fish it hard and thoroughly. The inside curve of the same bend is usually shallow and silted. Trout won't often be found in such unsuitable habitat so pass it by. Float inside, cast to the outside, and you'll take fish.

The "mixing zones" where main currents meet slower sidewaters should be thoroughly fished. Often trout will lie in the quiet water, just outside the faster flowing main current, waiting for the river to send a choice morsel within inches of their noses. A flick of the tail and lunch is served.

. . . pausing to fish all *the pocket water in rocky runs once you get there . . .*

Take advantage of this situation by fishing downstream. Drop your lure in the water at the top of the run, play out line slowly, and allow the current to carry the offering in a natural manner. If you take care to keep the lure tumbling along the edge of the main current, no trout will be able to resist it.

The sidewaters in the main channel downstream of feeder streams of flowing springs are also good trout hides. Colder water, high in oxygen content, will sometimes draw trout from hundreds of yards away.

Once, while fishing a slow stretch of the MacDonald River in northeastern Quebec, I took a limit of five brook trout, all over 2 pounds, from a hole no more than 10 feet in diameter off the mouth of a tiny, unnamed brooklet that flowed from inland springs.

Often, it pays to explore up the mouths of the larger feeder streams. In late summer, that's where the trout will be. And don't overlook any dry streambed that enters the main river. Usually they're nothing more than outwash channels for spring runoff waters. But occasionally you'll find a beaver dam farther inland. Discover that and you're into a float fisherman's Mother Lode.

My favorite trout-taking places are what some have dubbed "lunker logs." These are the downed tree trunks, deadheads, and old logs that have one end anchored in the bank with the other jutting into the stream. I've yet to find a lunker log on a trout river that doesn't conceal a fair-sized fish. Take a trout from under a lunker log today, and a replacement will have moved in by tomorrow.

To fish a log properly, drop your lure near the bank on the up-stream side, allow the lure to wash down with the current, then retrieve quickly along the length of the log from bankside to mid-stream.

Snagpiles, accumulations of flotsam and patches of foam often hide good trout. Drop your lure on the upstream side and work it carefully under the obstacle. You'll lose a few lures but the technique does take fish.

Other places that shouldn't be bypassed without an exploratory cast or two are tailwaters below dams, eddy currents downstream of culverts and bridge abutments, and the shadowed water beneath a bridge or large tree. The shade acts as a security blanket for trout. Drop a lure in the darkest part of the shadow and you'll sometimes take good trout even in

. . . carefully fishing the good trout hides under bankside snagpiles . . .

. . . "feathering" the course of the craft to take the inside bends when the good holes are always on the outside . . .

the bright sun at mid-day.

The trout hides commonly overlooked by float fishermen are the main river channels that meander under wide, straight stretches of river. Often, the fish that live here are larger than average. But they lie deep, hovering just off bottom where the flow is much slower than on the surface. Ordinary fishing methods and lures won't budge them.

Find these channels by searching across the water's surface from one side. Note where the water appears darker-hued. You should also see a variation in the velocity of the current. Water in the main channel will move slightly faster than the sidewater. Anchor in the channel, tie on a deep diving plug, weighted streamer, or live bait with enough weight to get it down fast. Hold your retrieve until the lure hits bottom, then reel in, at a speed that is somewhat slower than the surface current, directly downstream in the channel.

Anytime you see mid-stream rocks on a transition river be prepared for action. Approach the rocks carefully and from the side. Observe that the water downstream of larger rocks has a reverse current flow. Although the flow on either side of the rock is moving downstream in the normal way, the flow directly behind the rock actually flows upstream! The difference is important because trout lie with their heads into the current. Any fish in the main river will be facing upstream and any trout in the reverse flow behind a rock will be facing downstream or resting in the pocket of quiet water.

To take trout from rocky pocket water, cast across it from the side, retrieve through it at right angles to the flow, and your lure will take on erratic movements that trout can't resist.

An advantage of float fishing for trout is that you can carry an extraordinary amount of gear. You're not limited to what can be strapped on, stashed in a creel, or stowed in the tiny pockets of a fishing vest. You'll have room for several rods, a well-equipped tackle box, minnow bucket, bait box, camp stove and lunch, plus a cooler or two of liquid refreshments.

Wear rubber-soled canvas sneakers, quick-drying trousers, and wade wet if you find a likely looking spot. If the water is too cold for wet-wading, drop anchor and fish from your relatively dry mobile fishing platform.

It's good practice, when boarding or debarking from your craft, to do it on the upstream side. That way the force of the

. . . the result, a hefty brown like this, as Terry Kroll displays. (Looks smug-as-hell doesn't he? Why not? His canoe took him to a pool that few others venture to—And it was Opening Day!)

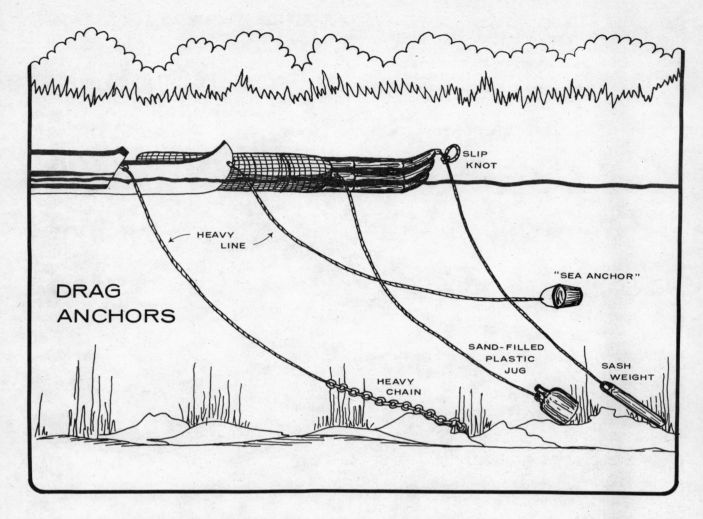

DRAG ANCHORS

SLIP KNOT

HEAVY LINE

"SEA ANCHOR"

HEAVY CHAIN

SAND-FILLED PLASTIC JUG

SASH WEIGHT

current can't trap you between the craft and a downstream obstacle.

To aid in handling the craft when you're out of it, tie a 15- to 20-foot length of heavy line on each end. The lines can be used as anchor ropes, mooring lines, haul ropes to get you off sandbars and snags, and will help in tracking the craft through shallow stretches that can't be floated.

Include an additional 50 feet of line in your gear for emergencies.

It's wise to secure the paddles or oars to the craft with a light line—I use nylon parachute cord—for it's surprising the number of times you'll drop a paddle overboard. If it hasn't been secured, it can lead to a merry chase downstream. Properly rigged, the tied paddles won't interfere with your ability to propel the craft.

Long hours hunched in a canoe, inflatable, cartopper, or jon-boat is murder on the back. To eliminate a visit to the chiropractor use some sort of backrest. Comfortable seat cushions are a must.

Don't forget raingear and a heavy jacket or sweater. Being soaked and cold, miles from the nearest take-out point, is downright miserable.

It's almost impossible to keep water from collecting in the bottom of the craft. Gallons splash in from bow spray. Quarts drip off paddles. Pints slosh off wet feet. Keep your gear dry by keeping it high. A few 1-inch wooden slats laid on the hull will do the trick. Cameras and food should be carried in waterproof bags. Heavy plastic garbage bags are ideal.

The most important piece of gear a float fisherman can own

is a life vest. It should be worn at all times and never used merely as a plush receptacle for an aching tailbone. When float fishing, there's always a risk of swamping or falling overboard. The slight inconvenience of wearing a life vest is worth the insurance it provides.

If you do swamp or capsize, don't fight the current to retrieve the craft. Simply hang on and ride with it until you ground in the shallows.

Another essential piece of gear is a drag anchor. Many floaters use heavy lengths of chain attached to the stern on a rope of the proper length to match river depth and velocity. The device prevents the craft from racing downstream too swiftly in heavy current and will hold it parallel to the flow.

But chain drags hang-up easily on bottom obstructions. Better is a gallon plastic bottle partially filled with sand. Its shape allows it to slip off bottom snags and rocks smoothly. Drag power can be easily adjusted by dumping or filling with sand. It can serve as an adequate holding anchor, too, when you want to stop and try stationary fishing. If one won't hold, simply add another.

Window sash weights, the oblong kind made of lead and often used in older homes, also work well. On a line of the proper length they will ride nose up over most bottom snags and keep the craft running true.

The trailed bucket you've seen pictured in many boating books is not a drag anchor but a sea anchor. It works well in open water when running before the wind. It is of no value in flowing water because the bucket, being light, is swept by the current.

Another good anchoring device to have aboard is a heavy wire, spring-loaded hook called a brush anchor. They're available at most canoe outfitters and boating stores. The brush anchor attaches easily to streamside brush and eliminates the need to drop an anchor overboard. When you want to get up and go, simply unsnap the springed hooks and you're on your way.

Load this assorted gear properly and your float fishing trip will be less of a hassle. Distribute it so the bow will ride slightly higher than the stern when running downstream. That way the flowing water will do most of the work of maintaining course.

If you must travel upstream for any distance, shift the load so the bow rides lower than the stern. In that position the craft can slice water easily without being whipped about by heavy waves, erratic currents, or wind.

Before embarking on any float fishing adventure it's a good idea to study a map of the stream. The U.S. Geological Survey topographic maps are most suitable for the purpose. They show dams, bridges, road crossings, and information that will be valuable once you're on the stream. If you're on a particularly long float or in a remote area, carry two maps. One can be tucked away in a watertight package. Use the other for route finding and for marking the places where you find fish. The information will be invaluable.

I have one map of a favorite lazy trout stream that not only shows 10 years' worth of fishing information but the dates and places we've found crops of wild berries, ruffed grouse drumming sites, whitetail deer runs, even some hidden geological formations that are a rockhounder's delight.

One rule to remember when planning your float fishing trip for trout is that it will take more time then indicated by the mileage on the map. I've learned from experience that all trout streams have crooks, curves, shallows, portages and obstructions that are unexpected and increase travel time.

Generally, 8 river miles a day is about the maximum you can cover on a transition stream. Anything longer will force you to hustle throughout the trip and that, in turn, means less lure-in-the-water time.

Properly planned and organized, a float fishing trip on a lazy trout river can be a serene, idyllic experience that will take you to places that cannot be penetrated any other way. Here, you'll find solitude. And each bend in the river promises new adventure. Different streams, you'll find, have different personalities. Adapt the methods we've discussed here to the special quirks of particular rivers and you'll take trout!

A limit of fat, sassy, rainbow trout is the succulent reward for a day-long float trip on a lazy transition river.

Downriggers Catch Deep Trout

by TOM OPRE

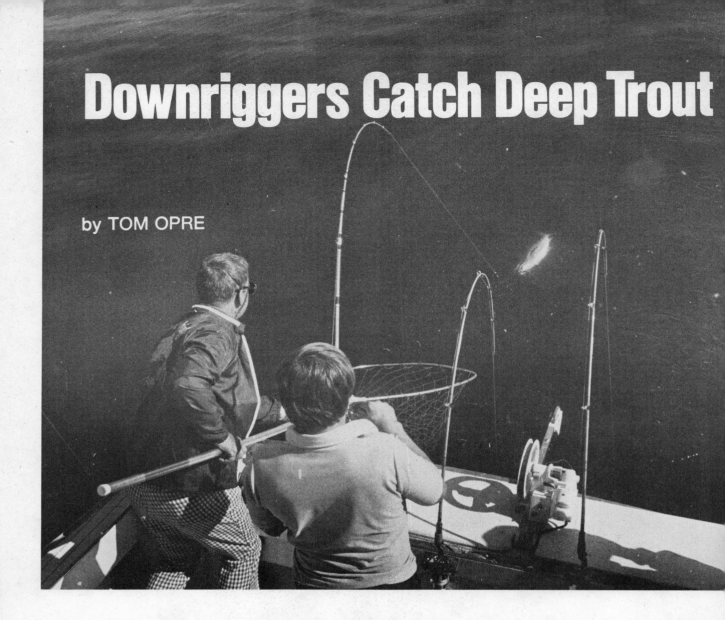

THE STERN of Captain Emil Dean's Lake Michigan charter boat bristles with bent-over rods as he trolls this huge inland sea for deepwater trout. I was watching the stern downriggers one afternoon when a deeply bowed corner rod sprang to attention. There's only one thing that makes that happen, "Fish on!"

I grabbed the bucking rod just as a silvery steelhead broke the surface behind the boat and skipped head over tail across the water. The rod was shaking in my hands and the line melted off the reel as the mixed-up fish tried to run a circle around the boat. People were ducking under my rod and the fish seemed determined to out-jump any other fish I've ever hooked. Three, four, five times that steelhead crashed into the air before he settled down to a hard knuckle fight in deep water.

Several minutes later I leaned back on the rod and the steelhead quivered his last in the bottom of Emil's large boat net. Congratulations were in order because it's not every day someone boats a 14-pound steelhead during midsummer's heat and deepwater fishing conditions.

We finished the day with a total of nine jumbo lake trout up to 15 pounds, the big steelhead and a pair of twin browns in the 9-pound class. Fishing expertise on the part of this

popular captain from Manistee, Michigan, certainly made much of our success possible. But, a great deal of the credit must go to the downrigger. Downriggers have completely revolutionized the sport of deep trolling for trout.

Downriggers aren't really as new as many Great Lakes fishermen would like to think. Some crude but reasonable facsimiles were in use by 1935 off portions of the East Coast.

Nowhere has their development been more precise, more impressive than along the shorelines of Lake Michigan, Lake Huron and Lake Superior since the advent of the Great Lakes salmon and lake trout programs. Today, downriggers are a way of life for most open water fishermen in the Midwest. They are as important as a sonar unit, a key part of the modern angler's arsenal.

The basic downrigger is merely a large metal spool capable of taking in about 2 feet of line on every revolution. Downriggers can be either manually cranked or raised and lowered electrically. Price is the determining factor.

The downrigger spool is filled with 125- to 150-pound braided wire line. At one end of the wire line is a heavy weight (cannonball) that scales from 7 to 12 pounds. Heavier cannonballs are used in deeper water to overcome drift-back at trolling speeds. Water resistance builds up on

A lunker laker comes to Captain Emil Dean's net. Note downrigger lines still set to the right of the fisherman.

the wire line and cannonball at greater depths and this pushes the cannonball farther back behind the boat.

The downrigger spool and crank or motor is perched atop a strong platform bolted to the boat's stern. Out-downriggers, made for fishing over either side, are made with longer arms and are mounted on the gunwales. Stern downriggers have shorter arms to keep the cannonball and wire away from the stern.

A release clip is normally attached to the downrigger wire just above the cannonball. The fishing line is attached to this release system and enables the striking fish to free the fishing line from the downrigger. There are literally dozens of fine release systems on the market that were devised solely for the downrigger fisherman.

Experimenting fishermen were quick to improvise and refine the downrigger to its present state. Many recent models now feature small digital counters that reveal at a glance how deep the cannonball is. Some downriggers have movable arms to facilitate easy line tending. One downrigger company is producing a model with a built-in thermometer sensor that gives an electronic readout—on the surface—of the water temperatures far below the boat.

The addition of tough electric motors eliminated the tedious job of cranking cannonballs up from depths as great as 100 to 150 feet. Mid-summer lake trout fishing is not uncommonly conducted at those depths, at least on Lake Michigan.

The primary reason for using downriggers in the first place is to enable the fisherman to fish his lures at a controlled depth. Most Great Lakes fishermen first take the water temperature to determine at approximately what depth the lake trout, steelhead and browns may be found. As a rule, lakers will be found in slightly colder water (50 degrees) while steelhead and brown trout normally frequent the 55-degree level. All three trout will be found moving between both temperature levels frequently.

Because of this, many fishermen have four downriggers on their boats. Lures can be staggered to cover both the high and low ranges of this temperature band and still have a couple of lines at the proper level.

Having four or more downriggers strung around a boat isn't a paved road to success, however. There are tricks to downrigger fishing just as there are in any other sport. These tricks often are the difference between taking trout when they're deep or just going for a boat ride.

Lake trout are great followers of a lure. Charter boat

Two types of downriggers; one is a stationary model used on the stern of a boat while the other is an out-downrigger for use over the sides. Note how this model can be raised by hand. Note the downrigger cannonball (heavy weight) hanging off the downrigger wire.

skippers like Emil Dean have watched lakers following a lure for a hundred yards or more by watching the fish marking a line on the chart recording graph.

These following trout will sometimes strike and many times they'll just peel off and head for bottom after tracking the lure for some distance. I've found it pays to experiment with a couple of tricks and often those following fish can be converted into a fish dinner.

One of these tricks is easy to perform with an electric downrigger. I'll just flip the up-down button and the downrigger will crank the cannonball up 3 or 4 feet and then I'll send it back down the same distance. Do this two or three times, up and down, and a following trout will often smack the lure.

What happens when this trick is performed is the cannonball pulls the lure and/or attractor toward the surface for several feet and then it flutters back down again when the cannonball is lowered. A trailing trout will see this rapid change in direction and often a strike is triggered.

Another trick that works well with manually-operated downriggers is to crank the cannonball up and down in the same manner. The hand crank is often faster to operate than the electric and this causes a quicker change in direction. This trick puts lots of trout in the box for fishermen.

Some downriggers have movable arms. Fishermen having this type of downrigger can merely grasp the downrigger arm and rapidly pump it up and down. I once had a 16-pound lake trout nearly break my wrist when it struck as I was pumping the downrigger arm up and down.

Another technique that works at times is to speed up the boat for 10 or 15 feet. A short, rapid burst of speed causes the cannonball to drift up and backwards from the boat. This lifting action can trigger slow biting trout into action.

After traveling 10 feet or so, slow the boat down to the normal trolling speed. This allows the cannonball and trailing lure to settle back to their original position below the boat. This increase and decrease of speed also has an effect on the flash of your lures and attractors. Many times trout will strike as the cannonball swings back beneath the boat.

Speeding up and slowing down of the boat causes a change in the action of the lure. A more vibrant wiggle or flash is created when the boat speeds up. The lure resumes its characteristic motion when the boat throttles back down.

There are times when trout are hitting savagely in a frenzied feeding period and a lure and attractor can be fished directly behind the cannonball. When the fish are really snapping, 6 feet between cannonball and lure is plenty.

But many times the fish are finicky, following and not striking, and this is when the savvy trout fisherman runs his lure 30 to 60 feet behind the boat before attaching the line to the release system. Often this distance is critical and the fisherman must experiment with distances before hitting on the proper combination.

It's been said many times before that trolling fishermen should always use lures with comparable actions. This is doubly true when downrigger fishing. Select lures with actions that work best at the proper trolling speeds.

It does little good to troll a Flatfish, for example, with its slow speed action at a higher rate of speed with a flashing spoon. The action should always be selected to correspond with trolling speed needed to induce strikes. And, speed is very important when deep trolling. Some days the

This fisherman cranks his bait down with the aid of a side downrigger. One hand controls the line from the reel while the other lowers the cannonball.

fish want a super-slow speed while other days only a faster troll will produce.

Much can be learned about downrigger fishing and success by comparing a recent trip of mine cut of South Haven, Michigan, with the *Mary E,* Emil Dean's charter boat. Dean's success with lake trout is fantastic, thanks to lots of experience and the modern array of fathometers, thermometers and downriggers.

"Being on Lake Michigan five or six days a week," he told me, "I usually know about where the thermocline is at any given time. We set our baits just above, in and below it for a start, providing the fathometer doesn't show the fish to be lying on or near the bottom exclusively."

Dean uses six lines at once; two are set on the gunwales— one on each side and four downriggers are set off the stern. A set of outriggers can accommodate two more lines and these are normally weighted with sizable weights on a sinker release system. Normally, the downriggers produce 95 percent of the trout.

We trolled for 15 minutes when the first line—one of the side downriggers—throbbed free. A laker had clobbered the fluorescent green Barber fly and rose out behind the boat as we continued on at trolling speed. Dean doesn't stop to fight a fish unless it is considerably larger than normal. He figures the fisherman can work it in carefully while the other lines are still fishing. It's a productive strategy.

Dean slipped the landing net under a fat 8-pounder which

Lunkers like Bonnie Dilts' 10-pound brown (left) and (below) author, Tom Opre's big laker are typical of some of the fast action possible with the use of downriggers.

is about average for Lake Michigan lake trout today. Four more lakers followed the first one into the fish box before noon.

"Lake trout are the charter skippers bread-and-butter fish," Dean told me. "We can count on them because their habits are easier to define and they aren't prone to roam all over the lake. They stick fairly close to identifiable areas throughout the summer," he continued, "and although they may or may not hit, the fish are still there. And that's important to the downrigger fisherman."

Our charter ended 2 hours later with a five-man limit of 15 lake trout. It was an easy day's fishing and the downrigger was what made it all possible. Fifteen big lakers from 90 feet of water would have been almost impossible without using this modern piece of fishing equipment.

Another method of downrigger trolling is called "long-lining." It's particularly effective for jumbo brown trout that tend to shy away from the commotion of a passing sport-fishing boat or the bubbling thrust of downrigger balls dragged through the water.

Anglers will let out as much as 100 to 150 yards of line with this approach before clipping it into the downrigger release. The cannonball and fishing line is lowered carefully to the desired depth. As more line is strung out behind the cannonball, water resistance increases, and the tension on the downrigger release must be adjusted accordingly.

Much of this long-lining is done in relatively shallow water, often in 15 feet or less. It has a great deal of merit because it presents a lure a long distance behind a moving boat and this lessens the chances of spooking the trout.

Often when a big trout strikes this combination he'll jump so far behind the boat you'll wonder whether that fish is hooked or not. About the time the fish crashes back into the water your rod tip will jerk upward from the released tension on the downrigger. It takes quite a while for the strike to travel up 100 or more yards of monofilament.

Many western and southern trout fishermen are finding a place on deepwater reservoirs or impoundments for downriggers. I talked with a chap that fishes Pyramid Lake in western Nevada and he's taken some huge cutthroats on downriggers. He said he often has to fish in 30 to 50 feet of water and the downrigger is the only way he can be absolutely sure he's covering the proper depths.

I'm firmly convinced that downriggers can open up new vistas for trout fishermen everywhere. The practicality of the device makes it simple to use, a beginner can learn to set downriggers in 5 minutes.

The device allows controlled depth trout fishing and this application will apply wherever trout are found. Many fishermen are taking a tip from Great Lakes fishermen who, thankfully, refused to be bound by tradition. Never have trout fishermen consistently taken so many trout.

In the evolution of sport fishing, many new methods and devices stand out. But none more so than the modern downrigger, a real key to trout fishing success that has a chance to spread worldwide among fishermen.

Big trout come to net over the stern of Captain Emil Dean's charter boat *Mary E.* Downriggers allow controlled depth trout fishing and open up new vistas for trout fishermen everywhere.

ING SUPREME

by MIKE MILLER

YOUR AIRCRAFT, a gutsy little five-placer on floats, banks hard, real hard, to the left as your pilot eyeballs the forest-rimmed lake directly below the wingtip. Your gaze follows the pilot's, down to the shimmering body of water, then you look around, as you have been for the past half-hour, at the surrounding countryside.

Wild country this is. A region of lush green forests and deep blue lakes and frothy streams—set amongst snowcapped peaks, alpine glaciers and lush mountain meadows.

The pilot gestures and you look to where he's pointing. At one end of the lake sits a solitary cabin, the first sign of human habitation you've seen since takeoff. "That's it," the pilot yells over the roar of the engine. "That's home-sweet-you-know-what for the next 7 days."

Minutes later, after a spiraling descent to lose altitude, the pontoons kiss the water as the pilot taxis the aircraft toward your cabin and a stretch of cleared shoreline before it.

You turn to the back seat of the plane and note that your companions are doing the same thing you've been doing—grinning, ear to ear, as they assess the lake and its wall of towering spruce and hemlock. Then, to one side, it happens. A fish breaks water, splashing in the sunlight in its quest for an insect. All of you feel more intensely than ever that marvelously overwhelming itch to get ashore, get gear in hand . . . and get fishing!

That's what it's like, the start of a trout fishing trip in Alaska. The end of the trip is no less satisfying, complete as it almost invariably is, with memories of good-sized, hardfighting fish caught amidst one of the last great wilderness regions under the American flag.

"In Alaska you'll find the finest rainbow trout fishing in North America. No place else comes close to it."

Those are the words of Rupe Andrews who directs the activities of the Division of Sport Fish within the Alaska Department of Fish and Game. And lest you think that Rupe's words have the ring of an Alaska-size brag, let me assure you I've heard similar statements from world-traveling East Coast sportsmen, from top anglers who hail from the Rockies, and from Canadian fishermen whose own habitat can only be described as prime trout country.

Nor is Alaska's superlative trout fishing limited to the feisty rainbow. Steelhead fishing in Alaska's more southerly waters offers you the challenge of trying to top Seattleite David White's 1970 world record steelhead which weighed 42 pounds, 2 ounces. He landed it near Ketchikan. White, incidentally, was only 8 years old at the time.

And if rainbows and steelheads aren't enough (technically, of course, these are the same critter, the latter being a sea-run version of the former) the list goes on to include cutthroat trout, lake trout, brook trout, Dolly Varden and Arctic char. These last four are members of the char family but usually they are viewed by Alaska anglers as trout and in fact vary only in the fact that they spawn in the fall, not the spring.

The best news is that a lot of this fabulous fishing—in still-untrammeled, unspoiled lakes and streams—can be arranged on a budget that most enthusiastic anglers can afford.

Take, for instance, the fly-in trip described in the opening paragraphs of this story. The wilderness cabin mentioned is one of more than 150 such units built and operated by the U.S. Forest in the southeast panhandle and in Chugach National

Opposite page—Pilot and sportsman load catch aboard a small aircraft in Alaska's bush country.

Right—This is the world's record steelhead trout—at 42 pounds plus—and the proud 8-year-old angler who caught him, young David White of Seattle.

Scenery along the Chilkoot Trail is surpassed only by its fishing. Here a sportsman pauses along the historic goldrush trail to try his luck at attracting trout.

Forest in the south-central region near Anchorage. For the trifling sum of $5 a night per cabin, up to a half-dozen sportsmen can enjoy the well-constructed, weather-tight accommodations which include bunks, stove, tables and chairs, plus out-back toilet facilities.

All the fisherman need bring is your sleeping bag, groceries, personal items and fishing tackle. Your only expense, other than food costs and the rental fee, is the charter for flying you out from a major community such as Juneau and picking you up. On a four-man fly-in excursion all these charges might total $100 or less per person—a modest charge indeed for the opportunity to spend a week of comfort in a wild section of top notch Alaskan fishing country where your only neighbors may be a wandering bear or moose.

If flying isn't your bag there is lots of good fishing to be found along the roadside in Alaska. But here's a tip knowledgeable Alaskans offer to auto-borne anglers: Don't do your fishing right where a stream crosses or adjoins the road. The fish, quite frankly, just won't be there, at least not in satisfying numbers. Instead, take a look at your watch and hike upstream or down for 45 minutes to an hour. *Then* put your line and lure in the water. Success is far more likely off the beaten path.

Actually, you don't have to fly or drive long distances to get into acceptable Alaskan fishing. Within greater Anchorage, for instance, Alaska natives and visitors catch trout at Jewel Lake, DeLong Lake and Campbell Lake plus Green Lake on the Elmendorf Air Force Base reservation and Otter Lake and Cluney Lake on the Fort Richardson grounds. Many folks, including most Alaskans, think the military lakes are reserved for military anglers. Not so. The state stocks about 35,000 catchable rainbows on these military reservations yearly and civilians are more than welcome to try their luck.

The two heaviest-fished areas in the entire state are the Kenai Peninsula, which meanders southwesterly below Anchorage, and the Matanuska Valley which is north of the state's largest city. On the Kenai the angler can combine fishing with some of the finest canoeing in the North Country—on the Swanson River canoe and portage system, and the Swan Lakes system, both within the U.S. National Moose Range.

Alaska is prime rainbow trout fishing country, however—and this is the locale Rupe Andrews described as "the finest . . . in North America"—is the watershed behind Bristol Bay on the Alaska Peninsula. This is the area the state has designated for *trophy fish* management. This is "Once in a lifetime" fishing country. Country where your daily limit is one fish over 20 inches and five under. Only artificial lures can be used and in some areas you are restricted to fishing with fly tackle.

It's not cheap, flying by jet to Bristol Bay and then flying out by bush carrier to premium lodges for guided forays into selected waters. But it's here that sportsmen may catch dozens of 12-, 20- or 25-pound rainbows, and perhaps elect to release them all, after recording the biggest catches on film.

Alaska encourages this. "It takes 10 to 12 years or more for a rainbow to grow to trophy size in the Bristol Bay country," says Rupe Andrews. "Growth rates are small. The food chain is limited. Only the region's previous isolation, and the state's recent management of the area as a trophy fish resource, has allowed these fish to attain their present size." The biggest fish Rupe has caught was 25 pounds. "I released him. He's still out there," Andrews notes. "And I hope I'll catch him again some day, maybe 5 pounds heavier."

As an enticement to encourage fishermen to release fish after landing them, the state publishes in its regulation booklet a simple five-step procedure for safely releasing trout and other species. In part the instructions say: (1) Do not insert fingers in gills; (2) Do use long-nosed pliers; (3) Do not try to remove a swallowed hook . . . Instead clip the leader off short . . . and the hook will dissolve later; (4) Do handle a fish with dry hands, and (5) Do not release an exhausted fish ("Hold it gently under water in a natural swimming position until it recovers and swims away.")

Alaska is so vast it's difficult to plan a fishing trip unless you break the state down into smaller regions for consideration. Following are seven such regions and a once-over-lightly recap of trout fishing opportunities to be found in each:

Southeastern

Two separate runs of steelhead occur in the "panhandle" region. In the lower southeastern a fall run enters creeks that have an accessible lake and these fish remain all winter, offering excellent cold weather trout fishing. Throughout

Roadside fishing is an added attraction in Alaska. A few minutes "work" with rod and reel is liable to produce food for the table almost any place in the 49th State.

southeast Alaska a spring run enters the larger creeks in April and peaks in May. Some of the better streams are Naha River near Ketchikan, Petersburg Creek near Petersburg, and a really hot river called the Situk at Yakutat.

Cutthroat and Dolly Varden are both year-round and migratory species. Some experts claim that southeastern is home of some of the last but best cutthroat fishing on the continent. Alaskans frequently seek these fish at Hasselborg, Thayer and Turner lakes near Juneau, Chilkat Lake in the Haines area, and Humpback Lake in the Ketchikan locale.

Eastern brook trout have been successfully planted in Salmon Creek Reservoir at Juneau; Green and Thimbleberry lakes, Sitka; and Grace Lake, Ketchikan.

Copper River-Prince William Sound

Your best time for lake trout in this region is immediately after the spring ice breakup and just prior to freezing. Fishing for "lakers" is productive in Louise, Susitna, Beaver, Dog, Paxson, Summit and Copper lakes, as well as along several small roadside lakes along the Denali Highway. Troll deep after the weather warms using Dardevles, Red-eyes, or Alaskan plugs.

The better rainbow fishing in this region occurs in roadside lakes such as Crater, Tex Smith, Blueberry, Thompson, Worthington, Sculpin, Strelna, Buffalo and Van. Cutthroat trout can be taken most readily after the ice has gone out of Eshamy and Eyak Lakes and again during the late fall. The best Dolly Varden fishing is located in streams near Valdez and Cordova.

Cook Inlet-Matanuska Valley

From late May through August the Deshka and Talachulitna rivers and lake and Alexander creeks offer the fly-in fisherman some of Cook Inlet's best angling for rainbows. Stream fishing for rainbows is available, as well, along the newly completed Anchorage-Fairbanks Highway on east side tributaries of the Susitna River such as Willow and Montana creeks.

Dolly Varden are not overly abundant in this region, however Lewis and Coal Creek near Coal Creek Lake northwest of Tyoned does produce a number of "Dollies" and additional catches of this species can occasionally be brought home from Theodore, Chuit and Talachulitna rivers.

Shell Lake near Skwentna is a fine fly-in destination for the angler seeking lake trout. It is recommended that you take along a small rubber raft, motor mounted, for trolling.

Kenai Peninsula

The Anchor River, Deep Creek, Ninilchik River and Stariski Creek are popular waters for steelhead from August through October. Rainbows are found in almost all the waters of the western peninsula and are available throughout the year. The Upper Russian River and Russian Lakes produce rainbows running up to 24 inches.

Dolly Vardens abound in most coastal streams from July through November. Particularly "hot" waters include the Anchor River, Ninilchik Creek, Salmon Creek, Deep Creek, Ptarmigan Creek and—for some real lunkers—the Kenai River.

Arctic Char are popular with Alaskan winter fishermen in this region, but are frequently caught in the spring and fall as well. Summer fishermen will locate these "cousins" to the Dolly Varden in the lakes of the Swanson River drainage but in the summer months you have to troll deep. Lake trout are commonly caught in good numbers at Hidden Lake during spring and fall by trolling the shallows with spoons or flatfish.

Kodiak Islands

Dollies appear in large numbers in virtually all the rivers and creeks in this area. Particularly popular with locals are Buskin, Afognak, Saltery and Pasagshak rivers, in May and again in September. Rainbow trout can be fished in no less than 26 lakes on the Kodiak road system. Near the city the following are productive: Bell's Flat Lakes, Cliff Point Lakes, Hidden Lakes and lakes Genevieve, Margaret, and Abercrombie. Excellent trout fishing during early June may be found in most river-lake systems on Afognak and Kodiak islands. For steelhead fishermen the Karluk River in October is a long-time favorite. Fraser, Ayakulik and Saltery rivers also boast good runs of this species.

Bristol Bay

As noted earlier these are among the finest rainbow waters to be found anywhere. Frequently, rainbows from this region

Three excellent reasons for traveling to Alaska to fish—Dolly Varden caught at the end of Mud Bay Road leading out of Haines, Alaska.

are mistaken for steelhead. To protect spawning, fishing in the Kvichak watershed is closed from April 15 through the second Monday in June. Fishing is usually excellent during the balance of the month.

Though rainbows may be taken in good numbers all summer long, the angling is especially exciting from late August until freezeup. Better locations include the Kvichak River at Igiugig, Lower Talarik Creek, and the Newhalen, Iliamna, and Gibraltar rivers.

Fairbanks and Northern Alaska

Rainbow trout are taken throughout the summer season in the interior and northern regions of Alaska. Excellent angling for the species can be had in Quartz, Donna, Mark, Little Donna, and Rapids lakes near Delta Junction, with Quartz Lake producing trout in the 16- to 22-inch category. Rainbow Lake, across the Tanana River from Big Delta, has excellent rainbow but the lake is accessible only by float plane during the summer or by winter trail.

Arctic char and Dolly Varden are available in northern coastal streams throughout the season while inland some are taken in the Nenana River tributaries near the city of Nenana and the Tanana River tributaries near the Johnson River confluence. Trophy size Arctic char are found in the Wulik and Kivalina rivers and tributaries of the Noatak River, all near the Eskimo community of Kotzebue.

For lake trout the north and south slopes of the Brooks Range offer very productive waters (but also very unaccessible waters, except by air). The better lakes include Shainin, Chandler, Kurupa, Elusive, and Itkillik lakes on the north and Selby-Narvak, Wild, Helpmejack, Chandalar, Squaw and Walker on the south.

The locales listed above, of course, represent only a tiny percentage—only the barest tip of the iceberg—of the really great fishing holes and streams in Alaska. Hundreds more are identified in a free booklet, called *Alaska Sport Fishing Guide* which is available from the Alaska Department of Fish and Game, Sport Fish Division, Juneau, Alaska 99801. The guide contains strip maps and charts identifying proven fishing destinations along hundreds of miles of state highways and in various roadless areas as well. It's the single best source of

fishing information in the state. Fishing regulations may be obtained each year from the same address.

As far as technique is concerned there isn't a great deal of difference between fishing Alaskan waters and other good trout streams elsewhere. Just about any spinning lure, bait-casting lure, or fly pattern you've used other places would be effective here. The fly fisherman will probably want to bring along a wide selection of wet flies or streamers as opposed to dry flies. "Attractor" type flies seem most efficient.

If you had to choose one all-around fly that would take the most fish in the most locations, that choice would have to be the Muddler Minnow. A close second choice would be the Black Ant.

More information? At press time the Department of Fish and Game is compiling a listing of the more than one hundred fishing guides, guide services, and fishing lodges located in Alaska. The list, which readers may request from the Sport Fish Division, will indicate not only the name of the service and location but also prices, accommodations offered and—very important—a showing of which species of fish may be caught at each locale.

Information about the U.S. Forest Service wilderness cabins can be obtained, complete with maps and reservations procedures, from the Regional Forester's Office, U.S. Forest Service, Federal Building, Juneau, Alaska 99801. For general travel information about Alaska the best source of data is the Alaska Division of Tourism, Pouch E, Juneau, Alaska 99801.

Alaska is a great place to come visit for some fantastic trout fishing. So far, residents and visitors have treated the land pretty gently—as they should, for in spite of its great size and frequently rugged terrain, Alaska is surprisingly fragile land.

When you come, and those of us who live here hope that you will come, make a special effort to leave the wilderness as unspoiled and unpolluted as you find it. As the saying goes, "Pack it in, pack it out . . . Leave only footprints, take only photographs."

If you do, your children and your children's children will have the same grand wilderness and trout fishing experiences that awaits you in this last frontier. What better gift could our generation leave behind for our heirs?

EVEN THE huge cloud of mosquitoes swirling about my perspiration-drenched face couldn't stop me from staring open-mouthed as I parted the brush and stepped to the edge of the secluded beaver pond. A wader-clad fisherman, safely snuggled in a large inner tube, was being towed slowly around the pond by whatever was on the other end of his wildly thrashing fly rod.

Oblivious of my presence, he was alternately encouraging the fish with whoops of joy and making the surrounding woods ring with peals of jubilant laughter. His laughter was so amusing that I soon found myself chuckling aloud.

Just as the fish turned his inner tube so the angler was facing in my direction, I saw his rod tip snap to attention signaling an end to the fight. His leader had parted and the big trout was gone.

"Hey, that must have been some fish you had on," I called across the water to the stranger.

"Oh, hi," he yelled back. "Yeah, he was a good one. I've never been pulled around like that before."

As we talked, he worked his way to the bank and I gave him a hand so he could reach solid ground where I stood.

The stranger stepped out of his tube and started dismantling his rod and I had a chance to look at the device which had made it possible for him to fish every corner of this backwoods beaver pond.

The contraption consisted of a large truck tire inner tube covered with heavy canvas. Two leg holes were cut in the bucket seat formed in the center of the tube. An integral part of the canvas covering was a broad shoulder strap which permitted the wearer to walk in shallow water and on land without having to hold onto the tube.

The incident remains clear in my mind although it took place more than 30 years ago. It was the first time I'd seen such a float used and it was my first encounter with a truly dedicated backwoods beaver pond fisherman. During the intervening years, however, I've become well acquainted with both and thought I'd pass along some information which might help you in your search for backwoods beaver pond brookies.

Many states such as Minnesota, Wisconsin, Michigan, New York, Pennsylvania, Vermont, New Hampshire and Maine have excellent secluded ponds that contain a brook trout bonanza for the angler willing to invest a little time and effort to locate active beaver ponds.

Finding a good beaver pond is like having Christmas twice a year. To dedicated pond fishermen it's like money in the bank and food on the table and they guard their new-found treasures like pots of gold. Nothing short of a death threat will make them consider divulging the whereabouts of a productive brook trout pond.

Locating and getting to a beaver pond, where the succulent brook trout reside, is not unlike taking a trip on a commercial airline where getting to the airport is the toughest part of the trip. Pinpointing a pond and finding your way through the brush to get to it is the hardest battle in this type of fishing. And, some of this difficulty can usually be eliminated by following a couple of simple suggestions.

Most beginning beaver pond fishermen start by acquiring a good map of the area they want to fish and begin walking the stream banks in search of a pond. This can be a killer especially in hot summer weather. The best time for this type of exploration is during early spring or fall when the weather is cooler, bugs are scarce and vegetation is at a minimum. This makes it easier to visually follow the stream source without having to actually walk the route.

Be sure and check with the members of your state fish and game department, such as the local game wardens or conservation officers, surveyors, foresters and game biologists.

Backwoods Beaver Pond Brookies

by MARK C. DILTS

Flying is a fast, sure way of locating beaver ponds, but explain your wants to your pilot. It can save time and money.

Game biologists and game wardens are the best bets for giving you the type of information you are seeking.

Game biologists are in the field during all seasons of the year and have good knowledge of such matters. Game wardens enforce trapping laws and beaver ponds are a part of their beat. Most officers will know where ponds are located and the best way of getting to them.

The easiest and fastest way of locating beaver ponds is from the air. If you're not a flying sportsman, or lucky enough to have a friend that is, then you can rent a plane from the nearest commercial airport. Rental of a two-place, single engine plane, complete with pilot, will set you back anywhere from $18 to $35 an hour, depending upon how hungry the pilot may be at the time.

This may sound expensive to you, but for this sum you'll be able to cover more ground in 60 minutes than you can in several months of tramping brushy streambanks. It is possible to locate enough ponds to keep you in fishing territory for several years during a one-hour flight. And, believe me, the great brook trout fishing that can result makes it worth every cent of the cost.

If you choose to fly, take along a good map and explain to the pilot what you are looking for. Have him head for the nearest major river and follow it until you spot a pond along one of the tributary streams. Locate your position and mark the pond on the map immediately. Ask the pilot to circle the pond so you can locate a way into it. If you find one, mark it on the map at once. Everything looks completely different once you get back on the ground. Pay particular attention to any visible landmarks that could be seen from the ground.

Make your flight during summer months when the countryside is covered with lush vegetation. Beaver ponds will

Below—A fishing tube is easy to make (see text for instructions) and it gives an angler complete freedom when fishing a beaver pond.

stand out like long underwear at a nudist's convention. While the ponds are readily visible, access to them will be less apparent. Take a little time to try and spot a footpath or trail road leading in the direction of the pond. Either one can save a lot of extra work on the first trip into your newfound fishing site.

Fishing a beaver pond can be a trying affair. Many have brush-covered banks which negate almost any kind of casting. Practically all are silt-laden so they are next to impossible to wade. The water is usually quite deep and the soft bottom adds considerably to this depth. The end result is that you fish from shore, providing you can find sufficient room to do so or you fish from a boat or other floating contrivance.

Since packing a boat or canoe into a pond spells plain hard work, which most fishermen tend to avoid whenever possible, most serious pond fishermen use what they call a "tube" or "donut."

They purchase a large truck tire innertube and outfit it with a seat. The whole rig costs less than $15 even with today's inflated prices. A new 10.00 X 20 truck tube will cost about $13 while the wooden seat, and rope to hold it in place can be garnered from material usually found around the house.

In making the rig, the seat is fashioned to appear like the end of a house with a square bottom, two side walls and a tapered roof with the tip of the peak knocked off (see photo). Drill three holes for the supporting ropes or straps; one hole in each of the two base corners and one near the peak. Tie the base as close to the tube as you can get it, separating the wood from the tube by knots in the rope. Once you're tied the peak of the seat to the tube, there should be two sizeable openings on either side of the seat for your legs and your job is complete.

There are several commercial versions of this type floating gear which sell for about $30-$35. They are usually innertubes covered with canvas and have a shoulder strap for carrying the tube while wearing it. The canvas seat of this type lets you sit lower in the water giving you a lower center of gravity which is a good safety factor. The lower seat makes fly fishing more difficult because your casting arm is near the water and makes an 8½- or 9-foot fly rod mandatory.

Another commercial version of this float is made from a neoprene-coated nylon tube that can be inflated by mouth once you've arrived at the pond. This tube lets you sit even lower in the water than does the innertube-type, with the same disadvantages, but it's easier to pack through the brush.

Fishing from a tube or donut is a unique experience which can only be fully appreciated after it's been tried. They are easy to maneuver and are powered by a swimming motion of the legs which is easily learned in a few minutes. You can purchase a pair of metal or rubber flippers for your feet which permit you to propel yourself through the water with a walking motion. The flippers spread open on the backstroke, pushing you forward, and then fold flat to offer no resistance on the forward stroke of your foot.

What about puncturing the tube and sinking in the middle of the beaver pond? This thought seems to plague those unfamiliar with this type of fishing. The answer is—it's no problem.

Some punctures occur from having the tube pierced by a sharp stick or limb, but this happens far less frequently than most people imagine. Truck tubes are manufactured from sturdy stock and are not easily ruptured. It takes quite a healthy poke to put a hole in them, especially when you're on the water where resistance is very slight.

Punctures from fish hooks are quite common but are little cause for concern. The tiny holes, and the low air pressure in the tube, gives you plenty of time to get to shore before the air hisses out. A friend of mine recently punctured his tube shortly after he started fishing, but he finished the best part of

An ample application of a good insect repellant is a necessity for the well-being of any beaver pond fisherman.

the mayfly hatch before going ashore. He was in no danger at any time.

Although most dedicated beaver pond fishermen we know prefer making their own floats, a word of caution is in order for the beginning fisherman who wants to do likewise. The home-made variety of float—where the seat is tied high in the tube—can be tipped over. One should get the feel of it while in the company of a companion before embarking on a backwoods fishing trip alone.

The large tube has extreme buoyancy and virtually sits atop the water—if the fisherman leans too far in any direction he can quickly find himself suspended in a head-down position with no means of righting himself. To complicate matters, his waders will likely be filled with air which will increase his difficulty in trying to reverse his position.

"I've never had it happen to me during my thousands of hours of fishing from a tube," said my friendly, dedicated pond fisherman, Carl Salling. "But it's something you are always aware of when fishing. I guess it's something like fishing from a small, unstable canoe; you just don't make the moves that will tip it over."

None of the dozen tube fishermen we know consider the device to be the least bit dangerous, but all felt beginning fishermen should be made aware of the fact that tubes can be tipped over and can present a serious problem.

Before getting into the tackle bit, the first thing we recommend is an ample application of insect repellant before heading into the brush. We like to spray our hat and shirt with a liberal amount for the walk to the pond. The spray can stays in the car. The spray job keeps enough of the pesky varmints away until we get into the water. Once we've stopped perspiring, we apply a few drops of Cutter's lotion repellant to

Backwoods beaver ponds are usually secluded, but that's what keeps the fishing so spectacular.

the exposed portion of our skin. This usually keeps us unbitten for the entire fishing trip although an unusually hot day or night might cause us to use a second application.

Most pond fishermen of our acquaintance prefer using fly tackle utilizing wet flies or streamers early in the season and then turning to dry flies during the aquatic insect hatching period of mid-summer. They usually revert to wets and streamers again before the end of the season.

The wet flies or streamers are often of their own creation with colors leaning heavily in favor of red, white, black or green. Some of their creations look like something that would scare a selfrespecting brookie right out of his white-edged fins but they often work.

I've found that varying sizes of the Professor, Parmachene Belle, Montreal and Grizzly King wet flies have been good producers. Nine-Three, Muddler Minnow, Green Ghost, Grey Ghost, Black Nosed Dace and the ever-popular Squirrel Tail have been the most consistant streamers for me.

When the insect hatches are emerging, it's best to try and duplicate the size of the hatching insect and hope the color doesn't make any difference to the fish. So far, I've often found something in the right size Adams or Hendrickson will usually do the trick for me. When they don't I fall back on some of the local favorites which can be found in the nearest tackle shop.

It wasn't long ago a friend and I were fishing a beaver pond when a small mayfly hatch began emerging. We thought we were in for some really great fishing, but after trying just about everything we had in our fishing vests we still had only one small brookie to show for our troubles.

Our problem didn't lie in the lack of feeding fish—heck, we had them feeding in our hip pockets, but they weren't taking our offerings.

"I've been frustrated by browns before, but these brookies are making me look like a dope," growled Charlie Wetzel, one of my favorite fishing companions.

"Yeah, I know what you mean," I answered. "What do you suggest?"

"Let's head back to camp, grab some sleep, go to the local tackle shop in the morning and give it another try tomorrow night," he suggested.

The following day we visited the tackle shop and found the favorite local fly to be a yellow yarn bodied fly with red hackle tied palmer over the body. The wings were a tuft of deer hair and the tail three single hairs. It didn't really look like much but the shop keeper swore it was a killer.

Charlie and I, with our new supply of killer flies, made the trek back to the beaver pond that night with only a faint hope that the new fly would produce results.

The hatch was just starting to dimple the water as we approached the pond and Charlie was in his tube and making his first false cast before I could wipe the perspiration from my eyes.

"Yippeeee," bellowed Charlie, as he hooked his first brookie, "you'd better hurry or you'll miss all the fun."

An hour and a half later, when we clambered back onto the soggy shoreline, we'd hooked and released over 35 trout and kept 10 for our next day's meal.

That scraggly looking, locally-tied fly was truly a killer. At least on that particular beaver pond on that particular night. Beaver pond fishermen have learned to accept good fishing on certain days with certain flies while realizing that same fly may never produce again.

When it comes to fishing live bait for beaver pond brookies there are few baits that can top the plain red worm or night crawler. Some fishermen prefer to use them with a quill bobber and a tiny split shot but most brookie fishermen use extremely lightweight monofilament lines and the bait—no weight and no bobber!

Hardware fishermen confine most of their efforts using small Mepps spinners and an occasional wobbling plug such as the F7 Flatfish. A slow retrieve is deadly for pond brookies.

Carl Salling, one of the best beaver pond fishermen we know, has spent thousands of hours fishing beaver ponds from a tube. It is not unusual for him to catch a limit of 10 fish and have each of them exceed 15 inches, nor is it unusual for him to catch and release 50 brookies in a day's fishing.

"Backwoods beaver pond fishing for brook trout is just about the easiest and best fishing there is on this earth," says Salling. "And, the great part of it is that you rarely run into another angler."

To this we can only add a fervent "Amen."

Special Trout Tactics

by JEROME J. KNAP

SOME OF THE best trout fishing exists in tiny brooks—the smaller the better—that are usually overlooked by most anglers. Small streams never get the recognition—the name—and the heavy fishing pressure found on larger trout streams. Frequently small streams are overlooked because no one seems to realize they harbor trout. And even when it's known that trout lurk beneath undercut banks and overhanging willows or alders, conventional anglers, particularly fly-fishermen, pass them by. Conventional techniques will not take trout in these places. For small streams, you need special trout tactics.

Small streams seldom get heavy spring runoff. The watershed area they drain is small, so the water is seldom cloudy or murky. These waters are amply shaded from the sun by trees and brush. Frequently small streams are spring-fed. All this creates stable water conditions, with cool, clear water during spring, summer and fall. Under such conditions, trout are easy to find.

However, to catch them you need some unorthodox techniques. The only way I've found to beat the brush is to wade downstream. It's true, downstream! Wading upstream is fine for big streams where you are free to move about and have plenty of room to cast. But smaller streams don't offer that advantage. They are confining, not only because of their narrow width but also because of overhanging brush. Casting into holes, below undercut banks, and under submerged logs—all usual trout haunts—is all but impossible. By wading downstream, you're above the trout haunts and all it takes to get your bait into them is to let it drift. The current will carry it the rest of the way.

Sure, wading downstream can raise mud clouds that spook fish. So it's important that you wade as much as possible on firm footing and gravel that has little debris. The odd small cloud of mud won't hurt. Actually disturbing the bottom a bit may even help, as it dislodges nymphs, small crustaceans, and other trout foods.

You have three choices of tackle for small streams; an ultra-light spinning outfit; a light flyrod of about 7 feet; and an old-fashioned bamboo cane, also 7 feet long. In many ways, the cane pole is easiest to use, particularly if you're going to fish with live bait (remember, there's no such thing as casting on these tiny brooks). But, most of us would feel a bit embarrassed at being caught with a cane pole by our avid trout fishing buddies.

A spinning outfit is preferable in a really tight situation. The rod's short length gives you room to maneuver, room to fight a fish. The flyrod is the best bet when you need to put your bait right onto a snag-ringed trout lair. You don't cast with the rod; simply strip off a few feet of leader and use it as a glorified cane pole. The flyrod's sensitivity will let you immediately feel the slightest nibble.

Tiny brooks are generally rich in trout food. Nymphs, tiny minnows, and small crawfish abound. Hosts of terrestrial insects—grasshoppers, crickets, moths, earthworms, leaf rollers, and other types of caterpillars—wind up in the water at various times. All of these make good bait, whether artificial or the real thing.

When fishing with live bait, use large hooks—as large as No. 4. Trout in small streams are unsophisticated. They continue to swallow, even when biting into a steel hook. By using hooks of a fairly large size, you make certain that any trout too tiny to keep won't get your hooks down their gullets and kill themselves. With large hooks, you won't even hook the little guys.

One of the most deadly baits for small streams is the leaf roller. This is probably because many tiny brooks are over-grown with brush and trees from which leaf rollers fall with regularity. Artificial leaf rollers are one of the easiest "flies"

to "tie." All you need are some duck primary quills for the body, some No. 14 or 16 hooks, yellow and blue lacquer, quick-hardening cement, and a fine file.

To make a leaf roller, simply cut the end of a quill to the proper length. One to 1½ inches is about right. Drill a tiny hole, about one-third of the way from the tapered end of the quill. Cut the tip of the quill off. Next, push the hook through the hole that you've drilled so that the eye of the hook sticks out of the large end of the quill. Glue the hook inside the quill with a liberal glob of cement. Mix the yellow and blue lacquers to get a light green color, and paint the quill a light green. Your leaf roller is tied.

You'll find that this "fly" pattern can be fished equally well with an ultralight spinning outfit or a small, light flyrod. Basically you just let the roller drift and wiggle it back and forth with a bit of rod tip action.

A trick I've used often on small streams is to create a hatch of leaf rollers. Shake the smaller limbs of overhanging stream bushes to dislodge leaf rollers. As they fall into the water an imitation hatch brings out feeding trout.

The leaf-roller fly is not the only oddball tactic that produces trout. Various insects such as crickets, grasshoppers, hellgrammites, and others made of rubber or soft plastic for bluegill and bass fishermen are deadly for small trout. Yet few trout fishermen ever try them.

Most of these artificial insects are heavy enough to cast with an ultralight spinning outfit, and they sink to where the trout are lurking. Why more trout fishermen, particularly spinfishermen, don't use them is a mystery. The technique for best success is not to just let them drift with the current, but to impart a bit of jigging motion with the tip of the rod. Let the appendages of these rubber insects wiggle and jiggle. Occasionally a small grub or tiny piece of worm will spice up this type of offering.

Special tactics are also needed for late-season trout during the latter part of August and September. The waters are low and fall rains haven't come. At this time, conventional fishing methods don't work well. The insect hatches have thinned out and the low water presents different problems.

To enjoy success, the late-season trout angler must change his tactics. He must realize his quarry has changed habits. Food is much less abundant now and deep water is restricted to holes. Most of the trout left will be natives. The naive hatchery fish have probably been caught or have died out. The few survivors have adapted to a life in the wild and become more elusive, less willing to take a fly or a bait.

To begin with, you must use a long, thin leader—a 12-footer tapered to 6X, or the thinnest mono (2- to 4-pound)—for the wily wild trout. Heavy lines and leaders will scare off more fish during low-water periods than any other cause.

With the insect hatches being down now, trout feed more heavily on terrestrial invertebrates, minnows, and even small crawfish. That's what you need to catch them. Ants are abundant in late summer, and the Black Ant is one of the top flies. Midges are good too. So are jassids, crickets, and grasshoppers. I've found small salamanders to be one of the most productive late-summer baits for trout. Fish them deep and slow along the bottom and work them into dark pockets of water under banks near log jams and other hiding spots.

The shallow, clear water means another change in tactics. Ripples from wading will put trout down quickly so wade as little as possible in still water. The fish can see you better, so make yourself less visible by keeping your silhouette low. Crouch behind obstructions and stay under overhanging trees. Dress in drab colors—greens and browns. And be careful about too much movement. I've seen trout spook from the slight movement of a fly rod laying out a fly.

The fish are more spread out now so don't neglect any

To catch trout in small streams, you must develop some unorthodox techniques such as wading downstream to beat the brush.

water. Tails of pools are good holding waters, particularly for browns. The way to begin is to fish the faster water below a pool first. Keep your line short to avoid drag. Then fish above the fast water, keeping your rod high so that the line is not swept into the riffles. Next, cover the middle water of the pool, and lastly, the areas where overhanging vegetation shades the water.

The reason for leaving the sides until last is because these are the hardest places to fish. Casting there is difficult. You want to cover the easy water first, where there is much less chance of a bad cast which might scare the fish. The sheltered sides are, of course, prime spots for lurking trout.

Next, you can cover the fast water at the head of the pool. You can wade now because the faster water will hide the ripples and obstruct your movements. Cast into any tongues of current, including the sides. Pay particular attention to any stream of white water that flows into a pool. Trout occasionally lie just to the side of white water, waiting for food to be washed by. Drop your flies or live bait right into the eddies.

To catch big browns in the early fall or even in summer when water levels are receding requires more special tactics. Some of these may be unpalatable to flyfishermen, but then not all of us are flyfishermen.

Big browns in streams hang out in holes and tangles of sunken trees, logs, and stumps. They seldom venture out in daylight. And they are very leery of artificials—flies or lures—because they see countless numbers of them with each

passing summer. When you do hook such a brown on a flyrod or light spinning rod, he heads for his lair where he wraps himself around obstructions and breaks the line or leader. This, of course, adds immeasurably to his education process.

The deadliest method of catching trophy browns is at night, with minnows rigged on a treble hook. The rig is easy to tie. Take a dead minnow of a fair size; say about 4 inches. Remember, you're after big trout. Run a heavy darning or carpet needle through the minnow's mouth, into its intestinal tract, and out the anus.

Now have a treble hook ready on a leader of monofilament about 18-inches long. Take the monofilament, insert it into the eye of the needle, and pull the needle out along with a piece of the monofilament. Pull the leader up through the minnow until the shank of the hook is snug inside the minnow's body. Attach the end of the leader to the line on your reel with a snap swivel. You're all set.

The tackle to use is a bayou bass outfit—a revolving spool reel and a fairly stiff bait-casting stick. The line should be heavy—15- to 20-pound monofilament—something you can bust brush with if you have to. Nighttime browns have a flair for busting tackle and the fisherman needs all the leverage he can get when he goes after lunker browns once the sun sets.

Cast the minnow into the current and let it bump along the bottom. If you are fishing still water, impart a little action to the minnow with your rod tip. You'll find that the trout strike at the minnow from the tail, and because the minnow is free to slide up and down the leader, it frequently doesn't suffer much damage. Just slide it down on the hook and you can use it again. Sometimes you can catch several trout on one minnow.

West coast steelheaders use a similar rig to catch steelhead when the water is high, cold, and roily and the trout need extra stimulation. They use a double-hooked needle harness. These gadgets are simply double, long-shanked hooks with a sharp-pointed eye that is threaded through the body of the minnow. It helps keep the minnow hanging straight and natural looking on the line.

The best bait fish to use in western streams is a sculpin, a small, strange-looking fish that resembles a bullhead. Stomach sampling of western trout by biologists has revealed that the sculpin is a favored food. The sculpin is a bottom dweller and lives under rocks. It seldom exceeds 2 inches in length. The fish, incidentally, preys on trout and salmon eggs during the spawning season.

The way to fish a sculpin-baited rig is with a split-shot about 10 inches above the double hook, and a sliding sinker above the split-shot. The sliding sinker must be heavy enough to keep the sculpin down close to the bottom.

The special tactic here comes in hooking the sculpin. It should be done by shoving the sharp eye of the hook through the fish's mouth and out somewhere near the tail. The hooks then protrude from the sculpin's wide mouth. The reason for this is that trout generally pick up sculpin head first, because of the bait fish's sharp dorsal fin. The hooks are in an ideal position, even if the trout only mouths the sculpin lightly. Another bonus of rigging the sculpin on the hooks this way is that the sculpin is carried down the current to the fish head first, in a life-like manner.

When winter begins to loosen its grip and the melting snows make even slow-moving streams flow like torrents, the trout fisherman must also adopt special tactics to fish successfully. The biggest problem is to keep your bait close to the bottom. If you use too much weight, you can hang up. If you are using too little, then the sculpin drifts too high. Remember that during spring runoff, steelhead, and probably all trout, tend to hug the bottom. Ideally you should have enough weight to allow the current to bump your bait abong the bottom in a natural manner. You must be prepared to experiment a bit on how much lead you need.

Secondly, you must cast upstream to allow your bait to sink. Casting at right angles to the pool you are fishing won't do it. The water pressure on the line will lift the bait off the bottom. At the same time, you must learn to control your line so that the sculpin or whatever bait you are using drifts along naturally and through likely holding water. This means learning how to read the river bottom through the tapping of your rod tip. Learn how to walk your bait downstream naturally and you'll catch more and larger trout.

In the spring with fast water, trout seek slower-moving waters to take up feeding stations. If you let the current have its way with the bait, it will take it where the water reaches its greatest speed and volume. That's exactly what you don't want. You have to direct your bait.

One way to direct bait is to take the line or to let line slip off the reel. Holding the rod tip high, if necessary even with your arms up, will reduce line drag and give you more control. By watching where your line enters the water, you can get a pretty fair idea of the position of your bait. One good thing about a high rod tip is that you can get slack line instantly by simply dropping the tip, if a fish runs with the bait.

One thing that many fishermen fail to realize is that the less line you have in the water, the less there is for the current to grab and exert pressure on. It also gives you more sensitivity in feeling both the bottom and bites. This is extremely impor-

You have three choices of tackle for small streams; an ultra-light spinning outfit; a light flyrod of about 7 feet; or an old-fashioned bamboo cane. This trout fell to spinning gear.

Above—The way to catch trophy browns at night is with a minnow, rigged on a treble hook with an 18-inch leader of heavy monofilament.

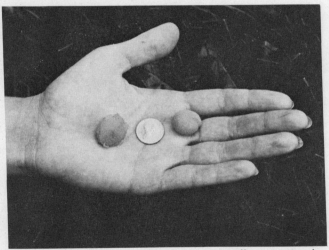

Foam balls come in both orange and yellow—note size in comparison to a dime. They're available in ready-made balls or in solid blocks for those who wish to cut their own.

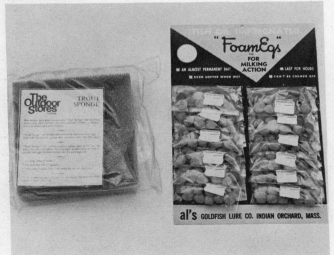

tant, since trout in cold water are more likely to pick up and mouth a bait gently than to run with it. Successful high-water trout fishing is, to a great extent, a matter of feel. If you can't feel the bites, you're not going to get many fish.

The high water facing the early season trout angler also requires special tactics. Perhaps special savvy is a more apt description. Riffles during normal water conditions become fast-flowing cataracts when the water is high. The normal runs of quiet water become inhospitable for trout. The fish seek new areas of quiet flow where obstructions will cradle them from fast water. You have to find these new holding waters. Remember, trout need comfort and this involves either cool water in warm weather or a haven from the heavy current forces— or a combination of the two.

Another point to remember is to place your bait close to these spring fish. Cold water makes them a bit lethargic so they won't do much searching for food. The fast flow inhibits their movements even further.

At this time, the trout will lie in the deepest pools, not at the head or in the shallow tail. Since the water is cold, it will be rich in oxygen and trout are happy to seek quiet, backwater flows where slowly moving water is deflected from the main current. Look for reverse eddies, quiet reaches above small dams, and even deep overflow channels.

Trout seek faster water cascades and ripples only when the water has warmed up and carries less oxygen. At that time, fast, loping water becomes important to the trout because it has more oxygen than slow-flowing streams. But in the spring, they stay away from very fast water so that they don't have to fight it. You must keep your bait away from it as well.

One good thing about early season trout is they tend to school. They are not feeding as much, so they're not competing for food. Chances are that where you find one fish you may find others.

Any treatise on special tactics for trout must not neglect the odd-ball baits—marshmallows, cheese, doughballs, and bits of synthetic foam. Ten or so years ago the thought of using doughballs for trout, particularly steelhead, was unheard of. Doughballs were carp bait, and so were marshmallows and cheese. But now these baits are being used for steelhead.

There's no special technique with fishing these baits. They are all fished close to the bottom. The doughball addicts have their favorite mixtures. One favorite mix is bread, oatmeal, and sugar, with enough water to make a stiff dough. Another popular recipe is a mixture of vanilla with bran flakes or wheat flakes. To make it, just pour a small bottle of vanilla into a bowl. Then add the breakfast flakes and knead until you have a gooey ball of dough. The dough will keep for a long time if you store it in an air-tight container in the refrigerator. But hide it. The concoction is quite tasty, and if your kids find it they'll probably eat it before the trout.

Cheese baits are generally mixed with flour and also made into balls. Soft, gooey cheeses are best. Commercial cheese-balls have the pungent odor of limburger.

The secret to cheeseball and doughball fishing is to make the balls fairly small, certainly no larger than an acorn, with some as small as peas. The hook should be of fairly light wire and well buried into the bait ball.

I suspect the reason why trout can take cheeseballs is because they look like fish eggs. The visual attraction is probably, again, the reason why small foam balls have been successfully used as steelhead bait. Foam balls look like single fish eggs when bounced along the river bottom. Many fishermen soak the foam in cod-liver oil. Commercial foam eggs are also impregnated with fish oil.

The trout fisherman who is willing to try special tactics on a river or lake is normally the man who always manages to come home with some fish.

Trout in the Southwest

by JIM TALLON

WHEN I LEFT Kentucky 25-years ago I was a bassman who had never set a barb in a trout. But I had a love for trout, fired up by hundreds of articles I had read in the outdoor magazines. I knew about the Madison, the Yellowstone, the Big Hole, and other Big Name Western streams; and the great tackle-busting *salmo* jockeying for space in their bellies. But I forsaked them all, spurred on by the flowery Southwestern descriptions of Zane Grey—a better salesman than the trout story writers—to settle in Arizona.

In the Southwest I expected to find a barren but beautiful land of red rock, sparse grass—for cattlemen and sheepmen to fight over—countless square miles of sand, hundreds of thousands of cactus, the Grand Canyon . . . and no trout. I was wrong. Zane Grey had a penchant for shifting specific landscapes to where he wanted them. So that must have been Arizona's neighbor state to the east, New Mexico, that he was talking about. Right? Wrong. Again.

Presently I can think of only one range war going on in the Southwest and that concerns a Navajo and Hopi Indian court battle over some grazing lands out in the Painted Desert. "Countless square miles of sand" is too much. And I know of no place in the Southwest that can be truly described as "barren." It does have the expected hot desert lands with Arizona's getting a bit hotter than New Mexico's, which is called "lower Sonoran," plus five more of the seven climates of the U.S. including Arctic alpine. This latter is found on mountains like 12,670-foot-high San Francisco Peaks, near Flagstaff, Arizona; and 13,161-foot-high Wheeler Peak, north of Taos, New Mexico. These are the highest points in these states; a number of other peaks, though, approach them in elevations above sea level.

The country that slopes up to these peaks are generally forested with juniper in the lower reaches but as you climb higher you find pinyon and ponderosa pines, spruce and firs. Thousands of miles of streams meander through them and lakes, both man-made and natural, are abundant. In this high country, the Southwest doesn't look like the stereotyped Southwest at all, rather like the Northwest.

Combined, the two states take in 235,419 square miles of highly-diversified real estate. In that much space you can fit the states of Rhode Island, Massachusetts, Connecticut, New Hampshire, Vermont, New York, New Jersey, Maine, Pennsylvania, Delaware, Virginia and West Virginia and still have 1,650 miles left over. Now, you say, there has just got to be some fine trout fishing in the Southwest. And you are right.

Fish management in the Southwest actually began about the turn of the century with the old U.S. Bureau of Fisheries hustling specially-built, fish-holding railway cars to stock lakes and streams. But with the marginal knowledge of fish habits and habitats, sometimes the wrong fish were stocked in the wrong waters. And the results were problems. By the time I moved to Arizona, fish management had progressed; but it has been since then that the major changes have been made—knowledge has been acquired that can turn sterile waters into highly productive ones. Such modern fish management techniques have made the Southwest an outstanding place to fish for certain species, including trout. That means rainbows, German browns, Eastern brook, black-spotted cutthroats, the elusive and beautiful Arizona native and its lookalike, the Gila trout (relatives of the golden trout); and such coldwater brethren such as Montana grayling, coho and kokanee salmon.

Most of Arizona's trout fishing is centered in the forested lands of the northern and eastern parts of the state. In New Mexico, trout fishing waters are basically grouped in three areas: north-central, west-central and south-central. However, both states have excellent trout fishing in waters surrounded by landscapes strictly foreign to that in which trout are supposed, and expected, to live. Among them, and perhaps the most prime and modern examples, are Glen Canyon Dam on the Colorado River near Page, Arizona, which impounds Lake Powell; and Navajo Dam on the San Juan River in northwestern New Mexico, which impounds Navajo Lake. Prior to construction of these dams, both rivers were great funnels of mud and silt incapable of trout life. Now these reservoirs act as great settling basins and cold, desilted water released from the dams has created excellent habitat for trout, both downstream and in the reservoirs themselves.

With these waters at relatively high elevations, Glen Canyon Dam about 4,000 feet above sea level and Navajo Dam at about 5,500, despite un-trout-looking vistas, trout fishing still seems plausible because of the relative coolness of water associated with these elevations in the Southwest. New Mexico's lowest point is 2,876 feet above sea level, and though eastern folks may regard that as high, cool country, the lower-Sonoran climate of these elevations gets summer hot. And with Arizona's desert lands dropping to just 70 feet above sea level, you can bet that is gets even hotter. But, despite the heat and aridness, some remarkable trout fisheries have come into existence.

New Mexico's largest trout stream is the Rio Grande River, which bisects the state vertically from Colorado to Mexico. In the upper elevations, together with its tributaries and other nearby waters, it forms roughly an inverted triangle, with Santa Fe at its upside-down apex, of fine trout fishing country.

When the Rio Grande drops to lower elevations, it slows to a wide and shallow Western river in which no one expects trout could exist. And they can't, except where Man has made inroads in river control. Flood- and irrigation-damming and modern fish management have created a number of good trout fishing areas along the Rio Grande. Several of these are near Albuquerque. Further south, near Socorro, is Escondida Lake. At Truth or Consequences are Elephant Butte and Caballo reservoirs; and about 50 miles north of the Mexico border, Burns Lake and Del Rio Drain.

The Arizona counterpart of the Rio Grande is the Colorado River, which enters the state in the form of Lake Powell at Page, and departs from it at Yuma. This is the same river that helped to carve Grand Canyon. From Lake Mead southward, it butts up against Nevada on the west bank for about 60 miles, then flows against California for about 180 miles, then crosses into Mexico and fans through its delta into the Gulf of California.

Using a canoe, these fly fishermen work the waters of Lee Valley Lake, in the White Mountains of Arizona, for Montana grayling.

The Colorado is one of the most controversial streams in the world, with every state and Mexico and dozens of state and federal agencies trying to claim a share of its waters, or control them. It has become an apparently unsolvable problem of satisfying everybody; and it has been said that those who attempt it will surely end up in the booby hatch.

One of the major complaints of conservationists has been the continuing efforts of the Bureau of Reclamation, aided and abetted by the Corps of Engineers, to make a "straight concrete gut" out of the Lower Colorado River. Their primary effort has been to store as much water as possible in impoundments; and move it as fast as possible so that evaporative losses are minimum. Someone at the Bureau once said, "The only way to do that is in concrete-lined aqueducts." And there has been some attempt to do just that, with oxbows, where fish species congregated because of the slower-moving water, being cut off and eliminated with straight channelization; and sterile sand dredged into the marshes where waterfowl—some rare species—once lived and rested. However, from a Southwestern trout fisherman's viewpoint, some of the damming of the Lower Colorado River has not been 100 percent bad. The desilting by the dams has turned the erratic and usually muddy Colorado into a stream where trout can live and thrive, at least in some of the impoundments and the immediate tailwaters below the dams.

Though this is hardly intended to be a treatise on the pros and cons of dam building, I felt it necessary to establish some sort of perspective on it in relation to trout fishing in the Southwest.

Thus, we have trout fishing where none existed before, in as unlikely a trout country as you would ever expect to see. Often the blistering heat raises thermometers to the erupting point; and often it rates as the hottest place in the U.S.

Before departing from this theme, I would like to mention another unlikely, but good, fishing place for trout. Summer heat here may be only a couple of degrees cooler than lower Colorado River area temperatures. I have in mind a short stretch of the Salt River, another multi-dammed stream, below impounded Saguaro Lake, about 50 miles northeast of Phoenix. The Arizona Game and Fish Department (AG&F) has made a "sometime" trout fishery of it. Rainbows are stocked in the cooler months when water temperatures drop low enough for trout survival. Any trout not caught before the summer temperatures raises water temperatures may die. Interestingly, this idea has worked quite well because fish grow rapidly with the longer feeding season of this part of Arizona, a lot of trout are caught, and remarkably, some survive the summers to put on a lot of weight and size. Each year a few trout fishermen are stunned by the dimensions of these survivors.

The trout fishing hotspots in the Southwest are too numerous to mention without writing a whole book. But we can touch on a few of the higher-rated waters. Starting with New Mexico, let us reflect back to the Rio Grande, where we find an 80-mile section near the Colorado line that is frankly considered to be "fabulous fishing waters." Here rainbows and browns are abundant with fish to 8 pounds being landed frequently and lucky anglers netting others in excess of 15 pounds. In the Sangre de Cristo mountains, which hosts some of those 13,000-foot peaks mentioned earlier, are some fine alpine lakes and streams, including the upper reaches of the Red River. Perhaps trout aren't consistently as big here, but this part of New Mexico must be rated as one for "quality experiences," where a trout fisherman gets primitiveness with his fishing. Some of this is above timberline so you'll need warm dress even in midsummer.

Eagle Nest Lake, about 40 miles east of Taos—where TV's Marshall McCloud is supposedly from—is privately owned and a commercial operation; it has excellent trout fishing. The two Charette Lakes near Wagon Mound belong to the New Mexico Department of Game and Fish (NMDGF) and supplies trout fishermen with some of the best rainbow action in the state.

Fishermen find fast action on rainbows and browns on the Pecos River, and other streams in the vicinity of the town of Pecos. Then working higher into the Pecos Wilderness Area, you'll see a primitive setting of mountains, meadows and streams—some with beaver ponds. These hold hungry rainbows, browns, brookies and cutthroats. And there you'll also find excellent high country trout lakes such as Katherine, Lost Bear, Encantada, Baldy and Santiago, to name a few. North of Tres Pedras, the beaver pond enthusiast will find some of the natural impoundments, and they're highly rated for trout fishing.

Another of the remarkable achievements of modern southwestern trout fisheries management occurs at Bluewater Lake, about 45 miles southeast of Gallup. A privately-owned irrigation reservoir, its owners were paid $92,000 by the NMDG&F to hold its water level high enough to support trout populations. That pay-off one year was 50,000 pounds of trout from 1,800 pounds of catchables stocked. That's a return ratio of better than 25 to 1. Most of these fish taken by troutmen were 2- to 3-pounders.

Just across the border in Arizona lives a fish just a spot or two different from the gila trout, and this one is called the Arizona native, or Apache native trout. Until just a few years ago, the gila trout and the Arizona native were thought to be the same species.

The primary reason for the decline of the Apache native was hybridization with the rainbow. This fish has been put on the endangered list, but unjustifiably, for the concerted efforts of the AG&F has brought it back to fishable numbers. Although presently denied the fisherman, legislation may soon make Apache natives fair game once again.

Turning to some of the best trout fishing spots in Arizona, we can start with the upper Colorado River. At the Utah border, we find Lake Powell, of Colorado River birth; Arizona can claim but a few miles of the lower part of the lake, but interestingly, it is this side that gets the best rating for trout fishing; most of the lake is considered essentially a bass and crappie fishing hole.

Below Glen Canyon Dam we find some of the finest rainbow trout fishing in Arizona. Fish up to 6 or 8 pounds are common. Continuing downstream, the Colorado winds through Marble and Grand canyons. Here it doesn't really qualify as a trout stream, but its side streams may provide excellent fishing. I well remember the 18-inch rainbows and browns, fat, beautiful and sassy, I used to catch (and mostly release) out of just about every pool on the lower 5 miles of Bright Angel Creek, adjacent to Phantom Ranch in the bottom of Grand Canyon. A few years back, a cloudburst caused a wall of water to violently rake this paradisiacal stream, killing or carrying away its trout populations and changing many of its desirable characteristics. However, happily I have had some recent reports that some 20-inch rainbows are once again being netted in Bright Angel Creek. Some other good Grand Canyon trout streams are Thunder River, Tapeats and Havasu Creek.

Farther down the Colorado we find Lake Mead, Willow Beach and Lake Mohave. Impounded by Hoover (Boulder) Dam, you can not really call Lake Mead a trout lake. An occasional rainbow or some of the recently-stocked coho

Left—The Rio Grande River in the upper reaches is one of New Mexico's best trout streams. Here it drops through a canyon on its way to Mexico.

Below—Everyone likes to fish and trout beauties such as these are regularly taken in New Mexico's waters.

Left—At Knoll Lake, on Arizona's Mogollon Rim, a trout fishing lady contemplates the scenery before casting for rainbows.

show up in the angler's creel and these are usually very good fish. Below the dam are 11 miles of river that has excellent trout fishing; the state rainbow record of 21 pounds came from here and 10-pounders are numerous. Access to these waters are through Willow Beach. Next we come to Lake Mohave which has very good trout fishing during the cooler months; you can catch them at warmer

In the depths of Grand Canyon, a river-rafter fly fishes in the Colorado at the mouth of trout-producing Deer Creek.

(and hotter) times of the year, but you must fish very deep to do so.

Making a big jump across Arizona to the highlands of the Mogollon Rim and the White Mountains, we find great concentrations of trout streams and lakes. On the Rim are Bear Canyon, Woods Canyon, Knoll, Chevelon, Black Canyon and Willow Springs Lakes. This complex was created by the AG&F in conjunction with the National Forest Service, and it offers quality fishing rather than quantity fishing. These lakes, at elevations of up to 8,000 feet above sea level, have been stocked with rainbows, browns, brooks, cutthroats, Arizona natives and Montana grayling.

Most of the many lakes in the White Mountains belong to the Apache Indians and are managed by the U.S. Bureau of Sport Fisheries and Wildlife (BSFW). Judging by the productiveness of these lakes, the BSFW may have "overstocked" them. But nobody is complaining. Sometimes even the smallest of the Apache lakes will shock troutmen with the number of tackle-busters in them. Among these winners are Sunrise, Hurricane, Drift Fence, Pacheta and Reservation. Some livestock watering tanks hardly larger than a washtub, and often unnamed, will give troutmen many surprises.

Just off the east side of the Apache Reservation are several very good trout fishing lakes, with the better known being Big Lake and Becker Lake.

Looking toward the north-central part of Arizona, near Flagstaff, three good trout lakes are certainly worth mentioning—Ashurst, Kinninkinick and Long. This latter is a rare example of successful "multi-management" with rainbows, browns, largemouth bass, northern pike, yellow perch and panfish; and though competitive species, they all seem to be doing very well.

West of Flagstaff, in the Williams area, are Kaibab, Whitehorse, and J.D. Dam Lakes. And southwest of Williams, Prescott has Lynx Lake. All are stocked with rainbows and some fine browns come out of J.D. Dam Lake. However, to fish the above, it takes a cut above average trout fisherman to make them pay off.

Since license fees and types, and creel limits are subject to change regularly, we won't discuss them here. I will say that New Mexico trout fishing rules and regulations are more complex than Arizona's. In the former there are trout seasons and specific ones for specific areas; in Arizona there are no trout seasons; you can fish for them year-'round. You should have up-to-date information to stay legal, and you can get it at license dealers in the two states, or by writing to the Arizona Game and Fish Department, 2222 West Greenway Road, Phoenix, AZ 85023; and New Mexico Department of Game and Fish, State Capitol Building, Santa Fe, NM 87503.

I would like to recommend an excellent fishing guide to Arizona called *Fishing the 100 Best,* which is printed by Phoenix Publishing, 4707 N. 12th Street, Phoenix AZ 85014. New Mexico may have a similar guide I'm not aware of.

Fishing southwestern lakes and streams take the same skills as in other parts of America, and maybe the world. The fish in them will smash a Royal Coachman or Wooly Worm, or mood permitting, a Mepp's Spinner or Dardevle. In some waters first-time fishermen will limit out; in others it takes the artful trout fisherman to fool wise fish into striking.

Since coming to Arizona, I have managed to wet a line in a number of other Western states, fishing even big name waters for trout. Taking into consideration the number, size, species, readiness to strike, in relation to available trout waters in a pair of water-poor states, Southwest trout fishing may be the best in the world.

Try Spinners for Big Trout

by NICK SISLEY

Four different species of Pennsylvania trout; rainbow, golden, brown and brookie, and three Montali Crazy Horse spinners used to take them.

TROUT WERE rippling the surface in the flat, calm waters behind the lee of an island—I mean huge trout. They were feasting on big mayflies. The spot was Lake Mistassini in far north Quebec—up above the 52nd parallel. My guide was slowly sculling the boat toward a rock outcropping that I had pointed to a few seconds previously. All my thoughts were concentrated on a trophy size fish working in that area.

The bail on my spin reel was already open. My whole body was poised, ready for the cast as soon as we were close enough. We'd spent all week catching a fish here and there but we were looking for a tailor-made situation like this. One where big trout were feeding and where the onus was on the angler to present a lure accurately and entice them to take. If he could, a wall mounting size trout would be his. As the rock outcropping drew closer, I shot a cast 10 feet beyond the spot where my prize was feeding. I was using a No. 3 Weaver spinner with a unique purple crackle finish on the blade.

The bail clicked shut, and soon I could feel the spinner blade pulsations through the rod tip. As the lure passed the feeding area the light wand jerked down tight, and the battle with the brute fish began. Four times I brought him to the boat. He was almost ready for the net the last time—almost turned on his side. Then he found the strength for one more speedy run. Luck found him a sharp submerged rock that nicked the 4-pound-test line and ended the battle. I sat down, a little sick, a bit wobbly in the knees. I didn't pick up my rod for a half-hour or more. I estimated his weight at 8 pounds—the guide estimated his weight at 9 pounds. Oh yes, what kind of trout was he? He was a brook trout—a brook trout to end all brook trout!

On another trip, this time even further north in Labrador, I was chucking spinners with an ultra light outfit, fishing below a waterfall that had already produced a stringer full of 2- to 4-pound landlocked salmon. We had more than enough for the frying pan. Now we were concentrating on the catch and release game. It was one of those memorable mornings when the fishing was exceptionally good.

This time I was tossing a Mepps Black Fury No. 2. A vicious strike almost tore the tiny 2-ounce rod from my grasp. This fish fought deep, not leaping like the ouananiche I had been stinging with sharp hook points all morning. It never entered my mind that the fish was anything but a land-locked salmon, but it was obvious that this one was going to be much bigger than others I had taken that morning. I finally landed him among the rocks and he was a lake trout with a small body and big head—obviously an old-timer. It was a week later before we reached a butcher's scale in Goose Bay. We kept the fish fresh by burying him in Labrador's permafrost. His weight at that late weigh-in was 9 pounds, 2 ounces and he was landed on 4-pound mono. He would have made the *Field and Stream* 4-pound record that year if the outfitter had sent me the signed affidavit in time.

On yet another far-flung trout angling adventure, this time in Ecuador, South America, spinners turned the trick for me again—this time I used Dardevle No Tangle Ospreys. We were fishing La Mica, a beautiful Alpine lake in the high Andes, and it was loaded with rainbows. We trolled and cast these unique spinners and even the locals got their eyes opened with the amount of fish we were able to take.

I relate these three anecdotes to impress you with the fact that spinners take trout, especially big trout. Whether fishing lakes or streams, this lure type can contribute to significant success. Many anglers have become reasonably successful at catching fish with spinners, and no wonder. They are very easy to fish with. However, as with any specific facet of angling, there are numerous little secrets that make it possible for a sportsman to increase his catch even more. Putting all these tips together will help you catch more trout with spinners. That's what this article is all about.

Spinners originated in Europe—along about the time Europeans also came up with the fixed spool or open face spin reel. This reel type and the rods that were eventually made specifically for them made it possible to cast the little ⅛-, ¼-, and ⅜-ounce spinners. Spinners and spinning tackle didn't reach North America until after World War II when returning GIs brought back the first models. Up until that time, spinners were too heavy to cast with fly equipment and much too light to cast with revolving spool, "thumbed" baitcasting reels.

But spinners and spin fishing did more than fill in a lure weight void. They made fishing easier. Novices were soon catching stringers of trout as long as seasoned veterans.

Spinners themselves involve a wire shaft to which a loop is twisted circular on top for attaching to the line from the reel or a swivel snap, and twisted circular at the bottom to enclose the eye of a hook—usually a treble. The spinning blade itself is a concave piece of metal that can have one of many different shapes. It is attached to the wire shaft by a small piece of metal called a clevis. Casting weight is added to the wire shaft below the spinner. Different types of weights can be used—glass beads, lead, metal tubing, brass, the list goes on.

Trout, especially in streams and often in lakes, are found in deep water. The primary reason spinners have been so

Above—This huge laker went for small spinner presented in shallow water. Left—A big laker swirls the surface as guide readies the net.

successful for so many years is these lures get down to the bottom, where the fish are—fast! There are times when fish will swim up several feet to take a lure or a fly, but they are not accustomed to feeding in this manner. Consequently, the occasions where you find them doing so are the exception, not the rule. To take trout (and almost any other fish species as well) it pays to put the lure at the depth the fish are. Never forget that fact, especially when spinning for trout. When stream fishing, learn how to feel the lure as it skims over the rocks.

One reason many anglers don't catch as many trout as they could on spinners is because they retrieve too fast. The retrieve should only be fast enough to keep the lure from hanging up on the bottom when stream fishing. I've watched many anglers let their lures sink properly, then they begin a retrieve that brings the spinner further and further away from the bottom until soon the spinner is buzzing just under the water's surface.

Spinning lures that are retrieved too quickly can cause line twist—even if a quality swivel is used. Most of these lures twist slowly as they come through the water. As the speed of the retrieve is increased, they tend to revolve at a faster rate. As the spinning blade, attached to the clevis, revolves around the shaft, the clevis, because of friction, tends to turn the entire shaft. A quality spinner will revolve less than an improperly designed one. I recommend using a good swivel with all spinners, as this helps remove line twist. When line twist occurs, it can cause untold casting miseries.

In working lakes for trout I like to begin the morning fishing by maneuvering the boat just off the shore line and cast towards the shallows. Begin the retrieve immediately. As soon as you feel the blade pulsating through the rod tip, slow the retrieve in an effort to have the lure sink slowly as

Left and above—Noted outdoor movie maker, Wally Taber, battles a trout in the Canadian wilderness and displays the fat lake trout he managed to take with his spinner.

Andy Montali, spinner manufacturer from Avonmore, Pa., tussles with a Pennsylvania trout hooked with one of his spinners.

it comes back—staying close to the bottom. When the sun gets high, I like to troll drop-offs fairly close to feeding areas. Split shot or other weight must often be added to get the spinner to travel at the proper depth. At times one must also let out plenty of line so the lure tracks deep. Slow boat movement during the troll also forces the lure to go deeper. A good way to accomplish even slower boat movement is to turn around and troll backwards—so that the flat transom rather than the pointed bow rushes against the oncoming water.

Although I've had wide experience fishing trout in streams with spinners, a fellow who lives fairly close to me in western Pennsylvania, Andy Montali, invented and markets a unique spinning lure that he calls the Montali Crazy Horse. Andy has fished spinners exclusively for trout for many years. I arranged to spend a day on the water interviewing and fishing with him, observing his techniques so that I could pass his tips and advice to you.

The patented Crazy Horse is unique in the following aspects. It uses a piece of copper tubing on the spinner shaft for casting weight. More importantly, Andy puts four slight but unusual bends in the spinner blade itself. One bend is at the very top of the blade, and three other, almost minute bends, are put into the bottom of his spinner blade. These bends give a unique fluttering action to the spinner. It does more than merely revolve around the shaft. It oscillates or flutters as it turns. Andy designed it because he feels it imitates a crippled bug more than a minnow. If regular spin lures are designed for slow retrieves, the Crazy Horse is designed for even slower ones. If you acquire one of these lures, experiment with it in slack water with slower and slower retrieves until you get the right fluttering action for which it was designed.

Andy essentially fishes his lure in the same manner that one would use with any other spinner. He occasionally fishes upstream, but he'll usually only cast to a good looking spot and then move on quickly. When he is walking upstream, his intention is to get a favorite spot, then start working back downstream. That's when he begins to fish slowly and thoroughly. Different trout holding spots, amount of stream flow, overhanging brush, and many other factors affect where he casts, but for the most part he prefers casting quartering downstream. He engages the reel bail immediately but does not start the retrieve until he feels the lure is close to the bottom. During this "dead" period, which Andy calls the "float," he encounters maybe 10 to 20 percent of his strikes. Watch your line! Once the lure is "swinging," enough speed is maintained to keep it riding deep, just over the bottom rocks. A small percentage of hits are felt as the lure travels on its path. As the lure comes to the "end of its swing," the majority of strikes are encountered. Once the spinner has reached the end of the swing Andy will often move his rod tip to the left or right so that the lure comes back toward him through the most likely looking trout holding water.

Andy has made his Crazy Horse, for his own use in virtually every size, shape, and color. However, he only markets sizes No. 2 and No. 3 with three different color combinations—he has found that these three combinations far out-perform any others. On cloudy days he prefers a spinner with a silver blade and silver body. On bright days he uses lures with a brass blade and bodies of either black and white or yellow and orange.

Andy also has some interesting theories about snap swivels. He only uses one next to the lure early in the season or when he encounters cloudy water conditions. When streams are low and/or clear, he clips off an 18-inch piece of mono from his reel. He ties a snap swivel to the line from the reel,

This laker was taken on an ultra-light outfit and tiny spinner while author, Nick Sisley, was casting for landlocked salmon. Evidently it was an old-timer—for it had a relatively small body to go with a massive head.

the piece of leader to the other end of the snap swivel, then attaches the lure to the short piece of leader with an improved clinch knot. He is certain that taking the swivel away from the position next to the spinner is a small factor in increasing catch success but he is also convinced it is a definite factor!

All properly designed or balanced spinners should come through the water so that they track straight and look realistic. If the weight on the lure is too heavy or too light, it comes through the water in an unnatural manner. It is usually necessary to attach split shot to the line in order to have a spinner run at the proper depth. Andy feels his spinner, for its size, is lighter than most. He never fishes the Crazy Horse without at least one split shot. Sometimes he uses two or more. He prefers his split shot to be 12 to 14 inches up the line from the lure. If more than one shot is attached, he separates them—2 to 3 inches between. Some add two, three, or more split shot so close together that they touch each another. Andy feels that this makes too much of a "glob" that looks unnatural and can spook fish. He doesn't deny that fish can see split shot, but he does feel that they can see two of them together just a little easier than they can see two that are separated. Again perhaps it's a minor factor, but still a factor—and it's the combination of all the secrets experts use that permits them to catch more fish than the novice.

At times, especially on big trout, a direct upstream cast can be wicked. The idea is to flick the lure upstream, or quartering upstream, then, with the combination of properly elevating the rod tip along with turning the reel handle just fast enough to prevent hanging up, you are likely to encounter some remarkable catches. As spin fishing goes, upstream angling is one of the harder aspects to learn. It takes a while before one acquires the proper feel—being able to keep from getting hung-up and to refrain from retrieving too fast.

A too-fast retrieve after an upstream cast can spook trout. It seems to give fish the impression that the oncoming spinner is "after" them. But if the blade revolves very slowly as the lure tumbles downstream over the tops of the rocks, look out. As I said, it can be wicked!

As a rule, spinners can be acquired in seven different

sizes. The teeny ones are denoted by the number 0. Even the No. 1s are extremely small. Probably the No. 2s and No. 3s are used in more trout fishing situations than any other. Sizes 3 and 4 are often used for bass. Then there are 5s and 6s, the latter the largest spinner blades that I have come across.

Spinners also come in numerous shapes. Probably the most popular are the Colorado and Indiana shapes. Aerodynamics experts claim that the longer, slimmer Indiana-type blades revolve faster. Of these two most popular blade shapes, however, I'd hazard a guess that the Colorado type is used on more spinners than any other blade type.

Once the spinner manufacturer decides on the blade design he wants to use, what he can do to make the blade unique is endless. Different types of metal can be used, although brass and chrome plate seem to be the most popular. The blade can also be painted—virtually any color of the rainbow. The Weaver spinners (alluded to at the beginning of this story) with their "crackle" finish, have produced exceptionally well for me. However, the unusual paint job on these spinners often wears off after several big trout have gnawed on its finish.

In addition to painting spinner blades, the metal can be hammered, stamped in a fluted design, stamped with a scale finish—well, no matter how many different ways I might mention, I am sure some new spinner manufacturer will come up with something else a week later.

Although spinners are not expensive when compared to quality plugs and some other lure types, it is possible to save a few dollars and while away enjoyable hours during the off season by making your own. It is relatively easy to learn how to do. A minimum of inexpensive equipment is required, and many fish tackle catalog houses will supply all that is needed.

Perhaps most of you readers have already found that employing spinners while trout fishing has been a productive way to increase your catch. Hopefully I've offered even experienced spinner fishermen a tip or two that they might be able to employ on their next outing for big trout. For the novices among you, I suggest you study and restudy how to fish spinners, because it is the quickest way to add big trout to your stringer.

AMERICA'S LITTLE KNOWN TROUT

by RICH G. LAWRENCE

ALMOST everyone has heard of or caught rainbow, brown, brook or lake trout. Many others have caught or at least heard of steelhead, golden, cutthroat and Dolly Vardens.

These trout are fairly common in their specific regions. The western states host steelhead, golden and cutthroats. Steelheads, browns, brookies, rainbows and lake trout are common to both eastern and western United States and Canada.

As common as the aforementioned species are, there are several little known trout in North America that also are part of our angling heritage. With one exception, these fish are scarce-to-extremely rare in population. Many are located in very small or remote areas.

Often thought to be sub-species by many fishery biologists, some biologists feel these trout are a separate and distinct race of fish. Most of these "little known" trout are small in size, due perhaps to their isolation. Also, the fact they could possibly be sub-species or much smaller editions, may be why most of these trout seldom attain any noticeable length and weight. Few of these unheralded trout species attain a length of much more than 12 inches except in the one odd case.

One of the "little known trout" is the aurora trout (*Salvelinus Timagamiensis*). The aurora has been listed in the Ontario fishing law books for many years. It belongs to the char family, the same as the brook trout (*Salvelinus Fontinalis*).

The aurora is fairly rare to scarce. Some biologists feel this trout is just a slightly different colored brook trout while

The beautiful and extremely rare gila trout of New Mexico.

others maintain it is a distinct sub-species.

This trout is found only in Ontario. There are only a few lakes near Timagami that contain aurora—most are found in White Pine and Clearwater lakes north of Timagami. There are also a few auroras in several lakes adjacent to White Pine and Clearwater. Some aurora are also found in Ontario's Gamble township in Temiskaming district.

This fish resembles the brook trout in general appearance, it is characterized by the absence of red spots on its sides and tends to have pale or silvery sides. It has a truncate tail.

Auroras are small trout generally, but on occasion they will reach a maximum of 20 inches. The aurora is very rare and could be extinct now or completely interbred with brook trout.

Another of the lesser known trout is the gila (*Salmo Gilae*). This small member of the trout family is found only in small headwater streams in Arizona and New Mexico.

The gila trout was first described and classified as a separate species by Dr. Robert R. Miller in 1950. Many people previously assumed it was just a small cutthroat. At that time, the only known population of gilas was in Diamond Creek in New Mexico.

This trout's original range was in the headwaters of the Gila River drainage. Most of the waters that now contain gila trout are within the boundaries of Gila National Forest, near Silver City, in southwestern New Mexico.

Gila trout have the same general appearance as cutthroat, which is why many thought it was just a smaller version. The gila usually reaches a length of 6 or 7 inches and seldom grows to more than 10 inches.

Recently the only pure strain of gila trout existed in Diamond Creek. Most of the previous gila trout streams were either fished out or the gila hybridized with rainbow trout.

This has seriously restricted the range of the pure strain of *Salmo Gilae*. The presence of rainbows, suckers and chubs were also a deterrant. The fact that many of the streams that held these fish were very shallow and occasionally dried-up in the summer months limited their range and numbers.

In November, 1970, with the combined efforts of the New Mexico Department of Game and Fish and the U.S. Forest Service, gila trout were shocked from Diamond Creek. The fish were netted and transferred by helicopter and pack mule to McKnight Creek. About 3,500 trout were recovered from less than 4 miles of stream. The transplant consisted of 307 trout. All of the fish survived the shocking, netting, helicopter and mule ride and are in good shape now.

The gila trout has a dark olive green back that shades to a yellowish belly. It has many small black spots on the tail and dorsal fin. It does have parr marks and has no spots on the lower fins. It has a longer upper jaw and head than does the cutthroat and has a very long adipose fin when compared to other trout.

The gila spawns in the spring, usually laying 150 to 200 eggs in the redd (spawning bed) on a gravel or rocky bottom. This amount of eggs is indicative of the smallness of this species of trout.

The older, mature gila trout has a dark, golden back with golden yellow sides and light golden belly. They have a golden-orange color on their jaws.

Several small populations of pure gilas have been found in other small creeks that have natural barriers, such as McKenna and Spruce Creeks. There are no other populations of rival fish in these creeks. There are plans to re-plant these trout in other isolated streams to help maintain the species.

In 1972, gila trout were stocked in Sheep Corral Creek, a small tributary of the Sapillo Creek. This is located roughly 20 miles north of Silver City, N.M.

The gila trout is still on the endangered species list, but with the efforts of many groups, the concensus is the gila will make it.

Jumping from the southern part of the United States to Canada, we find the Quebec red trout (*Salvelinus Marstoni*). This is also a member of the char family. This little-known fish has a very small, limited distribution within the confines of the Laurentides Park in Quebec and in some of the lakes in the Charlevoix country of Quebec.

The Quebec red is also found in the Rimouski country and some lakes south of the St. Lawrence river. They are also present in several lakes northwest of Quebec City and is quite widespread in the Gaspé Peninsula.

The red is basically a deep water fish and is normally found in the shallow lake water only during spring and fall months when the water temperatures are cold.

The red trout males have very bright red sides, especially during spawning time. The spots are usually very pale. These fish have red anal and pectoral fins with a white leading edge. The tail has a pronounced fork. The red trout has no black in the lower fins like the brook trout. Occasionally these fish will assume a rose-colored tint on their sides.

During summer months, most fish are caught by fishing

This world record tiger trout was caught in a northern Wisconsin stream by Charles Mattek. It weighed 10 pounds and measured 27 inches in length. This fish is a cross between a brown and brook trout.

The aurora trout of Ontario.

very deep. Either still-fishing with minnows, jigging with small spoons or Swedish Pimples or nightcrawlers will produce when fished near bottom.

They can be caught early in the spring just after ice-out by fishing the rocky shallows with a light line and small spoons or spinners. Trolling will cover more area and will place your lure in front of more fish during spring months.

Quebec reds spawn from mid October through November which is much later than brook trout. They spawn in the shoal waters of lakes.

The females do not make any attempt to build a nest but merely deposit their eggs at random in rocky crevices. This probably is one very good reason for the scarcity of this colorful fish. The amount of eggs deposited from a 12- to 14-inch female is usually about 900 to 1,000. Average weight is about 1-pound.

Another trout that is becoming more common in the U.S. and Canada is the splake. The splake is also called wendigo in certain parts of Canada. The splake takes its name from the SP of speckled trout (as brookies are called in Canada) and lake from lake trout. The name was originally suggested by the Ontario Department of Lands and Forest.

The splake is a hybrid but is different in the sense that it is a fertile cross and these fish can and will reproduce.

In appearance the splake is slightly slimmer than the speckled (brook) trout and heavier than the lake trout. The body spotting is a pale yellow like a lake trout with no red spots from the brookie. Belly and ventral areas of these fish will often have the red color of the brook trout.

Splake can assume physical characteristics of either trout. I've seen splake with forked tails like a lake and body and fin coloring of a brook trout. Others can look like a lake trout but possess the square tail of the brook trout. Several types of splake colors and configurations can be observed. These fish will mature at a younger age than lake trout—they also attain a much larger size than brook trout.

Splake were a natural hybrid in Ontario. The State of Michigan and some of the other Great Lakes states have planted splake in many inland lakes as well as the Great Lakes.

This hybrid has a temperature preference similar to lake trout and feeds heavily on minnows, smelt, shiners and chubs and will feed on alewives in the Great Lakes. Fishing for splake is usually very deep and near bottom during the warmer months. Early in the spring and late in the fall, when the water is cool, they will move into the shallows to feed or spawn.

Fall is spawning time for the splake when they will deposit fertilized eggs in rocky, shoal waters. While lake trout spawn at night and the brookie spawns during the day, the splake will spawn either day or night.

The sunapee trout is a little known member of the char family (*Salvelinus Aureolus*)—it is also called eastern golden trout, white trout or American saibling.

The sunapee has a fairly isolated range. It is only found in a few lakes in Maine, New Hampshire, and Vermont.

It is located in Sunapee Lake and Big Dan Hole pond in New Hampshire, Floods pond in Maine and Averill pond in Vermont. A few other lakes and ponds near these lakes may have remnant populations of sunapees.

The sunapee has a dark back with no vermiculations (worm-like markings) as does the brook trout. The spotting on these fish are very pale, sometimes either pale pink, yellow or red.

During spawning, males have a gold or yellowish-orange cast. They have a white leading edge on the lower fins with the rest of the fin orange and they have a forked tail.

The sunapee world record is a 11½-pounder that measured 33 inches. This is extremely large for these trout which seldom range over 12 to 14 inches long. In fact, the sunapee is now protected by a 12-inch size limit with a bag limit of two fish.

A hatchery is maintained in Grafton, N.H., strictly for sunapee trout. This hatchery will hopefully preserve the species for future generations and provide a passable fishery.

Being a deep water fish, trolling with spoons, cowbells and minnows or jigging will produce. Much of the fishing for these trout is in 60 to 100 feet of water. Occasionally they are caught on smelt in the winter months.

Sunapee will spawn in October in shoal waters, usually in 3 to 6 feet of water. Many of these fish are caught by the Conservation Department staff and stripped of eggs and milt and raised to fingerling size. This seems to work better than allowing the fish to propagate naturally.

The sunapee trout is very rare, seldom caught, and needs the protective measures that are currently placed on it.

The last of the little known trout is a hybrid known as the tiger trout. This fish is produced from a female brown trout and a male brook trout. Its name is apt because of the markings, feeding habits and the quality of the fight it puts up.

The fish has tiger-like markings on the sides. These fish are much more aggressive than either of their parents.

Approximately 35 per cent of the young are able to mature because they are prone to diseases which are inherent to the sac-fry. This cross occurs occasionally in nature but these fish are unable to reproduce.

Tiger trout have been produced on a very small scale in hatcheries and these fish have been planted in some states. Wisconsin has made fairly extensive plants in Lake Michigan. Private clubs have also planted them for their private use.

Tiger are considered to be a fine game fish because the fish is relatively easy to catch. They are very aggressive and bite readily. They feed on the surface and are easier to catch than their parents.

The tiger trout has large tiger-like markings that look like vermiculations. They have an overall yellowish-orange hue on the body with a brownish tail that has some spots and vermiculations. The lower fins are a reddish orange with a leading edge of white.

There have been many trout that haven't been included in this listing such as kamloops and piute trout.

If a person is interested in fishing for any of the listed trout, a word to the wise, contact the Conservation Department in the state, states or provinces involved. A letter or phone call would help in finding out the availability of the fish, where or when to go and what methods to use.

In areas that permit fishing, the best idea is to trophy fish, take one for mounting purposes and carefully release all others. This way perhaps someone else may share the same thrill as you did in catching one of America's little known trout.

Late Season Trout "Cool It!"

by BOB POOLE

THERE'S NO WAY to know how long it might be before I again catch late-summer trout and bury them behind me in a snow bank for "cool keeping," but at least I have this memory to sustain me on such days at other locations.

It happened on a glacier-fed lake high in Washington's Olympic Mountains where the season didn't even open until early July. When I was taking a limit of beautiful brook trout and refrigerating them on the spot, it was August, and I had no illusions as to how vastly different this was from anything I'd ever experienced in the way of trout fishing.

Actually, it doesn't take this sort of extreme situation to turn me on in regard to trout fishing during the tag end of the summer, because I've learned just how productive this period can be if certain judgments and tactics are employed.

Frankly, if it hadn't been for an eastern United States mountain background—trout were the first species I ever went after—I'd probably share the same opinion that most trout fishermen have of the late summer months. But, in roaming the mountain waters as a boy, I learned a lot that was strictly the product of zeal and a mind unencumbered by the moods and prejudices of adults. I fished when I could, and I used whatever methods the conditions warranted. I also fished practically any kind of water that was sufficiently deep to hold a fish.

It turned out that late summer fishing became one of my specialties, since June and July usually were occupied to a large extent by things such as Boy Scout camp, a visit to my grandparents, and things like that. August was pretty well "my month," and I spent most of it on trout streams. I didn't consider my tackle—a steel telescoping rod that would have

Some tributary streams look small at one location, but have better water elsewhere.

The approach in small streams is of the utmost importance, because the fish are easily spooked. Here the author gets set to net a nice brown in a small Appalachian stream—It was a late-season fish that moved into a tributary to stay cool. He took this nice brown on a nymph in a stream he could practically leap across.

handled anything from bluegills to barracudas—a disadvantage; it was all that I had. Besides, most of the streams I fished were hardly suited to long, delicate casts with tiny dry flies.

With no biases to restrain me, I stalked trout in places where they weren't supposed to be: tiny rivulets that I could jump across, and in the cool, deep holes on larger waters that had been swum in, whipped to a froth by almost every ordinary angler that came along, and ignored by the rest. Young boys are patient only in the outdoors; heaven only knows how quickly they might advance in other areas if this virtue got uniform application!

At any rate, through experimentation and plain common sense, I discovered the startling truth that trout and human beings are similar in at least one respect: they make every attempt to stay cool in hot weather. We do it with air conditioning; trout use "water conditioning." Fact: never fish in lukewarm water for trout unless you're simply trying to get away from it all and don't care about catching anything.

Using this axiom as a beginning point, it is simple to discard some of the places you might be inclined to fish if this rule wasn't applied. It reduces the number of possibilities and thus clears your mind to allow your imagination to work.

Thinking small helps. Little streams that occupy only vague niches in your memory are worth considering, even though they were inconsequential in the spring when your

favorite big waters paid off regularly. These often are in the form of tributary streams that flow into these same waters, and since they are usually spring-fed, they are cool, shady sanctuaries. Fish move up them once conditions become unbearable at their preferred places of residence.

It is true that such places are ordinarily tough to fish. About half of them resemble tangled tunnels, and sometimes it's a "crawl-in-and-dabble" challenge that would test the agility of a contortionist. The happily surprising thing is that often the washtub-size holes in these tiny nooks hold trout of startling proportions. After all, they're there for the temperature, not the amount of living space available. People do the same thing when they escape to pint-size cabins in the mountains when low-country weather becomes unbearable.

One of the best ways to get results in this manner is to explore every tributary that flows into a larger trout stream, regardless of its size. Don't just look at them where they flow in; walk upstream and see how they look, and if the character of the water improves. I've seen little streams that were totally unimpressive at one point, but which turned out to be terrific upon further examination upstream. One such stop-gap effort of this sort put me on a stream that I fished for several years without ever seeing another person, much less another fisherman.

It happened out of desperation, mostly. I had come to the place where I was convinced that some of the larger waters that had been fine producers earlier in the year were beyond hope. Heavy angling pressure along with warmer, lower water made them seem barren of fish. I was running through my mental index of places to try, and nothing had come up rosy yet.

I was driving back along one of the last of the larger

waters that I had in mind when I came to a place where the road crossed a small stream that glided out of a narrow valley just before joining the bigger creek. I remembered seeing it many times in the past, and I also recalled how unappealing it was: shallow, and with minimal water flow.

Only because I had nothing better to do, I parked the car and walked up to the edge of the laurel thicket from which the stream came. There was a small pool within view back in the shadows, and I eased up toward it, keeping an eye out for any movement of fish. I didn't see any, but when I reached the pool, I could look upstream and see several more in sequence. The nature of the stream changed dramatically in a short distance, becoming a tumbling, cascading brook that was instantly exciting to contemplate.

Back at the car, I put together a fly rod and tied on a weighted nymph with all of the thumbs I ordinarily have at the outset of the season. I hustled back up into the valley, enjoying the nervous feeling all of the way. It felt good after the summer lull.

The first pool didn't produce, probably because I snagged the nymph on the second drift and had to wade in to get it. The next pool quickly changed things.

I had no sooner dropped the nymph into the frothing water at the head of the pool than I had a fish on. The strike was solid, and a second later a frisky rainbow arched into the air and flashed brilliantly in a shaft of sunlight. In the limited amount of space it had, it gave a good account of itself before I netted it.

The trout was a chunky 9-incher with all of the color only a native or stream-reared fish can exhibit. It was also apparently the sole occupant of the pool, because a dozen more drifts didn't produce another strike.

There was a succession of nice, dark pools in the next hundred yards, and I caught and released three rainbows that would have passed for 6-inch triplets. I missed one fish that felt encouraging, and saw another flash in a pool that never displayed any interest in my nymph. The action was gratifying, though.

A cool breeze drifted down the valley, and it seemed more like a spring morning than a day in August. After taking a few fish, my excitement level lowered, and the beauty of the location began to capture my attention.

The fact that I coud make out only a faint trail along the stream pleased me, and it showed no evidence of use, anyway. When I noticed a small patch of ginseng growing right beside it, I realized that obviously only game traveled it. Because ginseng was heavily hit by herb hunters in the early years, and is still sought because of the market value of the roots, I realized that the little valley had remained isolated for a long time.

Any touch of solitude pleases me, so I took time to sit down and absorb all of it that I could. The sunlight filtered through the top of a tall hemlock tree above me, and a boomer, the small, saucy red squirrel of the mountains, scolded a jay that had invaded its territory. The first faint touch of fall was apparent in the tinge of yellow creeping into the poplar leaves, and the deepening blue sky looked like a preview of the coming attractions of old October. The boomer had quieted down, only to have the stillness shattered by the clatter of sound made by a kingfisher as it rocketed downstream. It made me realize just how close I was to napping.

I completed a limit of seven trout in the next couple of hundred yards of stream, with the largest, a fat 11-incher, taken in the last pool I fished. Actually, in the years afterward that I was to fish this same water, a 13½-inch rainbow ended up being tops in the size category. But I took quite a number of limits in late-season when it remained the best alternate I had to the existing conditions on other waters.

This story is but one example of the potential of such out-of-the-way places, and what they can produce in hot weather pinches. These kind of places exist on trout areas all over the nation, since the low-altitude waters of the West suffer the same effects when conditions cause the fish to seek out more favorable habitat.

I fished a famous Oregon trout river one late summer at a time when a fairly large number of anglers present were at the near zero level in results. Once I determined this, I went in search of side streams where two delightful things occurred: first, I caught an amazing number of 10- to 12-inch trout that were concentrated in the little streams in numbers that were astounding; and, second, I didn't encounter even one other fisherman in the process. Maybe the lure of the big water was too much to resist, or perhaps the small streams didn't interest them. Whatever the reason, I was thankful for my early experiences.

It's well to recognize that there's a certain kind of psychology that's associated with this kind of fishing. For instance, there are some advantages in fishing the small

Angler tries a small stream that might be bypassed when larger waters are productive.

Late season trout are often found hiding under logjams such as this.

streams that may not be immediately apparent. Trout in such waters generally have less access to an abundance of food—and less room in which to seek it. Because of this, they aren't as selective; in fact, they tend to take about anything that comes their way that is presented correctly.

This is a time when natural baits are indeed "natural" in both senses of the word, and fishermen who can delicately handle bait have a special opportunity. In places where a fly or lure can't be cast—and this is often the case on very small streams—bait can make the difference between a full creel and an empty one.

I carry some very small hooks and tiny split shot for such occasions, because I have found that if caddis, mayfly or stonefly nymphs can be located in the water, the rest is simply a matter of presentation. Trout will take these when practically nothing else will work. This may give purists the shudders, but when conditions demand flexibility, the choice is obvious.

There is also relative simplicity in determining where trout will be in little streams, because in the absence of shoal and riffle water of sufficient depth, the pools are the only satisfactory hiding places left. It isn't as easy as that, however.

Water clarity in late-season makes it necessary for the angler to exert special caution, principally in the approach to the pools. A low profile is required, sometimes even to the degree of crawling, so it's best to use tactics that you best remember from boyhood days when the business of stalking fish was your usual procedure. Actually, you'll find that it's fun, and it's one of the things that give this kind of fishing a particular flavor.

Tackle selection is something that requires some consideration, since the conditions can vary a great deal. Some of the waters will be better suited for ultra-light spinning gear,

while others will be OK for fly rods, but it's best to be prepared to go either way according to what the cover on the stream looks like. One thing for certain: short casts will be the rule rather than the exception.

I use a 6½-foot fly rod that is highly effective for this kind of fishing, and I have a 5½-foot fly rod to back it up in case of even tighter situations. My spinning gear is ultra-light, of course, and in the true definition of the term. It is short, with a fast action that permits casts with the flick of the wrist. I stick with 1/32- and 1/24-ounce lures, mostly of the spinner-fly variety.

Another helpful thing: If you're planning to explore for small streams in an area you're not to familiar with, the best aid you can obtain is a set of sectional topographic maps that cover the region. These enable you not only to determine the location of all of the streams, but the elevation lines help you get an idea of the type water you can expect.

Usually such a set of topo maps will prove to be an eye-opener, in that you'll find some streams in the area that you weren't at all aware of, regardless of how long you've lived in the locale. I found two little streams that proved to be excellent brook trout waters while looking over the maps trying to find some ruffed grouse range. I noted their location, then visited them the following spring. I forget if I ever found the grouse spots I was looking for, but I certainly remember the streams!

In a way, seeking out the small streams in late summer can be more challenging—and just as much fun—as early season angling. Because of the special tactics necessary, as well as the extra caution involved in stalking the fish, it can do a lot toward making one a better fisherman in the process.

And in the places you'll be, you can "cool it," just like the trout are doing!

Trout Fishing's Golden Triangle

by NORMAN STRUNG

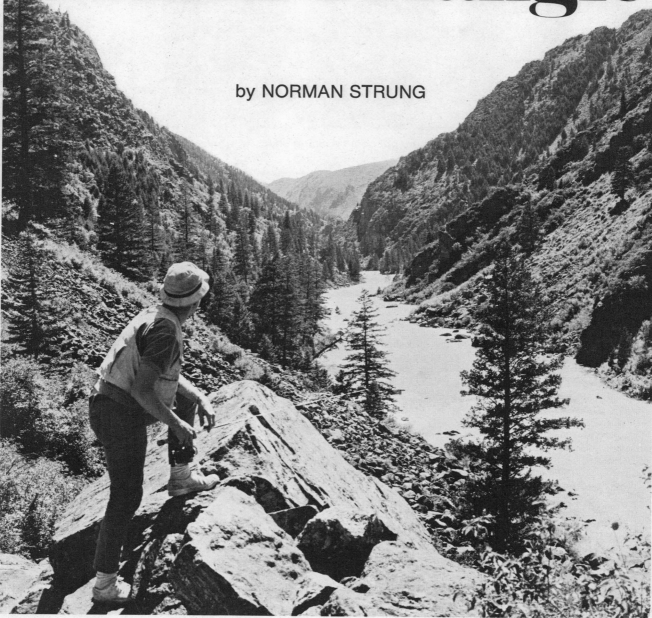

THE THREE corners region of Montana, Wyoming and Idaho supports the finest trout fishing in the contiguous 48 states. This isn't idle conjecture, but established fact, and there are reasons. It is mountainous country with some of the tallest peaks in the United States, and those high elevations gather heavy winter snows, which in turn, feed streams with pure, cold, highly-oxygenated water throughout the year. These watercourses also flow through lands rich in nutrients. They dissolve in the water, and stoke the food chain, producing a rich harvest of aquatic insect life to feed the trout that dwell there. It is also one of the least densely-populated sections of the country. The combination creates the kind of trout fishing anglers hope to find in paradise; large concentrations of husky fish, and a variety that includes brooks, browns, rainbow, cutthroat and the rare grayling.

There are a few rules of the road that can be stated about this region as a whole. Chest waders are of immeasurable help, but you'd better carpet the soles of your boots or wear felt creepers. The water is swift and the bottom is paved with greased cannonballs. You'd also be wise to choose your line or leader from the heavy end of the trout spectrum. My standard spinning line is 8-pound test, my normal fly leader is 4. This rule has its exceptions, like when you fish crystal headwater tributaries in late July and August, but generally you're better off to go heavy. The fish aren't particularly shy, but they are big, and they have the additional leverage of swift water.

Except when fish are plainly feeding on top, you're always wisest to start fishing deep, and I mean literally dredging bottom. Sinking tip or full sinking fly lines, weighted flies, and large, heavy spoons are the kinds of equipment that regularly take fish. Distance is also important. These are really trout rivers, not streams, and the reach of a 6½-foot

Opposite page—The Beartraps of the Madison is a granite gorge where access is by foot or a dangerous whitewater float. The largest fish in the river swim here. Above— The trick to catching Beartrap lunkers is to go deep with heavy spoons or bait.

spinning rod or a 7 or 8 weight fly rod with weight-forward line is needed to cover all of the water.

Beyond those universals, there's specific tricks to fishing each of the major rivers, so let's look at them by the numbers.

The Madison is number one, literally and figuratively. It's rated by anglers as the top trout stream in the nation, and it's my personal favorite—as much for the varied beauty of its shores as the big browns and 'bows that swim in its waters.

The Madison begins in Yellowstone National Park at the confluence of the Gibbon and Firehole Rivers. For most of its 20-mile journey through the park it is strongly reminiscent of English chalk streams and eastern waters. It is a deep, swirling river, that meanders slowly through meadows and around car-sized boulders.

At this point, the Madison is classic fly water and for this reason, park regulations limit fishing to flies only. If you're not a fly-fisherman, don't despair. Spinning rods are legal as long as there's a fly on the end.

Best times to fish this stretch are June 1 to 15, and September 15 to October 30. These times are mainly based on the tourists. The Madison gets whipped to a froth in July and August, and the fish are shy beyond belief.

There's also the matter of moss; August finds great wands of moss growing, making for difficult fishing conditions. It disappears with the first frosts of fall.

If you're a fly-rod angler, the most productive patterns will be nymphs. Caddis and mayfly variations in No. 12 to No. 16 are the most important foods, though I've done extremely well with the big No. 8 stonefly nymphs at times. There are some spectacular evening hatches on this river too. Adams, Blue Dun, and the lighter Wulff patterns in No. 12 to No. 16 are my regulars.

If you're a spin fisherman, you can't go wrong with a Muddler Minnow behind a heavy pinch of shot. Work it as you would any spinning lure, though you should try to impart a little extra action by regularly jerking the tip. Except when a big hatch is on, this technique will out-fish conventional fly gear two to one.

After the Madison leaves the park, it enters a broad valley. The river flows straight, and drops rapidly over a bed of large cobbles, and the entire river looks like one big riffle.

This 40-mile stretch is tough fishing for the uninitiated; the bottom is slick and the fast water makes for dangerous wading. Then too, there isn't a conventional "hole" in the river.

The trick to taking trout here is to work the water right next to the bank, or the pockets behind midstream rocks. Spinning with a Mepps or hammered brass Dardevle is the most efficient tackle. If you want to fly-fish, you'll need sinking line and large, weighted nymphs, like the No. 6 Wooly Worm in brown, black or green, or Montana Nymphs. Bait fishing on this stretch is impractical if not impossible.

That section of the Madison between the Ennis Bridge and Meadow Lake deserves specific mention because it's one of the few places in the West where you can catch grayling. Concentrations of these fish with the huge fin occur at the mouth of O'dell Creek, and where the several fingers of the Madison enter Meadow Lake. Grayling dine on a nearly exclusive insect diet, so nymphs, wets and dries amount to the best terminal tackle. The pattern I always start with is a Bailey Nymph in olive green, or black. If you're strictly a spin-fisherman, try tiny spinners with a lot of flash. Ultra-lite class Panther Martins and Mepps in black and gold are two lures that will turn up fish, but again, flies are more dependable.

The most frequent mistake made when fishing western trout rivers is neglecting water close-in to the bank (upper Madison). ▶

The Beartraps of the Madison begins by Meadow Lake Dam. It is a 20-mile granite gorge cut by the river. Access is by foot or a very dangerous raft trip. Because of its limited access, the biggest fish in the Madison swim here; browns and rainbow in the 12-pound class have been pulled from 'Traps waters.

Large, heavy spinning lures like the Kamlooper, Doty Raider, and sinking Rapala dredge up the biggies from the bottom. Work any deep, slow-moving water by quartering a cast upstream and retrieving just a little faster than the water is moving. This keeps the lure close to the bottom. Expect a strike just as the lure rounds the bend and starts upstream.

Fly fishing is difficult in the 'Traps because of steep walls and bankbrush. It's excellent bait-fishing water, with bullheads (sculpin), nite crawlers and large stonefly nymphs productive in that order. The most effective baitfishing technique employs a single baitholder hook, behind a pinched shot just heavy enough to bounce the bottom. If you hang up a lot, you've got too much weight. If you don't feel bottom, you've got too little.

The bait is offered to the fish on a 30-degree arc, the center of which is perpendicular to the shore. Quarter a cast upstream. The bait sinks and bounces bottom. At the end of the arc, the pressure of the river on the line lifts the bait from the bottom, and you retrieve and cast again. The trick to recognizing a bite is to watch your line. When it stops moving with the water, yet you still feel the bounce of bottom, there's a fish gnawing on the bait. Set the hook firmly; this technique interests big fish with hard mouths.

The Beartraps open up into the lower Madison, and here the river again becomes a meandering stream. There are access problems because of posted land, however, the river is a navigable waterway, and can be fished by floating. The Greycliff Fishing Access lies midway along the lower Madison, and it's a perfect spot for a pickup if you float down the Beartraps, or a put-in if you want to float to the highway bridge at Three Forks. Both floats are full-day affairs if you are serious about fishing, and I'd pick the Greycliff-to-Three Forks leg as the most productive.

Spinning, fly-fishing and baitfishing all work on this section of the Madison. Like the Beartraps, the trick to catching the lunkers is to go deep with lures or bait.

The Yellowstone River is my second choice when I think about trout. It can be roughly divided into three sections: the park, Paradise Valley, and the Lower Yellowstone.

The park section flows from Yellowstone Park to Yankee Jim Canyon. It is primarily cutthroat water, with fly fishing only along much of the river. It's just as well; cutts prefer flies over bait or lures anyway. Cutts are not, however, particularly avid surface feeders. They feed close to the bottom, snatching nymphs that crawl out from under stones. Fly patterns I've learned to lean on for cutts include green wooly worms, spruce grubworms, breadcrust and caddis.

Paradise Valley is a classic piece of trout water that stretches from Yankee Jim Canyon to Livingston. The Yellowstone dances across riffles and swirls into deep holes along this course and the water is easy to read. The places I always start prospecting are the sharp drop-offs at the foot of riffles, and the steep cutbanks on the outside of the riverbends.

The Muddler Minnow is the fly that's credited with catching trophies on this stretch of the Yellowstone, and Dan Bailey's "wall of fame" testifies to this fact. About half of the

The Gallatin, like most western rivers, produces the largest fish in its lower reaches.

4-pound-plus browns and rainbows outlined there fell victim to this pattern. If Yellowstone trout turn their nose up at a Muddler, it's nearly a sure thing that they'll be interested in a large No. 4 to No. 6 stonefly nymph with a yellow or orange belly.

Mepps, Dardevles and Rapalas all work well on this part of the river, and so does a rather offbeat technique for trout; jigging. I've done extremely well standing in a thigh-deep riffle, and jig-retrieving a feathery jig called a "Golden Girl" to the riffle foot. This trick is particularly effective when the water is very cold; usually the months of April, May, October and November.

The baitfisherman will find plenty to his liking on this stretch too. Either still fish the rotating bank eddies, or drift your hook through deep, swirling channels. Remember you must get down to the bottom. Sculpin and worms work best in the spring and fall. In midsummer these trout can't turn down a big grasshopper, though they are oddly selective about the species they favor. The big 3-inch, all brown grasshopper locally known as "clackers" will out-fish the yellow hoppers 10 to one. This, incidently, partially explains the year-round success of the muddler; it can be mistaken for a bullhead or a clacker.

The lower Yellowstone starts below Livingston and peters out as trout water around Columbus. Here the water flows slower and deeper than above. The fish are fewer, but they're consistently bigger than on other sections of the river. It is an excellent stretch for a float that will take fish if you cast a hammered brass spoon shoreward. Drop it as close to cut banks and rock cliffs as your accuracy allows, let it sink to the count of five, then begin a slow, measured retrieve. There are many 5-pound browns caught just this way. The largest fish, on the average, fall prey to a less-than-exciting technique; bank fishing the deep holes with sucker-meat on a No. 2 or No. 4 baitholder hook. Every week some old cowpoke with a rusty baitcasting outfit ties into an 8- to 10-pounder while practicing this patient pastime.

The Gallatin River flows from Yellowstone Park, to the headwaters of the Missouri River. Along its midsection, it twists through a spectacular canyon of rock and whitewater. Access is no problem here as the river is paced by an all-weather highway. The upper reaches of the river hold cutthroat, and as you get to lower elevations, rainbow begin to predominate. After it enters the Gallatin Valley, browns make up the majority. In general, the further up the canyon you get, the smaller the average fish.

Ultra-lite spinning tackle and lures that show plenty of flash at slow speeds is the killer combination on the upper river. Except during spring run-off (late May through June), this is much clearer water than most of the other major rivers, so it is also the place for light fly leaders. The general appeal of nymphs over other fly types still holds true. In midsummer, however, it pays to carry some dry flies in light grey, honey brown and dun colors. The eternal Royal Coachman is another fly I'm never without on this river at this time.

The canyon section of the Gallatin is swift, deep water, and the big trout will be in the larger holes. Small fish stick close to the bank. Here, and in the lower river, weighted Wooly Worms in brown and green are regular producers. When fish are feeding close to the surface, try a Goofus Bug. Spinning lures that I turn to along the lower reaches of the Gallatin are the Crocodile, Thomas Cyclone and Mepps Fury.

Above—The Firehole is so named for the many geysers and hotpots that feed it. Its warm waters produce maddeningly erratic insect hatches. Right—Still-fishing deep holes with suckermeat isn't particularly exciting, but this patient pastime regularly turns up the lunkers. Below—Jigging the foot of riffles turns up some fine trout during the colder months on the Yellowstone.

The Muddler Minnow is one of the top flies in the West. It's appealing because it can be mistaken for a sculpin or a grasshopper.

That part of the river that flows through the Gallatin Valley holds the largest fish. In fact, this is a reliable generalization about any of the rivers in the area. As rivers hit these valleys, their pitch decreases, they begin to meander, and a combination of lots of bank cover, food, and slow water puts on the pounds. As in Gallatin, however, most of these valleys are farmlands, and there are some access problems due to posting.

While I'm hardly a trout purist, I am of the opinion that fly fishing is the most enjoyable way to catch these fish. I suppose I would be a purist except for a pragmatic streak in me. There's too much excellent trout water that can be fished more efficiently by spinning.

When I think of this first love of mine, however, two streams stand out as meccas; the Firehole and the Henry's Fork of the Snake.

The Firehole is one of the tributaries of the Madison, so named because it is fed by fiery geysers and steaming hot-spots. It is slow, slick water, and oddly maddening because of its warm nature; hatches on this river are unpredictable. Insects that normally come off other rivers in August can hatch on the Firehole in early June. I once snowmobiled into the Park in January, and sure enough, fish were rising to caddis then. The air temperature was about 15 degrees.

Although this river's unpredictability finds me bringing every pattern I own when I fish it, so long as the trout aren't rising to identifiable flies, I always start prospecting with the same rig; a No. 10 Wooly Worm rigged on a dropper ahead of a No. 6 Muddler. I fish from the middle of the river into the bank, retrieving the flies in a jerking, downstream loop as I walk slowly with the current.

Like most of the park waters, the Firehole comes under heavy pressure during July and August, and grows an incredible amount of moss. So I usually fish my favorite stretch from the mouth of Nez Perce Creek to Firehole Falls in the months of June and September.

The Henry's Fork of the Snake is more of an all-summer venture. Neither the moss nor the tourists get particularly bothersome in the summer, though I'd better warn you that the mosquitos do. Of all the western rivers I've fished, it is this one that is most typically eastern in nature, with extensive hatches, including a green drake strongly reminiscent of the Beaverkill. However, the most memorable hatch you'll ever find on the Henry's Fork is strictly western. Huge stoneflies come off the river in late June and early July, and if you hit this hatch on the nose you'll have stories to tell your children about. Trout gorge themselves at this time, and refuse to be put down.

Other patterns that will produce on the Henry's Fork all through the summer include: Adams, Blue Dun, light Cahill, Goofus Bug, the lighter Wulff patterns, and the Royal Coachman in No. 12 to No. 16 hook sizes.

The Missouri River from its headwaters near Three Forks to the tiny town of Toston is probably the most overlooked piece of prime trout water in the West. It is a huge river, in places more than a 100 yards wide, that gently flows through canyons and meanders across farmlands. It is accessible via dirt roads from the tiny town of Trident, though you'd be wisest to drive a pickup truck in. By far the best way to fish this river is by a float. It is safe enough water for the greenest boatman.

The largest fish I've taken from the Missouri to date was a 7½-pound brown, and I took him on a ⅝-ounce gold and fluorescent Kamlooper spoon. I have no doubts much larger fish lurk there, and am convinced that someone with patience and a hankering for a record could well catch a trophy there. One of my future projects is to spend two or three days on the Missouri, dredging its deep holes with outrageously large plugs, fished steelhead-style on a three-way swivel with a heavy sinker, for that's the only way you could get down to the bottom of some of them.

While the mere thought of the fish that wait there makes my blood boil, I still haven't performed the experiment, which in itself is a comment on the fishing in this tri-state region. There's so much good water that you'll never get to fish it all . . . not even if you live there.

Hawaii's Little-Known Trout Streams

by MORT MICHAELS

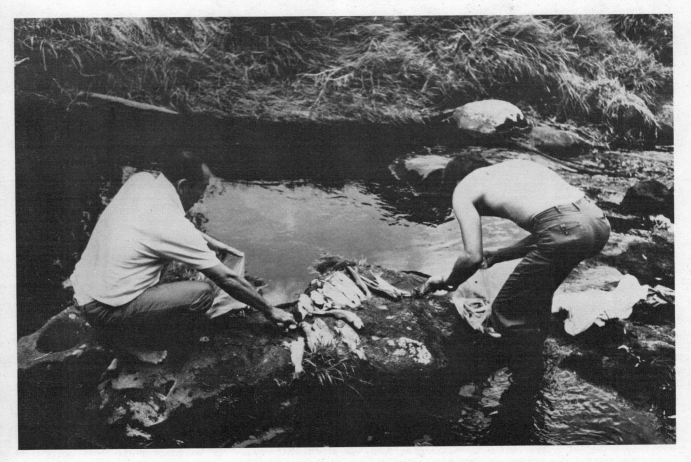

These fishermen clean a husky limit catch of rainbow trout from one of Hawaii's little-known trout streams.

FIRST, THE BAD NEWS about trout fishing in Hawaii: The season here is extremely limited. If you're not planning an August or September visit to the Islands, don't bother to pack your trout gear. Hawaii's trout-bearing waters are very limited—to a half-dozen or so streams or tributaries on one island.

So much for the bad news. The good news is that trout fishing, Hawaii style, offers as much fun, excitement and challenge as you'll find anywhere else in the country. Plus, there's an additional ingredient—the exotic locale with its colorful tropic rainforest.

Where else can you cast your line, watch it zip and whir through the water, fight a frothing, diving, dancing rainbow trout, and bring it to net against a jungle backdrop literally crawling and hanging with foliage, fruit blossoms, tree growth and bushes in a myriad of sizes and beautiful colors.

The place where all this fine sport takes place is Kauai, Hawaii's northernmost major island. It's the island best re-

membered by most visitors as the place where they viewed Waimea Canyon, the "Grand Canyon of the Pacific." It is along tributaries of the canyon's Waimea River that Kauai's 20 miles or so of trout fishing water are located. High above the river and the canyon's bottom, at 3,000 feet of altitude, are streams called Kauaikinana, Kawaikoi, Waiakoali, Mohihi, Koaie, and Waialae. The first four of these are reachable by jeep road from nearby Kokee State Park. The latter two are accessible only by foot. As you might guess the fishing is best, because the fishing pressure is less, along the Koaie and the Waialae. As a general rule, however, the fishing is good in all streams.

The trout are rainbows, not overly large by mainland standards but just as full of fight as any you'll tie into elsewhere. The trout are not native to the Islands. They are imported annually in the form of eggs, from federal fish hatcheries at Winthrop, Washington and Ennis, Montana. They're raised to the fingerling stage at nearby Sand Island after which they

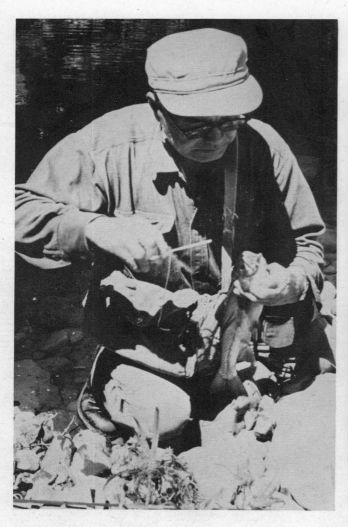

Below—This Hawaiian angler has just beached a fine rainbow trout from the Waimea River on Kauai, the nothernmost island. Left—A chunky 1-pound rainbow provided a thrilling mid-summer scrap for this angler.

are transported to Kauai and released by helicopter.

Techniques for hooking into Hawaiian rainbows is basically the same as you'd use anywhere else—with one major exception. Virtually no one uses fly fishing gear on Kauai. In the first place dry flies have no appeal to Hawaiian trout since mayflies, stoneflies, and caddis flies do not occur naturally in Hawaiian streams. Just as important, the lush tropic tree and bush growth, right down to and over the water's edge, makes spin-casting the most practical gear by far.

Light spinning lures or spinners with worms are most often productive. The use of corn for bait is specifically prohibited.

The size of rainbows you'll catch in Hawaii varies greatly from one season to another. Some years, heavy rains wash away large numbers of young fry, leaving only a small population in the streams. With little competition for food and forage, these fish grow to relatively large size by Hawaiian standards, perhaps 2½ to 3 pounds or more. Other years, when heavy rains do not decimate the population, a lot more trout grow to maturity— but food is hard to come by. The trout grow slowly and achieve a much smaller size.

The thick forest and undergrowth on Kauai dictates at least one item of equipment not usually required for most trout fishing expeditions: a machete. This slashing/clearing device can be particularly useful in coping with blackberry brambles and other thickets which have a way of overtaking trails hereabouts.

The complete angler on the Islands wears a long-sleeved shirt and long trousers because of the vegetation. Hip boots or

waders are not particularly useful. Locals usually just wear leather boots or wade wet in the streams.

And, say Hawaiian anglers, it's a real good idea when you're moving from place to place in and around the fishing grounds to stick to the established roads and trails and major streams. If you get off the beaten path it's easy to become disoriented and lost.

The nearest and most convenient accommodations are housekeeping units available in Kokee State Park—at extraordinarily low daily rental rates. The cabins are within a half-hour's drive of Kawaikoi stream, the first of the trout-planted waters.

Seasons, as noted earlier, are short. For 16 days after the first Saturday in August each year, trout fishing is permitted daily. From the 17th day on through the balance of August and September fishing is allowed only on Saturdays, Sundays, and state holidays. Each fishing day begins at 5:30 AM and ends at 6:45 PM. Daily bag limit is seven trout with no minimum size.

For more details about regulations, and for a copy of *Freshwater Fishing in Hawaii*, a free 20-page booklet describing the dozen or so freshwater fish species available in the Islands, write to the Division of Fish and Game, Department of Land and Natural Resources, Honolulu, Hawaii 96813. For details concerning the cabins at Kokee State Park, write to Kauai District Office, Department of Land and Natural Resources, P.O. Box 1671, Linhue, Kauai, Hawaii 96766.

The Kokee Public Fishing Area

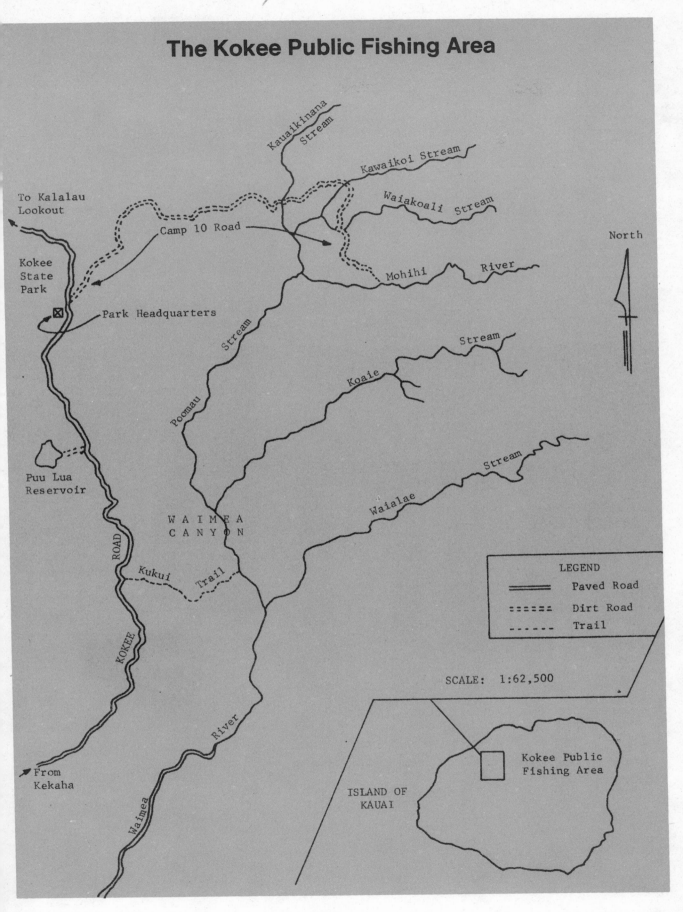

How to Wade a Trout Stream

by JIM STABILE

A TROUT fisherman's wading skill often determines whether he attracts fish, spooks them, stays dry or gets his backside wet.

Someone new to trouting often makes his first mistake on the stream bank before he sets foot in the river. He never assesses the river, its current flow and potential wading hazards. He walks into the river oblivious to all dangers, often he pays for his stupidity.

An experienced fisherman knows his best chances of approaching a feeding trout, getting within casting range, lies in wading upstream. So, whenever possible, he wades in that direction. The rushing current covers his approach.

Trout spend most of their time facing upstream, finning lazily against the current, watching for food to swim or drift down to them. They are in position to clearly see danger coming from ahead and above. That's one of the reasons you should approach from the trout's blind side.

Another reason for wading upstream is to prevent giving the trout an early warning—a factor important when you're fishing an extremely clear or heavily fished stream.

If you wade downstream, you will most likely dislodge sand, silt and debris, sending clouds of discolored water floating down to the trout. This indication of foreign intrusion in the stream can quickly panic a feeding trout and send him seeking the safety of cover. Many times it will be hours before that fish will feed again.

The upstream approach also helps when you hook a fish. Hooked fish seldom head upstream; they almost always wind up downstream from where they were hooked—either because they immediately head down when you hook them or they drift down with the current as they tire.

If you fish downstream, the trout you hook will almost certainly spook other fish from the water you had hoped to cover. By fishing upstream, your hooked fish won't put down other trout much above the site where it was hooked and the played-out fish will come down into water you've already covered for easier landing.

There are times, however, when you must wade downstream because of obstacles or, in the case of steelhead fishing, because the best way to work spawning steelheads is from above. The angler must learn to adapt to prevailing river conditions and wade accordingly.

Wading is an acquired skill, one that is not only essential to trout fishing, but also necessary to keep the fisherman safe and dry.

Safety is an important factor worth considering before entering a stream. It's easier to wade down with the current, but if the current is heavy (strong), you stand a much better chance of losing your footing by wading downstream than upstream.

When you're heading downstream, it's easy to misstep and the heavy current, coupled with your momentum, is enough to tumble you headlong into the water.

If there's one wading rule you should always observe, no matter which direction you choose, it is *move slowly*. Speed in wading should always be avoided.

Once you've chosen your path, step carefully and make sure each foot is firmly anchored before you take a step with the other foot.

Never take long steps in strong currents. Anchor that first foot solidly, then lift the other just high enough to clear the bottom. The higher you step, the more likely you'll get wet.

Choose each footstep carefully and, if possible, try to step behind large rocks because there is usually sand or silt there—material safer than slippery underwater rocks. Large rocks often have a small pocket of calmer water which makes wading easier.

Polarized sunglasses are very helpful in seeing stream bottoms. Be sure that what you think is a dark, silted bottom isn't a deep hole. If you can't see the stream bottom, you should either stay on the bank, probe extra carefully with each step, or use a wading staff to probe ahead for the bottom dropoffs, clay ledges, etc.

The choice of whether to use a wading staff or not is personal. Some anglers swear by them; others dislike them. A stout limb can serve as a wading aid, or you can make you own or buy one in sporting goods stores. Some fishermen use a

Above—Three anglers demonstrate the proper method to cross a stream using a long pole. Left—Firm bracing against a strong current is a must.

fiberglass ski pole, without the bottom ring, as a wading staff. Sturdy lengths of old bamboo canepoles, cut to size, are also an inexpensive substitute for a commercially made wading staff.

If you decide on a homemade model, be sure to fasten a leather thong to one end so you can put your arm through the loop and be free to use both hands while fishing.

Make sure your staff is long enough. A 5-foot length is about the right size.

Plant the staff firmly before stepping, then use it as a third leg—anchor, step carefully; anchor, step carefully; anchor, step carefully. A staff can be a nuisance in shallow water, but it's valuable in deeper water, especially when crossing a heavy currented stream.

Before crossing a stream, consider the downstream side of your line of travel. A heavy current could force you

For added safety a flotation vest or life preserver
worn along with the waders is a prudent precaution.

downstream further than you intended, so avoid crossing on the upstream lip of deep pools. Steer away from loose gravel in heavy currents; pebbles can roll underfoot.

A straight line may be the shortest route to the other bend but it's not always the safest. Take your time wading and stay dry.

If you're fishing with a couple other fishermen and have to cross in heavy current, try the pole method. All you need is a strong limb about 12 feet long.

With one fisherman holding each end and one in the middle, the leading fisherman can move slowly while the other two hold onto the pole so he has a firm handhold.

Now that you know how to wade, let's consider what you wear while wading.

Hip boots are more comfortable than waders, especially if you have to walk long distances back to your car. But unless the stream is shallow, hip boots will give you limited access in wading.

Chest-high waders will get you to a lot more trout hotspots than will hip boots.

Pay attention to a proper fit when choosing waders or hip boots. Loose fitting boots or waders will probably result in blisters on your heels. A too-tight fit can cut circulation as well as cause discomfort. A blistered heel has canceled many a fishing trip for anglers.

Try on your boots or waders while wearing the same weight socks that you'd wear fishing. Many fishermen select their hip boots and waders while wearing a heavy pair of insulated socks.

If you're buying waders, be sure you have ample room in the crotch. You should be able to raise one foot onto a chair to be comfortable. Try kneeling on one knee to determine if the crotch binds. Be sure you can bend your knees easily.

Generally, the lighter the wader, the easier it is to puncture. If you want durability, you may have to sacrifice light weight for a heavier type of waders that is relatively resistant to snags, sharp tree limbs or a chance encounter with barbed wire.

In addition to boot-foot waders, there are also stocking-foot waders. With the latter, you'll need wading shoes. Stocking-foot waders have an advantage over boot-foot if you buy two different types of wading shoes: One with rubber cleated soles; the other with felt soles. The type of bottom you'll be wading dictates the type of sole to wear.

The plain rubber-cleated soles are fine on most streams. This is the type of sole you'll find on most hip boots and waders. Felt is hard to beat, however, if you'll be wading on extremely slippery rocks or ledge rocks in heavy current.

Felt has a gripping quality that's outstanding. Felt soles will quickly wear out if you have to walk a road back to the car or do a lot of dry-land walking.

Replacement kits for felt soles come with directions simple enough to make almost any fisherman a good boot or wader retreader. Or, if you have regular rubber soled boots, you might want to try separate felt soles that you can attach and detach to your boots as the occasion warrants.

Whichever boot or wader or sole you choose, it will pay in the long run to buy the best you can afford. Beware of bargain prices on merchandise that usually costs far more.

If your waders do not come with a belt, get one. Before you enter a stream while wearing waders, be sure to tightly fasten a belt around your middle, over the waders.

By now, most people have probably heard the old wives' tale about the danger of putting a belt around your waders. This false tale would have you believe that if you get into

Right and below—With a belt tightened around your waders, you can float like a bobber. Note that angler also wears wet suit for added protection.

Fisherman is afloat while fighting a trout. The proper and safest technique is to angle toward the downstream bank letting the current do all the work.

water over your head while wearing waders, your feet will bob to the surface, buoyed by the air trapped in the waders, while your head is submerged. No way!

The belt will keep some air in—and also keep a lot of water out of your waders. This trapped air can act as a safety factor to a wallowing trout fisherman. Keep your knees up, which traps in the air, and allow the current to carry you to safety.

The one thing that drowns a wader-clad fisherman is panic. If you find yourself tumbling downstream, keep your head and don't panic.

Go with the current and angle toward a downstream bank. It's far easier to use the current to help you drift to shore than to fight the current and tire. Even if you're wearing hip boots and get into water over your head, try to go with the current.

When you're wearing chest-high waders, there's an important danger sign you should guard against. It comes when you're in deep water that's inches from the top of your waders.

When you begin to feel lighter than usual on your feet and find yourself bouncing along or moving down with the current faster than you'd like, get ready to angle toward the nearest bank; you're close to floating.

If you're unfortunate enough to get dunked in a swift current of a stream that has a lot of rocks or boulders, try floating downstream feet first. This will ward off dangerous bumps against rocks.

For added safety, consider using a flotation vest when wading. One of these lightweight vests and some knowledge about what to do if you should get into trouble while wearing waders will greatly improve your chances of reaching safety.

Your waders can also help you, in an emergency, to get across deep water. If you somehow get stranded and must return across a stream that's 6 or more feet deep, you can take off your waders on shore or in shallow water, trap air in them and use them as you would use an inner tube to cross the deep water.

Wading can get you to fish and it will help you find fish. Many anglers have found that "wading wet" is a good way to find trout during extremely warm weather, in streams where the water temperature gets high enough to make the trout seek cooler flows.

Some of these flows, such as cool feeder brooks, are easily visible. Often you can find trout congregating in these feeder streams when other river water has warmed into the 70-degree-plus range.

If you wade such streams while wearing ankle-high wading boots or even sneakers, you can often discover underwater springs simply by being alert to sudden coolness in areas below these springs.

You may have spooked the trout from these spots by wading into them, but if you wait for a while, the trout will return.

But if you want to stick to conventional wading, remember to take good care of your gear. Body heat and the coolness of the water which you wade will invariably result in condensation accumulating in your boots or waders. Sunlight also takes a heavy toll on waders; particularly rubber boots.

After fishing, always try to hang your waders by the heels in a dry, shady place. Dampness will speed the deterioration of the inner portions of the boots and waders. You can shape a boot or wader hanger out of a wire shirt hanger or buy readymade hangers for your footgear.

An important accessory for all who wade is a patching kit. These kits will enable you to make streamside repairs in case you puncture the rubber or fabric.

Finding leaks isn't too difficult, but if you have one that's only the size of a pinhole, and you don't need your wading gear in a hurry, you can locate the leak by filling the boots or waders with water. Watch for the leak, mark it, and patch it.

A trout fisherman's ability to consistently take fish is often governed by his expertise in wading. Wade slowly, step carefully, study the river before wading and you'll find more trout falling to your casts.

Troll The Inland Lakes

by JOHN DAVEY

WE HAD JUST rounded a point on Utah's Flaming Gorge Reservoir when the vibrant throbbing of the rod tip changed into an angry bow as an unseen brown scooped up the lure and headed for the surface.

Line was ripped off the reel as a brown vaulted through the surface of the lake and hung suspended momentarily before crashing back into the water in a huge splash. I held the rod tip high, forcing the trout to fight the bend in the rod, but he kept snatching yard after yard of line off the reel. The spool arbor was beginning to show before I could swing the boat around and begin recovering line.

I gained enough line so the brown seesawed back and forth 40 feet below the boat. A couple of other boats moseyed over, stayed a discreet distance away and watched the fight. Western anglers always seemed to be amazed that lunker trout can be taken by trolling instead of stillfishing or casting along the shorelines.

This brown produced a slam-bang fight underwater for several minutes before boiling to the surface with the string of Cowbells bouncing off his noggin. One short half-hearted run tuckered out the old warrior and he came slowly to the net.

Flaming Gorge, although currently holding the North American brown trout record with a fish weighing 31 pounds, 12 ounces, is just one example of how productive fishing inland lakes and reservoirs can be. My 12½-pounder was my largest brown from this reservoir bordering the Wyoming-Utah line but I managed to pull out a couple limit catches of 6- to 10-pound fish over a period of 2 days. This feat can be accomplished in widely scattered locations around the United States and Canada.

Trout lakes and other impoundments are located throughout eastern states such as New York, New Hampshire, Pennsylvania, Maryland, Vermont and Maine. Tennessee, Arkansas and Missouri are three more examples of states with heavy concentrations of trout water.

Midwest states such as Minnesota, Wisconsin and Michigan are liberally dotted with trout lakes that look like finely cut diamonds nestling in a sea of pines.

A trout fishery exists in many of these states on an almost year around basis. The more southerly or southwesterly lakes and reservoirs are often ice-free 12 months of the year and provide a thrilling fishery during any season.

Above—This lake fisherman has his trout fishing program together. He's using a sonar unit to keep track of changes in bottom contour and he's using an electric motor to troll super slow.

Much of the secret of taking trophy trout from these areas lies in knowing how to fish a trout lake. This usually means trolling deep. Trophy trout are commonplace in many lakes but a large percentage of them will live to a ripe old age without ever having been hooked. In this day of overcrowding on many streams, a lake fishery that has been untapped is a tremendously valuable source of pleasure.

Many of the better trout lakes and reservoirs around the country serve many purposes; most are two-story lakes that support a cold water (trout) fishery in the depths and a warm water fishery in the shallower areas for bass, panfish and northern pike. Some lakes have only trout populations and the angler may find rainbow, cutthroat, brooks, browns, lake trout or splake. Some of the higher altitude lakes will support populations of golden, cutthroat or rainbow-golden crosses.

Trout fishermen that wish to determine which lakes in their state have fishable populations of trout should contact the Fisheries Division of the Department of Natural Resources and ask for specific information on planting sites, numbers of trout planted, size of the lake or impoundment and species of trout. All of this is important in determining which lakes are "hot."

The first thing trout fishermen should realize is that trophy trout in inland lakes are extremely conscious of water temperature. A trout's metabolism operates at peak efficiency at a specific temperature range. At this level a trout will be actively feeding and the angler has his best shot at catching a big fish.

An electronic water thermometer is essential for lake fishing. I use one to locate the 60-degree water browns and rainbows prefer; splake and lake trout usually seek out 51-degree levels; brookies favor 58 degrees. It should be pointed out that these preferences will vary from the Midwest to the Southwest and anglers should use them merely for reference.

The majority of larger trout lakes and impoundments are sufficiently large enough to stratify into the well known "thermocline." I've found this comfort level in some western impoundments down 60 feet. A few of the lakes I've fished in the Midwest have thermoclines forming at 20 to 25 feet during the heat of summer. An electronic water thermometer will enable the trout fisherman to quickly locate this food and oxygen-rich thermocline in any lake. The location of the cool water is the first step toward filling a limit of big trout.

All inland trout lakes have peak periods of activity when big trout are taken consistently. The best month in the Midwest is June while May and October are good times to be fishing in Tennessee and Arkansas. That North American record brown I mentioned earlier was caught in January; not exactly a bumper month for consistent fishing, but an example of more southerly impoundments being able to produce good trout fishing year around.

Trout fishermen new to fishing a lake will be astounded to learn that much of the fishing will be done in depths from 10 to 40 feet. This can best be accomplished by trolling. Lake trout, jumbo cutthroats and Dolly Vardens in western states are often taken at depths well below these figures. Big trout live to become trophy size by spending the bulk of their time in deep water where most anglers seldom fish.

We've learned that trout must be fished in water of the optimum temperature. Another important factor to consider is that trout in lakes are *normally* bottom oriented.

This means they'll be found hovering on or near the lake bottom at the water temperature preference for the particular species of trout in question. This is why you must first determine which species of trout is found in a lake.

It would make little sense to fish 60-degree rainbow/brown temperatures for lake trout. You'd spend the day fishing far above any lake trout and trout seldom come up far for a bait or lure in a lake.

I've found that trout prefer certain types of lake structures and that the bulk of my trout will be taken in areas such as those listed below. Changes in bottom structure are important to trout and they lead the way to feeding migrations. A hydrographic map of the lake or impoundment is a tremendous asset to the lake fisherman.

A hydrographic map of the lake will show wide and narrowly spaced lines which indicate either quick changes in water depth or broad flat stretches of uniform bottom. Of the two, trout much prefer to hover along the edges of quick dropoffs. These areas afford comfort, food and safety of deep water close at hand.

Edges of submerged weedbeds in 15 or 20 feet of water are excellent spots to try for trout. Look for the deeper edge of the weedbed to be most productive providing the thermocline is present at that point.

One of the best areas in any lake or reservoir is a point. A point jutting out into a lake is a concentration and gather-

Lunker lake trout often fall to a well presented lure or minnow near bottom. Slow trolling speeds are the key to success.

ing spot for jumbo trout. I once located a school of rainbows off a point in Tennessee's Dale Hollow Lake that must have totaled 100 fish. They laid just off bottom and near the edge of the point where it dropped sharply into 30 feet of water. A limit catch of 'bows was easy that day.

Points can provide fantastic fishing almost anywhere along their length providing the water of the proper temperature and/or deep water lies nearby. Many points meander out into a lake in a long gradual point or bar or in a quickly breaking series of sharp dropoffs. Some points are wide and flat and these seldom are good producers of trout. I've found my best successes in point fishing lies in fishing points with a sharp dropoff into deep water or one where deep cold water butts right up against the side of the point. Trout will then be found either just off the point's dropoff or along either deepwater edge.

Trout often follow a long narrow point up out of deep water for a daily or twice-daily feeding excursion. These feeding migrations to shallower water are often easy to fish if you happen to be fishing the point at the proper time of day.

When's the best time? I don't know, although I've hit these feeding migrations quite often just after daybreak.

Western lakes and impoundments often produce good catches of trout along rocky shorelines, especially if the water near bottom is of the proper temperature. I've seen lakers and browns in western lakes lay down amongst the rubble next to shore and pound the daylights out of anything that dares intrude into their area—rocky areas are like magnets to trout.

An elevation or underwater hump near deep water is another prime location. These areas are often small and are usually conspicuously marked on hydrographic maps. It pays to troll the edges and across the tops of these humps until trout are contacted.

After the fisherman has checked a hydrographic map or inquired locally for information on where trout can be found, the next step is to take the water temperature. Locate the depth of water containing the temperature you're seeking. If 58-degree water is located at 22 feet, then you are going to have to fish just off bottom in water of that depth. The same principle applies in any depth water. Find the right water temperature and concentrate your fishing efforts in that area.

A sonar unit becomes vitally important at this stage of the game because without one you'd be all over the lake and seldom fishing in the proper depth. I use a Vexilar Sona-Graf because it gives me a quick look at the bottom contour, the depth of water is always indicated and it marks trout on the sensitive recording paper.

A flashing type of sonar unit is used by many fishermen and they find it entirely adequate for following bottom contours. The fisherman must be able to follow these contours exactly or the best lures and baits won't put many trout in the fish box.

Changes in bottom structure can occur rapidly in inland lakes or impoundments and the fisherman needs to keep a constant eye on his unit and learn how to anticipate changes. The normal impulse is to over-react with the boat and correct too far one way for a contour break. A day or two of trolling and structure reading will make any fisherman competent in this role.

The best advice is to make a trolling pass through a piece of water and make mental notes where changes occur in the bottom contour. I've got places lined up on a dozen lakes where I know exactly where to turn in or out on a specific trolling pass to keep my bait working through the best water. This comes both from experience and a bit of mental disci-

Big rainbows are commonly taken by fishermen trolling the shallows of inland lakes early in the spring.

pline. Line up contour changes with easily identifiable landmarks on shore. Trolling passes can be triangulated with three marks on various shores. Some fishermen know the best areas to troll and have them marked so well in their mind, that they can fish without having to use a sonar unit to keep track of the bottom.

Since the best method of taking trophy trout from inland lakes includes the art of trolling, we'll briefly discuss what constitutes good trolling gear. I prefer a 6- or 6½-foot baitcasting rod and a medium sized baitcasting reel with star drag and free spool. I prefer either 20- or 30-pound braided Dacron because it has a no-stretch quality I prefer when fishing deep water. A long line behind the boat in 40 feet of water means monofilament has far too much stretch to adequately anchor a hook in the jaw of a big trout. I don't want stretch; I want a firmly hooked trout after a violent strike.

The braided Dacron is marked at intervals of 60, 100, 120 and 150 feet by tying small pieces of brightly colored yarn into a blood knot. The yarn should be kept small so it doesn't bump going through the guides. Knots should be tied slowly and carefully. I've never had a knot come undone and I've landed lake trout up to 25 pounds on this rigging. It's important to measure this line carefully because it is a key in knowing how deep your line is running.

Deep water trolling for trout necessitates the use of an attractor and I've found the SunFlash Cowbell (Les Davis) to be the top producer. A 50/50 brass-chrome, all copper or all brass Cowbell is your best bet on bright days, while a

Lake trout such as these come easily for anglers that troll Cowbells and minnows at the proper depth.

bright chrome Cowbell works well on dull, overcast days.

It takes a varying amount of weight to take a Cowbell and bait down to the proper level. Weights up to 2 or 3 ounces can be wired to the Cowbell's rudder without detracting from its effectiveness. If more weight is needed to take the offering to the bottom strata, attach a wire leader ahead of the Cowbell and attach necessary weights ahead of the wire leader. This prevents the weight from swinging back in front of the Cowbell.

Minnows obtained from the lake being fished are the best bait for lunker trout but some states and/or lakes prohibit the use of minnows. Where this regulation is in effect I normally resort to using an imitation minnow such as a Rapala or Rebel. Attempt to match the body finish of the lure to the color of minnows prevalent in the area.

I prefer to obtain fresh minnows just prior to fishing a lake. A minnow trap, baited with Saltines, can be set near shore and the trap emptied of bait within a half-hour. These fresh caught minnows represent the best approach to offering a big trout something he's used to feeding on.

Shiner minnows are preferred in many areas and they are common in many trout lakes. Chubs (small ones) can be used, although they aren't as good as shiners for bait. Two- to 3-inch sizes are best for most trout although a larger 4- or 5-inch minnow can be used for lake trout or Dolly Vardens.

Once the Cowbell is attached to the end of the braided Dacron, tie a 16- or 18-inch length of 10-pound mono to a No. 4 or 6 treble hook—make sure the hooks are needle sharp. Buy stainless steel surgical needles from a medical supply house and use them to sew the minnow onto the line. Place the loose end of the leader in the eye of the needle. Run the point of the needle through the vent of the minnow and out its mouth. Pull the leader through the minnow and push the hook shank up the anus and pull the leader straight. The minnow should have a slight curve which will cause the bait to roll and wobble behind the Cowbell.

The proper trolling speed is slow—put-put slow. The proper speed is ascertained when the Cowbell puts a deep throbbing pulsation in the rod tip. Adjust the trolling speed until the blades of the Cowbell just turn over in the water. I normally run mine beside the boat until I can idle the motor down sufficiently to bring out the pounding beat of the Cowbell blades.

The big secret to this fishing is to obtain the proper trolling speed, fish in the proper depth and keep the Cowbell and minnow combination throbbing slowly just off bottom. This is accomplished by letting out the Cowbell and sewn minnow slowly until the weight touches bottom. Once you can feel bottom consistently, take up two or three turns of line and the bait will be rolling along just off bottom.

You should release line occasionally just to keep in contact with the bottom. If you can't feel the weight occasionally ticking bottom let out more line until you feel it hit and then reel up a bit of the slack. You have to stay within that productive zone found within 2 feet of bottom. Fish too far over that and most trout will ignore the bait.

I prefer to gauge my depth of Cowbells and minnows by referring to my marked line. I've learned over the years that a certain amount of line in the water in combination with a specific amount of lead will take my bait down to a specified depth at slow trolling speeds. The newcomer to this sport will have to experiment with trolling speeds and weight/line length combinations until he works it out for himself. Just remember to troll very slowly and close to bottom at the preferred water temperature.

There are other tricks the lake troller uses to hang big stringers of trout. I like to troll in a modified zig-zag pattern with sudden quick changes in direction. Following trout often pounce on a minnow that makes a quick sashay to the right or left.

A sudden burst of speed for a few feet will often inspire a following trout into striking. The Cowbell and minnow will spurt ahead for a brief instant and then flutter down slowly as the boat slows to the normal trolling speed. Trout often slam the bait either as it speeds up or slows back down. Either way, the strike is savage.

A trick I've learned to experiment with when trolling inland lakes for trout is to utilize the old-fashioned "chugging" technique. Lake trout fishermen used to chug for hours. This involves lifting the rodtip to a vertical position and then quickly lowering it. Fish often strike as the Cowbell and minnow settle after the rod tip is lowered.

You'll seldom encounter a mild-mannered trout in this type of fishing. The fish slam the bait, put up a tremendous arm wrenching battle and jump often. I've seen rainbows and browns 3 feet in the air with a Cowbell jangling in the sunlight. The hardware doesn't slow them down a bit; if anything, I think it makes 'em madder and harder to subdue.

It's difficult to comprehend just how many trout lakes and impoundments across America are virtually unfished. The number is probably staggering. All I know is I've applied these principles in trout lakes in a dozen states and managed to catch bragging size fish from every lake I've sampled.

I know that many trophy trout are not being harvested because too few anglers know how to fish a trout lake. Follow these tips and you'll soon be catching those lunkers other fishermen tell stories about, but seldom see.

The Fly Angler's Ultimate Challenge

by S. R. SLAYMAKER II

A NEW ENGLAND fly angling acquaintance tells an amusing tale about a distinguished fellow angler, the Duke of Edinburgh. His Royal Highness was fishing a brook trout lake in the northern reaches of his wife's Canadian wilderness with a party, including my friend.

As they set out in canoes, the eager anglers began whipping Silver Doctor and Dark Montreal wet flies with happy abandon in all directions. After unlimbering his fly rod the Duke appeared confused and reticent about casting. He finally did so, but uncomfortably. One of the group managed to elicit the difficulty. The Duke was nonplussed on seeing the others flailing away aimlessly; targeting their casts, as it were, at the lake in general. It seemed to him a monumental exercise in wasted effort. Why, he probably wondered, don't these overly energetic Yanks give trout a chance to rise and then fish to them?

There's no question but that the time-honored British practice of "fishing the rise" affords the epitome in angling pleasure. It's infinitely more rewarding to single out a feeding trout and fool him with a facsimile of his natural food than it is to "fish the water" blindly in hopes that you'll raise something!

Fishing the rise in England is facilitated by the prevalence of chalk (limestone) streams flowing placidly through pastoral country. Thus, even the most subdued rise or "dimple" can be seen easily from great distances. In North America the preponderance of fast flowing and sharp riffled freestone waters was conducive to the American custom of "fishing the water."

True, since the introduction of the dry fly in the late 19th century, American fly anglers have revelled in the joys of matching insect hatches for rising trout. But the practice generally never gained the status of a tradition in the United States and Canada.

Then, during the early 1950s, British chalk stream techniques came to the States. Not by importation, however. They sprang full blown from the heads of two eminently practical American anglers, Vincent C. Marinaro and Charles K. Fox. And the Marinaro-Fox techniques—beyond being pragmatic in a typically American way—were revolutionary. For in all their years of chalk stream experience the British never discovered the important part terrestrial insect imitations could play in duping their wily brown trout. More's the pity since terrestrials floating on the surface, or in its film, are conducive to rising trout!

America's prime limestone trout streams are mostly located in central and south central Pennsylvania. The large streams of the Allegheny Mountains such as Spring Creek, Penn's Creek, and Spruce Creek have been meccas for trout fishermen for many years. The smaller southcentral streams, not so well known until the Marinaro-Fox terrestrial breakthrough, are Falling Springs, Letort, Green Spring Creek, Big Spring, Boiling Springs and the Yellow Breeches, the largest of this region's trout streams.

These streams have the characteristics of England's chalk rivers. Between undulating limestone-based hills they meander slowly, their placid water cooled by strong underground springs. These limestone fed waters, highly productive of zoo plankton (the microscopic basis of the aquatic food chain), are responsible for a phenomenal volume of both aquatic and terrestial fish food; fry fish, minnows, mayflies, caddis flies, and stone flies—together with a variety of beetles, bugs, ants, crickets and grasshoppers. The rich insect food supply is replaced during winter months by an immense amount of sow (or cress) bugs and fresh water shrimp. As a result, limestone trout are extraordinarily well conditioned and quickly reach large proportions.

From the time of the first pioneers, trout have been taken from these lovely streams on all manner of rigs. Theodore Gordon, the patron saint of American fly angling, fished them with flies, as in later years did many others. Few, however, tried to match natural insect hatches and thus experience the pleasure of stalking rising trout in the British manner. Fewer, if any, realized that terrestial insects represent a substantial amount of the food consumed by limestone trout. If some observant souls did take note of the fact, they made no known effort to imitate terrestials. It fell to Vince Marinaro and Charlie Fox to do so and to contribute scholarly writings on the subject which justify their being ranked with fly angling giants such as Walton, Cotton, Halford, Skues and Gordon.

Anyone desiring in-depth knowledge of limestone trouting theory and practice should read the seminal work of Vince Marinaro, *A Modern Dry Fly Code,* (Crown) and two charming classics by Charlie Fox, *This Wonderful World of Trout* and *Rising Trout* (Freshet).

It's customary for dyed-in-the-wool freestone fly anglers to literally get the shock of an angling lifetime when they first experience fishing the rise on a limestone stream. My own introduction to this pleasing art form was no exception.

Fifteen years ago I was visiting Charlie and Glad Fox at their home on the banks of Letort Spring Run in Cumberland County, Pennsylvania, a stream Charlie and Vince immortalized with their terrestial insect experiments and discoveries. Japanese beetles were very much in season that beautiful summer day and a smart breeze was consistently blowing them into the stream. My first shock came when I saw the large size of some of the trout that were lazily devouring the beetles. It seemed impossible that such big fish could inhabit so small a stream. And in such great numbers!

The second shock came when Charlie attached a 10-foot leader tapered to the unheard of (to me) size of 7X! Shock number three came when 20 feet above us, a pair of immense brown trout rose ever so slowly and menacingly—

Charles K. Fox on the banks of the Letort examines weeds and finds heavy deposits of fresh water shrimp. He locates a feeding trout, presents an imitation of a fresh water shrimp, hooks the fish, and lands him.

for all the world like two U-boats in a wolf pack—until their up-tilted snouts budged the surface. Each drank in a beetle and settled back into the depths.

Charlie silently singled out the largest for me to tempt with one of his split coffee bean beetle imitations. I insisted he try his hand for my edification. Like a stalking Indian he crept noiselessly up the left bank. The fish lay in a channel bordered by a bed of watercress against the right bank and a parallel strip of elodea in center stream. After measuring the distance with a couple of false casts Charlie dropped his beetle at 2 o'clock, about 15 feet ahead of the trout's lie. It floated true, smack into the "take" zone. I almost heard my heart beat as the big brown began his slow rise. For a second he looked over the lure. Then, perfectly conned, he sipped it in. As Charlie struck, the brownie—as if momentarily electrified—sped upstream as the screeching reel drowned out the dreamy chirp of cicadas.

Charlie fought the fish for several minutes. But it got too firmly embedded in elodea and broke off. While he landed two smaller trout before a tangerine-colored sun sank behind the Allegheny foothills, it was obvious that Charlie's real pleasure lay in duping the trout rather than landing them. In order to do this his presentation had to be letter perfect. Were the drift off target, had the beetle alighted too close to the fish, or if the leader had been delivered in a bunched or coiled state, these trout would never have been fooled. It was plain to see that this kind of fly fishing was demanding of a high degree of skill.

Perhaps a dawning inferiority complex was responsible for my bad showing. With very little effort, I managed to make each of the above-mentioned faux pas (bad floats, "close in" casts, sloppy leader delivery), and I paid the price of putting down every trout to which I fished. Not one was hooked.

Had I been typical of some dedicated freestone anglers, one such limestone outing would have been enough. I would have foregone this potentially exciting kind of angling for more familiar mountain streams where gurgling rapids and singing glides are so thankfully forgiving of mistakes! Fortunately, I was not so dedicated a "mountain man" to give up on these wary, pastureland fish. First of all, they were close to home. There was plenty of time to practice over them whenever I got the urge. And there was the pleasing, old-world charm of limestone waters. The effect was hypnotic. So I went back. Over the years I've learned to cope well enough to fool these fish occasionally, which, as I learned that first afternoon, constitutes a more important challenge than landing them.

My experience is proof positive of the fact that the average fly angler should never forego an opportunity to

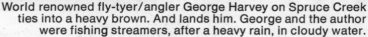

World renowned fly-tyer/angler George Harvey on Spruce Creek ties into a heavy brown. And lands him. George and the author were fishing streamers, after a heavy rain, in cloudy water.

challenge limestone trout because the degree of difficulty involved demands high expertise. But a stranger to this kind of fishing should be sure to *allow more time than he normally would on unfamiliar water to get acclimated!*

I discourage anglers visiting the limestone region from "dropping by" to wet a line for an afternoon or evening. They should spend at least a long weekend—preferably longer—to become familiar with the different angling idiom. It's not necessary to be an experienced water reader; especially since, under normal conditions, you will be fishing to surface-feeding trout. You don't have to be a tournament caster or one practiced in bizarre forms of presentation. But you must be a *careful* caster. Accurate presentation is mandatory; your flies should drift naturally on a given trout's normal food carrying channel. Thus, neophyte limestoners require plenty of time to practice unhurriedly. Then they will begin to get results. And they can be sure that the satisfaction involved will prove unmatchable.

The uninitiated often have the erroneous impression that in-depth knowledge of insect life is a prerequisite to success in limestone trouting. Any angler who fishes flies on free-stone streams can cope very easily. All he needs is accurate information germane to the locale he is fishing.

Limestone streams in north central Pennsylvania have some large mayfly hatches such as the legendary green drake hatch on Penn's Creek, not to mention those on Spruce and Spring Creeks. On these creeks also from early season to mid-July there are ample to large hatches of the sulphur, blue quill, little olive and caenis.

An angler visiting these particular waters—after checking with native regulars who are always easy to find—can easily learn what imitations to have in his fly book. And if flies aren't coming off the water at a given time, he will know what *should* be in the process of hatching. So he can use nymph imitations. This is exactly the procedure he would follow on a freestone stream.

In the south central limestone watershed mayfly hatches are not so heavy or varied, although there is an excellent early season hatch of Hendricksons on the Yellow Breeches. Also the sulphur and little olive are important flies, as is the caenis on Falling Springs.

While terrestrial insects are important trout fare in the north central region (especially later in the season) they are always a bigger factor to the south, thanks to the relative sparseness of the mayflies there. Since minute imitation terrestials require such great care in presentation, a beginning limestone fly fisherman would do well to sample north central streams before taking on those to the south. The northern streams more resemble freestone waters and there's more opportunity there to fish the more familiar mayfly imitations.

From mid-summer to early fall cricket and grasshopper imitations are safe bets on all limestone streams. Smaller facsimiles of common terrestial food are less easily detected as phonies during daylight hours, such as size No. 16 to 22 ants, jassids, and beetles, so these patterns are consistent favorites.

Most fly anglers' catalog houses and the better tackle stores carry a full range of terrestial imitations. Visitors to the south central area would be well advised to visit Ed Koch's tackle shop at Boiling Springs. Here gather experienced limestoners, some who fish the surrounding waters on a virtually daily basis. Information on what, when, and where "they're taking," along with a complete array of relevant fly patterns and equipment is available at Ed's shop.

While fly rods of all standard lengths are used in limestone trouting, I find the experienced anglers favoring rods of 7 to 8 feet. I've come to agree with their contention that midge rods—my own favorite on most trout waters—make for too much work on many of these streams. On the Letort, for example, roll casting and the ability to fish around and over obstacles is often necessary. Longer rods can better facilitate such work.

Recently, while fishing the Letort with Charlie Fox, I was working over a nice brownie from the only available casting location, a 90 degree angle, cross-stream from the fish. It was a 16- to 17-incher, lazily finning, hard against the far bank. Since I was in a totally unfoliaged spot, I knelt and roll cast with the 6-foot rod. The fish's lie was over 40 feet distant. The casts fell just short of my mark. Impatiently I went into a crouching position and placed a forward cast. The brownie immediately sensed the rod's movement and

Above—Art Lee, Director of the American League of Anglers, drifts a sow bug on the Letort. The limestone streams of Central Pennsylvania draw anglers from great distances, among them, well-known author/anglers.

Left—The author with a 19¾-inch, 3-pound stream bred brown trout taken with a Yellow Marabou from Spruce Creek.

was gone. Charlie Fox feels the new graphite rods, with their reputed extra kick, should make ideal rods for long roll casts. I surely will have one, or at least one of my old 8½-footers, the next time I fish the Letort!

Long, finely tippeted leaders are mandatory on smooth limestone waters. Ten to 12 feet of stepped-down leader with a 6X tippet is usually satisfactory for evening dry fly fishing while 7X is generally considered better during daylight hours. For wet fly fishing 5 or 6X tippets are often used.

A great boon to limestone anglers has been the opening of some prime Pennsylvania water for year-round fly fishing; namely, sections of the Letort, Penn's Creek, Spring Creek, Yellow Breeches, and Big Spring. This move by the Pennsylvania Fish Commission makes sense. The strong, high volume springs empty into these streams at about 51 degrees so this water is abnormally cool in summer and quite warm in winter. This situation promotes a longer seasonal span for aquatic insect life. As noted, the volume of fresh water shrimp and sow bugs is phenomenal at all times and trout gorge on them year 'round!

Of fairly recent date shrimp and sow bug imitations—size 18 became available from commercial tiers. Fresh water shrimp are free floaters so they can be convincingly fished with the dead drift method used for nymphs and dry flies. Sow bugs make for fascinating situations and they are handled in the same manner.

Trout sometimes can be seen making disturbances in beds of watercress or weeds. These fish are called "rooters." They literally shake the tiny sow bugs from vegetation so that they can be devoured while floating free. A sow bug imitation is cast carefully into a trout's feeding channel until he is either put down by a bad cast or he takes it.

Sometimes an untutored angler will give up and replace his sow bug lure with another pattern on the theory that the fish might want something else. This approach to finicky trout is common on freestone streams when various flies are on the water. But it is often a serious error on limestone water, particularly when trout are seen rooting. Sow bugs are what they want. If they don't take yours right away, it's simply because the fish in question hasn't had time to get around to your counterfeit! So long as you don't put him down, keep presenting your sow bug until you're really convinced that something about it doesn't look right to the trout. Not long ago I worked over a rooting trout on the Letort for at least 10 minutes before he "took."

Western out-of-staters will find it easy to reach both Pennsylvania limestone stream areas. East-west U.S. Route 80 traverses the center of the state in the vicinity of Springs Creek, Spruce and Penn's Creeks. The south central region is bisected by the east-west Pennsylvania Turnpike, Route 76.

Much of Pennsylvania's limestone water is restricted to Fly Fish Only and Fish for Fun regulations. These are changed periodically so visiting anglers should contact the Pennsylvania Fish Commission, Harrisburg, Pa. 17120, for current information.

Strangers to these fabled streams who are willing to take time to become familiar with them will be entranced with this very special kind of trout angling which some of us have come to call "the ultimate challenge."

GATHER YOUR OWN TROUT BAIT

by MITCH EGAN

WHEN I WAS a youngster there was a man in our community with a talent for always catching the largest trout. Other fishermen tried to follow this man and learn why he enjoyed such success while others were going fishless.

Huge stringers of lunker browns, rainbows and brookies were taken by this fisherman within several miles of town. The townsfolk knew he was using bait . . . but what kind? There were no bait dealers within miles of town and everyone knew the fisherman didn't care to part with money.

One day I followed the oldtimer. He made a brief pause at his garage, threw a wire screen into his car and headed down the road with me in hot pursuit on my bicycle.

By the time I'd caught up with him he was thoroughly engrossed in seining wigglers (larvae of the mayfly) from a gooey muck bed near shore. His movements and accompanying noise hid the sound of my approach so I had a chance to watch the operation unobserved.

He'd strain water and muck through the small mesh of the window screen and place the kicking wigglers in a small pail of cold water. I'd been there for 5 minutes when he looked up from his work, spotted me and asked, "Learnin' anything?" I nodded, but I didn't know just what it was I'd learned.

He finished his work and clambered up on shore and squatted next to me. "Know what those are?" he nodded at the pail of wigglers. "Them's the best summer trout bait in these parts."

The oldtimer must have decided that a youngster wasn't

going to reveal his special tactic of gathering his own trout bait, so he invited me along on an afternoon fishing trip. He was a wizard at bouncing the wiggler downstream on light line and into the haunts of big trout. By dark he had taken another limit of mixed trout and left me with a parting piece of advice: "When trout are finicky and hard to catch, gather your own trout bait and give the fish something they're used to feeding on."

Since that time I've spent many hours gathering trout bait from fields, trees, rivers and lakes. The number of trout I catch on these natural baits is astounding.

There are a number of advantages in gathering your own trout bait: it's an excellent way to save money due to the rising cost of buying bait from dealers; you're assured of a continuing supply when bait dealers run out of the choicest items; and some of the best natural trout foods are not handled commercially by dealers. Last, but not least, the task of obtaining these baits is fun and easy once you know how, when and where to look.

Nightcrawlers

The most common natural bait is the nightcrawler. This husky worm represents an epicurean delight to a free feeding trout, especially during or after a summer rainstorm. Rains wash generous amounts of crawlers into rivers and trout feed avidly on them.

The best time to locate crawlers is either after dark or following a rain. Heavy drenching downpours make crawler picking easy because the big worms are found crawling about the highways and driveways.

Fairways and greens of golf courses represent some of the best worm picking areas. I've found football fields are also good areas to search. Always secure permission to hunt crawlers in advance. Police take a dim view of being shagged off to a golf course after dark only to find a fisherman armed with a flashlight and a can of crawlers.

An empty milk carton filled with dark, moist soil or sphagnum moss is a suitable container for keeping worms fresh and healthy. A flashlight should be covered with red cellophane to avoid spooking the crawlers with the naked white beam. Avoid training the beam of light directly on a nightcrawler and he'll seldom scoot back down his hole.

Back strain is the only danger to hunting crawlers and this can be avoided by squatting instead of bending over. I prefer to squat and move the beam of light around on all sides of me. Crawlers glisten in the soft glow of flashlight. Once I've spotted a crawler protruding from its hole I keep the worm in sight with the outside edge of the beam.

Usually just the forward portion of the crawler will protrude from its hole. The flat tail equipped with tiny gripping spikes will be buried and ready to pull the exposed portion of the worm back into the ground at the first sign of danger.

Never reach long distances for crawlers. They'll either get away or you'll break them in half. Move slow and quietly until

These youngsters empty a minnow trap of its prized trout bait—live shiners and chubs. This means of gathering trout bait is quick and easy and saves money.

Above—This fisherman has just dipped a netful of smelt for later use as trout bait. Spring is the best time for dipping. Below—A quick dip and two spawning suckers have been gathered for use as bait.

the worm is within easy reach. Pin the wiggly creature to the ground with your fingers to prevent it from escaping. Pull the crawler slowly from its burrow—lift until you feel resistance and then just maintain steady pressure on the worm until you feel his muscles relax and then pull him free at that point.

Collecting crawlers after a rain is easy but there are ways of making the little rascals show themselves. One method is to thoroughly drench the lawn a couple of hours before you go worming.

A shovel is a handy tool for gathering worms by digging in gardens or low-lying moist areas. Shovel fans have the option of being able to select only those worms best suited for their method of fishing.

A fascinating method of bringing nightcrawlers to the surface is to use an ax and a 2-foot length of flat board that is sharpened on one end. The sharpened board is pounded into damp soil to half its length. The flat part of the ax is drawn across the top of the board which sends vibrations down into the ground. Worms appear within minutes. There is even an electrical device on the market that works on basically the same principle. A probe is stuck in the ground, the cord is plugged in and worms and crawlers bounce to the surface in a hurry.

Minnows

Minnows are a popular and highly effective trout bait. There are hundreds of different species of minnows, but some of the most popular among trout fishermen are shiners, chubs, suckers and sculpin.

Baitfish can be collected easily with either a minnow trap or a seine or other type of net. Minnow traps (the glass types are best) can be baited with white bread or soda crackers and

Left—A strainer or piece of screen is handy for sifting through sand and other debris on the river bottom. Below—Aquatic insects are excellent for trout. The author found some caddis larvae on the underside of this stream rock.

placed wherever baitfish congregate. A day's supply can be trapped in just a few minutes. Shorelines or small shallow streams are the best spots to look for minnows.

I like to seine minnows from streams. Colder water makes the minnows hardier and they make much better trout bait. Two fishermen can work a seine or net downstream with the lower edge of the net hugging the bottom. The poles holding the seine should be tilted back at a 45-degree angle. At the end of a sweep work from deeper water into shallow and herd the fleeing minnows against a bank or sand bar where they can be easily netted.

Seining a lake shore for shiners represents a more difficult proposition. Shiners frequent areas around docks and water from 2 to 4 feet deep. This necessitates a weighted seine and two husky fishermen to sweep the net around the school of minnows. One pass with a seine will usually yield several dozen shiners or enough to last out a week's vacation on a trout stream or lake.

A lift net is useful in lakes. I've used one many times and find the best place to drop the net is off the end of a dock. Once the net lies flat on bottom the minnows can be encouraged to congregate over it by throwing bread crumbs on the water. As soon as the crumbs begin soaking up water and sinking the minnows will begin feeding and this is the best time to lift the net.

In areas where smelt and suckers are abundant during spring months they can be gathered with either a dip net, by hand or by spear. Large concentrations of both fish are normally available and are easily harvested by trout fishermen for bait.

Suckers are generally too large to be used as trout bait but thin slivers of sucker meat are often used to add flavor to

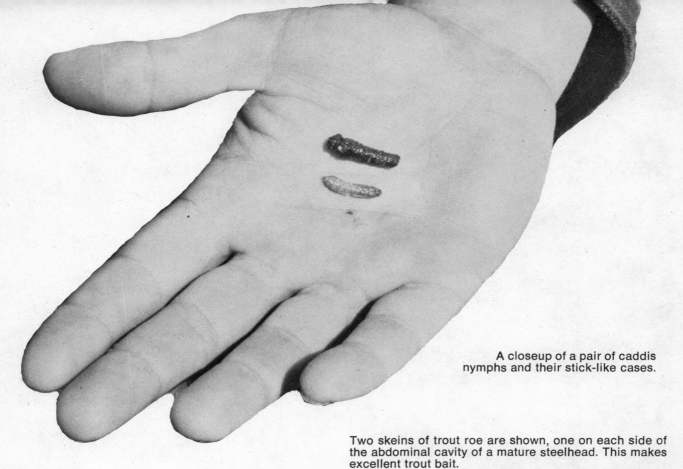

A closeup of a pair of caddis nymphs and their stick-like cases.

Two skeins of trout roe are shown, one on each side of the abdominal cavity of a mature steelhead. This makes excellent trout bait.

jigging or trolling baits. One sucker, kept on ice, will offer enough small fillets for lures to last quite a while.

Smelt, either live or dead, are some of the very best trout baits known. Big lake trout, rainbows and browns actively feed on smelt in the Great Lakes and other midwestern states and this large odorous minnow rates a high place in my list of preferred trout foods. Smelt in the 4- to 8-inch class are best and can either be fished whole, through the ice on tipups, or the tails will add a delectable taste to a jigging lure.

Regulations on collecting bait and rough fish vary from state to state. It is wise to check on local restrictions before gathering a supply.

Larvae and Nymphs

The aquatic larval and nymph stages of certain insects are topnotch natural trout baits. Many aquatic insects may be found attached to the bottoms of rocks in midstream. Others burrow into sand, silt or accumulations of other debris on bottom. This is why the oldtimer at the beginning of this story knew that wigglers would be found in the muck bed near shore.

Some of the more common types of nymphs and larvae you'll encounter are immature stages of the caddisfly, dobsonfly, mayfly, stonefly and dragonfly.

Caddisfly larvae are the easiest to identify. They are encased in a small stick-like case of twigs or grains of sand. Dobsonfly larva, commonly called hellgrammites, look like an aquatic version of a centipede.

Mayfly and stonefly nymphs are similar in appearance. Both have a forked tail which gives them the appearance of having an antenna on each end.

Collecting nymphs from a river is easy. Assemble a fine mesh screen (such as a window screen) between two poles or sticks. Hold the screen just downstream from rocks and logs

Above—The materials needed to tie spawn bags—roe, shears, thread, paper toweling and nylon stocking. Left —Gather up all four corners of the nylon and twist into a ball. Below left—Spawn bags compared to the size of a dime.

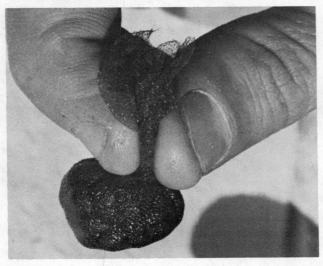

and turn them over rapidly. Nymphs stuck to the bottoms of the rocks and logs will drift off in the current and be trapped in the screen. The screen can be used to sift through sand and silt for wigglers and other nymphs.

Insects

Land dwelling insects also produce excellent results when used on trout. Trout are used to feeding on terrestrial insects that have fallen or been blown into the water. Smart trout fishermen rely on land insects during summer months when trout are hard to take.

During a mayfly or salmon fly hatch large quantities of these choice morsels can be gathered from limbs and bushes along rivers and lakes. These insects often gather on window screens beneath porch lights or under street lights and night-time gathering can be fast and easy.

Grasshoppers and crickets are two of the top choices for the summer trout fisherman and both can be easily collected. Crickets are found by turning over stones, boards or other debris in sunny fields.

Grasshoppers are more lively than crickets during the heat of day. A butterfly net increases the odds of gathering a supply of trout bait. The easiest way is to look for hoppers early in the morning when dew is still on the grass. They are sluggish at this time and can be plucked from their perches on blades of grass. I've collected some grasshoppers at night with a flashlight.

Hoppers and crickets can be transported in a pop bottle fitted with a trimmed cork to allow entrance of some air. A woman's nylon stocking is a handy method of carrying hoppers. Their feet tangle in the nylon and it makes escape difficult.

A variety of other land-bound creepy crawlers such as beetles, caterpillars and inch worms also work wonders on

Crayfish are deadly trout baits. Use small soft-shelled crawdads.

trout. Look for these types of insects in or under rotting logs, grassy fields or on the leaves of trees and bushes.

A novel method of collecting trout bait involves placing a piece of netting or wire screen across the grill of your car. An evening's drive will produce an abundant supply of ready-to-use bait.

Fish Roe

One of the deadliest natural trout baits is the roe from fish. Trout or salmon eggs are highly preferred although I've had some success using northern pike eggs tied into spawn bags. Rainbow and brown trout eggs rank high among fishermen although lake trout and coho or chinook eggs certainly are productive.

Obtaining trout roe for bait involves first obtaining a mature female in spawning condition. The roe is removed by making a surgical cut down the belly. One skein of eggs will be on either side of the abdominal cavity.

Roe can be used two different ways for trout bait. If raw roe is to be used, cover the skeins with powdered Borax or boric acid crystals. This toughens the membrane and preserves the eggs. After a period of 1 to 7 days in a refrigerator cut the skeins into chunks about the size of a strawberry or a marble. Treat the chunks with preservative again and they'll be ready to use. Spawn baits cared for in this manner will last a month or more in the refrigerator without spoiling. Larger amounts of processed spawn can be frozen for later use.

Fully mature single eggs or chunks of raw roe can be tied into spawn bags. Women's nylon stockings, cheesecloth or bridal veil are popular material for tying spawn bags. Square pieces of this material should be cut in 2-inch sections.

A small piece of eggs should be centered in the material and all four corners of the fabric closed tightly around the eggs. Roll the eggs slightly between finger and thumb to make a round ball and to remove all wrinkles from the material surrounding the eggs. Twist the four corners of the material to tighten the sack and then tie the neck of the bag shut with thread. Excess material is trimmed off to leave a marble-sized bag.

Preservative can be added once the bags are tied although I

Left—Note the goldenrod gall found on this stalk. Look for the white grubs inside. Below — Goldenrod grubs, a deadly bait for trout.

don't care to do this. I'd rather use untreated spawn bags and tie just enough for each fishing trip. Spawn bags can be refrigerated or frozen after tying.

Other Baits

Crayfish are perhaps the deadliest trout bait known but very few fishermen collect crawdads and even fewer fish with them. Crawdads are found under rocks or logs in streams, rivers and inland lakes. They can be found at night by shining with a flashlight. Their eyes shine red when hit by the light beam.

A wire trap baited with a bloody piece of meat or the entrails from a trout often produce large numbers of crayfish when set after dark. Soft shelled crawdads in the smaller sizes produce best for trout.

Many trout hatcheries have ponds full of crayfish. When the ponds are cleaned yearly the crawdads are removed. This can be an excellent time to secure a supply of this fine bait.

Winter trout fishermen have a need for natural trout baits and there are many available that produce exciting strikes for icefishermen. Goldenrod grubs is one example of a common bait that is deadly for trout. Look for goldenrod along roadsides and in fields. The small white grubs spend cold months inside some stalks. Look for a noticeable swelling or gall on the goldenrod stalk. Cut this open and remove the grub.

Cornborers are small white grubs that infect field corn left standing during the winter. Break or cut open any corn stalk that has little holes on the outside. The grub will be found nestled inside the stalk. I've seen as many as a half-dozen cornborers in one stalk. This particular bait is expensive and often sells for upwards of a dollar a dozen.

Lumber yards are another hotspot to check for winter bait. The larval form of the June bug can often be found in piles of sawdust. Golden grubs and mealworms can be harvested from under sacks of grain at a grain elevator or grist mill.

Wasps are dormant in their nests during winter and they can be used for trout bait. Look for nests under the eaves of buildings.

Trout bait is available year around in most areas and is often no farther away than the nearest field, log pile or stream. Every time someone complains to me about their inability to catch trout I remember sneaking up on the oldtimer harvesting wigglers. He taught me a trick about trout fishing that any angler would be wise to learn.

HOW TO CATCH TROUT IN JIG TIME

by ROBERT JACKSON

YOU'VE SEEN the type of hole I'm talking about—the kind that just has to contain a lunker trout. It was a long slanting affair with deep water toward the tail. Cedar boughs hung over the water and shaded the pool from heavy sunlight. A brisk current swept into the head before dumping its load of water-borne insects into the mouths of waiting trout.

I'd beaten the pool to death with a variety of insects on a hot sultry summer afternoon. None of the imitations had drawn as much as a nibble. The trout were apparently deep and sulking in the heat.

I crawled back up the hill in the hot California sun and beat it back to my car to sit in air-conditioned comfort and try to work out a solution to my problem. The trout were there. I could see an occasional flash deep in the pool but flies, spoons and spinners failed to turn the trick.

A though suddenly struck me; why not try jigs. They work in deep water conditions and possibly they might produce a strike under these circumstances. My Canadian tackle box, filled with walleye and northern pike jigs, was in the trunk. I grabbed a handful, started for the river and with a brief after-thought returned to the trunk for a bottle of Uncle Josh porkrind. If it's good enough to fool a big walleye it should fool trout, I thought.

I tied a Gapen Pinky jig onto my 8-pound mono and felt a bit foolish as I poked a cast under the overhanging cedar boughs. The ¼-ounce jig sank quickly and was soon bouncing along the bottom. I fished the pool for 15 minutes before stopping to assess why I wasn't getting any action. I knew the jig was working down through the trout. Why weren't they hitting?

I took a small piece of white porkrind from the bottle and attached it to the jig. I made a long cast to the head of the pool, allowed the jig to sink to bottom and began working the bait back in short hippety-hops. A trout lambasted the jig on the fourth hop and cleared the water in one smooth motion.

The rainbow ripped line off my reel in a screeching downstream run that had my line hanging from the lower branches as I charged along, trying to keep up with the beserk trout. The 'bow paused briefly in a shallow pool and I was certainly surprised to note it was a fresh run summer steelhead.

The steelie lit out on another scorching run and did two head standing leaps before settling down in a large deep pool for a drawn-out battle. Several minutes later I slid a prime 10-pound summer fish onto the bank. The jig hung from his bottom lip like the stub of a burned out cigar.

Since that day several years ago I've learned to try jigs and jigging techniques for trout whenever the fish are deep and reluctant to strike. There seems to be something about a jig that triggers a strike from lazily feeding trout.

Jigs come in all shapes, sizes and colors. Some are dressed with plastic grubs or beetles. A popular model with me is the Ugly Bug. It certainly looks ugly with its tiny rubber legs wobbling in the water but trout look upon it as something worth eating.

I prefer standard jigs in the ⅓-, ¼- and ½-ounce sizes. The larger sizes work very well in rivers or lakes where fishing has to be done either in swift deep water or at the greater depths of a lake.

I've found that white, white and red, yellow or yellow and red jigs are the most productive colors. I've had limited success with pink jigs and very little with chartreuse.

Jigs come in a variety of shapes but I honestly believe it makes little difference which shape is used. Jigs are meant to be activated by rod tip action and retrieval speed so the shape has very little to do with its fish catching ability.

It is important to vary the retrieve and jigging action when trout fishing. Like the opening anecdote points out, once I changed my casting position and tried a different approach to the pool, the trout would strike.

This is very important to jig-fishing a river. Trout will be found lying only in certain locations and the fisherman must experiment with different casting positions *and* jigging actions in order to completely cover the water.

I normally approach a pool and begin covering it with an across and upstream cast while standing somewhere between the head and the middle of the pool. Cast the jig quartering upstream, allow it to sink and bump it downstream with the current by lifting gently on the rod tip. This will cause it to lift over underwater obstructions and provide it with certain action.

Jigs dressed with feathers, marabou or bucktail are best for this purpose because the dressing will dance and weave in the water current.

If this opening technique doesn't produce I'll normally wade down toward the tail end of the pool and try the same cast there. Normally, actively feeding trout will be found frequenting the lower stretches of a pool.

My next approach would be to cast almost straight up stream. Allow the jig to sink to bottom, reel up the slack and jig it downstream toward you. Allow it to sink again

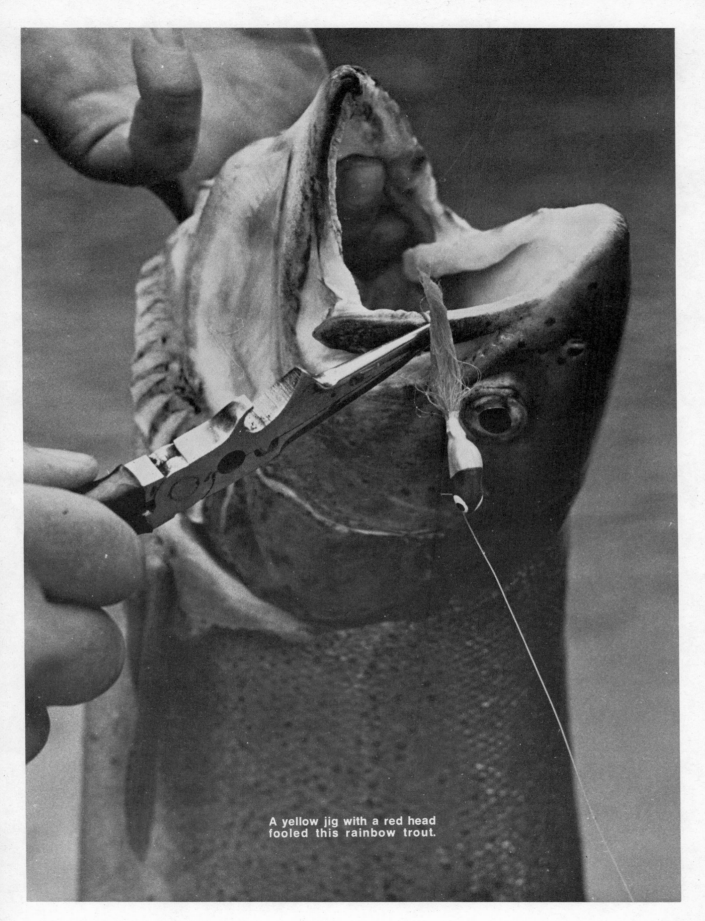

A yellow jig with a red head
fooled this rainbow trout.

and then jig once more. Work the jig back to you in this manner. If you have no takers, try casting closer to the opposite bank. A fairly wide pool will need a half-dozen upstream casts to effectively cover all water. It's important to strain all possible holding water with your casts.

A jig is just the berries for working tiny isolated pockets and deep holes beneath an undercut bank. I was working a ⅓-ounce yellow jig beneath a hemlock in Maine once when I felt a surging strike. I set the hook and the fish darted back and forth beneath the hemlock roots.

I couldn't give line because the fish would be tangled in the roots in an instant. I held firmly, hoping my 4-pound mono wouldn't pop, and finally I could see the brook trout beginning to play out.

A few seconds later I reached down and lipped a 14-inch brookie. The head of the minnow baited hook was barely visible down its throat. The brookie had literally engulfed the minnow and jig. The combination proved extremely effective that day when a limit catch of specks fell to my dabbling casts beneath the hemlocks.

This brings up an interesting point about jig fishing. Jigs are extremely versatile lures. They can be fished as is or they can be dressed up with porkrind, minnows, nightcrawlers, salamanders, or strips of fish flesh. It may seem sacrilegious to many fishermen but one of the top baits that can be added to a jig is the throat latch of another trout.

This throat latch is located under the chin of a trout just ahead of the gills. It is shaped roughly like an inverted "V" and can be cut from a dead trout. This thin membrane, when hooked at the apex of the V, will wave and float in the water. The tiniest twitch of the rod tip will set the throat latch in action. It's especially deadly for big trout.

One of the deadliest baits to add to a jig is a small minnow. Shiners or suckers are common in many eastern streams and sculpins are common in the West. Select a 2-inch minnow and hook the bait from the bottom jaw and out through the top of the head. When the lure is jigged the minnow will give extra action and provide a seductive drawing appeal that big trout cannot resist.

Salamanders offer trout a look at a bait they seldom see. This small lizard-like bait can be found by turning over logs or heavy piles of stones. They can be hooked in a manner similar to minnows. Smaller salamander generally produce better than the larger sizes.

Jigs will work almost anywhere trout are found. One of the favorite locations for jigs has always been below an impoundment dam. Dams drain water off the bottom of the impoundment and this cold water is forced through the turbines, which produces electrical energy and mincemeat of any small forage fish.

Trout lay downstream, just off the main current flow, and pick off free drifting pieces of food forced downstream through the turbines. This drifting food attracts smaller fish as well as trout. Lunker trout often forego the pleasure of eating the drifting morsels and concentrate on the smaller minnows.

The jig-minnow combination is deadly below power dams. I've used this rig in Arkansas, Tennessee, Michigan, Wisconsin and New York. It undoubtedly would work well anywhere trout are found congregating below a hydro dam.

Lake fishing can be exciting fishing for trout when jigs are employed. Trout in lakes often make shoreward migrations at certain times of day for feeding purposes. These areas are normally associated with points or areas containing quick dropoffs close to the lake shore. Trout move along this structure as they head for the shallows to feed. The feeding migrations vary from day to day and this can be the most difficult part of finding a good jig fishing area.

Once a path from deep to shallow water has been determined it becomes necessary to locate an area where trout disperse. Structure fishermen call this a scatterpoint. Migrating trout will scatter once they reach this point. Scatterpoints are often the last break in the bottom contour before reaching shallow water. Many times a scatterpoint may be a large rock or submerged tree at the edge of deep water.

Locate an area like this and anchor quietly. A heavier jig can be used in lakes to aid in quicker sinking in deeper water. I like yellow jigs dressed with either yellow or red hair for lake fishing.

A minnow or small white porkrind is very effective in fishing deepwater lake structure. Cast the jig out to cover all portions of the scatterpoint. Allow the jig to sink to bottom and let it rest momentarily without movement.

Begin swimming the lure back in very short jigging hops. Do not sweep the rod tip way over your head to jig. The most productive jigging movement is a short 3- to 6-inch lift of the rod tip. Keep the rod tip low to the surface. This aids in setting the hook.

Jig and quickly reel up the slack line. Keep the line tight at all times. Allow the jig to settle to bottom briefly before jigging again. Work the scatterpoint thoroughly from all angles. Fan your cast out to cover both the deep and shallow water sides of the area. When trout move up on structure from deep water and then scatter, you may encounter them at any depth.

Trout usually sock a jig pretty hard when they are encountered in deeper water. Set the hook sharply and try to work them to the boat as quickly as possible. Trout on a scatterpoint do not stay long in the area. It is imperative to get them into the boat and the lure back in the water quickly. Five or 10 minutes is usually all you'll have to make your catch.

These feeding trout will often spend a ½-hour to an hour in shallower water feeding and then they make a leisurely retreat back to deep water. Some of the fish will follow the same path back and you can encounter them at the scatterpoint before they drop off into their deep sanctuaries. Some trout will merely disperse over the dropoff and into deeper water without following their earlier route.

I've had some excellent very deepwater fishing with jigs. The heavier ½- to 1-ounce sizes work well when jigging for lake trout in depths of 50 to 150 feet. In water this deep it becomes necessary to jig the lure constantly to attract attention. The tail of a smelt or a piece of flesh cut from a sucker or shiner minnow is often added to add an olfactory attraction.

One time I was jigging for lakers in a remote Ontario lake. The fish, the guide told me, were deep—down 60 feet. I baited up with a yellow Ugly Bug, tipped it with a small minnow, and lowered the bait to the bottom. I'd been jigging and drifting with the wind for an hour before my rod tip was smashed downward from the force of a vicious strike.

I tried to set the hook but the bottom-hugging laker slammed into the lure again. This time he was firmly hooked and he took off on a slow deliberate run.

I worked the fish slowly and after a 20-minute battle the laker was doing small circles below the boat. I pressured the fish to the surface and my guide scooped the fish into his oversized net. The big trout later weighed just over 20 pounds.

Jigs are a versatile lure and many trout fishermen should realize that a properly fished jig can be just as deadly for trout as a spoon, spinner, fly or live bait.

This year try fishing jigs for trout when the fish are deep and sulking. The technique works equally well in either river or lake. I consider jigs my secret weapon for big trout.

Left—A jig fooled this leaping steel-head into striking. The jig had been worked through a deep resting pool.

Below—Jigs are especially productive during cold water period such as shown here on a winter steelhead stream.

Bottom—Rod bending action with big lunker trout can be yours by fishing a jig deep through holes.

Trout on Ice

by RICHARD P. SMITH

AN HOUR had passed since we'd pulled our first 3-pound brown through the snow-choked hole in the ice. After a period of inactivity, the gentle jigging of the Rapala was second nature. My mind was wandering and I daydreamed about a warm meal and dry clothes to replace the sleet-soaked ones I was wearing.

A trout struck with a solid jolt and slammed my rod tip down into the hole. Line ripped off my open-faced spinning reel with a howl as hollow as the crisp northwind. This was a good fish.

I was fishing with a 7½-foot rod and 6-pound mono and I had to jockey from one side of the hole to the other to keep the wispy line from sawing across the ragged edges. I could kiss my winter trout goodbye if my line caught on the solid rime of ice at the waterline.

It took several minutes of pumping and reeling to work the hefty fish up underneath the ice but he was nowhere near played-out. I had time to identify it as another brown before the spotted bulk slid past the hole on its side.

The battle see-sawed back and forth for several more minutes before I could slide the weary fish headfirst onto the ice. Two trophy winter trout in a matter of a couple of hours adds up to plenty of winter thrills for trout fishermen willing to brave the elements and icy conditions for a shot at their favorite fish.

Actually, winter trout—although ice bound—feed very well and trout fishermen across the northern tier of states can extend their fishing season considerably by taking to the ice. Trout tend to concentrate a good deal during winter months and many times the main problem in catching them lies in first finding a concentration. Once a group of feeding trout have been pinpointed, the rest is easy.

Before a fisherman can fully enjoy his winter trout fishing he must be fully prepared to spend the better part of the day on the ice. This necessitates dressing properly for the existing conditions. No other form of trout fishing will place such high importance on clothing selection as does ice fishing.

Too many icefishermen dress with whatever odds and ends they find lying about the house and as a result they are often chilled within an hour. Icefishing for trout demands concentration and nothing dulls your ability to concentrate faster than being cold. Dress properly, stay warm and you'll catch more trout.

I personally prefer dressing from the inside out . . . and this isn't a carelessly typed remark. A warm fisherman begins with warm waffle-weave or cotton-wool long underwear. A suitable, although heavier substitute, is down underwear. I opt for the old fashioned long underwear if the weather promises to be mild with little wind. If below-zero temperatures and a wind chill factor that looks like it was born in the Arctic

are factors, then I select my down underwear and wear this over a pair of cotton shorts and T-shirt.

Light cotton socks topped off with a light pair of virgin wool socks will do nicely toward keeping your feet warm. I then place a good pair of wool trousers over my down. A cotton shirt comes next and occasionally I'll wear a dickey or turtleneck shirt to keep some of the warmth from escaping from around my neck. On really cold days I'll add a heavy wool cruiser shirt for extra warmth.

The next three items are absolutely mandatory for winter icefishermen: a quality snowmobile suit, a warm cap and warm waterproof boots. Skimp on quality on any of these items and you're apt to be one darned cold trout fisherman.

I prefer an expensive 8-ounce snowmobile suit with plenty of pockets and a hood. The best suits are windproof and a fisherman can stay warm all day in one with a reasonable amount of activity.

Keep your head warm and the rest of your body will stay warm. This advice comes from many seasoned Arctic travelers and it's true. I like a wool stocking cap that can be either perched atop my head or pulled down over my ears if the weather turns sour.

Waterproof boots are an asset when augering holes in the ice. Unless you are super cautious even a hand-held auger will drench your boots when the bit goes through the bottom of the hole. The result, wet cold feet inside of 15 minutes. I like rubber galoshes with removable felt inserts inside. An extra pair of wool felts for a midday change is like having coffee and cake served to you on the ice. Nothing can beat good felts for keeping your feet warm.

Warm gloves or mittens complete the list of clothing needed for icefishing. A pair of handwarmers in your side pockets are often a wise choice on blustery days when gloves become soaked quickly.

The tackle needed for icefishing for trout is relatively simple and can range from an open-faced spinning rig (which I prefer) to the more simplified jigging sticks. Where trout run to large sizes I find the spinning rig to be much easier to use when playing fish. The tip is more sensitive to light takes and a big fish can be played expertly through the hole without too much danger of losing him.

A jigging stick is merely a curved wooden stick with mono tied to one end, threaded around two loops to hold the coils in place and then out the other end. The fisherman manipulates the lure by jigging the stick up and down. It works well for smaller fish but it's clumsy to use when trying to play a big trout. The stick has no give and I've seen too many beautiful winter trout lost because an angler tried to hurry the fish to the hole with a jigging stick.

Augering holes can be a backbreaking and time-consuming task. I've finally admitted I don't care to hand auger holes through 36 inches of ice and have purchased a Jiffy power ice drill. A hole is bored quickly and efficiently and gone is the labor that drives many fishermen from the ice after one episode at augering.

Opposite page—Before you can enjoy winter trout fishing, you must be prepared to spend the better part of the day on ice and snow.

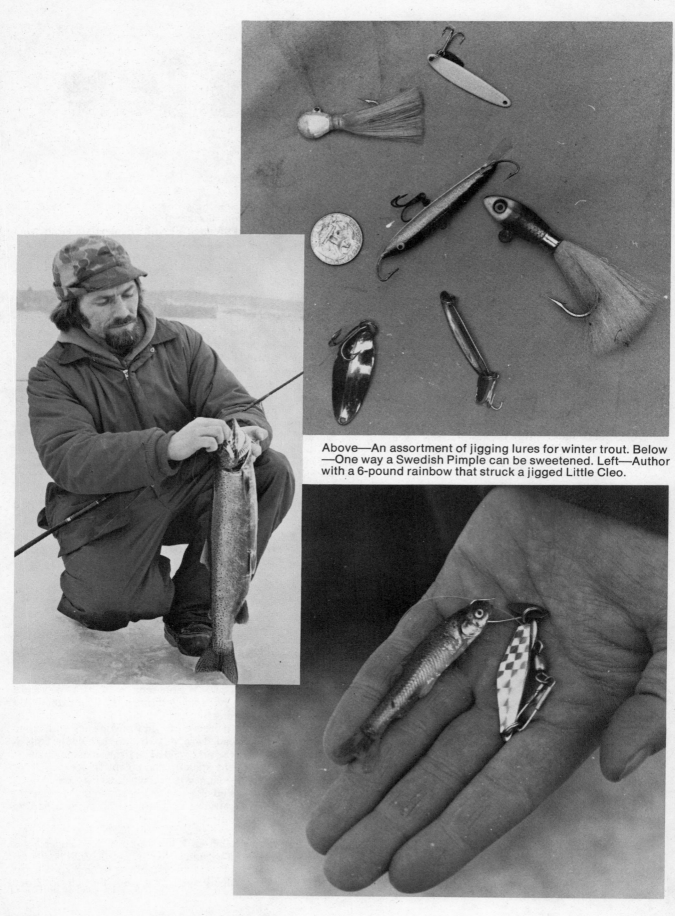

Above—An assortment of jigging lures for winter trout. Below —One way a Swedish Pimple can be sweetened. Left—Author with a 6-pound rainbow that struck a jigged Little Cleo.

Big fish like this lake trout need a gaff for landing. Trout of 10 pounds or better are commonly caught during the winter.

A pocket full of lures, an ice strainer, a seat to sit on and a bucket to hold your catch are about all the trout fisherman needs to get into icefishing. Other things such as lanterns, heaters, windbreaks, gaffs, bobbers, etc. are merely frosting on the winter cake.

Jigging is by far and away the most prevalent and productive method of taking trout through the ice. A good man on a jigging stick or with a light action spinning rod can do tricks with jigs that will have big trout sliding out of their hole with regularity.

There is a wide array of artificials that have proven themselves to winter fishermen. Excellent success can be had by jigging Rapalas, Swedish Pimples, Devle Dogs, Little Cleos, maribou or Barracuda jigs and the piggy-back jigging lures that have to be "sweetened" with a piece of fish flesh before being used.

Jigging one of these lures involves nothing more than lowering the lure to the bottom. This is where most winter trout will be found. You've got to drop it into their dining room before the combination of action, flash and possibly taste from the small piece of fish flesh can do its work.

Once the lures rests on bottom, tighten the line slightly so the hooks are hanging straight down. Slowly raise and lower the rod tip or jigging stick a few inches to impart motion to the lure. The key to success is to produce a struggling baitfish action to the lure. A series of short, sharp jerks can be utilized to give the illusion of a sick or injured baitfish.

One method that often works for me is to try and move the lure sideways in the hole. It's difficult to accomplish, but it often gives the lure a very faint motion that turns on big trout.

Occasionally an exaggerated motion will produce an erratic action to a lure. A group of long hard pulls will send the lure into a frenzy of activity which often pulls in trout from some distance. Lures such as the Swedish Pimple, a famous Midwest jigging lure, can be fished by sharply raising a foot or two and then dropping the rod tip or jigging stick rapidly. The flashy lures will flutter enticingly back to bottom. Ice-bound trout often strike on the downward flutter.

Almost any jigging lure can be improved upon by the simple addition of a small piece of meat carved from another fish. Smelt or sucker meat is very good. Slice a tiny sliver of flesh from the side of a minnow and place it on the hooks. Too-large a piece will upset the action of the lure.

If an angler has the opportunity to fish from an ice shanty he can often view trout coming in to jigging lures. This type of first-hand observation is important to determine the exact type of jigging technique needed to elicit a strike.

I once caught a limit of splake from a small inland lake only after experimenting for an hour with jigging techniques. Once I hit the magic combination, fish after fish began darting into the hole to grab the flashing lure. I'd often have one splake on and have one or two others pecking at the same lure. Limit catches are easy on days like this.

Depth of presentation is something jigging fishermen must also experiment with. Most of the time trout will be found hovering on or just above bottom. There are times when the trout may suspend themselves anywhere from 10 to 50 feet off the bottom although in the latter case, this usually happens when the icefisherman is fishing near a river inlet. Flowing water is warmer than lake water and often contains good things to eat. Trout commonly cruise beneath the ice in this flow of warmer water and feed avidly.

I normally begin fishing near bottom. If no action occurs within a couple of minutes I begin moving my lure a foot at a time toward the surface. This type of experimentation is important and time consuming. In this end it pays to have a light-proof shanty where the angler can view the action through the shanty hole.

A trick that often works well with lake trout is to jiggle the lure vigorously in the bottom mud. Where trout feed on sculpins and other bottom dwelling fish, this mudding technique occasionally brings the fish in.

Jigging is the fastest known method of icefishing for trout, but there are a couple of other ways of taking trout through the ice that deserve special mention.

A tipup is a spring loaded flag containing a built-in reel that triggers automatically whenever a trout grabs the bait. Tipups are normally baited with minnows such as small suckers, shiners or dead smelt.

Live minnows are much preferred for tipup fishing because they offer both action and a natural taste to prowling winter-hungry trout. Baitfish can be hooked in one of three ways that cause a minimum of injury and still provide excellent hooking action. I prefer to hook my minnows through both lips, although hooking either just beneath the dorsal fin or through the anus brings out the best action of the minnow.

Tipup lines are usually 20- to 50-pound braided Dacron with a 6- or 8-foot monofilament leader testing at 10 to 20 pounds. Use a small (No. 10 or 12) treble hook for minnow fishing and you'll find big trout sucking the minnow deep without hesitation. A small treble hook will catch as many or more large trout than a big hook and it's easier to conceal in the baitfish.

One or two split shot above the hooked minnow is usually enough to keep the bait near bottom. If a minnow is unusually active and keeps tripping the flag on the tipup, try cutting one lobe off its tail. This will upset the minnow's balance and keep him down near bottom.

Since the bulk of tipup fishing is done within inches of

Right—Ice shanties allow anglers like Charles Lunn to see and catch his limit of fine eating splake. Far right—A limit of splake for these two fishermen was possible because they knew enough to fish off a point (in the background) and because they dressed properly. Note heavy snowmobile suits and wool stocking cap.

bottom it becomes imperative to know just how deep the water is. I have an easy method of determining the depth. I attach an 2-ounce bell sinker to the hook and lower it until it just touches bottom. Grab the line where it enters the water and pull up about 12 inches. Tie an overhand knot at this point around a paper match. When the bait is lowered to bottom, position the match so it's just on the spool of the tipup and your bait will be nudging bottom.

Lower the minnow-baited hook to bottom, set the tipup flag so it'll trip on a strike and stand back to await action. On cold days I kick snow into my tipup holes to prevent them from freezing solid. Once a strike comes I don't want to be chiseling away at my tipup trying to free it from the ice. Some fishermen pour glycerine or antifreeze into the hole after the bait has been lowered. This effectively keeps the holes open although a baitfish cannot be brought up through this contaminant without impairing the natural flavor.

Once a strike occurs the important thing to do is nothing. That's right, nothing. Allow the trout to run with the minnow until it stops to swallow it. That's one reason why you need up to 200 yards of line on your tipup spool.

Many times a trout may run only several feet before turning the minnow in its mouth and swallowing it and other times I've seen them peel off 75 yards before stopping. Allow the fish to take line without resistance until it stops. This is the critical time; too many icefishermen get the jitters now and set the hook before the trout has had time to swallow the bait.

When the line begins peeling off again allow it to come tight in your hand and give a good jerk when you feel resistance. Be prepared to give line at any time if there is a good trout on. I've seen big lake trout and browns slug it out for 10 minutes before finally giving up. A hand-over-hand retrieve is best when the trout gives up and can be led to the hole. Just be careful with blowing lines at this stage; a trout often sees the bottom edge of the ice coming at him and recovers enough to streak off on a short run. If the line has blown around some jagged ice fragments at the hole it could mean a lost fish.

Smaller trout can be taken effectively with icerods similar to those used by perch and bluegill icefishermen. Small bite-sensitive rods coupled with tiny lures and 2- to 4-pound monofilament can make a 1-pound trout feel like a whale.

This type of fishing calls for small natural baits such as cornborers, wax worms, gall worms, wigglers, elmwood grubs, mousies and others. Tiny jigging spoons such as the

Tear Drop in hot colors such as red, chartreuse, orange, green and blue are great for small trout.

Winter trout are extremely finicky when in shallow water and this is where light tackle fishing of this sort is best. I prefer to fish in 6 to 8 feet of water. This means silent approaches to avoid spooking fish and a minimum amount of motion once the holes are drilled.

A trick that often works for these fish is chumming. I'll often drop a half-dozen corn kernels or salmon eggs through the hole to stimulate their appetite. Although they feed actively on the corn or salmon eggs, the small flashing spoon and grub baited hook still hold a deadly fascination for them. Hard strikes and occasional broken lines are par for the course in this brand of icefishing.

Jigging techniques with the smaller spoons are basically the same although the movements of the rod are minimized. Too much flash and action in shallow water will spook winter-weary trout. Keep jigging movements slow and deliberate.

Icefishing hotspots vary from area to area although some generalities occur. Search out points or islands in lakes for a starting point. Mid-winter trout concentrate in these areas. A rapid change in depth occurs near points and islands when shallow bars drop off into deep water. The edges of these dropoffs are hotspots.

Inlets and outlets of a lake or river are good spots to try. Trout concentrate nearby to prey upon food washed into the lake. The warmer water and higher oxygen content is another deciding factor.

Timing can be an important factor for winter trout fishermen. Early morning or just before dark are usually the best times although a sudden change in the weather can bring about a feeding spree at any time of day.

The best advice for icefishermen trying for trout on an unknown lake is to either obtain specific instructions from someone familiar with the lake or punch as many holes as possible. I've found that 15 or 20 holes augered over a wide expanse of a lake will almost always locate some feeding trout. A power auger makes this child's play and eliminates much of the time that used to be spent prospecting for fish.

Trout are fun to catch and just because someone lives in an ice-bound area doesn't mean he has to forsake his trout fishing. Bundle up properly, locate a good trout lake in your area and have a go at one of winter's liveliest sports—ice fishing for trout.